Claude Welch

GRADUATE EDUCATION IN RELIGION

A CRITICAL APPRAISAL

A Report of a Study Sponsored by the American Council of Learned Societies with a Grant from the Henry Luce Foundation, Inc.

UNIVERSITY OF MONTANA PRESS
Missoula

BL
41
.W4

"Libri Montani"

Library of Congress Catalog Number: 70-181353

© 1971 Council on the Study of Religion

All rights reserved. No part of this book may be reproduced by any means, electronic or mechanical, including photo-copying, without permission in writing from the Publisher.

PRINTED IN THE UNITED STATES OF AMERICA
PRINTING DEPARTMENT, UNIVERSITY OF MONTANA, MISSOULA, MONTANA 59801

93915

ADVISORY COMMITTEE

JAMES T. BURTCHAELL, C.S.R.
Provost, University of Notre Dame

ALLAN CARTTER
Chancellor, New York University

GERSON COHEN
Jacob H. Schiff Professor of History, Jewish Theological Seminary,
New York

JAMES E. DITTES
Director of Graduate Studies, Department of Religious Studies,
Yale University

WALTER HARRELSON
Dean, The Divinity School, Vanderbilt University

RAY L. HEFFNER
Provost, University of Iowa

PAUL JOHNSON
Graduate Student, Department of Religion, Duke University

EDWARD A. LANGERAK
Graduate Student, Department of Religion, Princeton University

J. A. MARTIN
Chairman, Department of Religion, Columbia University

WILLIAM F. MAY
Chairman, Study of Religion, Indiana University

J. BOYD PAGE
President, Council of Graduate Schools in the United States

JAMES N. SETTLE
Executive Associate, American Council of Learned Societies

KRISTER STENDAHL
Dean, The Divinity School, Harvard University

Statement by the Advisory Committee

The Advisory Committee wishes to express its appreciation to Claude Welch, Director of the Study, for the care, sensitivity, and directness with which he and his colleagues have conducted the study and reported their findings. The Committee, appointed by the American Council of Learned Societies, has been involved in the study in a number of ways. It offered many comments concerning the design of the study and the questionnaires and other instruments used. The Director provided the Committee with copies of drafts of chapters and asked for individual comments and for counsel by the Committee as a whole. Revised drafts of the manuscript were discussed at length, and many proposals were made for revision, curtailment, and expansion. In particular, the Committee proposed that the Director hazard an evaluation of the individual graduate programs and indicated its readiness to share responsibility with the Director for the inclusion of such an evaluative section in the final report.

The task of the Advisory Committee was to advise; the Director was not required to accept advice tendered. The interpretation and assessment are those of the Director. However, the Committee did have ample opportunity to render its best judgment concerning the method, form, style, and contents of the report, and therefore it wishes to recognize its share of the responsibility for such flaws or limitations as the study may have.

Preface

1. THE POINT OF THE STUDY

When the study was first conceived, in 1967, the educational escalator still seemed to be running. Education was "the greatest growth industry in the country." The great upsurge in the study of religion in colleges and universities allowed dreams of ever onward and upward. Now that the study has come to the time of delivery, the world is different. The academy has been under attack from a dozen sides and from within. Even in the strongest of institutions, the words are "financial crisis" and retrenchment." This may not alter the shape of some of the problems for graduate education in religion, but it surely puts them in a different context.

Since World War II the academic study of religion has been changing rapidly at all levels, posing important issues for public and educational policy. Religion has emerged vigorously in the colleges and universities as a field of studies distinct from theological training in a seminary or divinity school. In what Robert Michaelsen has aptly called a "quiet revolution" (McLean, 1967, pp. 9 ff.), departments of religion and interdepartmental programs have multiplied and expanded in both private and public institutions of higher learning.

Expansion has been particularly noteworthy in the public sector since the United States Supreme Court decision in the Schempp case (1963), which in effect legitimated the formal study of religion for all United States public education. Associate Justice Clark, in the majority opinion in that case, wrote:

> . . . It might well be said that one's education is not complete without a study of comparative religion or the history of religion and its relationship to the advancement of civilization. It certainly may be said that the Bible is worthy of study for its literary and historical qualities. Nothing we have said here indicates that such a study of the Bible or of religion, when presented objectively as part of a secular program of education, may not be effected consistent with the First Amendment.[1]

At the undergraduate level, the academic study of religion has now been significantly, though not yet massively, established in public universities in both the United States and Canada, including some of the largest and pivotal schools (see Chapter 9). The formal study of religion has also begun to be introduced into public secondary schools. In several states, curricula are being shaped and teacher training programs established.

Graduate studies in religion, formerly carried on almost entirely in or in close association with theological schools, have also been rapidly changing. Numerous

[1] Abington School District versus Schempp, 374 U.S. 203,225 (1963).

vii

Ph.D. and master's programs have been established in universities having no theological schools. Some older programs have been radically restructured.

Theological schools have also been in a state of ferment and reappraisal. One powerful tendency has been to form "clusters" of institutions, both Protestant and Catholic, in close relation to universities, providing new combinations of resources and offering both promise and problems for graduate and professional studies.

This study arose from the judgment that the clue to the future of these changes lay in graduate education: in the training of the scholars who are to be the teachers and researchers in this field. The body of useful literature that has so far emerged deals largely with undergraduate studies in religion and its principles, though the course of that development and the prospects for the future have remained largely uncharted and undirected.[2] Almost nothing has been written concerning graduate studies in religion, as distinct from theological education. Religion, for example, was not included in the 1964 Cartter assessment of quality in graduate education (ACE, 1966), nor in the 1969 report by Roose and Andersen (1970), though for some time more earned doctorates in religion have been awarded than, for example, in philosophy, classics, art, linguistics, French, German, or Spanish—all of which were included.[3] Neither Berelson (1960) nor Walters (1965), in their studies of graduate education, took account of the field of religion. Even the Niebuhr, Williams, and Gustafson study of theological education (1957) mentioned doctoral-level programs only briefly (and inadequately).

Further, in the recent general studies of higher education, neither the magnitude of undergraduate and graduate religious studies, nor the changes that have taken place in them, has been noted or interpreted.

As a major attack, therefore, on the problems of the development of religious studies at all levels, we proposed a critical review of graduate programs in the field of religion in the United States and Canada. Our intention was both to assist in the formation of policy for the future and to provide a body of reliable information and assessment to which educators, administrators, and public servants could turn.

2. DEVELOPMENT OF THE STUDY

The initial proposal for the present study came from a task force of the Society for Religion in Higher Education. The idea gathered momentum and endorse-

[2] See the Bibliography. Among the most valuable studies are Holbrook, 1963, Michaelsen, 1965, and Ramsey and Wilson, 1970.

[3] The reason for the omission of religion from the graduate program assessments is apparently that religion doctorates have been more highly concentrated in a few schools. Twenty-seven of the institutions included in the survey by Roose and Andersen offer Ph.D. degrees in religion (not including those in Hebrew or Near Eastern Languages). This is a smaller number of institutions than for any of the fields included except for Russian. Nonetheless, these twenty-seven institutions include the largest producers of religion Ph.D.'s.

ment from a variety of scholarly groups, including the Council on Graduate Studies in Religion, the American Academy of Religion, the Fund for Theological Education, the Society for the Scientific Study of Religion, and the Commission on Religion in Higher Education of the Association of American Colleges. The American Council of Learned Societies (ACLS) offered to serve as the official sponsor and administering agency.

In July, 1969, a generous grant was secured from the Henry Luce Foundation, Inc., sufficient to support the project in its entirety, and the study was begun in the fall of that year. An ACLS advisory committee was appointed, whose members both individually and collectively have assisted in planning the study and in reviewing the materials and drafts of the report.

Although the special focus of the investigation was to be doctoral programs, these had to be set in the context of the quantitative and qualitative changes taking place at the undergraduate level. Thus a first task was to secure information concerning as many as possible of the undergraduate religion programs. In this portion of the study, we were assisted particularly by the Center for Research on the Acts of Man, directed by Professor Samuel Z. Klausner of the Department of Sociology of the University of Pennsylvania. From responses to a simple screening questionnaire, sent in the winter of 1969-1970 to the heads of 2,335 institutions, a list of 1,311 four-year accredited colleges in the United States and Canada was compiled.[4] Of these, 873 claimed to have a special program or department of religion, and to them was sent the final form of the undergraduate questionnaire in March, 1970. The questionnaire asked for information on approximately 75 items relating to the general character of the institution, its religious affiliation (if any), the structure of its program or department of religion, the purposes of the department, the numbers of faculty and student enrollments over a period of fifteen years, the full pattern of courses presently offered in the department, and certain characteristics of each present faculty member (see Chapter 9).

Our second task was to define more precisely the limits of the study at the graduate level. "Graduate programs" was defined to mean courses of study leading to the research and teaching degrees, that is, primarily the Ph.D. degree and in some cases the earned Th.D. (Doctor of Theology), S.T.D. (Doctor of Sacred Theology), and D.H.L. (Doctor of Hebrew Literature or Letters). M.A. programs were to be strictly a secondary concern, and programs leading to "professional" theological degrees (such as B.D., S.T.B., S.T.M., M.Div., M.H.L., D.Min., and D.Rel.) were not to be reviewed.

The universe of doctoral programs to be studied thus finally included 69 institutions of higher learning in the United States and Canada. Of these, 50 are universities or other Ph.D.-granting institutions (some of which also grant the Th.D., S.T.D., or D.H.L.) and 19 independent theological schools granting

---

[4] Of the 2,335 schools, 1,024 were eliminated as not being four-year colleges or universities.

the Th.D. or S.T.D. Altogether 75 programs have been reviewed (see Appendix A). The difference in numbers here results from the fact that several institutions offer two or more programs that needed to be included (among them, Chicago, Graduate Theological Union, Harvard, Montreal, and Ottawa) and that three of the degree-granting institutions (Emmanuel College, Knox College, and Trinity College in Toronto) have joined their Th.D. programs in the Toronto Graduate School of Theological Studies. Certain Th.D., S.T.D., and D.H.L. programs have been omitted from the study because these were explicitly defined by the respective institutions as intended to prepare for professional ministerial, priestly, or rabbinical service rather than research and teaching (e.g., the Claremont Th.D., the San Francisco Seminary S.T.D., the Garrett Theological Seminary S.T.D., the Boston Th.D., and the Hebrew Union College D.H.L.).

To collect the maximum amount of information about the graduate centers, we have done extensive visitation and used a battery of questionnaires. Between November, 1969, and October, 1970, I visited 59 of the institutions involved, plus several others with proposed or related programs. Those interviewed included department chairmen and directors of graduate study, graduate school deans or other senior administrative officers, the chairmen of other departments in the humanities or social sciences, various members of the faculties, often members of the library staff, and occasionally a group of graduate students. These consultations proved to be of great value, and the faculty and administrators were almost invariably open and responsive.

As a special investigative project, my research associate, Harold Remus, conducted extensive group and individual interviews with doctoral students at seven institutions, chosen to give representative variety and geographical distribution: Princeton, Duke, Harvard, Catholic University, Southern Baptist, Iowa, and Chicago (plus a few interviews with students in Judaica at Columbia and Jewish Theological). Interviews were planned for the West Coast, at the Graduate Theological Union, but these were not carried through because of the campus disruptions of May, 1970.

Five types of instruments were used for securing statistical information and other responses from the several institutions: a summary report form filled out by the department chairman or director of graduate studies and his aides; a questionnaire for each faculty member involved in doctoral instruction; a questionnaire for each doctoral student in residence or writing a dissertation; a report on the library resources and holdings; and a card for reporting certain information concerning each recipient of a doctoral degree in the five-year period 1965-1969. These procedures have inflicted a considerable burden on departmental chairmen and offices, and we must be deeply grateful for their cooperation. Only in a few instances, and for varying reasons, were institutions unable or unwilling to supply most of the information requested.

Our net has thus gathered the following: summary information from nearly all institutions; an almost complete account of the approximately 1,400 doctoral degrees awarded between 1965 and 1969; 1,965 responses from present doctoral students (that is, approximately two-thirds of the total number of students); and 614 responses from graduate faculty (a somewhat smaller percentage of the total). Among the most valuable materials have been the comments, often extensive, made by faculty and students concerning graduate studies in general and in their particular fields.

3. THE REPORT

Our goal in this report has been a statement that will inform, interpret, critically analyze, and make proposals for the benefit not only of faculty and students in the fields of religious studies but also of the larger publics to whom the academic study of religion must be responsible: the educational, the religious, and the civic communities. The task of interpreting and even of simple reporting is important because of the large public unawareness of the "quiet revolution" in the study of religion during the past two decades. Critical evaluation is essential because of the ferment, uncertainties, and now severe pressures under which the whole academic world labors.

For the structure of the report itself, instead of the presumably logical order of development, from history to exhibition of the evidence and then to conclusions, I have decided on a reverse direction. Chapter 1 consists of a concise summary of conclusions and recommendations. Here I have tried to formulate proposals for improvement and reform as briefly as possible. Other kinds of conclusions are also drawn in the course of our analysis, for we have been concerned not only with change but with interpretation of an academic discipline and the characterization of its present state. The resulting descriptive generalizations and positive evaluations are important, but I leave them for discussion in succeeding parts of this report. Application to specific programs or institutions is likewise deferred for later notation (especially Chapter 5). In the general recommendations I simply try to designate as succinctly as possible the primary areas of need for change. The relevant chapters discussing the issues or providing important information are indicated in each case.

The conclusions inevitably overlap with other proposals that have been made concerning graduate education as a whole. I have firmly resisted the temptation to incorporate all suggestions that might apply to graduate studies in religion— for example, those bearing on foreign language requirements, examination processes, and the nature of the dissertation. Many of these are relevant, but no more so in religion than in other fields of study. I have tried instead to focus on matters particularly germane to studies in religion and theology. Nor is the list of proposals intended to include all the difficulties in the field (for instance, in the area of research and publication). Our concern is, rather, specifically with the needs and reform of programs for the academic study of religion, though with the hope that proposals which are of value here may also be relevant to other academic disciplines and to graduate education as a whole.

Part II of the report surveys certain major areas of tension and conflict in a changing discipline, out of which the recommendations emerge. In those chapters, I have attempted to state the issues as sharply as possible and to make judgments as specifically as is responsible. At such points particularly, I would much rather be wrong than to produce a report that could not meet with disagreement.[5]

Parts III and IV go on to more descriptive accounts of various "contexts" for present doctoral studies in the United States and Canada (historical backgrounds, the European scene, and undergraduate studies), of the doctoral student, of the fields of study, of the demography of doctoral studies, and of directions of research.

4. ACKNOWLEDGMENTS

Throughout the two years in which this investigation has been conducted, I have depended heavily on the assistance of many others.

The Advisory Committee appointed by the American Council of Learned Societies has been of invaluable help in reviewing the work from the design of the study through the drafting of large sections of this report. (This was, incidentally, the first ACLS Advisory Committee to include graduate student members.) The criticism and counsel of these associates has much improved the final product. In spite of the Committee's willingness to assume some responsibility for the outcome, however, I must insist that any blame for errors, for misjudgment, and for plain wrongheadedness is mine.

To the staff of the ACLS, especially Thomas Condon, James Settle, and Ruth Raborn, I owe a special debt for assistance in the administration of the project. The ACLS is not, of course, to be held responsible in any way for the conclusions of the investigation, but the active interest of the Council in sponsoring the study, and the encouragement of its officers, have been a source of deep pleasure.

Charles Y. Glock, Chairman of Sociology at the University of California, Berkeley, has been a regular consultant, particularly for the survey of undergraduate programs but also for other aspects of questionnaire development and interpretation. Not only has he been a helpful guide for one unskilled in data gathering; he has also been a hard critic, for which I am all the more grateful. To Professor Samuel Z. Klausner of the University of Pennsylvania, and his staff in the Center for Research on the Acts of Man, I am indebted for handling most of the development, distribution, and preliminary reporting of the undergraduate survey. I am grateful also to Dr. Martin Trow of the University of California, Berkeley, for permission to use selected data from the study of higher education being conducted by the Carnegie Commission on Higher Education in cooperation with the American Council on Education.

The University of Pennsylvania contributed greatly by granting me a year's leave of absence and by providing facilities for the project.

Five noted European scholars, who are properly identified at the beginning of

---

[5] Some elements of this assessment were offered in a preliminary form in my article (1971).

Chapter 8, most graciously agreed to formulate brief statements concerning advanced studies in religion and theology in their countries, in order that the patterns developing in North America could be seen in the context of current trends abroad.

During the study I have been continuously assisted by Harold Remus, who was willing to interrupt a most promising graduate career to spend a year and a half as full-time research associate, by Bridget Gibbons, project secretary, and by Joseph Eckenrode, who undertook a number of special assignments. They deserve a particular reward for good humor, excessive labor, and unusual competence. Among other contributions, including stringent attention to detail, Mr. Remus is the author of Chapter 7 and largely of Chapter 10. Mr Eckenrode brought together the materials and drafts for Chapter 13. Others who have contributed in important ways, often by quite tedious work, include Wayne Aoki, Arnold Eisen, Elhanan Peleg, and Thomas Welch.

Penultimately, I want to offer special thanks to all my fellow department chairmen and their secretaries and assistants, on whom we have inflicted considerable burdens, to the deans and other administrators whom we have consulted, to the librarians, and to graduate students and faculty, for their ready and uncomplaining cooperation. They believed the study to be important, and although some will be distressed by parts of this report, they have all urged that the hard things be said. I hope they will judge their confidence not to have been misplaced.

Finally, though also first, I am indebted to the Henry Luce Foundation, Inc., which by a generous grant made the project possible. The Foundation Vice-President and Executive Director, Martha Wallace, has been as encouraging as one could wish and has left us entirely free to pursue the study and develop its results.

CLAUDE WELCH, Director

Philadelphia, Pennsylvania
30 June 1971.

Table of Contents

III

CONTEXTS

IV

DEMOGRAPHY AND DESCRIPTION

List of Tables and Figures*

*All tables and figures refer to 1969-1970 unless otherwise labelled. The numbers indicate tables (the first numeral designating the chapter) except as noted.

PART I

I

Prescript:
Summary of Conclusions and Recommendations

CONCERNING THE SHAPE OF THE DISCIPLINE

1. Graduate education in religion is going through a crisis of identity requiring redefinition of the basis or core material that is presupposed by advanced and specialized studies.

Formerly the base for advanced studies was almost invariably a program of professional theological studies, leading to the Bachelor or Master of Divinity, the Licentiate in Theology, the Rabbinic ordination or their equivalents. The continuing validity of the professional degree as one avenue of approach to advanced study is not to be denied. But the field of religious studies has been rapidly broadening to include much more than was traditionally assumed as the core of professional studies and to overcome the restriction of study to a single tradition, such as Jewish studies, Christian studies, or Buddhist studies. Growing numbers of students enter advanced studies in religion without benefit of professional school preparation and without interest in ordination. Therefore, appropriate substitutes and parallels for the former bases in professional studies must be identified.

These bases ought to include more extensive exploration of the several methodologies for the study of religion: linguistic, historical, philosophical, sociological, anthropological, and phenomenological. They also require both renewed concern for the coherence of the field and cross fertilization of the various subdisciplines, transcending the distinctions of the religious communities and of Eastern and Western cultures. (See Chapter 2.)

2. A new integration is needed between graduate study in religion and undergraduate studies.

Such integration is made possible by the expansion and the improvement in quality of undergraduate academic programs of religious studies. It is necessitated by the growing independence of graduate studies from the work of the pro-

4 PRESCRIPT

fessional schools. The appropriate interrelation will require responsiveness at the graduate level to the changing interests and patterns in the undergraduate study of religion. It will also require sharper definition (though not uniformity) of the kinds of undergraduate studies that can provide an adequate foundation for advanced study.

It is obvious that some shortening is desirable in time required for the doctorate in religion, since both in years of academic enrollment and in elapsed time, that period is now the longest of any field. The only way to attain reasonable compression of the time span, without sacrifice of quality and of depth in specialization, is through more adequate integration of undergraduate with advanced studies. (Chapters 2, 5, 9.)

3. Both graduate and undergraduate studies in the Eastern religious traditions, in Islam, in African religions, and in the religious experience of Blacks in North America must be strengthened and expanded.

Support for such efforts is particularly important in view of the economic and social pressures now threatening the existing college and university programs in non-Western studies generally, and in view of the relative weakness of the academic study of religion in the East itself. Undergraduate studies outside the Judeo-Christian tradition have grown, but too much of the expansion has been only of the token variety, and further attempts have been hampered particularly because graduate studies cannot be carried on without the immediate access of students to adequate training in the appropriate languages.

Close coordination is here required between the work of religious studies programs and that of departments such as oriental studies and Asian studies, so that treatment of religion in the latter can more adequately reflect the work of those who have been concerned with religious phenomena on a broad scale, and on the other hand, so that the advanced study of non-Western religions in religion programs can be fully grounded in the linguistic and other competencies of the collateral departments. Departments of religious studies should not try to develop all the latter resources within themselves.

Several of the presently existing programs which purport to offer specialized study in non-Western religions do so without adequate supporting resources in the university. In some major institutions, where the cognate language and area study programs are already available, programs in the history of religions have been insufficiently supported and have received too little attention from both the department and the institution as a whole. A few other institutions, already in possession of strong collateral resources, should be encouraged specifically to develop graduate religious studies in non-Western religions. (Chapters 3, 4, 5, 9.)

4. Graduate studies in religion need to be strengthened by fuller attention to the social-scientific approaches to religion, including those of sociology, psychology, and anthropology.

There is growing interest on the part of graduate religion programs in the study of religion and society, in comparison with the traditional literary and "history of ideas" approaches. Yet there is frequently lack of good interaction between the social-scientific study of religion and the humanistic study of religion. This lack is most evident in relation to the sociology of religion and the psychology of religion (though that discipline has tended to languish anyway, except in relation to counseling and therapy) and secondarily in relation to anthropology. The problem of interaction is more serious than in the case of Near Eastern studies, oriental studies, and area studies, since these, with their focus on language and cultural studies, are generally more closely akin to the prevailing humanistic orientation of religious studies. Social scientists, however, presumably in the interests of methodological purity and in order to maintain close relations to other types of sociological study and to practicing psychologists and researchers, have tended to draw away from effective interaction with humanistic modes of the study of religion.

A consequence of this bifurcation is that while specialists in ethics and society or social ethics or religion and culture, from the side of religious studies programs, do frequently attain depth in formal sociology of religion studies, students in other religion fields do not find it possible to explore the social-scientific avenues, even though they should, for the illuminaton of their own specialized studies. On the other hand, work in the sociology of religion, as frequently carried on in departments of sociology, often lacks acquaintance with the historical and theological-philosophical approaches that are also essential for the understanding of religion. (Chapter 4.)

CONCERNING PROGRAMS OF STUDY AS SUCH

5. Training in teaching and participation in the teaching process can and should be incorporated into the program of graduate study itself.

This is as true for the Ph.D./Th.D. programs that emphasize research as for Doctor of Arts or other programs oriented specifically to teaching, since research in religion is inseparably connected with written and oral communication and since the overwhelming majority of graduate students in religion hope to enter the teaching profession.

The need may be no greater here than in some other areas of advanced study, but it is at least as true in religion as in any other field that teaching and scholarship dare not be separated and that teaching must be recognized as a primary purpose and responsibility of programs of advanced studies. Relatively little has been done in graduate religion programs to fulfill this responsibility, either by extensive attention to what constitutes effective teaching, or by making the teaching assistantship a useful educational device, or by participation in internship programs. Doctoral students who plan to enter academic careers need to have available carefully designed programs for preparation for teaching. In particular, there is need for more extensive participation in the teaching process as a mode of learning within the graduate program. (Chapter 3.)

6. Better communication and direction of research are required with respect to dissertation study.

The field of religion shares the common problem of wide variation in the conception of the nature of the doctoral dissertation. Dissertation studies seem particularly plagued by the duplication of research, by inadequate attention to what is being done or has been done elsewhere, and by the lack of cooperative research endeavors that can draw attention to neglected or new areas of study and organize projects for investigating them. New modes for the communication of the results of research need to be explored. (Chapter 13.)

7. Master's-level programs require increasing attention and definition.
The several interests and purposes of M.A. studies are often neither clearly distinguished nor appropriately presented, with the result that master's programs become a potpourri of course offerings. The various purposes include: the creation of an adequate basis for advanced and more specialized studies; a period of further study for persons seeking largely to explore religious questions for the resolution of their own life problems; advanced study for clergy and other religious leaders; cross-disciplinary studies for persons from other disciplines; and preparation for teaching at the secondary school level. These purposes are not all incompatible with each other, but the same program is plainly not equally suitable to all, and individual institutions need to delineate more precisely the purposes their M.A. programs are intended to serve. (Chapter 2.)

8. There is room for much experimentation in the role religious studies can play in interdepartmental or interdisciplinary graduate programs.
This is important both because of the close involvement of religious studies with cognate disciplines and because graduate study in religion will remain numerically a relatively minor field, compared, for example, with English, history, and foreign languages. The study of religion can appropriately be a major focus within interdisciplinary Doctor of Arts and Ph.D. programs in the humanities or social sciences. (Chapters 4, 6.)

9. Arrangements for greater mobility of students and exchanges between doctoral programs need to be extensively developed. (Chapter 5.)

10. Efforts should be made for the greater participation of women and minority groups in advanced religious studies. (Chapter 10.)

CONCERNING RESOURCES AND SUPPORT

11. Devices are badly needed for over-all planning in the use of resources and for the allocation of responsibility for the development of particular fields of specialization.
It is not enough to say there is need for more rational planning among institutions, for there has been simply none at all. Each institution has proceeded in its own way, usually without consultation and always without review by others, and with insufficient attention to the question of what an institution is able to do distinctively. The result has been too many attempts at a simple duplication of traditional programs by institutions of second and third rank. On the

other hand, some of the efforts to move in new directions have been imprecisely defined and inadequately supported by collateral resources. Graduate programs in religion have the special responsibility of developing in relation to the strong cognate resources available in a given institution or area. Doctoral programs in religion can indeed be sustained only in institutions already possessing, or able and willing to develop, strong graduate programs in closely related areas of study. (Chapters 4, 5.)

12. Universities with theological faculties that carry a large burden of the graduate program in religion at these schools should consider whether such doctoral programs are too much an appendage to the professional school studies and at the same time too much of a drain on the resources of the theological faculties for the health of either the professional or the doctoral studies. That is not to deny the continuing important role of theological faculties in doctoral education; these and theological libraries are major resources for research and advanced study. But doctoral programs need to be integral parts of universities, and their operation needs to be more free from professional school interests. Special support should be given to some nonseminary-related programs. (Chapters 3, 4, 5.)

13. Levels of financial support for graduate students must be raised, even though it is desirable at the same time to reduce the total number of students.

Only about half the doctoral students in religion receive any sort of financial aid whatever from their institutions. In only a handful of institutions do a majority of the doctoral students receive substantial financial aid (that is, tuition plus significant fellowship stipends). With the current decline in federal support for graduate students, the constriction of graduate fellowship funds, and the reduction or cancellation of several of the private fellowship programs that had been important in the past, the financial situation of graduate students in religion has deteriorated. Continuation of this trend will lead to an unhealthy increase in the amount of part-time study and further elongation of the period of study. (Chapters 5, 9, 10.)

CONCERNING STRUCTURES FOR INTERPRETATION AND ACCOUNTABILITY

14. Since the academic study of religion at all levels is now extensively developed outside the areas of church-related schools and professional interests, it needs more careful attention by academic associations and in particular by public authorities. (Chapters 2, 5, 9.)

15. Effective organs are required for representing the academic study of religion to the several publics to which it is responsible, in particular to the civic community. The Council on the Study of Religion and its constituent professional societies should particularly be encouraged to undertake the task of more adequate interpretation of the study of religion and theology both to governmental agencies and to other academic associations. (Chapter 5.)

16. Close coordination is needed between the several regional accrediting associations and the American Association of Theological Schools (AATS) in the

8 PRESCRIPT

certification of doctoral programs in religion and theology, with the former assuming responsibility for university-administered Ph.D. programs and the AATS assuming responsibility for certification of the Th.D., S.T.D., and D.H.L. degrees offered by independent theological faculties. Together, these agencies should discourage all nonuniversity-related theological faculties from offering the Ph.D. (Chapters 3, 5.)

17. The Council on Graduate Studies in Religion, in concert with the learned societies in the field, should be encouraged to take up intensively and systematically the questions of the need for developing particular areas of study, of the availability of resources, of unnecessary duplication, and of cooperative arrangements among graduate programs. The Council ought to assume responsibility for insisting that schools allocate fields of specialization and that each institution open itself to the judgment of others with respect to work in a given area.[1] (Chapter 5.)

CONCERNING EXPANSION AND CONTRACTION

18. The number of doctoral candidates in religion should be allowed to decline by at least one-third, with more rigorous standards of admission being applied. This would improve the quality of graduate studies and would at the same time make ample provision for training the faculty needed both in universities and colleges and in theological schools. (Chapters 5, 6.)

19. The number of doctoral programs in religion and theology should be reduced significantly, though in a few instances new programs should be encouraged and supported.

At least a dozen of the fifty-two Ph.D. programs must be regarded as marginal or inadequate because of faculty or library deficiencies, unavailability of collateral and supporting resources, difficulty in attracting good students, or uncertainties in definition of purpose in relation to the needs of the discipline. Still others are in need of serious self-discipline and delimitation of goals.

Ph.D. programs should be encouraged only in universities that are able to support superior graduate work in many areas. The major burden of doctoral studies in religion and theology can and should be carried by such institutions.

Even apart from the question of supply and demand, it is evident that some presently existing doctoral programs should be abandoned. Many should be reduced in size. Nearly all the very large programs have become inflated in numbers of students to the point where the quality is endangered.

The number of Th.D., S.T.D., and D.H.L. programs could well be cut in half. Some are sadly deficient in resources for advanced studies; some are not fundamentally oriented to either teaching or research; some are only appendages to theological school studies. It is doubtful whether any Th.D., S.T.D., or D.H.L.

[1] The Council might well also undertake to encourage somewhat more uniform definition of the areas of specialization and the use of standard terminology, without discouraging flexibility and experimentation.

program should be encouraged to continue in the absence of an effective working relationship with a major university.

At the same time, the movement of religious studies into the public sector needs to be more adequately represented at the graduate level. A small number of additional programs should be established in public institutions. They should particularly emphasize the presently underdeveloped areas of religious studies. There are major public institutions (like the University of Toronto and the University of California at Berkeley) where extensive resources are already in existence for the study of religion, including the non-Western religious traditions. These universities should be encouraged strongly to organize and develop these resources. (Chapters 4, 6.)

PART II

TENSIONS AND ISSUES
IN A CHANGING DISCIPLINE

2

Identity Crisis in the Study of Religion?

I. The academic study of religion has firmly established its identity.

II. The academic study of religion is going through an identity crisis.

I want to defend both of these theses, for I believe both can be shown to be true.

1. IDENTITY

The value of the scholarly study of religion in college and university has now been so widely acknowledged that it need no longer be a subject for anxiety. In this sense, the period of emergence of a discipline of "religious studies," as distinct from theology, is coming to an end. In principle, of course, the argument was always easy, since to deny the propriety of studying religion is to restrict the freedom of investigation that belongs to the very idea of a university. What has changed is that this principle has become generally accepted and that the validity and quality of the studies actually being done have been widely recognized.

1. James Gustafson has commented that "very few, if any other, fields are as preoccupied with their legitimacy and as introspective about their self-understanding as religious studies" (Ramsey and Wilson, 1970, p. 330). That statement may be somewhat overdrawn. After all, other changing disciplines have agonized over their nature and role, and some are still struggling for self-identification and acceptance. But, as Gustafson notes, in religious studies there has been a "special burden from the past to bear" in that "the scholarly study of religion has historically been bound up with the propagation of faith and with the apologetic interests of religious institutions." Teachers in religion have been (sometimes rightly) suspected of covert intentions to proselytize. Would-be friends of the study of religion have occasionally confused its purpose with

pastoral care. Proponents of the study of religion and organizers of academic programs have sometimes been overly self-defensive.

One cannot quite say that the study of religion has attained that degree of acceptance which would bring acute embrarassment to any university or college not possessing a program of religious studies. But some striking evidence has emerged in our examination of undergraduate programs of the degree to which the legitimacy and importance of this area of study have now been acknowledged. Departments of religion are no longer confined to the religiously oriented or church-related institutions, but have become prominent in both private and non-sectarian and public colleges and universities. In both of these kinds of institutions, religious studies have expanded rapidly in the past two decades. Religion has come increasingly to be looked upon as a proper field of study in the liberal arts curriculum, rather than a subject so bound up with the confessional interests of religious groups that it could not be dealt with responsibly and directly in the academic community. Moreover, there seems to be a definite correlation between the academic quality of an educational institution and the likelihood of its having a program of religious studies.[1]

The purposes of the study of religion in church-related institutions have also been undergoing rapid redefinition. Formerly, religion programs were often viewed as preludes to theological seminary studies, or as direct professional preparation of religious education workers, or as religious training of laity. The reasons for the inclusion of religion courses and requirements in the curriculum of church-related institutions were predominantly "evangelical" or "catechetical": they were intended to instruct in the faith, or even to convert, and thus to provide support for commitment to the religious community and a religious and moral basis for life. (And these were precisely the reasons why, in many private as well as public institutions in the decades following World War I, there was strong reaction against religion courses.) These motives were also important in the establishment of the many schools of religion adjacent to college and university campuses.

Increasingly, however, except in the religiously conservative institutions, such purposes are being rapidly abandoned in favor of quite different understandings of the role of religious studies, and the patterns of teaching are changing accordingly. Confessional claims on either faculty or students have been more and more abandoned. In part this is associated with the increasing secularization of private colleges, but even in institutions seeking to maintain close ties with the religious communities, the departments of "theology" or "religious education," with their former confessional and/or professional orientation, are being transformed into programs that are at least transconfessional or "ecumenical" or pluralistic and that seek to deal more inclusively with religious phenomena. Religion is viewed as a field in the humanities (or social sciences), the study of which is justified simply by its contribution to any liberal education that proposes to take into account the whole range of human experience. Correlatively,

[1] On both those points see Chapter 9.

religion requirements have been reduced or abandoned at an increasingly rapid rate. In Roman Catholic institutions this has largely been a phenomenon of the 1960's, as a consequence of the revolutionary forces unloosed by the Second Vatican Council.

Concurrent with the changes in the understanding of the purposes of undergraduate religious studies and with the growth in undergraduate departments, though also antedating those changes and certainly helping to effect them, has been the determined attempt to improve the quality of instruction and faculty. One early landmark in this movement was the establishment of the Kent Fellowship program in 1923, to provide financial support for doctoral work by students concerned about the relation of religion and higher education. Though not restricted to students in religion, this highly selective program did center for years mainly on those who entered teaching in the area of religion, and through the association of the Fellows of the National Council on Religion in Higher Education (in 1963 merged with the Danforth Fellows group into the Society for Religion in Higher Education) it played a decisive role in the upgrading of the quality of religion faculty in Protestant and private nonsectarian institutions. More recently, this concern has been taken up actively by the several professional scholarly societies in the field—witness the reorganization of the National Association of Biblical Instructors into the American Academy of Religion (1963) and the formation by seven societies of the Council on the Study of Religion (1969), with the assistance of the American Council of Learned Societies.

One of the clearest and strongest points of convergence in the new study of religion is the understanding of the requirements laid upon the scholar-teacher. The demands are essentially those that obtain in any other area of scholarly inquiry. The faculty member may or may not be a convinced member of a religious community; his scholarly qualifications are not determined on those grounds. Rather, his competence is judged by his knowledge of the field, his critical powers of discrimination, his possession of the appropriate tools of investigation, and his integrity in their use. The field of religion may well be a particularly useful place of testing for the common ideals of scholarship, just because of the nature of the subject matter and the plurality of authorities (public, academic, and ecclesiastical) to which the scholar may be subject; but the ideals are truly common.

In Roman Catholic institutions, a special symbol of academic improvement has been the frequent change in name from department of "religion" or "religious education" to department of "theology"—this because "theology" was the word commonly designating graduate-level specialized studies, whereas "religion" suggested catechetical and high school instruction. Thus we have the paradox that nearly opposite changes in nomenclature have represented actually similar developments: in Protestant-related institutions the movement has been away from departments of "Bible" or "Bible and theology" toward departments of religion or religious studies, whereas in the same interest of academic quality many

Roman Catholic institutions have changed from departments of religion to departments of theology. Both shifts symbolize the wider movement of the tradition of serious scholarship beyond the theological schools into the colleges, private and public as well as church-related.

2. A further dimension in the establishment of the identity of the new mode of religious studies is the widespread rejection of several inadequate and even dangerous notions about the teaching of religion. I am thinking here particularly of the "zoo" theory, according to which religion can be dealt with only by exhibiting representative members of the various species; likewise, the "insider theory," according to which no one except an adherent can legitimately interpret or even understand a religious tradition; and further the "ecumenical institute" whose function it is to provide the religious communities opportunity to debate with one another and come to an understanding. Also, fortunately, the temptation to look upon the study of religion as a specially valuable means to the redemption of the university has been resisted.

The "insider" theory has been the most beguiling of these conceptions. Crudely put, the theory is easy to refute. Simply to adopt the principle that Catholic studies must be taught by a Catholic, Hinduism by a Hindu, Buddhism by a Buddhist, and so on, is to open doors to all the claims for "equal time" and if applied in the university generally would require a Democrat to teach about the Democratic party, a Hegelian to interpret Hegel, and a Marxist to treat Marxism. Further, it imposes a condition of employment that runs precisely contrary to the university's principle of freedom of investigation. Is one not to be permitted to examine and interpret that in which he does not believe? Further, interesting questions are raised about what would happen, for example, if the Hindu engaged to teach Hinduism should become converted to Islam. The ultimate absurdity of this principle is exemplified by the actual instance in which a Japanese religionist was brought to lecture for a semester, even though he could not speak any language but Japanese and no one at the university could understand the language.

The "insider" theory, however, actually works more subtly than this. For example, since non-Catholic institutions have in fact tended to give somewhat short-sighted attention to post-Reformation Roman Catholicism, it is desirable that an expert on Roman Catholicism be included in the faculty. Those qualified in the field are likely to be Roman Catholics; hence the curricular need is most likely to be satisfied by the appointment of a Roman Catholic. Then the conclusion seems to emerge that the desideratum is to appoint a Roman Catholic to a chair of Catholic studies. Further, since it is important to have diversity among the faculty, it seems desirable to have confessing Roman Catholics as well as members of other religious traditions. But then very subtly the occupant of the chair of Catholic studies becomes viewed, as Preller has put it, as "a spokesman for Catholicism, a purveyor of Catholic interpretation, or a supporter of Catholic truth claims." Preller draws the appropriate conclusion: "In order to see how intolerable such an interpretation is, we need only substitute 'Near Eastern' for

'Catholic.' An expert on Near Eastern studies is not taken as a supporter of Near Eastern truth claims" (Ramsey and Wilson, 1970, p. 144; see also Holbrook, 1963, pp. 181 ff.).

The problem is simply that in such a theory academic criteria are confused with nonacademic criteria. There are good reasons for having diversity in faculty perspective as well as in areas of specialization, but these are not the same as arguments for faculty appointments on the basis of confessional allegiance.

On the other hand, of course, it is not to be denied that the study of religion cannot be simply disentangled or disengaged from the practice of religion. Neo-positivist postures of indifference and "value-free objectivity" are no more valid here than elsewhere. College and university religion teachers, in the interest of establishing "academic respectability" for their work, may indeed have often leaned over too far backward in avoiding religious associations or commitments and have sought a false "objectivity." But to suppose that scholars in religion should be simply unconcerned about the life of the religious communities and their professionals is like saying that the political scientist should take no serious interest in political processes or politicians. And to forbid the religion teacher any articulation of concern and commitment is to adopt a restriction not assumed by anyone else in the academic community and at the same time to open the way for distortion by unacknowledged presuppositions.

3. The establishment of the identity of religious studies is also marked by the resolution of the "legal question" concerning the permissibility of the academic study of religion in public universities. This question, once hotly debated, has now been firmly settled in both the United States and Canada. As noted earlier (Preface), a great turning point in the United States was the Supreme Court decision in the Schempp case (1963) in which the majority opinion in effect legitimated for all public education the teaching "about" religion (as distinguished from instruction "in" religion). Enough of the leading state and provincial universities have now established departments or programs of religious studies so that no serious question is likely to be raised again about the constitutionality of such action (at least as regards the United States Constitution). Significant beginnings have also been made in introducing formal courses in religion into the public secondary schools. The problems that remain are those of interpretation to persons who have not yet caught up with either court decisions or actual practice and to others who use the "legal question" as an excuse for not facing directly the substantive issues.[2]

4. Finally, the new identity in religious studies is marked by definite changes in the objects and patterns of study. These include growing attention to the religious traditions outside the Judeo-Christian orbit—notably the religions of Far Eastern origin, Islam, and primitive religions. The range of religious phenomena is being rapidly expanded to include far more than the belief systems, rites, and behavior patterns traditionally called religious.

[2] See Katz, "The New Legal Climate," in McLean, 1967.

Within the traditional areas also, significant alterations are taking place. A historian of American religion writes:

> In the field of American religious history, the central development probably is the slow but decisive movement away from "church" history of the traditional, subtly apologetic sort, and toward a "religious history" in which the history of the Church is one strand. . . . By and large, religion programs have heretofore supervised the work on American religion that could be pursued under the church history rubric, and have left it to history departments to teach those who wanted to work within a context of American cultural history. I think that is changing.

A similar shift is symbolized by the tendencies to reshape the former Old Testament and New Testament studies into study of the religion of Israel (or ancient Near Eastern religion) and of Christian origins.

2. IDENTITY CRISIS

The process I have described in Section 1 may properly be viewed as the second of three stages in the twentieth-century development of religious studies. First, there was an essentially parochial orientation and purpose in Catholic and Protestant schools alike, up through the 1920's and 1930's, with the interests of the religious communities basically in view. (As built up after World War II, Jewish studies have basically continued that sort of interest, even perhaps with intensification in the 1960's.) The second stage was the emergence of religion as an authentic area of study in the family of academic disciplines. Even though religious studies were still organized largely along lines derived from the earlier stage, new moods and patterns of study emerged and the battle for recognition of the integrity of religious studies in college and university was largely won. That stage is now coming to an end, and the third stage is beginning, involving a search for new styles and approaches consonant with a fuller understanding of the nature of religion. Intertwined with the patterns of growth and the positions apparently secured are evidences of a real struggle in which the issue is not yet resolved. This I have ventured to call an "identity crisis" in religious studies.

1. The evidence for such a crisis comes only in part from the mass of "hard data" now in hand concerning undergraduate and graduate programs, students, and faculties. My conclusion rests as much on a network of symptoms of tension and change and on a long process of direct observation and consultation, which has partly reinforced and partly reshaped my own convictions. Thus I am not proposing so much to draw direct inferences from statistical summaries (though my judgment has been informed by these) as to offer a reflective analysis drawing on many kinds of evidence set forth throughout this volume. The symptoms include such diverse phenomena as striking experimentation at the undergraduate level with new ways of conceiving the pattern of religious studies, and the development by graduate students at more than one institution of their own infrastructure to provide a kind of learning that existing approved patterns do not afford.

The term "identity crisis" is not intended as hyperbole. I mean it to denote a critical situation through which a new sort of identity is being realized. In part we may think here of the sense of "loss of identity" or the fundamental uncertainty that the phrase "identity crisis" has currently come to connote. But more than this, I have in mind that kind of turning point or confluence of forces out of which a new and more mature identity can be realized.

The center of the crisis, out of which a new sort of identity may be emerging for religious studies as a whole, I would locate in this kind of question: How can a proper coherence be attained and expressed in religious studies, particularly at the graduate level, though all levels of religious studies share the problem? Note that I say "how" rather than "whether." There is an alternative—namely, to take the line of those who say that academic disciplines in general are "at bottom nothing more than an administrative category," with the "various sub-disciplines within biology or history or psychology, for example, having only the most limited intellectual relationship to one another . . ." (Jencks and Riesman, 1969, p. 523).

Yet I cannot believe that we can rest content with such a situation, if it does exist. Even though the notion of a neatly defined field with a single methodology is a quite illusory goal, to be satisfied with a simple unrelatedness of the areas and patterns of religious studies is to slide toward greater and greater isolation of our efforts from one another, precisely at the time when we ought to be finding and exploiting the points of contact.

a. That this is a major problem for religious studies is painfully manifest. The larger graduate religion faculties are characteristically organized into "departments" that operate almost independently. In a number of institutions faculty seem to have no interest even in trying to talk with one another. A perceptive colleague from a related university department reports that to him the most striking characteristic of the graduate religion program in his institution was this: from a student's being in the program one could infer almost nothing about the intersection or overlapping of his interests or competence with those of other students in the program. To that observation, we can add our own report that graduate students in religion programs are frequently objecting both to the lack of intellectual community among their teachers and to the barriers among themselves that are erected by narrow and inflexible requirements of the subdisciplines in respect of examination fields and the like.

b. The issue here is closely related to the nearly universal problem of breadth and specialization in graduate training, which has been intelligently discussed by Berelson and others.[3] But the problem of coherence has distinctive configura-

[3] Let it be quite clear that I have no interest in diminishing the demands for intensive specialized studies which will give the doctoral student a mastery of some particular area. That mastery cannot be given up in favor of the production of "Jacks of all trades": we have had to struggle too hard to overcome the naïve assumption of many, including college administrators, that anybody can teach anything about religion. Further, neither here nor in other areas is the problem of "overspecialization" to be solved by the mere addition of more study in more different areas. That is likely to be artificial and unproductive, resulting in what Berelson calls "interdisciplinary work by juxtaposition" (1960,

tions in the study of religion. In particular, it involves the question (already hinted at) whether we are prepared to talk about essentially independent areas of investigation called Christian studies, Judaic studies, or Buddhist studies, for example, or whether we are to define the study of religion in a less sectarian way.

This dimension of the problem has often been identified with the Protestant Christian orientation which made fine distinctions within one tradition by sub-dividing the study of it into a battery of areas of investigation in Bible, history of Christianity, and theology (mainly Protestant, of course) and then throwing everything else into one bag called World Religions. As Van Harvey has put it: "It is as though a history of science department were to offer a number of courses within the history of chemistry and then, as an afterthought, to add one or two entitled 'the Non-chemical Sciences'" (Harvey, 1970). This was a tendency even in private nonsectarian and public university programs, since initially most of those were staffed by scholars from Protestant backgrounds with Protestant theological training.

To change the metaphor, religious studies curricula have often looked like the Cape Codder's map of the United States. Like the distance between Chatham and South Chatham, small differences in the immediate neighborhood seem important and exaggerated; so the curricula carefully distinguish between New Testament and patristics or between Early and Late Reformation; each requires separate faculty appointments and sometimes separate degree programs. Judaism is perhaps like Massachusetts, a little more clearly recognizable and distinguishable. But just as the Cape Codder is alleged to have thought of Minneapolis and Indianapolis as the Twin Cities, somewhere near Spokane and Dallas, so all other religious traditions—nonliterate, classical, Asian, "etc."—are lumped in a single undifferentiated category largely beyond our ken.

The very caption "history of religions," frequently used to designate the investigation of religions other than Judaism and Christianity, is a prime illustration of the anomaly. Even if there were a distinctive scientific method for studying religion, as some defenders of the term "history of religions" believe, it would make no sense to apply it only to non-Western religion. I shall use the term for convenience, but it is a growing embarrassment. Perhaps now is the time to propose abandoning it as part of a thoroughgoing revision of nomenclature.

We are now being delivered from much of the parochialism. College departments are eager to add faculty in history of religions and non-Western studies even though the net result is still often no more than the assignment of the whole non-Western world to one man's responsibility—or an occasional "captive" Buddhist or Hindu (or Jew or Roman Catholic).

The problems here cannot be resolved, however, simply by giving more nearly "equal time" to other religious traditions. That can still leave religious studies with a schizoid personality. The issue is whether the fundamental organizing

p. 61). A desirable kind of breadth will at the same time be integrated: the breadth will be such as to pull together a variety of materials in relation to one or more specializations and thus provide mutual illumination (*ibid*).

principle ought at all to be "Christian studies" or "Jewish studies" or "Buddhist studies." Victor Preller, in the essay already cited, has outlined a powerful argument against "Catholic studies": such a division of study "can be academically justified only as a temporary solution to a problem contingently inherent in the present . . . transitional stage in the historical development of departments of religion" (Ramsey and Wilson, 1970, p. 145). That contingency, of course, is the frequent neglect of post-Reformation Roman Catholicism in many departments.

In a similar way, I want to argue that "Judaic studies" and "Buddhist studies" have their rationale mainly as temporary correctives to the traditional identification of religious studies with Christian studies. Or, I would add, they have a *raison d'être* simply as territories carved out for convenience and practicality in study.

But to use these divisions as the organizing principle for the study of religion is to deny to each of them the possibilities of mutual fructification and sometimes to isolate them from the method and content of such disciplines as cultural anthropology and sociology—as well as to risk falling back into the arms of confessional interests.

What is discouraging, as one looks at the recently established doctoral programs in religion, is the extent to which many of them have been content largely to repeat the traditional three divisions of Christian study: biblical, historical, and theological (including here philosophy of religion and ethics)—and this precisely at a time when undergraduate studies are beginning to move in quite new directions. The reverse side of the coin, of course, is the lack of resources in most institutions to do anything else.[4]

c. The preceding considerations lead immediately to a series of related questions: whether religious studies can legitimately be pursued in the 1970's in relation only to any single cultural milieu; whether there can be only one method in the study of religion; and whether the examination of religion at any level can be carried on except in close relation to the studies in "cognate fields," including anthropology, classics, history, literature, philosophy, sociology, Near Eastern studies, Asian studies, and so forth. If the answers to these questions are "No," we have to say that the present achievements fall far short of the goal.

2. In operational terms, the problem of this new sort of identity can be focused quite simply: what is to take the place of the theological degree as the base on which advanced studies in religion are built?

A distinctive feature of the tradition of graduate education in religion is that

---

[4] See below, especially Chapters 4 and 5. Contrast the 1971 reordering of courses at Yale, so that "scriptural and textual studies" include not only Near Eastern scriptures in their contexts but also Chinese Buddhist texts; "historical studies" include Buddhism, Christianity, and Judaism; "theological studies" include not only Christian and Jewish thought and the philosophy of religion but also Hindu and Buddhist thought; and "religious ethics" includes Jewish, Christian, and Indian ethics. So also Brown treats Judaism under the rubric of "history of religions."

there were important common bases. The traditional route to the doctoral degree, for Protestant, Catholic, and Jew alike, was through the seminary curriculum. This is still true of the majority of students in Ph.D. studies, but the majority is not large. Increasing numbers of students are going directly into graduate work in religion with indifference or even disdain for study in the professional theological schools. (See Chapter 10.)

The new trend poses a problem, however, because whatever the merits or demerits of the professional orientation of the seminary curriculum, the traditional route did provide both depth and breadth within the limits of a major religious tradition, on which it was possible to build a real specialization. There was, in other words, a common base or core of study. The biblical student had some significant exposure to the theological tradition and the sociology of religious communities and the philosophy of religion, just as the philospher of religion had some knowledge of scripture and of cult and of the theological options that had actually been explored. And the theological curriculum was by no means necessarily narrow in outlook.

But if the movement to by-pass the theological degree continues to grow (and it will), and if "religious studies" is to be defined as something other than strictly Christian studies or Jewish studies or Buddhist studies or Hindu studies, the situation is genuinely critical. Either we fall into a chaos of simply unrelated investigations, in which no one can finally talk to anyone else, or we search for new patterns of coherence which will both maintain the possibilities of communication and offer richer possibilities for the illumination of the subdisciplines in the field.

The quest for self-identification can properly be called a crisis. The term is particularly appropriate at the graduate level. Changes in undergraduate programs seem to be further advanced. In the graduate areas we are by no means agreed unanimously on the proper directions to take. There are places where something constructive is being attempted, but these are tentative and faltering beginnings, with widely varying degrees of intensity and success.

Further, it is dismaying to one who tries to observe the scene carefully to note a widespread lack of concern for this issue. I have mentioned the number of new programs that simply repeat the traditional areas of Christian studies. Judaic studies are in no better state. We should note also the resistance to change in the old, established programs, which, just because of their prestige and size, exercise the primary credentialing authority. According to the chairman in one such institution, serious discussion has never been held in the faculty whether students should be required to go outside their special fields for their general examinations or at any other point in their graduate preparation—and this is a university where graduate students are quite vocal in their unhappiness about the lack of opportunity for substantive exchange with related areas outside the department or even within the religious studies department as a whole. In more than one school, inertia and faculty conservatism are reinforced by a "senatorial courtesy" which precludes serious suggestions that a colleague might alter his devotion to "doing his own thing."

The difficulty is especially acute for institutions whose doctoral programs are built on the resources of a theological faculty, simply because the presence of massive resources in faculty and library in the traditional areas generate momentum requiring the dominance of those areas.

The present condition must be called critical also because of the constriction of university resources and the need for numerical retrenchment at the graduate level. These factors not only inhibit the potentially valuable development of graduate studies in the major state and private universities, in which there would be ample opportunity for fresh experimentation and definition. They have also, in the traditional centers, tended to restrict precisely those ventures into new areas that need most to be encouraged, simply because they have commonly been staffed by junior faculty who in a program of faculty retrenchment are the first to go.

This means, finally, that the difference between the lively experimental movements in undergraduate studies in religion and the dominant patterns in graduate study may become even greater, unless a vigorous attempt is made to continue reshaping the latter.

3. Thus far my diagnosis of the patient's condition. What are the prognosis and the prescription?

The condition is not one, I believe, that calls for a miracle drug, in the sense of some altogether new ideology for the study of religion. The basic difficulties are less theoretical questions about what sort of identity ought to be realized than practical problems of how the self-understanding can be adequately expressed and implemented. In this sense the prognosis is good. Though we do not have unanimity, there are some signs of emerging consensus about the directions in which to move. I shall note four areas of prescription, which suggest the contours of a proper self-identity for religious studies in the 1970's and which focus particularly on the problems of shaping the patterns of graduate studies.

a. As I have already implied, the basis for graduate education in religion must be more nearly cross-cultural, leading to a significant understanding of more than one religious tradition. The directions of present movement and the needs of the discipline lead me to side explicitly with Max Müller, who said, "Wer eine Religion kennt, kennt keine," and against Adolf Harnack, who responded, "Wer diese Religion nicht kennt, kennt keine, und wer sie samt ihrer Geschichte kennt, kennt alle."[5] The justification for this judgment is not the presumed desirability of learning more about different phenomena; that is likely to lead to the illusory breadth of mere juxtaposition. The real justification is simply the illumination that such a pattern of study can bring to the special problems being investigated.

The understanding of the Bible, for example, can be enriched by an awareness of the functioning of religious texts in the Buddhist or Hindu traditions—and

---

[5] Müller: "He who knows one religion, knows none." Harnack: "He who does not know this religion [referring to Christianity, especially in its Roman Catholic form], knows none, and he who knows this one, together with its history, knows them all."

some of the most interesting developments in the interpretation of the traditional Jewish and Christian scriptures have resulted from the discovery of the Dead Sea Scrolls and the Nag Hammadi Coptic texts. These studies, with the renewed interest in Gnosticism and other early Christian nonorthodox groups, have led to a widening of the field to take in all the culture of the Graeco-Roman world. (So also, in previous generations, Old Testament studies were greatly enriched and reordered from the study of Babylonian and other ancient Near Eastern texts.)

Similarly, religious reformation in one tradition and epoch needs to be studied along with reformation in other traditions and epochs. Interesting work is being done in the relating of such phenomena as Jewish eschatology, pre-Reformation millenarianism, Polynesian Cargo cults, and National Socialism (as a secular millenarian movement). Contemporary philosophy of religion can be better informed not only by fuller acquaintance with the theological traditions of the West but also by Eastern understandings of the esoteric nature of religious truth. In a related vein, a Christian ethicist notes as the most important new development in his field "the expansion of ethics programs into the non-Christian religions." This has moved him particularly into Jewish ethics and the ethics of Indian religions, thus toward comparative ethics.

The difficulty of breaking out of the purely Western pattern is not to be minimized. In spite of the brave talk about movement toward the study of non-Western religious traditions, most of what has so far been done must be set down as "tokenism." Among the sixty-nine institutions involved in our study, only six list areas of specialization specifically in one or more of the Far Eastern religious traditions (although another fourteen provide varying opportunities for such study under the headings of "history of religions," "comparative religions," and "world religions"). Only one institution lists for its religion department work in "primitive religion" (though it is always to be recognized that more studies go on than are noted in published statements). Barely six percent of the current doctoral students in religion have identified themselves as specializing in the areas of history of religions, Eastern religions, and primitive religions—although history of religions ranks a strong first among areas in which undergraduate departments want to make their next appointments.

The point is not at all that the student of religion should pretend to be informed about all the varieties and all the traditions. The omnibus world religions course and the handbooks of religions are of dubious value. Nor should we fall back into the mistakes of an earlier generation which was content to search simply for parallels and made too ready assumptions about common meanings. Rather, the time has come when the parochialism of restricting religious studies to a single tradition can no longer be afforded. The specialized investigations of the phenomena require the illumination provided by cross-cultural studies.

b. The study of religions at all levels must involve a plurality of methods. For example, one who comes to the study of early Christianity with a significant background in sociology and anthropology will be able to bring to it a different persepective than if he had only linguistic and literary tools. It is important to recall that significant study of this sort was carried on in the early decades of the present century, before the rise of the so-called neo-orthodox theology, and that Near Eastern and biblical studies now seem to be moving again in the direction of social and cultural studies.

This is not to say that anyone can try to manage all the possible approaches—historical, textual, anthropological, psychological, sociological, phenomenological, and philosophical/theological—any more than that one individual can treat all the parts of the field of religion. It is rather to say that no serious student of religion should be allowed to be content merely with one of the modes of inquiry into religious matters—which may conveniently be grouped into three families: the historical (and textual), the philosophical (and theological), and the social-scientific.

A pluralistic attack is particularly important if religious studies are intended to deal with the actual ways in which people act and believe and are motivated, rather than simply the normative *ideas* defined within the tradition. The "great books" and scriptural texts can no longer hold the sole dominant position in the materials to be studied; the methods of literary analysis and the history of ideas have to be related to other ways of looking at a much broader range of phenomena. The result will be that a coherent part of the field of religion—really almost any coherent part—may be viewed in its coherence.

c. It follows from the preceding points that graduate religious studies must increasingly involve interrelation with the "cognate areas." The resources of the related fields are needed both because religion is going to continue to be a relatively minor field of study (in numbers of students, faculty resources, and so on) in comparison with history, English, and the like, and because the nature of the discipline itself requires such interrelation. The severely practical problem is that the resources of these cognate fields, where they presently exist, are not being sufficiently exploited. Fully half of the institutions offering doctoral studies in religion make no mention of the desirability of collateral work outside the field of specialization. A few have modest requirements of work in a related discipline or a cognate area in religion. In some cases, however, this results simply in a juxtaposed minor area of study; in other cases the related area proves to be an immediately adjacent subdiscipline, such as Old Testament or patristics as the cognate areas for New Testament studies. Often it is merely suggested that a student "should be aware of possibilities that the university offers in such departments as. . . ." Examination patterns are rarely organized in such fashion as to involve several modes of approach, or differing parts of the whole field, or study in the "contexts" of the field of specialization. (It should be noted that studies in "religion and society" and in the history of religions areas are those most likely to draw significantly on the resources of cognate disciplines and departments.)

d. Finally, the questions of new bases for advanced studies in religion, and of the integration of cross-cultural studies and methodological varieties with specialized study, come to focus in the operational problem of building *continuing* patterns of religious studies.

"Bases" for advanced study cannot mean simply "preliminary" or "background." Nor can religious studies be organized in a simple vertical structure, in which *a, b,* and *c* always follow in that sequence and *d, e,* and *f* always presuppose *a, b,* and *c.* I have no interest in proposing a monolithic structure or imposing a single pattern. On the contrary, one may better liken religion to a broad field of more or less loosely clustered points with multiple interconnections, in which the task of formulating an intelligible program of study is that of encompassing related groups of points in their actual interconnectedness, for the purposes both of understanding something about the whole field and of an intense exploration of a definable cluster. Thus new patterns and groupings of study need constantly to be allowed to emerge.

But new bases for study do also mean first steps; and if those first steps are not to be taken in the professional theological school curriculum, they must come either at the undergraduate level or in new kinds of master's programs. The developing undergraduate studies in religion are increasingly offering a broader background than was provided by the theological school training.[6] Yet it is not at all evident that undergraduate programs have been appropriately designed to provide preparation for advanced studies in religion. This is not, of course, to say that undergraduate studies should be ordered primarily toward graduate study (or toward professional study). On the contrary, graduate studies must be better attuned to changes at the undergraduate level. And undergraduate programs in religion have several lively roles to fulfill. But if there is to be any coherence in undergraduate studies, they must involve structuring out of which something can develop. One of the legitimate purposes of an undergraduate major in religion is surely the laying of a foundation for advanced studies. Far too little consideration has been given to the shape and intensity of undergraduate studies that might be useful as such a foundation.

It is simply absurd to suppose that a responsible three- or even four-year doctoral program in religion can be built directly on a B.A. degree unless that degree has included an undergraduate honors major—honors both in quality and in depth. Such a program would necessarily include the following as a minimum: careful introduction to the development of modern approaches to the study of religious phenomena; a solid beginning in necessary languages, both modern and ancient; advanced work in more than one of the major patterns of study of religion (such as sociology of religion, philosophy of religion, or textual studies); a significant concentration of studies in one of the subfields (a religious tradition, or a geographical area), in which courses actually build on previous work; and a definite start in exploration of a religious tradition or area culturally distant from the primary field.

That kind of undergraduate preparation could provide a basis for continuing into graduate studies with both further exploration of the coherence of the field and an appropriate intensity in specialization, quite comparable to what can be attained on the basis of a first professional theological degree. On such a basis

[6] See also Chapter 9.

a three-year doctoral program is not inconceivable, although four years seem more likely, particularly in fields requiring extended language studies. The present difficulty, however, is that the average B.A. program rarely provides both the coherence and the concentration that are indispensable. The need will therefore have to be partly met either in the early years of graduate study or in the development of well-formulated master's degree programs. The latter, however, have even less identity than undergraduate programs, attempting at one and the same time to serve a multiplicity of different and even incompatible purposes. Hence there is rarely coherence. Most M.A. programs are of one year only, with ambiguous prerequisites, and consist of some requirement of distribution of work in several areas plus a special concentration. The same sort of structure is offered whether the intention is to supplement and inform work in other disciplines, to prepare for secondary school teaching, to provide a year of advanced study for persons in ministerial careers, to lay a basis for doctoral studies, or simply (!) to provide an opportunity for learning.

One cannot say that the two-year master's programs are much better. Sometimes these are described as alternatives to the professional theological degree, but again they largely collapse into simply specialized studies or into a juxtaposition of diverse courses with distribution guaranteed by the "pork barrel" principle in which the faculty members in each area are guaranteed some place in the curriculum. Plainly there is a variety of purposes that the master's degree can and should serve; but equally plainly, the same program cannot serve all purposes.

It may be that the master's degree should be simply given up as a foundation for doctoral study and rehabilitated in relation to the other sound goals of post-baccalaureate education.[7] But the substantive problem remains.

At the graduate level, a few attempts have been made to expose the student to a variety of subdisciplines, areas, and methods through the introductory seminar or proseminar at the beginning of graduate study—as at Columbia, Brown, and Ottawa—or the less formal and usually optional "graduate colloquim."[8] The growing number of such devices testifies to an increasing awareness of need. But so far these schemes seem in practice to have exhibited the same defects

[7] Interesting models that seem to point in this direction have appeared, for example, at Indiana University (especially in "the religious element in culture"), St. John's College, Minnesota (directed to religious educators), Waterloo Lutheran, Ontario (with "thematic courses" tying together Near Eastern studies and contemporary religious issues), and the University of the Pacific (again with emphasis on religious issues in contemporary culture).

[8] Columbia has had a long-standing course in history and theory of religion; Brown more recently has experimented with a theory of religion requirement; and Ottawa University has developed a basic course in religion and hermeneutics treating the approaches to the interpretation of religion in the nineteenth and twentieth centuries.

The Interdepartmental Seminar at Emory and the Doctoral Colloquium at Hartford are serious efforts to emphasize cross-disciplinary discussion, engaging students from the several areas of specialization.

as some older patterns of distributional examinations, resulting largely in the mere juxtaposition of areas with little or no integration. The introductory colloquium becomes "Mickey Mouse," since the real energies are devoted to work in special fields. The broadly distributed qualifying exams become simply a series of hurdles to be overcome, often resented as irrelevant to the actual development in learning. With respect to the prevailing patterns of distributional requirements (where they exist), Jencks and Riesman's observation is correct: "Ph.D. candidates must know something about the speciality of almost everyone in their department. . . . The problem . . . is not really that Ph.D. programs turn out nothing but specialists. The problem is that they turn out generalists who all have the same mix of specialized skills" (Jencks and Riesman, 1969, pp. 524 ff.). Or, I would add, no mix at all.

Much more promising is the pattern developed at Stanford, which includes a continuing cycle of seminars, required of all students, in the four perspectives or disciplines judged characteristic of the humanistic study of religion: the exegesis of religious texts; the history of religious movements, especially schools of thought; the comparative study of religious phenomena; and the philosophical-theological discipline of examining and comparing the ways of expressing religious meanings. The humanistic approaches are chosen, not because they are judged to be inherently better than the social-scientific, but because in that university the program has grown up in the humanities and connections with supporting resources are most fully established in these fields. This scheme is plainly an attempt to combine concentrations on identifiable areas of the field with a variety of distinguishable perspectives. The plan clearly envisages a continuing interrelation that informs graduate study up to and through its most specialized development. Yet most efforts in this direction encounter the other difficulty; namely, of defining and obtaining an appropriate intensity in specialization. As far as I can determine, no one has yet found the adequate devices for an effective combination of the essential ingredients. That I take to be one of the most pressing tasks for the next decade.

A related model that deserves extensive experimentation, but has nowhere been tried, is the "departmental seminar" for all students and faculty, which would constitute a substantial portion and focus of the student's learning from the beginning to the end of the graduate program—incorporating systematic study of the history of the discipline(s), the major perspectives and styles of approach to religious studies, and serious attempts to locate the frontiers in each of those subdisciplines in which a given department proposes to offer advanced studies. Such experiments would be feasible at least in programs of modest size, and there are valuable precedents in other disciplines, where, in some institutions, the continuing departmental colloquium or seminar has become a centripetal and fructifying force of great power.

There will doubtless be no single model or formula that will emerge as the resolution of these problems. It is neither possible nor desirable to specify a precise body of core material that *every* Ph.D. in religion should know. But it is possible and necessary to identify related clusters of problems and modes of approach that will make the concept of "religious studies" intelligible as something more than congeries of specializations.

Two elements at least seem indispensable for any effective solution that will allow varieties in method and cross-cultural studies to contribute to coherence rather than to mere proliferation of hurdles and juxtaposition of materials. These are: (*a*) some device for continuing systematic examination of particular areas of study in relation to other parts of the field and other methods of approach; and (*b*) the willingness of institutions and programs to focus on a carefully limited set of related specializations, rather than trying to encompass all the parts of the field. Of course, as long as each faculty member persists in simply doing his own thing (and replicating himself in the next generation), no amount of carefully designed curricula will do anything for coherence. A condition for any advance in the directions proposed is the willingness of faculty members actually to expose themselves to each other, to carry on their own study and teaching with a view to its relation to their colleagues' and students' work. Given that sort of self-discipline and mutual criticism, however, the prognosis for a new sort of identity in advanced religious studies is good.

3

Tensions of Graduate
and Professional Education

Advanced education in religion has been historically associated largely with theological faculties and the professional preparation of clergy. Studies have focused on the basic areas of primary concern to the religious community—scripture, history, and the systematic interpretation of cult, belief, and ethics—and for the most part have been based on European models of theological instruction. Religion was, of course, also investigated in other academic departments, such as history, philosophy, oriental studies, and anthropology, but graduate programs explicitly directed to the study of religious phenomena were conventionally the province of theological faculties.[1] Graduate education in religion and theology could thus happily be considered as "professional" in two senses: preparation for service in and for the religious community, and preparation for the profession of teaching and research.

The recent emergence of independent departments of religion in private nonsectarian and public institutions and the rapid transformation of religion and theology departments in church-related institutions has fundamentally altered this picture. In the spring of 1970, there were no less than nineteen universities in the United States and Canada offering Ph.D. programs in religious studies without any dependence on theological school faculties—and this does not include the numerous programs in such departments as Semitic languages and literature, Near Eastern studies, Asian studies, and Islamic studies. In addition, in at least half of the universities with a divinity school that offer a Ph.D. degree in reli-

---

[1] With the exception of the special area of "history of religions," the same thing continues to be true in European countries (see Chapter 8). Even in a place like the Netherlands, where the appointment of theological faculty in biblical studies and in history of Christianity has long been under the control of secular authorities, the relation in both faculty and student body between advanced studies of religion and the preparation of clergy has remained close.

gion, the program is administratively under control of the graduate school of arts and sciences rather than of the theological school faculty.[2] Such arrangements have often involved major changes in institutional structure, of which recent important instances are the establishment of departments of religious studies at Yale (1963) and McGill (1970).

The range of problems generated by these developments for the relation of "graduate" to "professional" education in religion may be divided into at least four distinct sorts of issues: (1) the question of the validity of the distinction itself; (2) the profusion of graduate and advanced professional degrees and their relation to each other; (3) the logistic as well as ideological problems of the seminary-based graduate programs; and (4) the weakness of graduate religious studies generally in preparation for the profession of teaching.

These issues I shall take up in order and state as sharply as possible, but let me emphasize at the outset that I do not see the desirable outcome as a simple separation of graduate, seminary, and undergraduate education. These have been and will remain elements within a complex system. The elements are being rearranged, and they need to be; but they can continue in healthy tension with one another.

1. "GRADUATE" AND "PROFESSIONAL"—AN IRENIC ESSAY IN DISTINCTION

Complaints are frequently heard that one should not distinguish between graduate education and professional education. After all, professional schools in law, medicine, and theology have long since generally required the B.A. for admission, and the trend is strong in schools of business, engineering, social work, and many others to follow the same pattern. Thus, professional education *is* graduate education.

Moreover, there have been strong tendencies in theological seminaries to conceive their role as that of graduate centers for the study of religion. Confessional allegiance is sometimes of little or no importance as a criterion for appointment, and many faculties have become by design interconfessional or religiously pluralistic. Similarly, claims upon students for religious commitments

[2] Unfortunately, this is a development that has largely escaped the attention of the major organs of interpretation and analysis of graduate education generally, which continue to assume apparently that graduate studies in religion are identical with professional degree programs. Thus the 1969 edition of the ACE guide to graduate programs classifies all religious studies programs under the heading of theology. The National Academy of Sciences reports on doctoral degree production classify all religion and theology doctorates as professional degrees, along with education and business. Lewis Mayhew's study (1970) offers a long rank-order list of master's and doctoral programs offered and projected, based on questionnaires returned from 368 institutions. In this list religion nowhere appears. All programs in theology or religion appear to have been lumped together under a separate listing of present and planned professional schools and colleges (p. 11, Table 1). The "quiet revolution" (Michaelsen, in MacLean, 1967) has apparently not been well understood by otherwise sophisticated educational interpreters. A similar confusion has bedeviled the attempts of legislators and government administrators in their attempt to provide support for higher education.

are rapidly being abandoned. This tendency has doubtless gone much further in Protestant institutions, but the trend also appears in Roman Catholic and Jewish schools.[3]

On the other hand, Ph.D. studies in religion are in fact largely directed toward the preparation of teachers in colleges, universities, and theological schools and therefore need explicitly to be recognized as professional preparation, largely for teaching, with the consequent obligation on graduate schools to take this seriously.[4]

These qualifications having been made, however, there is no good reason why we should not use the commonplace distinction between graduate and professional education. It is a distinction, not an antithesis. Divinity schools and seminaries, like schools of law and medicine, are commonly organized as distinct from graduate schools of arts and sciences, and there are obvious differences between the M.A. and Ph.D. religion programs in the latter and the Bachelor or Master of Divinity (and now, Doctor of Ministry) or Licentiate in Theology or Master of Hebrew Letters and Rabbinical programs that are directed toward the preparation of priests, ministers, and rabbis for ordination and ministry in religious communities.

We need to be aware of at least three sorts of distinctions in further relating graduate and professional studies in religion.

First, there are differences in intention and interest between theological studies in the professional school and the study of religion in the framework of arts and sciences. "Professional study" intends to prepare for leadership in a religious community. Thus, "the American Association of Theological Schools is an association of schools and groups of schools devoted to education for the Christian ministry or the Jewish Rabbinate" (AATS *Bulletin* 29, 1970, p. 9). There are many sorts of "ministries," of which teaching may be one. There is also great ferment concerning the nature of priesthood, ministry, and rabbinate and the preparation for them. Nonetheless this preparation is understood to take place, in part at least, in a context of some kind of commitment to a religious tradition.

The graduate study of religion in arts and sciences is carried on in a different context, one that does not ordinarily assume the validity of the truth claims of a

---

[3] There are also theological schools that have tried to become "little universities," with departments of psychology, sociology, literature, and the like. I do not question the need and hunger of theological students for work in the humanistic and social science disciplines, nor the importance of such study for the field of religion (see Chapters 4 and 5). And the relevant university departments have too often moved away from orientation to questions of fundamental human value and concern. But the theological school's effort to generate these departments within itself may also reflect an "arts and sciences complex" on the part of an institution that has lost confidence in the integrity of education for a profession and therefore seeks to emulate the prestige model of a graduate school. This is a matter for the professional schools to ponder.

[4] Ph.D. study is also professional education, according to the useful definition of "profession" as "an occupation that is relatively colleague-oriented rather than client-oriented. . . . Professionalism means that the practitioners seek the exclusive right to name and judge one another's mistakes" (Jencks and Riesman, 1969, pp. 201 ff.; see Hughes 1958).

religious tradition and may be neutral toward them. It certainly does not exclude religious commitment on the part of faculty or students, but it need not presuppose or require such commitment. All truth claims, if not bracketed, are at least open for examination. Faculty and students may indeed understand their work as contributing to the well-being of the religious community, and ventures in systematic theological construction may properly be a part of such study; but the intention of such programs of graduate education is ordinarily quite distinct from the preparation of clergy or rabbis for service in congregations.[5]

Both professional education and graduate education are obviously concerned for higher learning and the best in scholarship. The religious communities have a great deal at stake in this. Furthermore, "graduate education" may also properly refer to those programs in advanced studies beyond the "first professional degree," which are intended primarily to prepare faculty members for research and teaching in theological and rabbinical schools. Thus, the "academic" or "scholarly" study of religion is not a happy term to distinguish what is done in arts and sciences faculties from work in professional schools; the latter have as much at stake in being academic and scholarly as do graduate schools.

Second, the differences between graduate and professional education are partly symbolized by the distinction between the Ph.D. degree and the several advanced "theological" or ecclesiastical degrees. In the latter area there is a profusion, and confusion, of degrees—and one may lament the extraordinary proliferation of degree nomenclature in the field of theology as a whole.[6] The most common designations for the highest degrees are: Doctor of Theology (Th.D. or D.Th.); Doctor of Sacred Theology (S.T.D.); and Doctor of Hebrew Letters (D.H.L.). In general the Doctor of Theology terminology is used by Protestant institutions. In Roman Catholic institutions, the S.T.D. is the degree awarded by schools to which Rome has granted the status of a Pontifical faculty; this is the highest ecclesiastical degree that Roman Catholic institutions in North America are permitted to grant. The D.H.L. is given by Jewish seminaries. All these degrees are in part—probably in large part—intended to prepare for teaching and research. However, the Th.D. degree is also widely offered in the so-called "practical fields," that is, preparing for specialized competence in ministerial practice or teaching in those areas. Further confusion is introduced by the fact that the S.T.D. degree, while frequently an honorary degree (like D.D.), and so legally defined by New York State, is awarded by some Protestant institutions as part of a program of continuing education for ministers or for specialized training in ministerial practice (as at San Francisco Theological Seminary and Garrett Theological Seminary). Sometimes the Th.D. degree is restricted to the "practical

[5] This situation is complicated, of course, by the numerous recent proposals that the pattern of professional education for the ministry may well take the form of several years of study in a graduate program of religious studies, followed or accompanied by specific "professional preparation."

[6] One theological school, with a full-time faculty of 13 and a student body of 255, offers the following degrees: D.Min., M.Div., M.R.E., M.S.M., S.T.M., Th.M., M.A., M.S., M.A.R., M.S.R. This is but one extreme illustration of the problem that degrees have come to be so widely accepted as "reward symbols" for training and study.

fields," and the D.H.L. is sometimes described as not directed toward teaching and research (for example, at Hebrew Union College—though at Jewish Theological Seminary no distinction in principle is drawn between the Ph.D. and the D.H.L.).[7]

Third, there are important differences in institutional structures. Five kinds of doctoral programs leading to teaching and research degrees can be distinguished according to types of institutions: (a) Ph.D. programs in universities that do not have theological schools; (b) Ph.D. programs in university theological faculties or combined university-seminary faculties; (c) Ph.D. programs in independent schools of religion or theology; (d) Th.D., S.T.D., and D.H.L. programs offered by independent schools of theology; and (e) Th.D. and S.T.D. programs in theological schools that are integral parts of a university. Despite overlapping in program, these structures point to important distinctions (see also Chapter 11, below).

2. PH.D. VERSUS TH.D./S.T.D./D.H.L.?

Are there substantive differences between the Ph.D. and the Th.D./S.T.D. graduate programs in religion? Two patterns of differentiation seem to hold at the outset.[8]

First, there are important distinctions in areas of specialization between the kinds of study offered at universities without a professional theological school and the kinds offered in independent theological seminaries (see Chapter 11). The university programs make a large place for the history of religions (or comparative religions or world religions) and for non-Western religious traditions (sometimes also for Judaic studies). These are not to be found in the independent theological school Th.D. programs, with the sole exception of Princeton Theological Seminary, whose history of religions work depends heavily on resources of Princeton University. On the other hand, the theological school Th.D.'s regularly offer work in the areas of practical and applied theology—preaching, homiletics, liturgical studies, pastoral theology and psychology, religious education, and missions and evangelism—whereas these areas almost never appear in the university programs.[9] Judaic studies, Near Eastern religions, and Islamic studies are also nowhere to be found among the independent theological school Th.D. programs.

Second, the first professional degree (the Bachelor or Master of Divinity, or the Licentiate of Theology) is the standard prerequisite for admission to the

[7] In our study we have excluded direct examination of programs that were explicitly defined as not directed toward teaching and research.

[8] We may omit the D.H.L. from this discussion, since only at Jewish Theological Seminary is it defined as a teaching and research degree, and there the program is indistinguishable from the Ph.D.

[9] The exceptions are the new Notre Dame program in pastoral theology, the Catholic University Department of Religion and Religious Education, and perhaps the University of Iowa program in religion and psychology.

It is also striking that only one of the Ph.D. programs in universities that make use of theological faculties offers concentrations in practical theology: Northwestern-Garrett.

Th.D., and a significant proportion of Th.D. recipients have gone into pastoral work and church administration. On the other hand, increasing numbers of students are embarking on the Ph.D. without first attending theological schools. The traditional route to the doctorate in religion—the B.A. degree and then three or four more years of study for the Ph.D. (in the Roman Catholic tradition the pattern has been somewhat different and often more extended, but the principle has been the same)—is still the one that has been followed by the majority of present students in Ph.D. studies (see Chapter 10). But the pattern is changing, and a number of universities are actively encouraging entrance into M.A. and Ph.D. studies in religion directly upon college graduation. This kind of distinction is apparent, for example, in the doctoral programs offered at Catholic University, the one in the Department of Religion and Religious Education not requiring the professional degree, whereas those in the School of Theology and the School of Canon Law do.

Apart from those differences, however, there are few distinctions in the fields of graduate study proposed in the Ph.D. and Th.D. programs. Studies in Bible, in the history and thought of Christianity, and in constructive theology (or philosophy of religion and ethics) regularly appear—and a few of the university programs do not go at all beyond what forms the core of the theological schools' doctoral programs (for example, Baylor, Case Western Reserve, Marquette, and Notre Dame).

Difficulties in differentiation become acute when one compares the Ph.D. and Th.D. programs offered in the same institution, or in institutions drawing heavily on each other's faculties. The most instructive instances are the Graduate Theological Union in Berkeley (California) and Harvard University.[10]

At the Graduate Theological Union the Th.D. degree was established first (1962), the Ph.D. degree two years later. The fields of study proposed for the Ph.D. and the Th.D. are largely parallel. The Ph.D. areas are: biblical, historical, and theological studies, religion and society, religion and the personality sciences, theology and education, theology and arts, and the history and phenomenology of religions. The Th.D. areas are the same except that they do not include reli-

---

[10] The other relevant instances here are the University of Montreal, St. Paul (Ottawa), the interrelated programs at Union Theological Seminary (N.Y.) and Columbia University, and Jewish Theological Seminary.

At Montreal, the Ph.D. and Th.D. programs are almost indistinguishable: the same fields of study are pursued, the only difference being that the Th.D. student must spend a year longer in the theological school program proper, so that the total length of time in study turns out to be the same. At the University of St. Paul, Ottawa, one studies at the same time in the same program for both the Ph.D. and Th.D. and receives both degrees for essentially the same work, the Th.D. being awarded only after publication of a dissertation in some form. (The Ph.D. program in Religious Studies at the University of Ottawa, which is separate from the St. Paul programs, is of a quite different sort.)

The Union Seminary Th.D. and the Columbia University Ph.D. are different in the fields required for comprehensive examinations. The programs overlap in the areas of biblical studies and Christian thought and history, but differ in Judaica and Eastern religions.

The Jewish Theological Ph.D. and D.H.L. programs are academically indistinguishable.

gion and society, history and phenomenology of religion, and religion and personality sciences. But there appears to be no academic reason why these three fields could not be represented in the Th.D. program. The substantive differences seem to be that the Th.D. is more specifically theological in scope; studies in a given area are undertaken "in the context of the entire theological spectrum." Ph.D. studies are carried on "in the context of the university disciplines," students being expected to take substantial portions of their work in cognate disciplines in the University of California.

The two Harvard programs present even more of an anomaly. The Th.D. is administered by the faculty of the Divinity School; the Ph.D. in the study of religion is administered by a committee of the faculty of Arts and Sciences, including representatives from that faculty as well as from the Divinity School. However, the basic instructional faculty is that of the Divinity School. The areas of study are almost precisely parallel: religion and society is offered only in the Ph.D. program and applied theology only in the Th.D. Apart from this there are the basic six fields that are common: Old Testament, New Testament, church history, theology, ethics, and comparative religions—with only minor variations in designation (for instance, "Old Testament and Inter-Testamental Judaism" in the Ph.D. as against "Old Testament" in the Th.D., and "Christian Theology" in the Ph.D. as against "Theology" in the Th.D.).

In both of these instances, the question immediately arises, why maintain the distinction? More specifically, why not simply the Ph.D. degree, especially since in both institutions, as well as in the American scene as a whole, the movement is strong toward the Ph.D. rather than the Th.D.?[11] The Graduate Theological Union appears to have no particular interest in preserving the Th.D. At Harvard, apart from work in applied theology, the academic reasons offered for maintaining the distinction are that the professional degree prerequisite for the Th.D. ensures that the comparative religions student will have a grounding in Christian studies (whereas the Ph.D. student might work in a single other tradition or in several traditions but not including Christianity), and that the Th.D. student in theology will have studied Bible and the history of Christianity (whereas one can get a Ph.D. in "Christian theology" without working in those areas!). Beyond these, the reasons given for maintaining the distinction are "political" or "strategic"—e.g., administration of scholarship support, vaguely defined fears of control by the arts and science faculty, desire for "leverage" or, as one Divinity School faculty member put it, "If we gave up the Th.D. we wouldn't have a doctoral degree under our own control." The Harvard situation is further complicated by the fact that the majority of students in Old Testament are presently encouraged to take their degrees in the Ph.D. program in Near Eastern languages and literatures, the Old Testament faculty in the Divinity School being also members of that department.

The more general question now arises: what kind of future has the Th.D.

---

[11] Over the past fifteen years the number of Th.D. degrees awarded has remained relatively constant, whereas the number of Ph.D.'s has increased greatly. Similarly the great increase of students has come in Ph.D. programs (see Chapters 10, 12).

degree as a whole? Its only exclusive province seems to be studies in practical theology (even though this is not a complete monopoly). Yet just at this point an ambiguity arises with respect to the Th.D.; namely, whether it is to be understood as an advanced teaching and research degree or whether it is an advanced professional degree designed to provide specialized ministerial skills.

The problem is still further exacerbated—or perhaps it will be resolved— by the action of the American Association of Theological Schools (June, 1970) recognizing "the right of member schools to move toward the establishment of programs for a professional doctorate (D.Min.) provided that their academic and other educational resources warrant such a development" (AATS *Bulletin* 29, 1970, p. 27).

The movement toward the Doctor of Ministry as the first professional degree is sure to grow in strength. It is not within our province to discuss the propriety of this degree for professional education. Its emergence may, however, do the following: (a) provide a way for satisfying the (sometimes unfortunate) hunger on the part of both clergy and laity for the doctor title for ministers; (b) open the way for theological schools to concentrate more freely on the problems of professional education per se, without having to be preoccupied with the degree reward structure; (c) drastically reduce the applications for the Th.D. programs from those interested essentially in continuing education or in the doctor title (two deans of quite different theological schools indicated to me that adoption of the Doctor of Ministry as the first professional degree would probably reduce Th.D. enrollments in their institutions by two-thirds).

To these considerations, I must add my own judgment that approximately half of the present Th.D. programs are of dubious academic quality, either because of the lack of academic rigor or resources, or because they are programs pursued by part-time students and staffed by faculty who already have far too much to do in their professional school programs. Further, some Th.D. programs are carried on without the possibility of an effective relationship to a first-class university, thus without the abrasions and pressures from other disciplines that are important for quality graduate education. The strong Th.D. programs are almost entirely those in university-related institutions.

If there is a future, then, for the Th.D. degree, I believe it must be defined relative to four sorts of considerations.

First, some may wish to argue that there is need for a genuinely advanced professional degree for the development of specialized ministerial skills, or for study in those areas not likely to be accepted in university-related programs. But here there is the question whether academic degrees are the best means of certifying such training.

Second, certain advanced degree programs may be defined specifically in relation to the confessional interests of a particular denomination or group of denominations.

Third, it is sometimes held that there is a difference in kind between scholarship carried on in the context of a community of faith and worship and that pursued in the secular atmosphere of the university graduate school. This

assumes, for example, that the kind of biblical studies carried on by the faculty
of a professional theological school, concerned to prepare persons for religious
leadership, involves interests and questions of a different sort from those required for study of the Bible in an independent university setting. Since the
religious communities need scholars trained at the highest level of proficiency,
it would follow that there is a need for graduate studies carried on in the context of the professional school commitment, parallel to studies in the graduate
school. Apart from the specific claims of denominational allegiance, I believe
this third argument to be of dubious validity. It appears to attribute to scholars
outside the theological school walls a posture of neutrality, at best, toward the
claims of faith, an attribution that is surely unwarranted. A review of the
actual complexion of the faculties of nonseminary departments of religious
studies does not seem to show the kind of difference implied, and no good cause
will be served by trying to impose a neopositivist stance upon university programs. Further, many of the strongest pressures toward nonconfessional biblical
and historical study have come precisely from within the theological school communities. And there are strong arguments from within the religious communities that precisely the best sort of education for ministers in most of the traditional theological disciplines can come as these are carried on in the free
atmosphere of the university in relation to the other disciplines.

The fourth kind of argument for the Th.D./S.T.D./D.H.L. is more powerful,
emphasizing differences in the areas of study rather than in "point of view" or
in degree of commitment. Theological schools have an obvious and proper
interest in having faculty whose special competence is set in the context of
the whole scope of a religious tradition and its concerns and who also have
studied the problems of the profession and of professional education. Thus
(a) the Th.D./S.T.D./D.H.L. program may be defined as one presupposing the
professional degree and its interests, whereas the Ph.D. does not presuppose
that background and basis, but some other route and core of studies. Further,
(b) the distinction can usefully be drawn (along the lines of the Graduate
Theological Union definition) between the Ph.D. program as one set in the
context of university disciplines and emphasizing religious phenomena across
a broad range of cultures and historical periods, and the Th.D. program as one
organized in the context of "other theological" disciplines. Thus the Th.D. could
be maintained in selected instances as a program of high quality involving a
spectrum of studies not necessarily included in the Ph.D. This will be a far
better course of action than for independent theological schools to seek authorization to offer the Ph.D. The question still remains, of course, whether any
theological school faculty not related to a major university can have the
resources necessary for doctoral studies of high quality.

3. SPECIAL PROBLEMS OF THE SEMINARY-BASED PROGRAMS

Until at least the last decade, a few centers of study enjoyed an unthreatened
oligopoly in graduate religious studies in America. These were, as James
Gustafson has put it, "the established grandfather institutions [with] a status
in the academic market almost as dominant as that of General Motors, Chrysler

and Ford in the automobile industry" (Ramsey and Wilson, 1970, p. 340). These were the institutions with the massive faculty and library resources; they attracted the majority of students and they produced by far the largest number of doctorates.

Eight institutions, for example, produced two-thirds of the approximately 2,250 Ph.D.'s in religion given between 1952 and 1969. These were Yale (with 308 Ph.D.'s), Boston (288), Chicago (230), Columbia (167, with which should probably be associated 138 Th.D.'s at Union Theological Seminary), Duke (158), Harvard (126 plus 78 Th.D.'s), Drew (123), and Vanderbilt (108).

On the Th.D. side the situation is similar. Of approximately 1,500 Th.D. and S.T.D. degrees awarded between 1952 and 1969, five-sixths were given by seven institutions: Southwestern Baptist (266), Southern Baptist (256), Princeton (156), New Orleans Baptist (155), Catholic University (148 S.T.D.'s), Union Seminary in New York (138), and Dallas Theological Seminary (123). (The next largest producer was Iliff with 79.) [12]

If one leaves aside the large southern producers of Th.D.'s (Southern Baptist, Southwestern Baptist, New Orleans Baptist, and Dallas Theological),[13] which have served special clienteles, there is a striking concentration of graduate religious studies in a handful of theological school faculties that either are an integral part of the university or work in close association with an adjacent university.

The breaking of the oligopoly, through the establishment and rapid expansion of new Ph.D. programs in the 1950's and 1960's, together with the movement toward new conceptions of graduate religious studies, has not been without signs of serious strain and tension. The old and the new have each felt threatened by the other, and sometimes this threat has appeared within a single faculty. The newer programs have had to compete with the reputation and the greater faculty and library resources of the older programs, and they have therefore struggled especially hard to establish their own identity and to win a share of the market. The independent university programs could rarely hope to match the gross numbers of faculty in the theological schools. On the other hand, the seminary-based programs, in addition to the inevitable con-

[12] For fuller details, see Chapter 12.

[13] It is noteworthy also how relatively few of the Th.D. recipients from these four institutions are engaged in undergraduate teaching. We have information on the sources of the highest degree for 3,329 teachers in undergraduate departments in the United States and Canada. The institutions mentioned have contributed fewer than 150 of those highest degrees, though they have together awarded 800 Th.D.'s since 1952. Of course, they have also trained the great majority of their own seminary faculty and sent numbers of their graduates into the mission fields. But the basic pattern is confirmed by those schools' reports on first employment of their doctoral recipients, 1965-1969. Of twenty graduates, Dallas sent three into college teaching, eight into seminary teaching, six into the ministry. Of New Orleans Baptist's forty-seven degree recipients, fifteen went into teaching (two in seminaries) and thirty into parishes. Southwestern Baptist, with seventy-five Th.D.'s, produced fifteen teachers (two in seminary) and fifty-one ministers. Corresponding information concerning Southern Baptist graduates was not available.

cerns about the weakening of their own privileged position, have been fearful
(a) that the new university programs would be indifferent to the interests of
professional education and of the religious communities and (b) that the
movement to by-pass the intermediate professional degree would dilute the
quality of graduate religious studies.[14]

The changes of the past decade have also exposed some persisting problems
in the seminary-based programs—problems partly of an ideological sort, but
much more in resources and logistics. A brief glance at the structures at Yale,
Duke, Vanderbilt, Chicago, and Claremont may serve to illustrate the dimensions of the problems.

Yale organized the Department of Religious Studies in 1963 as an entity
administratively and budgetarily distinct from the Divinity School. The department is located in arts and sciences and has responsibility for undergraduate
instruction in Yale College as well as for the M.A. and Ph.D. degrees. The
Divinity School has responsibility for the Bachelor of Divinity, the Master of
Sacred Theology, and other professional degrees. As of 1969-1970 almost
half the members of the department were carried entirely on the departmental
budget; about the same number held joint appointments with the Divinity
School; three others held joint appointments with other departments in the
university. In 1970-1971, the distinction was made sharper, with two of the
joint Divinity School appointees being transferred fully to the department.
Graduate student admissions, fellowships (with the exception of teaching
fellowships in the Divinity School), courses of instruction, examinations, and
dissertation supervision are administered altogether independently from the
Divinity School, though some members of other faculties, including the
Divinity School, are regularly invited to participate in all aspects of the doctoral
program. Doctoral students register only in Graduate Arts and Sciences, not
in the Divinity School, although courses in the Divinity School are open to
them. Faculty in the Department of Religious Studies may teach courses open
to undergraduates, to Divinity School students, and to M.A. and doctoral students.[15]

---

[14] A similar "intramural" distrust and competition appears between the Baylor University
Ph.D. program and the Southwestern Baptist Th.D. program. The former was established
in 1966, presumably to offer a university-based program of graduate religious studies. Yet
in the areas of study proposed (with the exception of practical theology), in the characteristics of faculty (it was said by more than one faculty member at Baylor that no non-Baptist
could be appointed to the religion faculty, except possibly a visiting non-Christian or
Roman Catholic), and in the constituencies served, it is difficult to see any significant
differences.

[15] Prior to the establishment of the present structure, doctoral studies in religion at Yale
were supervised by a graduate faculty, which included members of other departments as
well as some faculty appointed primarily to the Religion Department at Yale College, but
the graduate faculty was to a large degree those Divinity School faculty members who
taught in the areas of graduate instruction.

The evolution at Yale toward the present pattern is symbolized by the changing schemes
for registration and tuition charges. The Ph.D. degree has always been awarded on recommendation of the graduate faculty rather than the Divinity School. However, twenty-five

At Duke, after several decades in which graduate work in religion was carried on as an adjunct to the Divinity School, with the members of a fairly large department of religion in the university playing very little role in it, doctoral studies were put in the hands of a graduate faculty, with an executive council chaired by a director of graduate studies who receives his appointment directly from the Provost. The executive council includes the dean of the Divinity School, the chairman of the Department of Religion, and four other elected members. Budgetary and appointive responsibilities remain in the hands of the Divinity School dean and the department chairman; hence the director of graduate studies exercises power purely by persuasion. The graduate faculty decide who will be members of the graduate faculty and what courses will be offered. The director and the executive council have responsibility for admissions and curriculum. Formally, at least, participation in doctoral instruction by faculty from the Divinity School and from the department is relatively balanced. In practice, however, this instruction is still largely carried on by the divinity faculty, although participation by the department is increasing, so that in 1969-1970 a dozen of the nineteen members of the latter faculty were teaching in the doctoral program. Also, since the establishment of the position of Director of Graduate Studies, all occupants of that post have been members of the Divinity School faculty.

In contrast to both Duke and Yale, responsibility for the doctoral program at Vanderbilt is more largely located in the Divinity School. The Department of Religion in the college is small (though now growing rapidly); it became a department only in 1969-1970, and two of its members held joint appointments in the Divinity School. As in the case of other professional schools at Vanderbilt, doctoral work is administered through the Graduate School, with the resources being provided by the Divinity School. The graduate chairman is appointed by the dean of the Graduate School, on recommendation of the dean of the Divinity School. Doctoral students are admitted to the Graduate School and are not Divinity School students. Fellowship funds for doctoral students come from the Divinity School budget. Faculty from the undergraduate department who are qualified for graduate instruction are members of the graduate faculty, but nearly all the graduate teachers are supplied by the Divinity School, since all members of the latter faculty (in the relevant areas) are listed in the graduate program.[16]

The University of Chicago Divinity School represents the formal identification of a theological faculty with the graduate faculty, so that the Divinity School has both fiscal and administrative responsibility for the advanced degrees. The Divinity School is as such the graduate faculty of religious studies

years ago doctoral students registered as members of the graduate class of the Divinity School and until the final year of doctoral studies paid the (much lower) Divinity School tuition. Then in the 1950's doctoral students began to be required to pay the full graduate school tuition from time of admission to study for the M.A. or Ph.D.

[16] It may also be noted, as an almost unique situation in a university-seminary combination, that the divinity library is housed with the general university collection.

and offers the A.M. and the Ph.D. degrees, as well as the Doctor of Ministry degree. Thus the same faculty supervises both the professional and graduate degrees through an A.M.-Ph.D. committee and a D.Min. committee, which direct parallel programs—parallel in the sense that students enter directly upon one or the other. All these degree students are thus students in the Divinity School. It should also be noted, however, that a Ph.D. program in New Testament and Christian origins is offered in the humanities division of the Graduate School and is staffed largely by Divinity School faculty. Further, several members of the divinity faculty hold joint appointments with other departments in the university.

The Claremont Graduate School, a relative newcomer to doctoral studies in religion, presents a still different pattern of relations among graduate, theological, and undergraduate faculties. Ph.D. studies in religion had been approved in the Claremont Graduate School earlier, but the proposal was not implemented until after the move of the School of Theology from Los Angeles to Claremont. As is usual in graduate departments at Claremont, three members of the graduate religion faculty are Graduate School appointees. Most of the other graduate programs draw heavily from faculty in the appropriate departments of the several Claremont undergraduate colleges. In the case of religion, however, the great bulk of instruction is provided by faculty in the School of Theology, and it is also in the School of Theology that the library resources have been principally built up in the area of Christian studies. There is a close working relationship between the graduate faculty in religion and the School of Theology, but little participation by religion faculty from the undergraduate colleges. Faculty from the Graduate School and the Theological School do some undergraduate teaching.

In all the institutional structures just described—and these are cited only as illustrations, not by any means as an exhaustive list of institutions in which the problems arise—three kinds of difficulty can be seen:

a. First of all, there is a persistent competition between the interests of the professional school and the graduate school. This is not primarily an ideological quarrel. The interests of arts and sciences department faculties and those of professional school faculties often overlap greatly, as also do their areas of competence and methods of approach. Members of departments of religious studies (especially in institutions with a theological faculty) are rarely indifferent to the concerns of professional education.

Yet there are differences of orientation and purpose that in numerous institutions have led to uneasiness and tension. The faculties in several theological schools have long been divided over the question whether their primary task was that of professional training of ministers or graduate studies in certain disciplinary areas. (Chicago Divinity School, in the formation and later breakdown of the Federated Faculty, has exhibited this tension more publicly than most institutions, but it is by no means the only one with the problem.)

Even in institutions where the administration of doctoral studies has been put explicitly in the hands of a "graduate faculty" as distinct from the theological faculty, students and faculty alike have frequently reported to us the tendency of the divinity school pattern to dominate their graduate programs. The majority of the faculty naturally come from the theological school. It is not necessarily the case that all theological school faculty will teach graduate students, but nearly all those joining the theological faculty hope to do so. The library collections are likely to be housed in the seminary, and the students tend to do their studying there. The graduate chairman is almost certain to be a member of the theological faculty, and many of the classes will be held in the theological school buildings. The existence of a separate graduate department office often seems a mere token distinction. Some graduate students are also concerned that the programs are not only oriented to professional school interests but, therefore, necessarily Christian-oriented: since the appointments that most heavily service the graduate program are effectively made by the theological school, its concerns tend to dominate. It is also clear that some theological school faculty and administrators, in the institutions mentioned above, definitely think of the graduate program as essentially the theological school's project.

Again, we are not here dealing necessarily with ideological conflict, but with tensions between differing legitimate interests. And numerous students are now entering theological schools, not with clear "professional" intent nor from religious commitment, but for much the same reasons that an undergraduate may give for majoring in religion. The tensions can be healthy and creative as well as destructive. They derive from the historical situation out of which advanced studies in religion have emerged. But they are no less real.

More important than differences in orientation is the simple competition for faculty time. The three-way division between undergraduate, professional, and graduate arts and sciences teaching magnifies all the usual struggle between undergraduate and graduate interests. This is a special burden for the occasional faculty member who tries to teach on all three levels at the same time; but the problem also affects a wider circle, since more of the faculty are necessarily drawn into the planning and operation of three distinct educational structures. Another kind of difficulty arises from the necessity of excluding some faculty members from graduate instruction, thus seeming to make them second-class citizens in the theological school which throughout purports to operate at the graduate level. Finally, while one can hardly say that the overloading of individual faculty members is a function peculiar to the involvement of theological faculties in doctoral instruction, it is plain that in many institutions, in spite of the apparently extensive faculty resources provided by a large theological faculty, an unusually heavy burden of doctoral instruction falls on relatively few members of the faculty, and indeed usually on those who are also most in demand for the professional school program.[17]

[17] A related problem of resources, which is at least as serious for the independent theological schools in their Th.D. programs as for the university-related schools, is the necessity to carry on a considerable portion of doctoral instruction in both seminars and lecture courses designed primarily for the professional degree curriculum.

b. A second kind of problem bears on the development of undergraduate religious studies. With the major exception of Duke, where a large and effective undergraduate department had emerged on the basis of required courses in religion (and until recently with little relation to the graduate program), it seems that in institutions where the doctoral program has been heavily dependent on a professional school faculty, the undergraduate program has been a neglected stepchild. The circumstances and causes are obviously not all the same, but it is striking that undergraduate programs in religion have not in the past flourished at Yale, Vanderbilt, or Columbia, an undergraduate program has only just begun at Chicago, and Harvard is only talking about the possibility of an undergraduate concentration in religion. Other illustrations could be offered of the apparent inhibition of undergraduate development.

It is also true, of course, that religion programs have generally been weak and neglected stepchildren in major universities until recently. But as religion departments have developed in the past ten to fifteen years, the large private universities with theological faculties have moved less rapidly than others to expand or introduce college programs, no doubt partly because of the large number of religionists already on the faculty.

The question may also be asked whether university administrators have sometimes mistakenly assumed that the presence of the theological faculty itself provided sufficient resources for all levels of study in religion and theology and that, therefore, undergraduate studies could simply be developed by drawing on the theological faculty. This is very like supposing that the whole university program in biology could be manned by the spare time of a medical school faculty.[18]

The problem of undergraduate studies in the university with a theological school is also that as the undergraduate faculties do develop, they tend to be distorted by being forced into non-Western, or at least non-Christian, studies, since Christian studies are presumably adequately represented by the theological school faculty. Vanderbilt is an obvious illustration of this situation, but the chairman of a department in another university also reports the difficulty of persuading his provost that even if the divinity school has three or four biblical scholars, the department of religion might also require one.

c. A further range of practical problems in the relation of graduate and pro-

---

[18] The inhibition factor we are describing here seems to operate even in cases where the theological faculties are not integrally a part of the university. For example, it must be asked whether the presence of Union Theological Seminary has not been used as a justification for Columbia University's relative inattention to its Department of Religion. (Jencks and Riesman, 1969, pp. 211 f., observe that for Columbia the theological affiliation "presumably . . . helps protect the University against charges of godlessness and helps appease the Trustees who are worried about the University's failure to teach morality and wisdom.") Also, the role of Garrett Theological Seminary faculty in the joint Northwestern-Garrett Ph.D. program may have inhibited the development of the Department of Religion at Northwestern, especially the participation of that department in graduate studies.

fessional education concerns the allocation of resources and the internal ordering of graduate studies. These are the perhaps inescapable consequences of the concentration of resources on the areas traditionally important to the respective religious communities. A university divinity school, for example, lists for 1969-1970 a faculty of six persons in biblical studies (including languages), five in the history of Christianity, eight in theology and ethics, six in the church and practical theology, and three in the history of religions (the school is atypical in this last feature).[19]

A casual inspection of the fields of specialization offered by the various types of institutions (see Chapter 11) reveals at once the enormous concentration of faculty resources in the traditional fields of biblical studies, historical studies, and theological studies (including ethics and philosophy of religion).

The results of these concentrations are at least fourfold. First, there is what can be described as either a "richness" or a "superfluous proliferation" of graduate courses in the field of religion at institutions with theological faculties, in comparison with other departments of the same universities. A graduate dean, for example, expressed amazement to me at the number of courses offered in religious studies at his institution relative to the number of faculty and students; that is, there were many more than in departments of comparable size in the sciences and in the humanities. One need not look far in university catalogues to discover that listings of graduate religion courses are in fact regularly longer than for other departments, a consequence partly of listing courses offered in the theological school at an advanced level as well as those designed by each faculty member specifically for doctoral instruction.

Second, it is commonly assumed that if doctoral studies are to be offered at all by the theological faculty, such studies should be available in all the areas in which the faculty work and in some proportion to their relative strengths (the area of practical theology being a major exception in the case of Ph.D. programs). Thus there are no less than sixty institutions in the United States and Canada proposing to train specialists in biblical studies. Each biblical scholar would like to have five students in his seminar to keep it going and, therefore, needs to press for the admission of doctoral students in the biblical area. Those pressures from individual faculty may be resisted to some extent, but it would be much more difficult to propose to an institution with, say, six faculty members in the history of Christianity and Christian thought that its doctoral program should not focus heavily on this area.

[19] Emory University lists: History of Religions (1); Biblical Studies (6); History of Christianity (3); Theology (3); Ethics (3); Theology and Culture (2); Practical Theology (1); Sociology of Religion (2).

The School of Theology at the Catholic University of America lists: Oriental Theology (2); Scripture Studies (6); Church History (4); Practical Theology (5) (this and the following list do not include numerous visiting faculty).

Jewish Theological Seminary lists: Talmudic and Rabbinic Studies (17); History of Judaism (2); Hebrew Literature (5); Biblical Studies (9); Theology (1); Philosophy of Religion (1); Pastoral Psychology (1); Religion and Education (2); Jewish Ethics (1).

Third, a consequence of the concentration in the traditionally important areas
is that few resources are left over or attainable for movement into such areas as
non-Western religions or the social-scientific study of religion. Further, the
present pressures for retrenchment will bear hardest on the newly developed
areas and those already only marginally supported.

The other side of this result, when combined with the interests in convenient
academic packaging and the desire to have at least two or three faculty members
working together, is the creation of the "catchall" areas to include advanced
studies that cannot be put under one of the standard categories. I do not
mean to impugn the validity of graduate studies in some of these areas; on the
contrary, they often represent new styles of approach and exploration that badly
need to be encouraged. My point is simply that many of them tend to be
lumped together under such headings as "religion and society" or "religion
and culture" or "ethics and society."

An interesting example of this pattern has been the organization of the
program at Hartford Seminary Foundation. Here, in addition to biblical studies,
theological studies, and history of religions (with the emphasis mainly on Islam),
there is the field called "human nature and religion." This area is plainly the
least well defined of the four. It involves serious efforts at interdisciplinary
work, relating ethics, psychology, sociology, religious education, linguistics,
and communications. Thus a way is found to incorporate elements originally
developed primarily for professional purposes, and almost no one is excluded
from participation in the Ph.D. program. There is ample room for experimental
and novel patterns of study—as well as for the attempt to do Ph.D. work simply
in psychology in the context of an independent school of religion. On the other
hand, the area is at best vaguely focused, and it remains unclear what kind of
coherence can be ascribed to it.[20] The question to be raised here, and in numerous other comparable instances, is how these fields or approaches are organized
in relation to each other. Perhaps it is too much to ask for integration, but at
least one needs to ask what the criteria are by which they are brought together
in a common category or heading.

Finally, doctoral programs that are built essentially on the resources of faculty
developed for the traditional professional school areas have a powerful built-in
resistance to change, somewhat beyond the ordinary inertia of graduate faculties.
At X University, for example, where a distinguished faculty member in biblical
studies is retiring, no one is seriously proposing to replace him with an appointee
in the history of religions or the sociology of religion, even though the need for
college and university teachers in those areas is patently much greater than in
the area of biblical studies. This problem is intensified by the fact that the
traditional styles and concentrations of resources are most firmly entrenched in

[20] A special feature of the Hartford development is that, because of the school's independent status, it has sought to represent in its faculty the areas that might otherwise be
supplied by other departments of a university (notably psychology, sociology, anthropology,
and linguistics).

the old and stable institutions, which have naturally the strongest credentialing power and thus make redefinition of the field and reallocation of resources even harder.

4. GRADUATE EDUCATION IS "PROFESSIONAL" EDUCATION

Graduate studies in religion and theology have been very largely preparation for teaching and research, thus for a profession. In this dimension the question of "graduate" and "professional" education is not at all a special problem of the relation to seminary education, but is present for all doctoral programs.

To be sure, the ecclesiastical doctorate has often served as a further training period for ministerial responsibility to a congregation or in a religious hierarchy or bureaucracy. To a lesser extent Ph.D. studies have also served such purposes, and it is argued in some quarters that Ph.D. recipients ought to look increasingly to a variety of vocations, including special community services and urban studies and programs, for which a highly developed understanding of religious phenomena, in particular from the social-scientific point of view, will be of value. However much such movements may develop, it remains the case that the majority of the recipients of an earned doctorate in religion (especially the Ph.D.) have become college and university teachers. Of the 898 degree recipients between 1965 and 1969, about whom we have information, at least 80 percent of the Ph.D.'s and 55 percent of the Th.D's went for their first position into teaching at the college level or above. Again, over three-fourths of our 1,965 graduate student respondents want to teach, and only three percent definitely prefer a nonteaching career.[21]

There is no reason whatever to oppose research to teaching in this area. Very few persons in religious studies go into positions that are purely research activity. And teaching needs constantly to be informed by research, just as much

[21] The proportion of doctoral recipients in religion who enter teaching seems indeed to have increased substantially during the decade of the 1960's. Even though its report base is different from ours, the NAS study, *Doctorate Recipients from United States Universities 1958-66* (1967), p. 84. shows the following important changing patterns of post-doctoral employment for religion and theology doctoral degree recipients in the years indicated:

Type of postdoctoral employer	Date of Degree		
	1958-60 %	1961-63 %	1964-66 %
College and University	50	59	70
Elementary and Secondary	12	5	1
Government	*	*	*
Nonprofit	29	25	20
Industry	1	*	*
Other	*	*	*
Foreign Employer	8	11	9
(Total with known employer = 100%)	(376)	(419)	(496)
(Unknown employer)	(46)	(37)	(54)

*= less than 0.5 percent. The NAS classification "nonprofit" includes pastorate, rabbinate, and church administration.

of the vital research that can be done in the field of religion, at least when it is an area of humanities study, requires constantly to be informed by a living relationship to students and their ways of posing questions.[22]

Furthermore, whatever may come of proposals to develop a Doctor of Arts degree, designed specifically to prepare teachers rather than researchers and perhaps especially appropriate to the growing numbers of community and junior colleges, it remains the case that Ph.D. and Th.D. studies in religion cannot be absolved from responsibility for the preparation of teachers. Also, the argument that institutions where faculty members have their first appointment should assume responsibility for helping them to learn to teach, since these schools have the biggest stake in the teaching effectiveness of their faculty, does not seem to me to relieve the doctoral programs of responsibility, even for the success of internship teaching programs.

What, then, is disclosed concerning the initiation of graduate students in religion into the teaching process? The answer is simply that, in spite of the widespread discussion in the past decade of the failure of graduate schools to prepare for teaching (see, for example, Berelson, 1960; Lee, 1967; Jencks and Riesman, 1969; Nowlis, Clark, and Rock, 1968), almost nothing has been done. In many institutions there are teaching fellows or assistants, presumably working under the supervision of a senior faculty member, and a few individual faculty members tell of efforts to guide their assistants in teaching. Some informal seminars or discussions have been reported. But the almost universal testimony of our respondents, both faculty and students, is that little is being done and that few institutions have assumed any responsibility for this aspect of graduate education.

Faculty and students, in conversation and interviews and on questionnaires, are agreed that the emphasis in graduate education in religion, as in graduate education generally, is on research and scholarship. Papers, examinations, and dissertations are what the student is judged by, and he sees that his professors' publications are what weigh most heavily in the academic balance and even that scholarly eminence seems in the mind of fellow faculty to be the sufficient qualification for effective teaching. While a professor may occasionally be denied tenure for lack of teaching skills, the student who would be refused the doctor's degree on such grounds would doubtless become a *cause célèbre*.

Faculty members' responses to questions about the effectiveness of their graduate programs in the preparation of teachers tended to fall into two categories. On the one side were those for whom the "Master-Apprentice" (or paradigm-imitation) model of creating teachers is the one to be preferred.

[22] William May has put it well: "Research in the humanities, while affording its own private pleasures for its participants, cannot be readily abstracted from the inherently social acts of writing and teaching. . . . research in the humanities reaches its fruition only as it issues in writing and nourishes teaching. Put another way, the content of research cannot be separated from its social form. . . . by and large every teacher in the humanities needs frequent exposure to the raw, unformed, non-professional questions of the classroom, as his own life as a researcher comes into contact with the culture of his age. Both ideally and in fact, research nourishes his teaching and his teaching vitalizes his research."

Those respondents also tend to assume that the human qualities necessary for effective teaching are "born, not made" and could not be communicated by pedagogical instruction. Many respondents expressed doubts about courses concerned with the teaching of teaching, and many think that the status quo is as effective as any system could be. I suspect that this is often a counsel of despair, if not of simple indifference.

The second group, on the other hand, judge their programs to be seriously deficient. Such comments as the following are typical: "At best we train graduate students as teachers only indirectly." "As yet we have not shown any creativity in this respect." "My feeling is that preparation of graduate students as teachers is widely ineffective. I am especially distressed by this feeling since my own research is in the area of improving teacher effectiveness, and I am thoroughly convinced that effective teaching is not accidental."

At greater length, one colleague writes with respect to his department that the program is in this area ". . . relatively ineffective. The fact that we have a group of very bright and alert graduate students mitigates the problem, but it is serious and may become more so." He continues, in language that is appropriate to many institutions:

(1) Graduate students do not have a chance at extensive, innovative teacher training and undergraduate contact, because our undergraduate teaching program is small as well as conservative in both content and procedure. This is at least partly due to its being overshadowed by the demands of the graduate program (as well as by the presence of a distinguished divinity school) and the resultant highly specialized kind of work within the faculty.

(2) There are no effective channels for general and regular communication between faculty and graduate students on the question of teaching. There is no general departmental seminar or colloquium on this matter, only occasional *ad hoc* programs.

(3) This university's pervasive and rigid departmental structure, the general absence of reflection on methods of education (we have no school or department of education!) combine to bar graduate students from access to any and all significant broad level exchange on teaching and on new educational programs, such as community colleges. In our graduate program, the effective ideal for learning to teach—if any at all—still seems to be that of master-apprentice relation. But even if this is still a pertinent ideal (and I am ready to agree that it is in some respects, but not in others) I do not believe that it is being carried out effectively; and certainly there are very few undergraduate classes in our department that provide the opportunity. But even if there were more of them, I wonder how much attention would be paid to the actual training-in-teaching of the undergraduate assistant. The first step would have to come from the graduate school, requiring professors to report on what they had done with their graduate assistants in undergraduate classes, and how the assistant performed. (For that matter it might not be a bad idea to have a report from the graduate assistant on the professor's performance as a teacher and a trainer of teachers.)

(4) We have not mastered the admittedly difficult problem of a successful balance between (*a*) narrow, expert specialization and (*b*) covering a broad range of interests and information, developing skills that will enable the student to make significant connections across the apparently disparate sub-fields in the vast arena of religious studies. Our sole concentration on (*a*) (especially on the

graduate level, but it washes over on to undergraduate teaching) does not necessarily contribute to bad preparation for teaching but it certainly maximizes the
risk.

(5) I doubt that many of us in our week by week classroom contact with our
students bear steadily in mind the question of their eventual effectiveness in
classroom teaching under a diversity of conditions. Certainly we don't shape our
topic with that issue in mind. We are subject-oriented, strictly and exclusively,
judging from my experience—and I hasten to add that this is a very good thing
in an educational structure in which there is constant temptation to devalue the
intellectual currency. But it is an excellence that involves being relatively in-
sensitive in some other respects—including the training of students as teachers.

At least two institutions in our study, Duke and Yale, have received foundation support for the development of programs to prepare doctoral students
as teachers, but neither program seems to have been effective for more than a
very few students.

Only in two instances have we found evidence of significant exceptions to the
prevailing weakness. One is at the University of Iowa, among teaching assistants
in the large undergraduate introductory course. Here the assistants are organized
for mutual assistance and meet regularly under the leadership of one student
who is employed as a coordinator. The consensus of the students is that they
are helped in preparation not only for teaching (and reinforced in their desire
to teach) but also for their examinations.

The second instance is a small but apparently effective program begun recently
at Union Theological Seminary in New York and directed by two faculty
members from Teachers College, Columbia. The group has been limited to no
more than eight doctoral students at Union and Columbia, mostly Th.D.'s, with
one tutor to handle the general management of the group. For the small group
of participants, this seminar is reported to have had excellent results—but as
one of the directors writes, "We find that it is terribly expensive. In addition
to two professors and one tutor it is necessary to have a technician to film the
students' teaching episodes and to be on hand to operate the equipment when
the professors and students begin their critical analyses."

One reason, therefore, for the paucity of creative experimentation in the
training of teachers is the expense and technical difficulty of such obvious
assistance as can be provided by video tape and other admittedly useful means
of providing opportunity for self-criticism.

No such obstacle, however, lies in the way of other concrete steps that can
be taken.[23] In view of the great fluidity in undergraduate religion programs
(see Chapter 9), the question arises whether it is not an essential part of
graduate study in religion to be confronted by the question of the appropriate
nature of undergraduate instruction—that is, whether the latter is to be a
carbon copy of existing doctoral programs or a departure from these and from

---

[23] I make no effort even to enumerate the various reasonably effective methods that have
been devised in some fields in some institutions for the training of teachers, but cite only
a few areas that seem particularly germane to the study of religion.

most present undergraduate programs in religion. I have argued elsewhere that undergraduate studies in religion should not consist merely of congeries of courses, often themselves organized along traditional (seminary) lines. An undergraduate major needs to have over-all cohesion and purpose, with students acquiring an understanding and appreciation, both critical and empathetic, of religion(s), of religious dimensions in cultural life, the nature of religious commitment, and so forth. It should have discipline, with students proceeding from elementary to advanced courses and acquiring firsthand knowledge in some depth of at least one specific religious tradition. Training for undergraduate teaching could, accordingly, lead students to study and reflect on the nature of an undergraduate program in religion. (If there are any such ventures now under way, we are unaware of them.) If doctoral programs themselves had more cohesion, as we have urged that they should, the task would, of course, be much easier. And if a part of doctoral study were a continuing seminar in which the theory of religion, and appropriate methodologies for the study of it, were the subjects of discussion, reflection on the nature of undergraduate studies in religion could well constitute an item on the agenda.

Another major factor, however, in the low state of preparation for college and university teaching is the almost universal failure to integrate the work of teaching assistants with their graduate studies. "The use of graduate students in teaching" is an all too revealing phrase. Almost invariably the work of a teaching assistant is something in addition to his program of study, and while it may be hoped that his will be an experience in learning to teach, rarely is it interpreted as a possibility for advanced study itself. Yet what could be more natural than to propose that a student pursue his graduate studies through the process of preparation for teaching in certain areas and actually doing it? The obstacle to this seems to be the assumption that graduate students learn only by sitting in classes taught by their professors.

In at least two departments of religious studies, in the University of Indiana and Wesleyan University, proposals for graduate programs have been made which would seemingly and consistently incorporate teaching into the process of learning. Both programs are as yet in the stage of projections. The most fully developed proposal is that at Wesleyan, where, from the beginning of his graduate career, a substantial portion of the student's graduate study would itself be carried on by working with a faculty member in the preparation and conduct of undergraduate courses, both those to be team-taught and class seminars to be conducted by the student himself.

Such experimental ventures ought to be widely pursued. At least in the case of institutions that already make use of teaching assistants, experiments would require no large-scale institutional financial commitments—only imagination and concern on the part of graduate faculty.

4

The University Context:
Religious Studies and the Cognate Fields

How is graduate education in religion to be related to research in other disciplines in the university? In depicting an identity crisis in religious studies (Chapter 2), I have already called attention to the importance of this question, and it will have to recur frequently. The issue is a perennial one because religion cuts across so many of the areas of study in the humanities and social sciences.

The difficulty is compounded by quite contrasting tendencies and arguments. On the one hand, it is argued that religion is still striving to establish itself as an independent discipline just at the time when all disciplinary lines are being questioned. On the other hand, it is said that religious studies programs have been so much concerned to display their interdisciplinary credentials that they have lost sight of their own primary subject matter. Again, it is alleged that there is in religion no special subject matter or method, but only a convenient collaboration of a group of scholars with overlapping interests. Against this, there are some who insist that the study of religion must be defined in relation to a unique object, a distinct aspect of human experience called religious, or the sacred or the holy, and that the investigation of this phenomenon requires a method uniquely appropriate to it.

Such debates that go on both within and outside the field are complicated even more by the entrance of religious studies into new areas—such as the relation of religion and the arts, religion and literature, and the theology of culture—and by the redefinition of traditional fields (see Chapter 13). This is part of the explosion of knowledge in religion.

I shall not attempt here to rehearse these arguments or to pronounce the last word on the issues. The tensions will continue and it is healthy for them to do so. But it is necessary to stake out three positions bearing on the nature and ordering of graduate studies in religion within the family of academic disciplines.

1. THE RANGE OF RESOURCES

It is a truism to say that much of the important research in the field of religion has been and is still being carried on in "other" disciplines and departments of the university, including nearly all the humanities and social sciences. Religion faculty have often come from those departments.

In many of the language areas, it is hardly possible to avoid the study of religious texts. The religions of the ancient Near East have been extensively explored in departments of Near Eastern languages and literatures, as well as in archaeology; and biblical studies has long established close connections with those departments. The study of Asian languages has focused on the texts of Hinduism, Buddhism, and the indigenous Chinese and Japanese religious traditions; and like Near Eastern studies, the various Asian programs have moved increasingly toward becoming departments of "language and civilization" or "culture and civilization." Slavic and Russian studies involve Eastern Orthodox Christianity. Classics may take up Greek and Roman religion.

In spite of the fact that historians of the modern period have often seemed systematically to ignore the dynamic role of religion—and a prominent historian says that, now awakened from his dogmatic slumbers, he is doing appropriate penance by reading extensively in theology—it has always been the case that investigators of Western civilization have had to be deeply immersed in religious history. (Thus the American Society of Church History, for example, has found its ties to the American Historical Association to be closer than its connection with the Society of Biblical Literature.)

Sociology, psychology, and anthropology have come more recently on the scene, but decisive advances in the study of religious phenomena have come from these areas. One thinks immediately of Freud, Jung, William James, Durkheim, Weber, Wach, Lévi-Strauss, Parsons, and Malinowski.

Theology and philosophy have been intertwined both historically and constructively. The history of philosophy in the West is hardly separable from that of theology. The problems of God and evil continue to occupy the philosophers. And need one comment on the importance of the Bible in Western literature or of other scriptures in the literature of other cultures?

At the outset, therefore, we have simply to make clear the extraordinary breadth and richness of the potential resources for the study of religion throughout the academy. It is hardly possible to find a college or university in which courses in religion have not long been offered in one department or another. And dissertations on religion appear from various departments. Any attempt, therefore, to identify all the places where religion *might* be seriously studied at the graduate level would result in a long list of departments in many institutions. But it would be an uninformative list, and unfortunately the presence or extent of the study of religion in departments of anthropology, classics, history, literature, philosophy, and sociology is often not indicated at all in published summary documents.[1] Only a detailed review of all these departments, going far beyond the possibilities of the present investigation, could provide a list of schools where, for example, sociology of religion or philosophy of religion is in fact offered.

---

[1] See, for instance, the ACE *Guide to Graduate Study, Programs Leading to the Ph.D. Degree*, 4th ed., 1969, which is the most complete general description of doctoral programs.

54   THE UNIVERSITY CONTEXT

For our immediate purposes, however, it is useful to note the collateral resources in institutions where organized doctoral studies in religion are carried
on. Of the universities involved in our study, twelve have anthropology departments that are widely recognized as adequate or better, twenty-six have history
departments so regarded, twenty-one possess such sociology departments, twenty-
five have comparable philosophy departments, and sixteen have classics departments so recognized.[2]

The possibilities for the study of religion in Near or Middle Eastern and in
Asian studies departments are much more limited. Near Eastern and Middle
Eastern doctoral programs are to be found at Brandeis, Brown, Catholic University, Chicago, Columbia, Dropsie, Harvard, Johns Hopkins, New York University, Pennsylvania, Princeton, and Yale—among the institutions with religious
studies programs. (Others exist at Bryn Mawr, University of California at Berkeley and Los Angeles, Cornell, Indiana, and Michigan.) Doctoral studies in Asian
or oriental studies may be found, among the universities in our study, at Chicago,
Claremont, Columbia, Harvard, Pennsylvania, Princeton, Stanford, Wisconsin,
and Yale. (There are others at Arizona, University of California at Berkeley and
Los Angeles, Cornell, Hawaii, Indiana, Michigan, Washington University, and
University of Washington. See also Section 3, below.)

The complexity of the whole matter is indicated by the practical difficulty of
deciding, for the purpose of the present study, what should count as a doctoral
program in religious studies. We have taken account, for example, of Johns
Hopkins' Department of Near Eastern Studies, formerly the Oriental Seminary
and a major training center for biblical scholars, but we have not included the
UCLA Islamics program (whose description in such documents as the ACE *Guide*
does not mention Islamic religion), or in general the Near Eastern and oriental
studies departments. The Brandeis and Harvard Near Eastern departments
needed to be counted because of their importance for biblical and Judaic studies.
New York University's Institute of Hebrew Studies has been included, but not
the N.Y.U. degree in Religious Education, nor other religious education programs in schools of education. The principle for inclusion has been the directness of involvement in preparation for research and teaching in religion. Obviously no final lines of demarcation can be drawn, and it is not important that
they should be.

2. WHY "RELIGIOUS STUDIES"?

In view of the wealth and diversity of resources for the study of religion just
exhibited, the question is frequently raised, what is the point of separating out

[2] See the ACE 1969 ratings of graduate programs, edited by Roose and Anderson
(1970). Canadian institutions were not included in that survey; nor were departments
of Near Eastern, Middle Eastern, Asian or oriental studies rated. Twenty-seven of the
thirty-six United States university graduate schools among our list of institutions with
religion doctoral programs were rated in the 1969 survey. We need not overlook the
limitations of the Roose-Anderson sort of ratings to recognize that they provide a useful
index of informed opinion.

religion as a special department or program? Is there anything that goes on in a department of religious studies that cannot take place in one or another of these cognate departments? I believe not. Except perhaps for constructive theologizing (and I am not at all sure that this is an exception), nothing appears in a program of religious studies that could not appear elsewhere. Yet there are two sorts of decisive reasons for the existence of graduate programs in religious studies: pragmatic reasons relating to the way universities operate, and substantive reasons arising from the nature of the study itself.

a. Let us grant that departments are dangerous and that departmental loyalties often interfere with education. Provost Richard Schlatter of Rutgers has put it nicely:

> Perhaps a more serious consequence of the separation among academic disciplines is the injury inflicted on the life of the mind, on the development of the rich and critical scholarship and fruitful scientific research. Departmentalization fosters more and more specialization, more and more pedantry, and more and more triviality. We all know, in the abstract, that much of the most original scholarship and research arises just in those border areas where traditional disciplines rub together and generate sparks of new knowledge. Every university administrator knows that he must foster interdisciplinary research centers and institutes . . . [yet] much of the time, the various specialists who sit together in the interdisciplinary research institute resemble nothing so much as the emissaries of enemy powers negotiating an uneasy cease-fire. Each one is jealous of the rights and privileges and prerogatives and budgetary independence of his discipline. Everyone thinks that joint appointments between two or more departments are a good thing, but the man who holds one may find himself in a no man's land where promotions are hard to come by (Hartzell and Sasscer, 1967, p. 18).

The same sort of thing can be said frequently about the subdisciplinary divisions in religious studies, which tend to operate as departments within a department.

But it is easy to score points against departmentalization. As Schlatter goes on to argue, departments have both practical and intellectual justification:

> Without departments, the intellectual establishment would be disordered and amateurish. The organization by discipline fosters a needed specialization and a concentration of intellectual effort. . . . In spite of the limitations which we all recognize, the organization of our intellectual establishment of higher learning along disciplinary lines has been a success and continues to be a success. We should break down the fences at some points; we should redraw the boundaries from time to time; and we may want to recreate new disciplines. But we need the disciplines all the same. . . . Unless a subject has the status and dignity of a departmental organization, students will conclude that the subject is of little intellectual importance. Without a department and without a major program which a department makes possible, the teacher of religion is reduced to a general service function which derogates his dignity and deadens his own intellectual growth.

The practical point is simply that in the university things grow only if they are tended, and that means being given an organizing center, a structure, a budget, some appointive control, and so on. This is patently the case with respect to programs of religious studies. Those that have been organized simply as inter-departmental or interdisciplinary operations have regularly failed to prosper.

b. The substantive arguments for special graduate departments of religion are more significant, however, than the practical considerations. If the phenomena of religion are to be responsibly investigated at the highest level, both kinds of study are essential: the sort that takes place in the context of other constellations of interest, and the kind that occurs when the range of religious phenomena is the primary focus. To say that religion can be studied significantly as part of a program in sociology or Near Eastern studies is not to say that it will be. The multiplicity of other disciplines that may involve the study of religion is both a problem for organizing this investigation and a reason for doing it. In other contexts religion is often not studied well, and sometimes not at all.[3]

We need not settle the question whether religious studies have a unique object of investigation in order to recognize, for instance, that Chinese Buddhist texts should be explored by those cognizant of the development of other religious traditions as well as by those whose interests are primary philological and literary. The Reformation needs to be investigated both by those whose primary focus is sixteenth-century Europe and by those who interpret the Reformation in relation to a continuing religious tradition. Similarly, the philosophy of religion will prosper only as it is carried on both by those who work also in the philosophy of science and the philosophy of art, in epistemology and metaphysics, and by those who are trained in the range of theological options that have been developed in the several religious traditions. It is just for such reasons that graduate education in religion has in fact now thoroughly established itself in the academic spectrum, and it is at least as unified a "discipline" as political science or sociology, which also had to make their place in the university curricula.

3. THE CONTINUING DEPENDENCE ON COGNATE
   DISCIPLINES: PROMISE AND PROBLEMS

It has been necessary for religious studies to be identified as a distinguishable and important area of investigation in its own right. But the viability of graduate education in religion also depends on recognizing the continuing dependence on adjacent disciplines and on reinforcing and exploiting the connections.

The testimony of faculty at this point is impressive. In response to the question "What do you regard as the most important new developments in your field?" no theme recurs with greater frequency than the outward movement and the expansion of the horizon of studies, precisely for the advancement of the specializations. That is where the "action" is. A distinguished historian of early Christianity in a theological school wrote:

[3] Professor Richard D. Lambert, of the University of Pennsylvania, who has made an extensive survey of area studies programs, both graduate and undergraduate, reports that of approximately 5,600 faculty who identify themselves as area specialists, only 132 report their discipline as religion.

The discovery of large amounts of new source materials, primarily in languages which New Testament students do not know too well, Hebrew and Coptic, [requires] more work in languages [and] skills in related areas such as archaeology and paleography. The study of the New Testament thus becomes the study of the sources for the history of early Christianity, which far exceeds the traditional "New Testament and Apostolic Fathers." The widening of the horizon of historical scholarship does not allow any longer that New Testament find its ultimate focus in "biblical theology." Instead, the history of the Greco-Roman civilization, the processes of development of the Christian movement, its cultural ramifications and sociological consequences—all this will occupy more and more of the time and energy of scholars and students. Such studies require the close cooperation of classicists, philologians, and historians in the education of doctoral students; they call for more competence in the traditional languages (classical and hellenistic Greek instead of "New Testament Greek"—a field which should go out of business!); study of the new methods of cultural analysis and historical methodology in general.

Faculty members, moreover, are "putting their money and time where their mouths are." One young scholar specializing in patristics spends a year in Vienna studying Roman classics. A historian of modern theology, investigating early nineteenth-century German thought, has been led into the ramifications of the myth of reunification of all things in the One in all of German Romanticism, thus less into the traditional materials for the history of doctrine and more into social and political history.[4]

If this is a critical demand and direction for graduate education in the future, two sorts of questions must be dealt with: (*a*) what is now being done and what can be done in individual institutions; and (*b*) what are the particular problem areas that need special attention?

a. In respect of the former question I have to observe first that not much has been done to date in the actual structuring of doctoral education. Half of the present doctoral programs do not even mention the desirability of studies in cognate disciplines. In a few instances there are strong recommendations and even formal requirements (among others, at Duke, Northwestern-Garrett, Southern California, Stanford, and Vanderbilt) for a minor concentration in a cognate field; but sometimes the teeth are drawn from such recommendations by allowing the option of a minor simply in another closely related specialization within religious studies. In other cases examination patterns are designed in such a way as to require cross-fertilization: for instance, at Southern Methodist, where one of the examinations for all students is "the philosophical, psychological and sociological study of religion," and at Chicago, where contextual exams are intended to ensure that students "can also work in two other contexts" (replacing the

[4] One of the most imaginative and fruitful means of encouraging this trend has been the program of postdoctoral fellowships for cross-disciplinary study funded by the Danforth Foundation and administered by the Society for Religion in Higher Education. In recent years grants have been made to a political scientist to study the Jewish Talmud, to an English professor to study contemporary theology, and to professors of religion to study political science, law, philosophical psychology, and sociology.

58 THE UNIVERSITY CONTEXT

former scheme of seven field exams, which were abandoned because they had been widely judged to be unrelated hurdles to be overcome).

McMaster has made an interesting attempt to structure the entire program around cross-cultural study, emphasizing the religions of Near Eastern origin together with those of India and China, also choosing to locate the department of religion in the social science rather than the humanities division of the university. Pennsylvania has required all students to be examined both in the philosophy of religion and in a second major religious tradition. Yale, in the "history of religions," has insisted on the investigation of more than one religious tradition and on a plurality of methodologies.

In fields going by such names as "religion and society," the exploitation of cognate disciplines is probably furthest advanced, with frequent requirement of work in psychology, statistics, and sociology. The resources of language departments, notably classics, Near Eastern languages and literatures, and oriental studies, have of course long been utilized in biblical studies and in the investigation of Asian religions.

Let us not suppose, of course, that either the existence of formal recommendations or the judgment of faculty as to what is desirable necessarily ensures that the education of graduate students will involve the utilization of cognate departments or fields. A sampling of reports from students taking graduate courses in 1969-1970 shows the widest variations. In some institutions, there is impressive evidence of extensive study outside the department. To cite only a few examples, at Chicago, 43 percent of the doctoral students were enrolled in one or more nondepartmental courses; at Columbia the figure was 52 percent, at Claremont 55 percent, and at Pennsylvania 76 percent. Yet in other instances, even in schools where significant collateral strengths were present, only a tiny minority of students, or even none at all, were actually enrolled in nondepartmental courses.

The other side of the problem, obviously, is how great in fact are the potentialities? A majority of the faculty respondents in the survey indicated that a prime methodological *ideal* is increased utilization of the resources of other departments and fields germane to the study of religion. But the achievement of this goal necessarily depends on the presence of useful departments, of faculty and of library resources. Such strengths are likely to be available only in a major university. Indeed, if we ask in what institutions are there wide ranges of strong or distinguished cognate departments, capable of supporting advanced studies in many of the subdisciplines of religion, the list is very short. Among institutions having programs of graduate education in religion, this list would include at most: Brandeis, Brown, Chicago, Columbia, Harvard, Johns Hopkins, McGill, Northwestern, Pennsylvania, Princeton, Stanford, Wisconsin, and Yale—though California (Berkeley) and Toronto should be added in relation to the Graduate Theological Union and Toronto Graduate School of Thelogical Studies. This is not to say, of course, that any of these institutions has supporting resources for advanced religious studies in *all* areas, or that other universities do not have significant collateral resources in some areas.

b. The other principal question concerning cognate fields is that of special areas of need or difficulty. These I believe to be found particularly in relation to the social sciences, to Asian studies, and to Islamics.

Extensive interconnections have traditionally been developed with classics, with Near Eastern languages and literatures, with history, and with philosophy. More recently, the study of American religious history, which has been of growing importance, has been carried on in effective interrelation with American studies programs. And I would say that the newly developing area of religion and literature or theology and literature, though not yet clearly defined, has also been a genuine joint enterprise, drawing on faculties in religion and in literature.[5]

(1) The relation to the social sciences constitutes a serious problem. What used to be called the psychology of religion has fallen on hard times. Some believe it has ceased to exist. Psychology departments have become increasingly divided between experimentalists, clinical psychologists, and social psychologists, with the latter existing somewhere between psychology and sociology. Closer relations are developing with psychiatry and psychoanalytic theory, drawing on the traditions of both Freud and Jung, but the attempt to carve out areas such as "religion and the personality sciences" remains confused, including such divergent tendencies as the exploitation of the deliverances of psychoanalytic theory for constructive theological articulation on the one hand, to developing the theory and techniques of personal counseling on the other hand.

Sociology presents a special difficulty. Within religious studies it is increasingly emphasized that religion must be seen as a social phenomenon and that the descriptive analyses of one or another of the social sciences must increasingly inform a wide range of areas of religious study. At the same time, there is evidence of a tendency on the part of some social scientists to draw away from effective interaction with other (humanistic) modes of the study of religion. This is presumably in the interests of purity or maintaining the "scientific" character of their study, and in order to maintain close relations with other types of sociological study and with practicing psychologists and researchers. A notable illustration of this tendency was the partial withdrawal of the Society for the Scientific Study of Religion in 1970 from participation in the Council on the Study of Religion. That action was taken partly for practical reasons (financial and organizational), but seems to have been motivated also by some fear of contamination by association with such groups as the American Society for Christian Ethics, the Catholic Biblical Association, the Catholic Theological Society of America, the College Theology Society, and the Society of Biblical Literature (apparently the American Academy of Religion, with a great diversity of subject areas, was felt to be less ideologically dangerous).

The consequence of this potential bifurcation is that just at the time when students of religion are generally increasingly aware of the need for a combination of methodologies in the study of religion, and in particular for the incorpo-

---

[5] For discussion of trends in the traditional areas, as well as further illustration of the problematic relations, see the treatment of new trends in research, Chapter 13.

ration of sociological studies, the resources of the latter tend to become less available. On the other hand, the sociology of religion as carried on in departments of sociology will be impoverished by lack of acquaintance with the historical and theological-philosophical approaches to religion. In the social-scientific area, above all, we find an illustration of the need to carry on the study of religion both in sociology departments and in religion departments—"in order to keep each other honest."

(2) The relation to Asian studies programs of all sorts constitutes a special problem of at least three dimensions. First, investigation of the Far Eastern traditions is not only increasingly popular in the American scene; it is also a special responsibility because the scholarly study of non-Western religions is only poorly developed in the East.[6] It is also true, of course, that although the serious beginnings go back a hundred years, the study of Asian religions in the West is only in its adolescence, and in some cases in its extreme infancy.

Second, Asian studies programs everywhere are under severe economic pressures in the university. They have unfortunately rarely developed strong undergraduate bases and are expensive to maintain. Further, there has been a decrease in opportunity for conducting research abroad, both because of the decline in available funds and because of restrictions in foreign countries.

Third, the mounting of any responsible program in the study of non-Western religions requires the commitment of major resources in language and cultural studies.

A review of the institutions giving doctorates in religion provides the following results. Altogether twenty schools were in 1970 proposing to offer work in one or another of the Eastern religious traditions, or Islam, or primitive religion, either with explicit identification of the areas for specialization or under such general headings as "history of religions" or "comparative religions." How many of these can actually call on important language or other facilities in cognate departments?

Chicago, Columbia, Harvard, and Yale belong to the traditional centers of religious studies, and each is an institution with extensive and highly developed resources—linguistic, historical, sociological—for the study of various religious traditions. Chicago, Harvard, and Yale have both Far Eastern and South Asian languages and literatures.[7] Columbia's Eastern languages and cultures emphasizes China and Japan, and there is an interdisciplinary program in Buddhist studies. The other programs that have been in existence for some time include: Hartford, with a special focus on Islam and to a lesser extent on Hinduism, going

[6] This is well reported, for example, in a 1961 study by Martin and Martin, privately distributed by the Association of Teachers of Religion in Higher Education.

For a useful delineation of the critical situation in the United States study of Japanese religion, see the February, 1970, report of the Social Science Research Council—American Council of Learned Societies joint committee, chaired by Professor John W. Hall of Yale, *Japanese Studies in the United States: A Report on the State of the Field, Current Resources, and Future Needs.*

[7] Yale is closing down its South East Asian studies, however.

back to the earlier work of the Kennedy School of Missions, with a strong tradition of language study in the Seminary Foundation; McGill, with its special relation to the distinguished Institute for Islamic Studies; and Princeton University (1955) and Princeton Seminary, which need to be considered together because the seminary program (with the exception of one faculty member) depends almost entirely on the resources of the university, notably in East Asian and oriental as well as Near Eastern studies.

Iowa has also ventured into the history of religions area, noting particularly the study of religion in India, China, and Japan—in which the work of two faculty members in the School of Religion is buttressed by that of two others in oriental studies and anthropology, respectively, and by language resources in linguistics and in Chinese languages and civilization (Indian languages are less strong, though Sanskrit is offered).

Among the programs newly established (in the 1960's), McMaster, Pennsylvania, Stanford, and Wisconsin give some clear specification of the non-Judeo-Christian areas proposed. Pennsylvania is without question the most richly endowed with collateral resources for study in a variety of religious traditions, and with proper development could join the first-mentioned group above: there are extensive language resources in Near East, South Asia, and Far East, with strong departments of anthropology, linguistics, oriental studies, and South Asia regional studies.[8] McMaster has focused specifically on Indian and Chinese religious history (mainly the former). Neither Near Eastern nor Far Eastern languages is offered outside the Department of Religion, it being expected that necessary language study can be secured at Toronto (a somewhat optimistic expectation, even granted the greater freedom of movement for Canadian students). The department itself, however, has tried to build seriously in the Indian area. Stanford's program proposes to relate specifically to Far Eastern religions, since East Asian studies are strong, whereas the university does not intend to develop Indian studies or Near Eastern studies. Wisconsin has focused specifically on Buddhist studies, in the Department of Indian Languages and Literatures.

The Ottawa Department of Religious Studies, under its rubric of "history and problematics of the science of religion," is the only religion program in North America explicitly proposing advanced studies in primitive religions, including both Africa and the religions of the North American Indian, in the latter case capitalizing on uniquely available resources for field study. (Both areas are offered in French only.)[9]

The other newly established programs are less specific in identifying areas of specialization. Catholic University announces the history of religions as an

[8] The newly proposed program at the Graduate Theological Union in history of religions could also draw on powerful supporting resources from the University of California at Berkeley. The University of Toronto likewise has the potential, in cognate resources, for the study of Near and Far Eastern religions (including both East and South Asia).

[9] The University of Chicago Divinity School program in the history of religions is also, of course, an important center for the study of primitive religions; and a student or two at Temple and at Hartford report work in this area.

area of advanced study, though no students seem to be specializing in it and support in Eastern religions seems to come largely from work in the Anthropology Department in South East Asian cultures and from introductory study in Chinese thought in the School of Philosophy, as well as some Sanskrit.

Claremont has developed its history of religions studies in close association with the interdisciplinary Ph.D. in Asian studies.

Fordham lists the history of religions, although there are no cognate language resources for Eastern religions except a course in Sanskrit.

Temple offers world religions as one of its main organizational areas, presumably including Hinduism, Buddhism, Islam, and primitive religions, though there are no supporting departments in Asian or Near Eastern studies.

Dropsie lists "comparative religion and philosophy" and "Arabic and Islamic studies," but without apparent resources. And John Hopkins has included Islamic studies among its areas of graduate study, though as of 1969-1970 only one faculty member and one course were shown.[10]

In sum, the list of institutions with strong supporting resources for the study of non-Western religions is very short. I find no institution with adequate facilities for advanced study in all the major Asian religious traditions. About half of the schools now offering doctoral work in history of religions can be said to have significant cognate language and literature departments for the support of research in one or two Eastern religions. Others have sought to operate with at best a marginal, and sometimes a quite inadequate, commitment to the development of the necessary language and cultural study and should not be encouraged to continue.

(3) Finally, I would offer Islam as a brief case study in problems and needs. Oddly, one has to search very hard in the readily available indices to discover where it might be possible to study Islamic religion (for example, the ACE *Guide* to doctoral programs lists only UCLA as offering Islamics specifically, although the summary of the UCLA program makes no mention of religion). One would not know from the description of the graduate programs in religion at Harvard that this university was in fact one of the strong places for Islamic studies (drawing particularly on Arabic and Iranian).

The other institutions with supporting doctoral programs for the study of Islam are: Brandeis (in Near Eastern and Judaic studies), Chicago (Arabic, in Near Eastern languages and civilizations), Columbia (under Middle Eastern languages and culture), University of California, Berkeley (Islamic languages, under Near Eastern languages), Indiana (Arabic literature, in the Department of Near Eastern Languages and Literatures), McGill (in the Islamic Institute),[11] New York University (Islamic civilization, philosophy, and theology, under Near Eastern languages and literatures), Pennsylvania (in the Near East Center), Princeton (in Near Eastern and oriental studies), Toronto (Islamic studies),

---

[10] To the list may now be added the Northwestern University program in the history and literature of religions, which has at least the possibility of drawing on some language studies in the Linguistics Department.

[11] Though the Islamics Institute is in serious economic difficulties.

and Yale (Arabic, under Near Eastern languages and literatures). To this list of possibilities may also be added Hartford's long-standing focus on Islam and one religion faculty member in Islamics at Temple.

In other words, supporting resources in Arabic are not unavailable, but rarely do these seem to have been extensively utilized for the study of Islamic religion. Islam is one of the least well developed areas in North American religious studies. Of 1,760 religion doctoral students reporting their areas of specialization, only eleven cited Islam (these were students at Chicago, Hartford, Harvard, Temple, and Yale). Islam would seem to be a field particularly in need of encouragement and of the creation of structures for interrelating religious with literary and cultural studies.

5

Quality, Quantity and Accountability

"As for the graduate schools themselves, they are astonishingly complacent."[1] That judgment may serve as a proper warning to us in any attempt to speak specifically to the questions of quality in graduate education in religion. It is true that the severe economic stringencies of educational institutions and the growing surplus of the graduate schools' prize product, the Ph.D., have begun to disturb the complacency. Self-satisfaction will not be as easy in the 1970's as it was in the expansionist period of the 1960's. These pressures will affect the graduate study of religion at least as much as other fields, making it both possible and necessary to raise questions of quality with a new urgency. But on the basis of interviews with graduate religion faculty, students, chairmen, and graduate deans at nearly sixty of the sixty-nine institutions offering doctoral work in religion, I see little reason as yet to exempt the field of religion from Jencks and Riesman's charge. There are new and responsible experimental programs, but the expansionist mood of the 1960's has also brought "new" programs that are in no way new or distinctive and whose sole reason for being seems to be the desire of faculty to teach graduate students. (The latter may be a valid reason for considering the development of the doctoral programs, but it is hardly a sufficient reason. One interviewee was even able to say with a straight face that the presence of fourteen Ph.D.'s in Bible in the geographical area had been cited as a sufficient reason for proposing to offer a Ph.D. in the field.) We have found a fair amount of ferment and distress among graduate students, but even they seem on the whole satisfied with the education they are getting (see Chapter 10), and most of their proposals for reform center in procedural changes. Graduate departments are generally willing to apply a few Band-Aids, but rarely to undertake major surgery. A few institutions quite candidly admit that they are simply trying to do at a B or C level the same kind of thing that others can do at an A level. The Council on Graduate Studies in Religion has met for twenty years of pleasant conversation among representa-

[1] Jencks and Riesman, 1969, p. 515.

tives of the prestige institutions, but it has done very little to attain its stated objective of raising the standards of doctoral studies.

In the institutions in which they exist, graduate programs in religion are believed by graduate deans and other departmental chairmen to be good. In some schools evidence is at hand—from comparative Graduate Record Examination scores, from high selectivity in admissions, from success in national fellowship competitions, and the like—to show that students in the religion programs rank high among an institution's graduate departments. But this only means that in most cases the religious studies program is about as good as the institution as a whole.

How does religion stand with respect to that other observation of Jencks and Riesman, that "the American graduate school has become the envy of the world, a Mecca for foreign students and a model for foreign institutions" (Jencks and Riesman, 1969, p. 513)? We need not discuss here whether that fine rhetoric requires qualification with respect to many fields; it is more nearly apt in respect of some of the physical, biological, and social sciences than in the humanities. Plainly it applies only partially in the area of religious studies.

There are good reasons for holding that in religion and theology the traditional European and British disdain for American scholarship has begun to give way to a growing respect. Further, there are certain areas in which North American scholarship has both levels of quality and distinctive styles of approach that place it in advance of some of its European counterparts—in anthropological and sociological approaches to religion, as well as in the whole conception of a scholarly study of all religious phenomena (including those of the Western traditions) which is less tightly bound to professional theological studies. (See the comments by Ninian Smart, Chapter 8.) In the idea of a department of religious studies, as distinct from a theological faculty, the American pattern has in fact begun to be a model.

But the North American graduate programs in religion are obviously not a Mecca for foreign students and scholars. About 7 percent of the three thousand doctoral students in the United States and Canada come from outside these two countries (roughly the same proportion as in United States graduate schools generally). A handful of institutions have more than 15 percent of foreign students in their doctoral populations (Catholic University, Hartford, Harvard, McGill, Vanderbilt, Princeton Theological, Southern Baptist, and Union Theological in New York). The foreign student populations tend to be concentrated in those institutions traditionally related to missionary studies (though not exclusively so), and they come more from Latin and South America, Africa and the Far East, than from Britain and Europe. There is a far greater movement of American graduate students to Europe than vice versa, and American faculty travel much more to Britain and Europe for advanced study than do their European counterparts to North America. Economic factors, of course, play a powerful role in this one-way movement, as well as the fact that the theological disciplines have long lived under the shadow of the great nineteenth-century outburst of scholarly energy in Germany.

At every point in this study, we are concerned with questions of quality. Here specifically, however, I want to focus on three sorts of issues. (1) What conclusions are to be drawn and what problems are to be noted from the application to graduate religion programs of the standard (or at least frequently cited) indices of quality in graduate education? (2) Are there special considerations bearing on the quality of graduate programs *in religion*—not necessarily unique problems, but questions of distinctive or peculiar importance? (3) What are the particular problems of accountability and accreditation in this field of study? Then (4) I shall offer a summary rating of the sixty-nine programs studied.

1. GENERAL INDICES OF QUALITY: SOME APPLICATIONS

The kinds of questions to be asked generally about quality in doctoral programs have been extensively developed by previous studies of graduate education, by accrediting agencies, and by such groups as the Council of Graduate Schools in the United States. We need not duplicate that work.

Some of the standard items are relatively quantifiable and bear on the "discipline" of graduate programs. These include selectivity in admissions and control over numbers of students admitted; decisions concerning size of doctoral programs; proportions of full-time versus part-time students, including students writing dissertations in residence or *in absentia*; length of time in study; loss ratios; and other indicators of efficiency or waste.

Quantitative measures can also be applied to some extent in determining the availability of resources for doctoral studies: the presence of senior faculty of maturity and proven competence in proposed areas of specialization; faculty-student ratios; teaching loads of faculty; availability of specific graduate course offerings and supervised research for doctoral students; library holdings, acquisitions, and funds; and financial support for both faculty and students.

Such criteria, however, must be set in the context of equally important indices that are essentially nonquantifiable, some of which also merge into special problems for the field of religion. For example:

degree and character of institutional commitment to the program;
responsibility shown in shaping a program in selected areas of specialization in relation to the needs of the field and the institution's resources (what is it that a particular institution specifically proposes to do distinctively?);
relation to other graduate programs, including the possibilities of study in the principal related disciplines;
imagination in curricular development;
flexibility and openness to change, e.g., relative to subdisciplinary lines;
the scholarly and teaching competence of the faculty;
the rigor with which requirements are applied (all statements of requirements look good on paper!);
the adequacy of advising procedures and the responsibility exercised in screening students during graduate study;
restrictions imposed by formal doctrinal requirements or special purposes that the institution seeks to serve.

I shall not try to relate all these indices to the programs studied, but ample evidence is available both to warrant significant generalizations and to allow some specific applications, beginning with criteria bearing on discipline in graduate programs.

a. Admissions

In 1969-1970, religion programs reflected the whole spectrum of selectivity in admitting applicants for doctoral study, ranging from a few institutions that were able (or willing) to exercise a high degree of selectivity to those who admitted nearly all comers.[2] Ph.D. programs were almost exactly divided between those admitting 50 percent or fewer of the students who had applied and those admitting over 50 percent; Th.D. programs were on the whole slightly less selective.

The most selective programs (those admitting fewer than 25 percent of the applicants) were these:

Ph.D.		*Th.D.*	
Harvard	16%	Harvard	18%
Johns Hopkins	20%	Union (New York)	25%
Princeton	20%		
Southern Methodist	19%		
Stanford	21%		
Yale	21%		

At the other end of the scale, more than 60 percent of the applicants were accepted by the following:[3]

Ph.D.		*Th.D.*	
Brigham Young	75%	Grace	67%
Catholic U.	100%	GTU	65%
Chicago (NT and		Lutheran Theol.	
ECL)	67%	(Chicago)	80%
Iowa	73%	New Orleans	100%
McGill	88%	Southwestern Baptist	89%
McMaster	65%		
Montreal	100%		
St. Louis	90%		
St. Michael's	80%		
Syracuse	64%		
Temple	66%		

[2] Precise information on the numbers of completed applications, admissions, and actual new students enrolled was supplied for 49 programs (37 Ph.D. and 12 Th.D./S.T.D./D.H.L.). No information was available from the following: *Ph.D.*—Aquinas, Boston University, Brandeis, Dropsie, Harvard Near Eastern Languages and Literatures, Jewish Theological Seminary, New York University, Ottawa, Pittsburgh, Rice, St. Mary's, Wisconsin, Yeshiva; *Th.D/S.T.D./D.H.L.*—Catholic University, Fuller, Iliff, Jewish Theological, Knox, Laval, St. Paul, Trinity, and Union (Va.).

[3] In relation to some Roman Catholic institutions, such figures must be viewed with

The quality of graduate student bodies, and their instruction, is also related to institutional policies concerning the total numbers of students to be admitted. In practice this means departmental policy. In interviewing graduate school deans in the spring of 1970, I was astonished by the widespread lack of interest of graduate school officials in exercising control over the numbers of students admitted to their various departments. Rarely (notably at Harvard, Yale, and Princeton University) have firm policies and limits been in existence for any length of time. In a few cases, controls have recently been imposed, particularly as a part of the general policy of cutting back on graduate school size. Yet in only three instances beyond those noted was there evidence of a graduate school policy on the number of students to be admitted (Chicago, University of California at Santa Barbara, and Stanford). Another eleven departments reported definite quotas of their own.

The older Ph.D. programs have in general exercised better controls over the numbers of students admitted. Over the ten-year span 1959-1969 only Columbia, Harvard, Princeton, and Yale maintained relatively constant graduate student populations in religion, and Harvard reduced its Th.D. enrollment by 50 percent. Boston, Duke, and Vanderbilt grew modestly.

Eight institutions expanded by more than 50 percent:[4]

Brown	(from	8 students to 24)
Emory	(from	28 students to 64)
Iowa	(from	25 students to 83)
Hartford	(from	31 students to 71)
Hebrew Union	(from	22 students to 36)
Johns Hopkins	(from	6 students to 16)
McGill	(from	5 students to 22)
Northwestern-Garrett	(from	10 students to 48)

Among the newer programs, that is, those established since 1959, a clear distinction appears between those that have grown at a controlled rate and those that represent an almost runaway inflation. To the former category, judging both from actual numbers of students and clearly articulated departmental policies, belong Marquette, Notre Dame, Pennsylvania, Southern Methodist,

caution, since frequently competitive procedures do not exist, candidates for graduate study being assigned by their ecclesiastical superiors to study in specific institutions, with correlative responsibility of graduate centers to accept such candidates.

[4] And for sheer numbers, Chicago should also be noted, increasing from 170 to 251. For 1969-1970 totals, see Chapter 12.

Drew increased greatly during the first half of the decade, but then reduced drastically as a result of the administrative controversy resulting in the departure of half the theological faculty.

It is mainly in the Ph.D. sector that questions of discipline in expansion may be raised, since that is where the great expansion of the past decade has come, rather than in the TH.D./S.T.D./D.H.L. programs. Ph.D. enrollments in religion increased 142 percent between 1959 and 1969. This compares with a total United States graduate enrollment increase in private institutions of 60 percent for the same period (ACE *Fact Book*, 1970, p. 70.35).

Stanford, Syracuse, and Wisconsin. Claremont, Graduate Theological Union, and McMaster have expanded rapidly, but not without some restraints. Apparently uncontrolled growth has characterized both Fordham (to 130 students since the establishment of the Ph.D. in 1967; there was an M.A. program earlier) and Temple (since 1961, to an estimated 173 doctoral students in 1969). In those institutions, the drive for sheer quantity in students seems to have quite overshadowed the concern for quality.

b. Full-Time or Part-Time?

Given the present organization of graduate education, the opportunity for students to pursue their courses, examination preparation, and dissertation writing on a full-time basis is a major factor contributing to quality in education. In about half of the programs for which sufficient data are available to make a responsible judgment,[5] two-thirds or more of the students were engaged in such full-time residence study (for the total religion doctoral population, the figure is about 60 percent).

The select group in this respect, with 75 percent or more of their students in full-time study, included: Columbia, Fordham, Fuller, Harvard, Notre Dame, Princeton, Southern Baptist, Southern Methodist, Syracuse, Union (N.Y.), Vanderbilt, and Wisconsin. (On the basis of less complete responses, it appears that McMaster and Stanford should also be included in the list.)

At the other end of the spectrum, warning flags may properly appear when the proportion of full-time students falls below 50 percent, as in the case of Baylor (33 percent), Chicago Theological (33 percent), Concordia (22 percent), Drew (9 percent), Grace (32 percent), Lutheran Theological (7 percent), McGill (33 percent), New Orleans (48 percent), Southwestern Baptist (26 percent), and Toronto GSTS (21 percent)—to which on the basis of less complete reports should be added Temple (45 percent) and Southern California (38 percent). (In some of these instances, students writing dissertations *in absentia* constituted a large fraction of the part-time population.)

Reports of full-time study often need to be viewed with mild skepticism and correlated with other factors, notably the availability of adequate scholarship and fellowship assistance and the need of students to engage in outside employment. *In only about a third of the institutions were 50 percent or more of the students pursuing their work without outside employment*: Catholic University, S.T.D. (50 percent), Columbia (66 percent), Emory (54 percent), Harvard (62 percent), Marquette (54 percent), Notre Dame (69 percent), Princeton (68 percent), Rice (75 percent), St. Louis (50 percent), Southern Methodist (61 percent), Stanford (75 percent), Syracuse (68 percent), Union (N.Y.) (54 percent), Vanderbilt (51 percent), Wisconsin (89 percent), Yale (73 percent). If we set aside students writing dissertations *in absentia*, a few more schools can be added to the list as having more than half of their resident students free

---

[5] Except as otherwise noted, I take account here only of institutions from which at least 60 percent of the doctoral students responded to the questionnaire.

from outside employment: Brandeis, Brown, Claremont, Duke, Fordham, Iowa, Pennsylvania, Grace, and Princeton Theological Seminary.

There is no present evidence to warrant hope for general improvement in this area in the near future. The decline in federal support for graduate education in the United States and the almost universal reduction of private and graduate school fellowship support will in fact make the situation worse, with larger proportions of students having to support themselves. The particular dimensions of this change will depend, of course, on the extent of reduction in the numbers of graduate students. And it may well be desirable to reconceive the ordering of graduate education specifically to provide for more extended (and interrupted) patterns of study.

Related evidence concerning program discipline and resources may be gained by identifying the proportions of students completing doctoral dissertations after leaving residence study. The 17 percent of all students responding who identified themselves as writing dissertations *in absentia* constitute slightly less than half of all students at the dissertation stage. This proportion does not seem to differ greatly from that in other fields of the humanities. There are, however, relatively wide variations among the institutions we have studied. On the one side are schools with more than 25 percent of their total doctoral student population engaged in writing dissertations *in absentia*: Catholic University (Ph.D.), Case Western Reserve, Concordia, Drew, Duke, Grace, Knox, Lutheran Theological, New Orleans, Princeton Theological, and Southwestern Baptist. (Again from incomplete returns we should probably add Brandeis, Jewish Theological, St. Michael's, St. Paul, and Montreal.) At the other end of the spectrum, schools with fewer than 10 percent of their total graduate population writing dissertations *in absentia* include Chicago, Harvard, Notre Dame, Southern Methodist, and Union (N.Y.).

The gross figures I have given may be generally too low, because they tend to underrepresent newly established programs, with small proportions of students having reached the dissertation stage. Thus some correction and amplification may be given by identifying the proportion of students preparing dissertations full-time as compared with those writing dissertations part-time. Most religion students write their dissertations on a part-time basis (60 percent of all those reporting). In only a handful of institutions do we find 60 percent or more of the dissertation stage students in full-time study: Harvard, Notre Dame, Southern Methodist, Syracuse, Vanderbilt, and Yale (counting only institutions with more than two dissertation students). The list of institutions in which fewer than a quarter of the students are writing dissertations full-time is longer: Baylor, Brandeis, Case Western, Drew, Grace, Iliff, Knox, Lutheran (Chicago), Northwestern-Garrett, and McGill.

c. How Long, O Lord?

Much has been written about the problems of the duration of doctoral study, particularly the contrasts between elapsed time and full-time equivalent study and the variations among fields. This tells us relatively little, I believe, about quality, but to the general discussion it is important to add a few comments and qualifications, since the relation of graduate and professional education in religion has frequently not been understood.

First, since the standard route to the doctorate in religion (whether Ph.D. or Th.D./S.T.D./D.H.L.) has been by way of the first professional degree, the normal range of full-time equivalent post-B.A. study has been from six to seven years (three years of professional school studies, two or three years in further course work, and one or two years of dissertation study). It can be argued that there has usually been considerable waste in this route to the doctorate, in time spent either on "practical theology" studies that are not necessary, and sometimes not relevant, for doctoral study, or in making up work that in other fields would ordinarily have been covered in undergraduate study. But if we can assume, for the better theological schools, that these years are all to be counted as graduate study, the actual full-time equivalent of graduate study spent in securing the doctorate considerably exceeds the medians frequently reported for full-time study in both the arts and sciences and the professional fields.[6]

Second, with the present radical reassessment of the need for doctorates in order to supply the demands for college and university teachers, the hue and cry of the 1960's to get students through doctoral programs more quickly has died down considerably. The problem of the duration of doctoral study may thus be considered more in the terms of quality of education and the problems of financing graduate study. These considerations *may* both argue for a shorter time span, but they may argue even more for better coordination of graduate with undergraduate or other prior study.

Third, relative brevity in the time required to secure the doctorate may mean greater efficiency or discipline in the conduct of a program. It may also mean laxness in requirements. On the other hand, longer periods of time may mean greater rigor in requirements (or more extensive language requirements, as in the case of biblical studies or non-Western religions); or they may result from

---

[6] The NAS report of doctoral study duration accurately reflects the greater than average periods of registered time in pursuit of the religion doctorates. The report *Doctorate Recipients from U.S. Universities 1958–1966* (National Academy of Sciences, 1967), pp. 66 ff., provides the following comparisons:

	All fields	Arts and Humanities	Religion and Theology
B.A. to doctorate, *total* time:			
1958–60	8.6	9.9	11.4
1961–63	8.8	10.1	10.8
1964–66	8.2	9.5	11.6*
B.A. to doctorate, *registered* time:			
1958–60	5.2	5.7	7.1
1961–63	5.3	5.7	7.1
1964–66	5.4	5.7	7.2†
Graduate school entry to doctorate, total time:			
1964–66	7.2	8.1	10.1

* The longest except for Education and Fine Arts.
† The longest of all fields.

the steeplechase conception of graduate study, in which many obstacles are spread out in sequence, to be overcome one by one; or they may be a function of part-time or interrupted study or departure from residence before completion of the dissertation.

The present situation in religion, on the basis of a comprehensive account of doctorates granted from 1965 through 1969, can be summarized in the form of a threefold tabulation of elapsed time, relating the number of years in the doctoral program itself to the time periods from B.A. to the doctorate and from the professional degree to the doctorate. (Differences in the numbers of cases result from variations in the items of information supplied.)

	Median	*Range*	*No. Cases*
Number of years in program			
Ph.D.	5.4	1–21	660
Th.D./S.T.D.	5.4	2–21	416
D.H.L.	5.0	0–13	19
Total	5.4	0–21	1,095
Elapsed time (years) B.A. to doctorate			
Ph.D.	11.6	4–42	669
Th.D./S.T.D.	12.3	5–35	285
D.H.L.	17.0	11–32	9
Total	11.8	4–42	963
Elapsed time (years) B.D. (or equivalent) to doctorate			
Ph.D.	7.3	2–28	580
Th.D./S.T.D.	7.2	3–32	290
D.H.L.	10.0	5–29	14
Total	7.3	2–32	884

The distribution of elapsed time periods is graphically represented in Figure 5-1.

About this general picture, two remarks suffice. First, it can hardly be said that the average doctoral student in religion spends too little total time in acquiring the doctorate. Second, comparison with the NAS reports (note 6, above) suggests that this situation has probably not deteriorated much in the past decade.

A full statement of lengths of time in study, by institution and degrees, is given in Chapter 12. It is clear, however, from a comparison of those reports with other factors such as full-time/part-time study, and institutional resources, that we must be cautious about conclusions as to the quality of a particular graduate program from the length of time that students have taken to receive the degree. Neither brevity nor length can be directly correlated with quality.

d. How Many?

Can anything be said about the optimum size of doctoral programs in relation to quality? Is there a "critical mass"? (Certainly there can be an uncritical mass.)

FIGURE 5-1

LENGTHS OF TIME IN STUDY, BY DEGREE TYPES

(1965-1969 Doctoral Recipients)

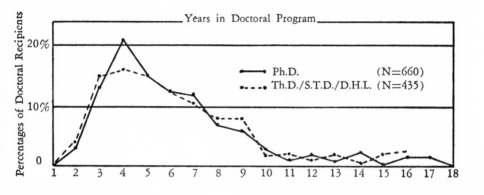

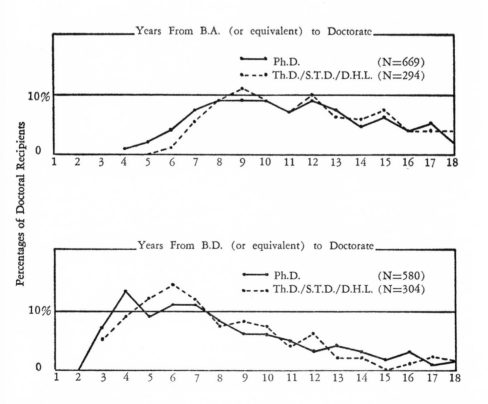

Little can be said in response to these questions in the abstract except the conventional wisdom. It is highly desirable to have two or more mature faculty persons in each area of specialization, so that students are able to encounter directly several points of view. It is also desirable to have a community of students to educate each other and to make possible specific graduate courses as well as tutorials, so as not to depend too much on courses designed for undergraduates or theological students. The argument has as much to do with the economics of graduate instruction as it does with quality. On the other hand, too many students can imperil the quality of graduate instruction, not only by overburdening the faculty but also because of the difficulty of relating to what other students are doing—though this can be a problem for a small department as well as a large one.[7]

Because of the multiplicity of subdisciplines in religion, together with the wide variations between the large seminary-based faculties in major universities, the independent schools of theology or religion, and the small or modest-sized religion departments in universities of first, second, third, or fourth rank, any attempt to devise universally applicable rules would be fruitless. The tasks of critical evaluation and policy formulation require relating the concretely available faculty and institutional resources to graduate student body sizes and to other faculty responsibilities.

Something of the diversity in graduate religion programs may be seen from the summary in Table 5-1 of the ranges of faculty resources in relation to total numbers of doctoral and other students in a few institutions, selected to illustrate several differences (very large and very small programs, old and new, geographical distribution). The numbers of doctoral students and of total faculty engaged in their instruction, and the estimated faculty full-time equivalent devoted to doctoral instruction, are those provided by the directors of graduate study. The number of other students (undergraduates or M.A. or professional degree) for which the faculty are *at least partially* responsible have been taken from responses to the survey of undergraduate programs and from the 1970 Directory of the American Association of Theological Schools.

From unqualified figures such as those in Table 5-1, it does not help much

---

[7] Allan Cartter contended in 1966 (*Journal of Human Resources*, p. 37) that "four-fifths of the nearly 250 universities presently awarding the Ph.D. are too small to be educationally or economically efficient. We might also ask whether public policy would be better served by consolidating and strengthening our existing graduate schools, rather than by encouraging another 10 or 12 new doctoral granting institutions to join the university ranks each year as is now occurring." This line of argument combines the consideration of economic and educational quality, and it is appropriately applied to the field of religious studies. The question is not only one of economics (cost of instruction) but of availability of first-rate faculty and students to populate a growing number of programs.

The Harvard Committee on the Future of the Graduate School (1969) believed there was less student dissatisfaction in the smaller departments, not because of differences in student/faculty ratios, but because "a group of twenty can more easily develop a sense of participation and fraternity among its members than can a group of one hundred and twenty" (p. 55).

TABLE 5-1

RANGES OF RELIGION FACULTY RESOURCES IN RELATION TO DOCTORAL AND OTHER STUDENTS IN SELECTED INSTITUTIONS, 1969–1970

	Total Faculty Engaged in Doctoral Instruction	Full-Time Equivalent Doctoral Faculty	Total Number of Doctoral Students	Other Students Taught*	
				Professional Degree or M.A.	Undergraduates (Fall 1969 Registration)
Chicago	32	21.1	251	157	†
Fordham	18	12.0	130	—	2,250
Graduate Theological	46	13.9	133	1,038	—
Southwestern Baptist	28	5.4	120	1,671	—
Yale	19	10.4	114	316	542
Claremont	21	7.0	78	243	†
McMaster	13	7.3	42	24	1,183
Notre Dame	27	12.3	51	—	2,962
Southern Baptist	20	6.7	52	1,041	—
Vanderbilt	19	10.9	59	257	†
McGill	6	1.8	22	78	—
Princeton University	13	5.1	22	—	669
Pennsylvania	11	4.1	28	—	497
Rice	3	1.5	16	—	90
Southern Methodist	14	2.8	17	320	—
Stanford	8	2.4	7	—	339
Syracuse	10	3.3	26	—	1,750

* Not exclusively by faculty engaged in doctoral instruction. Particularly in the large theological schools, a number of other faculty are involved.

† Some participation in undergraduate instruction.

simply to calculate faculty/student ratios. The availability of other university faculty resources is of decisive importance at several of the institutions listed. Further, the crucial questions may not emerge in relation to total faculty/student ratios, but only in respect of the particular subdisciplines.

Nevertheless, considering simply the gross teaching responsibilities of the faculties, the question does arise about most if not all of the large doctoral programs in religion *whether they have grown to the point of being unmanageable in size and an excessive load on faculty.* Among the large programs, Yale and Harvard have exercised more rigorous control than most over admissions, but they too have felt the strain and are cutting back, as also are Chicago,[8] GTU, and Princeton Seminary. Such reductions are obviously related also to general graduate school economics and the decline in the demand for Ph.D.'s.

Similar problems of sheer magnitude may also be apparent in somewhat smaller programs, as at Claremont, Emory, Iowa, and McMaster, all of which have expanded rapidly and have faculties with major undergraduate or seminary teaching responsibilities.

At the other end of the spectrum are programs with small doctoral populations (and sometimes small faculties), where the question of faculty resources can be weighed only in relation to decisions, whether made or not, about areas of specialization to be offered and in relation to particular faculty strengths, cognate departments, library resources, and support for students.

Much more than the small university departments, which do usually manage to develop a spectrum of graduate courses specifically for graduate students, the numerous small theological school Th.D. programs exemplify a kind of issue that is relevant to most of the seminary-based programs. To what extent is it appropriate to rely heavily on first professional degree courses for the instruction of doctoral students? Or, correlatively, to what extent is it essential to develop special graduate seminars?

Plainly the answer to these questions depends greatly on the quality of the professional degree students. It also depends on the degree of imagination in devising complementary means of instruction and the ability and willingness of faculty to direct independent study. Further, participation in seminary or undergraduate courses *can* be of value, particularly in collateral or minor areas of study. But it does not follow that doctoral studies can be added to an existing theological (or undergraduate) program without a major commitment of additional resources. Judging by reports from faculty of their actual teaching responsibilities in 1969-1970 (with the numbers of doctoral and nondoctoral students in each course), nearly all the small seminary-based Th.D. programs show a heavy reliance on seminary courses (that is, significant numbers of faculty reported

[8] Chicago requires special note, since the Divinity School has almost from the beginning placed greatest emphasis on doctoral instruction. Whereas the ratio of one graduate student (Ph.D., Th.D., or perhaps S.T.M.) to three or four first professional degree students has often been considered acceptable in seminary-based programs, the ratio in Chicago has been nearly the reverse. (Yet Chicago produces fewer religion Ph.D.'s than Yale or Boston. See Chapter 12.)

that most of the courses in which they taught doctoral students were more than 50 percent populated by other students.)[9] Sometimes numerous graduate seminars are listed, but few are offered—sometimes only one in a field per year.

e. Library

The variations in faculty resources relative to students in graduate religion programs are paralleled, if not exceeded, by the disparities in libraries.[10] The major research centers are few, and the costs of maintaining and creating research collections even in selected fields are escalating rapidly. Not a few institutions have seriously underestimated the kind of commitment required to develop resources adequate for doctoral study. The difficulty is now compounded by the growing necessity of major libraries to charge high fees to outside users. Some libraries are woefully weak in foreign language holdings; by contrast, in one important theological library, 60 percent of the current acquisitions are in foreign languages.

Three major types of library collections in religion must be distinguished: the university-seminary library systems, either of a single institution or of cooperating schools; the independent theological libraries; and the general university libraries. The distinctions, of course, correspond to the types of institutions offering doctoral work. Because of the traditional association of advanced study in religion with professional theological education, the large research collections have been developed mainly in the theological libraries, although some of these have tended to be restricted to Christian studies (except insofar as non-Western religions were dealt with in the missionary context). General university libraries, on the other hand, are often relatively stronger in the non-Christian areas than the theological libraries, but usually have collected sparsely in the systematic theological area and relatively little also in the histories of theology or of particular Christian religious communities.

In relation to these types, but without pretending to an all-inclusive listing,

[9] This is also a problem, at least in selected areas, for even some of the strongest schools: for instance, at Duke, in historical studies and ethics and society; Graduate Theological Union, in theological studies; Harvard, in historical studies; Vanderbilt, in historical and theological studies; Yale, in historical studies and philosophical theology; Princeton Seminary, in history and practical theology; and Union (N.Y.) in history. This is by no means an exhaustive list, but only illustrative of the problem.

[10] In order to get a picture of library resources, we asked librarians at each institution to fill out two documents: (*a*) a summary report (for 1969–1970 or 1968–1969, depending on the year for which figures were available) concerning total annual expenditures and holdings; number of titles, annual expenditures, and acquisitions in the field of religion, including periodicals; facilities for study; library policies concerning acquisitions in the various areas of religious studies; and special collections in the library; (*b*) a modest check list, cutting across the broad spectrum of areas of religion, of works likely to be found largely in research collections, in order to provide a moderate independent check on the depth of library holdings, including foreign language resources. Reports were received from fifty-one institutions, and these, together with information otherwise gained about nonreporting institutions, make some generalizations feasible.

we may group the libraries in the institutions with graduate religion programs into four classes:

(1) The major research collections, spanning a broad spectrum of fields in depth, are only five in number. All of them combine strong theological school and general university library resources, built up over a long period of time, and they are found in the oligopoly of large, traditional, and prestigious centers of theological studies. In order of importance, these are: Cambridge (mainly Harvard); New York (including Union Seminary, Columbia, and Jewish Theological); New Haven (Yale); Princeton (Seminary and University); and Chicago (especially University of Chicago).

At a considerable remove from those centers are other collections which still may be called important: Duke; Graduate Theological Union (in conjunction with University of California, Berkeley, and building rapidly); Toronto (a very promising future, with the combination of the university and the Toronto Graduate School of Theological Studies); and Vanderbilt. The Library of Congress is, of course, also a great asset in the Washington area.

(2) A different kind of library concentration consists mainly of those centered in theological schools and generally restricted to the traditional theological areas, such as (including only those with more than 100,000 volumes in religion and theology) Catholic University, Claremont, Concordia, Drew, Garrett, General Theological, Hartford, Hebrew Union, Pittsburgh, Southern Baptist, Southern Methodist, Southwestern Baptist (though weak in foreign language holdings), and Union (Va.).

(3) The number of university library systems that comprise both large general collections and even relatively good holdings in religion (independently of a theological school library) is again quite small. In this group we may count the following:

Pennsylvania. 2,181,000 volumes, 65,000 classified as religion; good but spotty; especially strong in history of religions, notably Hinduism and Buddhism (special emphasis and extensive collections also in canon law, ethnology, medieval and Renaissance history, Early Reformation and papacy); good acquisitions rate; there are also useful theological libraries in the area.

Stanford. 3,725,000 volumes, 46,000 classified as religion; weak but with a fair acquisition rate and expanding collections in history of religions, Bible and ancient Near East, history of Christianity, theology and philosophy of religion, and sociology of religion (special emphases in modern and medieval Christianity, and related collections in East Asia, anthropology, philosophy, psychology, and sociology, as well as art and music).

Iowa. 1,420,000 volumes, 45,400 classified as religion; a policy of comprehensive collection in history of religions, Bible and Near East, history of Christianity, Roman Catholic and Protestant studies, philosophy of religion, sociology of religion (related collections in anthropology and medieval and Renaissance history), but relatively low expenditures for religion.

Southern California. 1,400,000 volumes, 75,000 classified as religion; modest rate of acquisitions in religion.

Brown. 1,250,000 volumes, 48,000 classified as religion; strength in Judaism, biblical and Near Eastern studies, philosophy of religion, history of Christianity (extensive related collections in anthropology, folklore, medieval and Renaissance history), but surprisingly low budget and rate of acquisition in religion.

Notre Dame. 1,136,000 volumes, 56,000 classified as religion; a high acquisition rate; strong in philosophy of religion and theology, especially Roman Catholic (special emphases in history of American Roman Catholicism, liturgics, medieval studies and philosophy).

In relation to university collections, one must also note such special collections as those in Indian and Buddhist studies in the University of Wisconsin, and in Islamics at McGill.

(4) Is it reasonable to speak of any cutoff point, below which serious question must be raised about the adequacy of a collection in religion for doctoral studies? Any individual judgment, of course, must be made in relation to the quality of the collection, to the specific areas of specialization proposed for doctoral studies, to the program of library building, and to the presence or absence of easy access to other major libraries. Comparisons of the actual over-all holdings and expenditures in institutions now offering doctoral work in religion, however, suggest that holdings in religion of fewer than 40,000-50,000 volumes and a rate of expenditure, at 1970 prices, of less than $25,000 per year for acquisitions would indicate very meager resources for supporting doctoral studies, unless the program were defined in a highly disciplined and restrictive way. The following instances are instructive: Case Western Reserve, with religion holdings of 12,000 volumes in a library of 1,000,000 volumes and a budget (1969-1970) of $8,000 for books and monographs; Fordham, with 42,000 volumes in religion and an allotment for books of $8,900; Grace Theological Seminary, with a religion collection of 16,000 volumes and an acquisitions expenditure of $3,000; Rice, with 24,000 volumes in religion out of a total library system of 600,000 volumes, and $6,000 annual expenditure on religious studies; Syracuse, with 16,000 volumes in religion of a total library of 1,360,000, with total annual expenditure estimated at $11,000 for religious studies; Temple, with 24,000 volumes in religion of a total of 955,000, religion acquisition expenditures of approximately $10,500.

f. Financial Support for Faculty and Students

With respect to the levels of support for faculty in religion and theology doctoral programs, two conclusions may be drawn with confidence.[11] First, as is

---

[11] Chairmen and graduate directors were asked to provide, where institutional policy permitted (and in most cases this was no problem), specific information concerning salaries and fringe benefits of their faculty members together with average salary levels for the entire institution. No names were given; only designation by rank.

well known, with the exception of two or three theological faculties, there is a large difference between salary levels in independent theological schools on the one hand and in university departments and divinity schools on the other hand. This has been a matter of increasing concern among the theological schools. The difference is offset to some extent by the tendency in the theological schools for faculty to cluster at the higher professorial ranks, but important contrasts remain. For example, among the independent theological schools the average salaries for full professors in 1969-1970 ranged from $9,800 to $20,000, with the average at the median school being $14,000. In the university departments and divinity schools the averages for professors ranged from $10,000 to $22,500, with the median institution's average being $17,600.

Second, with four exceptions—including one prestigious institution, where the average salary for full professors in the divinity school was lower than the average reported to the AAUP for all ranks in arts and sciences—the salaries of faculty members in university departments and divinity schools were generally on a par at all ranks with those of the arts and sciences faculties generally.

Similarly, with respect to student financial aid, there seem to be no important differences between the support of religion doctoral students and those in similar academic disciplines. We shall defer to our discussion of the doctoral student (Chapter 10) a picture of the over-all financial situation of graduate students in religion and its relation to other disciplines, here noting only some of the widespread variations among the institutions (with the obvious correlation with the possibilities of full-time study).

Slightly over half of all Ph.D. students got some form of financial assistance from their institutions; the proportion among Th.D.'s was considerably less (34 percent).[12] In only twelve institutions did two-thirds or more of the resident graduate students get any financial aid from their schools: Brown, Case Western Reserve, Chicago, McMaster, Marquette, Northwestern-Garrett, Notre Dame, Princeton, Rice, Stanford, Syracuse, and Yale—and in four of these instances half or more of the students receiving help got tuition only, in whole or in part (Chicago, Northwestern-Garrett, Rice, and Syracuse). Harvard and Hebrew Union College were close to the two-thirds level. On the other hand, in an almost equal number of cases one-third or fewer of the resident students received financial aid of any sort from the institution: Aquinas, Fordham, McGill, St. Louis, Concordia, Fuller, Grace, and Knox.[13]

---

[12] From the latter figure, we have excluded the large number of doctoral students at Southern Baptist seminaries where no tuition is charged to doctoral students. Since these 186 students would have to be counted as receiving full tuition scholarships, to include them with the other Th.D. students receiving some sort of financial aid from their institutions would seriously bias the averages.

[13] In both these summaries, students writing dissertations *in absentia* have been eliminated from the calculations. The summaries are based on information concerning financial aid received from 1,959 students. Compare these levels of financial support with the proportions of full-time/part-time study and of outside employment (above and Chapter 12).

It can hardly be said that graduate programs in religion are overly supplied with funds for financial assistance to students.

2. QUALITY AND THE ALLOCATION OF RESOURCES

The special questions of quality in the graduate study of religion all seem to cluster around the wise use of scarce resources, where the problems of the economics and of the quality of graduate education merge. Particular foci include the relation to collateral or cognate resources and the special difficulties of the independent school of religion or theology, which must generate its own language instruction and so forth.

One symbol of the issues is the disproportion in the distribution of fields of specialization among the various graduate programs. For example, there are in the United States and Canada 60 different programs (in 56 institutions) offering specializations in biblical studies, 50 programs in the history of Christianity (or church history or history of Christian thought), and 46 programs in Christian theological studies—as against some 22 that involve specialization of any sort in non-Western religions and 6 that deal with Islam (of which Dropsie and Johns Hopkins are dubious), 17 programs in religion and society (or sociology of religion), and 7 in religion and culture or the arts (see Chapter 11). The former, of course, are the traditional loci of study in the Christian area, the fields in which the most faculty are available and the most courses have been taught at both the undergraduate and the graduate levels. The question is not mainly one of gross supply and demand (see Chapter 6). It is the question whether 60 different programs of good quality can be maintained. Are there enough good faculty and good students, and are they brought together in the right way? One faculty member writes as follows concerning what he believes to be "the relative weakness of many New Testament programs in the country" (I have deleted the names of specific institutions):

> The problems of programs in universities with only one or at best two good teachers and a small number of students . . . is: not enough first-rate faculty members in the field . . . X seminary has a good setting (with Y university) but in recent years has not been able to keep a good faculty in New Testament. Z university has several outstanding faculty members but little cooperation between them; students are left on their own, or just with the supervision of one faculty member only. P and Q universities have (or have had) at least one outstanding member of the faculty, but not enough, and have suffered from unclear relationships between the divinity school and the religion departments of their universities. C university has a weak faculty and no rigid requirements . . . .
> One comment on the students: the quality of applicants I have seen in ten years has improved immensely. But there are not enough good students to fill a dozen or more doctoral programs in this country in the field of New Testament. Half a dozen or less such programs would probably do all that needs to be done.
> The present application pattern does not help to improve the situation. A few major institutions compete for the best ten applicants in the field. Each of these is admitted by two or three institutions at the same time. But a number of almost as qualified applicants are not admitted anywhere [i.e., within these institutions] and go into a second rate program.

Another facet of the same problem is the fact that many of the newer doctoral programs have been largely content to repeat the traditional areas of Christian studies. For example, among the programs established in the past decade, the following have proposed areas of specialization that fall entirely within the orbits of biblical studies, history of Christian thought, Christian theological studies, and Christian or theological ethics: Baylor, Case Western, Fordham, Fuller, Marquette, Pittsburgh, St. Louis, St. Mary's, Southern Methodist (Notre Dame adds liturgics to biblical and theological studies). And to this list we might add the somewhat earlier established programs at Aquinas and Emory and the restructured programs at Montreal and at St. Paul (Ottawa).

The obvious query to be made with respect to any such new program is: what is the justification for another instance which is essentially more of the same? Unfortunately no one from outside the institution has been available or willing to ask such questions seriously. This is not to say that I believe all these programs to be unjustified, or of doubtful quality. It is to say that such programs and proposals have a special burden of showing that there is a real need for another center of study in the usual areas and that the institution has distinctive resources to contribute.

On the other side, however, is the question: who are prepared to do anything else—that is, to develop advanced studies in the less well-represented or the new and distinctive areas? Here arises with special force the problem of collateral and cognate resources.

The most obvious illustrations come from the fields of non-Western religions. As we saw in Chapter 4, only eleven of the twenty institutions proposing to offer doctoral work in these areas can call on major supporting resources in a university.

Religion is thus an especially good illustration of the pervasive problem in graduate education of identifying and using resources for study, thus of serious academic planning. There is great need for much more realistic calculation of what a given institution can responsibly propose to do, and what also needs doing. In a few cases, institutions have been unwilling or unprepared even to define the precise areas of specialization in which they judge themselves competent to offer advanced study—and a further number of the announced programs are not clear. The fluidity of development in religious studies, combined with a legitimate interest in providing flexibility, has often led to a confusing vagueness about just what is proposed. But the real issue is the exercise of discipline in limiting and focusing the areas in which individual graduate departments offer facilities and direction for genuinely advanced work. As I have already made clear, I believe it of critical importance to avoid reducing the study of religion to a concatenation of independent and unrelated modes and areas of investigation. It may be true with respect to the highest levels of intensive study that "the real unit of intellectual work is the sub-discipline, which usually has only one or two representatives on a small campus and seldom more than a half dozen on a big one" (Jencks and Riesman, 1969, p. 526). But with respect to the subdisciplines, it is questionable whether even the largest and strongest institutions can cover all areas. No weakness is more obvious in the North American scene than that too many graduate departments of religion are trying to be all things to all students. We can learn at this point from other disciplines, where the most distinguished departments are characterized by concentration on a quite limited number of areas of work.

A few of the relatively newer programs have made efforts to select carefully. McMaster, combining social-scientific studies with philosophical-theological studies, has chosen to concentrate on the Hebraic tradition and on Eastern religions, especially Indian. Stanford has sought to capitalize on its locus in the humanities program, emphasizing four related methodologies. Southern California has opted to concentrate on a single area, social ethics, working out relations with a developing urban studies emphasis within the university. Brown has identified Judaic studies, biblical studies, and western religious thought (largely Christian thought) as the areas for attention, though students have been more widely dispersed in their prime interests. Notre Dame and Marquette have restricted themselves to the more traditionally Christian fields of study (with liturgics as a distinctive special area for Notre Dame). Princeton has opted for history of religions (Hinduism and Buddhism in particular), history of Christian thought, and philosophy of religion and ethics, abandoning a former specialization in biblical studies. Pennsylvania, although listing a broad spectrum, actually focuses on history of religions, biblical archaeology, Christian origins and patristics, modern religious thought, and philosophy of religion. St. Michael's emphasizes Christian thought. Wisconsin restricts itself to Indian and Buddhist studies. Chicago Theological has proposed to concentrate on biblical studies, history of Christianity (especially Reformation and Free Church studies), and "theology and the study of man."

These examples are not intended as an affirmative judgment on the wisdom of any of the efforts, or their viability, but only as illustrative of some real attempts at self-discipline.

The issue here is not only a matter of allocation of various resources. It is that, but it is also a clue to the way a new sort of base, as I have called it earlier (Chapter 2), can emerge and be exploited effectively. Varieties in methods and cross-cultural study can contribute to coherence rather than to mere proliferation of hurdles and juxtaposition of materials if departments are willing in each instance to focus those methods and studies on a carefully limited set of intents and specializations—and also if faculty members are willing actually to expose themselves to each other, to carry on their own study and teaching with a view to its coherence with their colleagues' and students' work. If each persists simply in doing his own thing, no amount of carefully designed curricula will do anything for coherence.

The problem of resources, in respect both of waste and duplication and of scarcity, is obviously related to the questions of cooperation and consortia. Of the recent ventures in this direction, only the Graduate Theological Union appears so far to have effected a successful combination of resources at the graduate level. On the other hand, since the breakdown of the Federated Theological Faculties at Chicago, the Divinity School of the university has sufficiently iso-

lated itself from surrounding institutions that competing doctoral programs have
been encouraged. A professor from another university writes: "Our program could
be improved, if other area schools could be encouraged to call better scholars to
their faculties and if these men would be given status in our university's program
(this is only one example of the difficulties that exist with respect to the participation of good scholars who are legally not members of the institution which
supervises the degree program)."[14]

The other side of the same problem is the lack of provision for students to
pursue important segments of their graduate study in other institutions or to
move readily to other institutions when their interests change.[15] Even given the
discipline—which generally seems lacking—to admit students only in the areas
in which a school is genuinely prepared to offer graduate education, little provision is made for the student who decides after arrival that he wants to specialize
in an area in which the faculty do not believe it would be responsible for them to
train students. Devices such as the Traveling Scholar program at the universities
participating in the Committee on Institutional Cooperation (the "Big Ten" and
Chicago) seem sadly lacking, either to supplement graduate students' opportunities for study or to provide for students whose interests change. Graduate school
regulations are in these respects woefully archaic.[16]

3. ACCOUNTABILITY, CREDENTIALING, AND ACCREDITATION

The word "accountability" has come to have a faddish popularity, but it is
useful to indicate that certifying quality is a much broader matter than formal
accreditation processes.

a. Scholarship in the field of religion has the distinctive burden and opportunity of being accountable to three distinguishable communities: the religious, the
civic, and the academic. Paul Harrison has put it nicely with respect to the study
of religion in public institutions: "The scholar of religion in a public school, no
less than any other man, possesses a variety of commitments and loyalties and
interests, but he is in a precarious position of unusual sensitivity, for unlike the
priest, the politician, or the secular scholar, he cannot enjoy the privileges of a
primary and guiding commitment to a single institution, whether it be the
church, the state, or the academic community."[17] Except for the most sectarian
contexts, this statement applies aptly to the study of religion in nonpublic insti-

[14] It is good to note, however, that in the summer of 1970, the heads of seven university
schools of theology began to meet together to collaborate on programs of study, general
school planning, and funding. The schools are: Chicago, Graduate Theological Union,
Harvard, Notre Dame, Union (N.Y.), Vanderbilt, and Yale. It is too early to judge
the import of such collaboration, but it would appear that a number of gains for the
study of religion should be forthcoming.

[15] One exception, however, is SMU's program which was initiated with the constructive
proposal that a period of a student's graduate career, with SMU fellowship support, might
often be spent elsewhere.

[16] This is not to overlook the fact that the greatest obstacle to such mobility is often
the student's own unwillingness to make the necessary changes.

[17] Harrison, 1966.

tutions as well, since accountability means much more than formal submission for approval; it also means availability for testing in relation to the distinctive concerns of the several communities. That means the examination of the scholar's work in the academic community in accord with the methods that are available to everyone, regardless of belief. It also means that anyone who seeks to interpret a religious tradition is accountable to the adherents of that tradition for the adequacy of his interpretation.

This triad of loyalties and responsibilities has traditionally involved tensions. As Harrison goes on to say, "The Church and the State have been traditionally enamoured of authority and power. In contrast, the school and university, primarily because of their limited function, have been unable to acquire or even realistically hope for a monopoly over authority. So they have done the next best thing in jealously guarding and striving to maintain their freedom."

The problems have generally arisen from the failure to recognize the essential interaction of these three interests; that is, their need to act as checks on each other. On the one side, not only the claim for accountability to particular confessional interests but also the ideal of responsibility to religious communities in general has sometimes been made primary to responsibility to the scholarly community. I have heard it argued: "There are many mediocre churches and they need mediocre ministers," the implication being that there is a large role for mediocre theological schools. The same kind of argument, at a somewhat more refined level, has been offered as a justification for graduate programs in religion. Similarily, there is disturbing evidence that academic authorities of several sorts have occasionally not applied vigorous standards to programs in theology and religious studies because of the presumed interests of piety, or service to the religious community.

On the other side, the public interest has often been thought to be served by the deceptively simple disjunction of church and state—the "wall of separation." This is, of course, no simple disjunction at all, and it has led to all sorts of confusion in the public decisions with respect to the study of religion at the university and graduate school level; for example, the awkward attempts of Congress to define the limits of federal financial support, as in the Higher Education Act of 1965, and in the NDEA fellowship program and the National Endowment for the Humanities.[18]

---

[18] For example, the Higher Education Act of 1965 excludes support of work "primarily in connection with any part of the program of a school or department of divinity." This has on occasion been interpreted to apply even to the use of rooms in university buildings supported by federal funds for undergraduate courses in religious studies that have nothing to do with the preparation of clergy. Similarly, the National Endowment for the Humanities has excluded from consideration for senior fellowships any teacher "holding full or partial appointments in schools or departments of divinity" (even though the legislation itself does not include that restriction), thus leading to the anomaly of excluding a specialist in Buddhism whose primary status is in Sanskrit in a faculty in arts and sciences, because he also happens to have a partial appointment in a theological school. This policy was subsequently modified to allow that such an individual might apply for a fellowship in Sanskrit linguistics, though he would be ineligible to apply for a fellowship in

It ought, however, to be recognized that finally these varieties and tensions in accountability are healthy and creative. To cite Harrison again, the debate in the past has usually "circled around the issue of which commitment should be primary—the religious, the civic, or the intellectual. . . . The participants in the debate have failed to recognize that the integrity of the public scholar in religion could possibly be enhanced by virtue of his peculiar institutional relations. This scholar must remain continually and critically sensitive, not to one authority or to one power, but to the corrective discipline of the countervailing interests of church, state and academic community."

b. Accountability to the academic community, which is not simply separable from the responsibility to the civic and religious communities, though we must focus on it as our primary concern, is less a matter of formal accreditation processes than of the informal credentialing that goes on through recognition of the leadership of certain institutions and the approval or disapproval that is expressed by comparing the work of other schools with these.

Further, as I have already tried to make clear, the critical questions are not those of defining universally applicable general standards by which quality is to be measured. They are rather the problems of influencing decisions about the viability of actual and proposed programs in specific areas and in relation to particular needs and resources.

Yet there does arise the question of institutional structures through which responsible decision can be assisted. The Province of Ontario has developed a rigorous and sophisticated scheme for avoiding unnecessary duplication and for evaluating the quality of graduate programs (this in all fields). Even though approval by the "Appraisals Committee" is optional for institutions, it is not likely to be by-passed. Nothing corresponds to this, so far as I can discover, in the United States or elsewhere in Canada. At this point there has been a particular vacuum with respect to religious studies. The regional accrediting associations, in relation to religious studies, are widely believed to have been of less help than they might have been. This is (1) partly because the over-all accreditation process for a large university cannot hope to deal with every specific departmental graduate program, and (2) partly because of occasional confusion about the relation of the interests of the several communities to which we referred earlier. Further, there have been instances of regional accreditation of independent schools of religion to offer the Ph.D. degree, in which there has been in fact no university relationship and the competence of the institution is questionable.[19]

Buddhist studies—this again on the presumption that Buddhist studies are *ipso facto* intended to proselytize or to reinforce adherence to a sect.

[19] There has also been a relatively widespread movement for theological schools to seek regional accreditation, because students who do not finish the theological program or do not go into the priesthood, ministry, or rabbinate sometimes wish to continue studies in public institutions, many of which forbid transfer of credit from institutions not regionally accredited. It is widely thought that some regional accrediting associations have in view of this established a double standard, with lower quality requirements for theological schools.

The American Association of Theological Schools has for years (particularly since the Niebuhr, Williams, and Gustafson report, 1957) been concerned to improve the quality of professional studies and has also dealt with teaching and research degree programs in which the theological school faculties were involved. During 1970-1971, the whole range of AATS accreditation standards has been reviewed and revised. With the rapidly increasing participation of Roman Catholic theological schools and the awakening interest of some Jewish institutions, the AATS is in a position to be effective in relation to programs administered by theological schools as such. However, the AATS cannot properly deal with university-administered programs, which constitute by far the bulk of those offering doctoral studies in religion and theology.

The professional societies in the field—of which the largest have been the American Academy of Religion, the American Society of Church History, the Society of Biblical Literature, and the Society for the Scientific Study of Religion —have had no structures for raising the questions of accountability, and they have made no efforts in this area. A further problem is that professional societies in the field of religion have been so separated, at least prior to the formation of the Council on the Study of Religion in 1969, that they could not have exerted significant pressure had they wanted to.

The Council on Graduate Studies in Religion was formed two decades ago by the directors of graduate studies in a dozen of the prestige institutions, with a view to defining and maintaining high standards in Ph.D. programs in religion. The Council has in fact formulated a statement of standards for the Ph.D., the acceptance of which is a condition for membership in the Council. It has also published a useful report of dissertations in religion, 1940-1952, and it has maintained (largely for the benefit of its members) a continuing dissertation title index of dissertations completed and in process. But the Council has grown slowly, to a membership in 1970 of twenty-two institutions,[20] and until 1971, while it has served a useful function of exchange of information among member institutions, it has sought little influence on other existing or developing programs. Recently, however, the Council has proposed to take action by putting serious questions of capabilities and intentions both to its own members and to other institutions.

Insofar as structural resolutions to the problems of accountability are relevant, the vacuum in credentialing responsibility may best be filled by the combined exercise of responsibility of all four of these groups. The AATS committee on revision of the accreditation standards for teaching and research degrees has taken a major step forward by proposing, with respect to the institutions for which the AATS can properly assume responsibility, to shift from over-all accreditation of an institution for graduate teaching and research degrees to the definition of particular programs or types of programs, for which specific fields the resources and competence of an individual school will be evaluated.

[20] Boston, Brown, Chicago, Claremont, Columbia, Drew, Duke, Emory, Fordham, GTU, Harvard, Iowa, McGill, McMaster, Notre Dame, Pennsylvania, Princeton University, Syracuse, Temple, Union (N.Y.), Vanderbilt, Yale.

Close collaboration between regional accrediting associations and the American Association of Theological Schools seems essential in any actions by the former in granting accreditation to independent theological schools or schools of religion. One of their joint tasks should be to discourage nonuniversity-related theological faculties from offering the Ph.D.

Neither the regional accrediting associations nor the AATS, however, can reasonably be expected to meet the needs of the university-based doctoral programs in assessing their competence to offer advanced religious studies in specific areas or in assisting them to plan for further development. Something is needed other than formal accreditation stamps of approval or disapproval, and it is not likely that the Ontario model of evaluation with respect to need and competence can be exported or developed on a widespread geographical scale. A more viable line of action would appear to be for the Council on Graduate Studies in Religion, perhaps in concert with the Council on the Study of Religion and the American Academy of Religion, to begin to take up in serious and systematic fashion the fundamental questions of needs, allocation of resources, comity arrangements, and cooperative ventures in the field of graduate religious studies.

4. A SUMMARY RATING OF DOCTORAL PROGRAMS

Throughout this and the preceding chapter I have been exploring criteria by which strength and weakness in graduate education in religion can properly be judged, and I have offered a number of illustrations of the application of such criteria, particularly at the extremes. Is it possible now in summary to draw together these bits of evidence in an estimate of the range of quality in the sixty-nine institutions involved in the Study?

Three cautions are essential: (1) The data are uneven and in some cases insufficient to allow a responsible judgment. Furthermore, it must be remembered that the statistical data come from the academic year 1969-1970. Some programs were so new as not yet to have awarded a doctoral degree. Others were then and have since been undergoing rapid change. (2) It would be patently unfair to compare directly the old established departments with the newly developed ones in relation to resources, reputation, and the like. Any groupings of institutions must take account of the fact that some twenty-five of the programs have come into existence since 1960. Some are quite small, and some are experimental. These have had little opportunity to prove their worth, even though we can make some judgment as to their relative potentialities. (3) This summary is not organized in relation to specific fields of specialization, where the final test of responsibility and adequacy must always lie (see the Concluding Note at the end of this chapter).

Given these qualifications, I believe doctoral programs in religion can be grouped into six major categories, relating age and size to several major indices of quality:

I. The older, large, and established programs of the first rank (though by no means necessarily equal in every field).

II. The older and established programs of the second rank.

III. Relatively newer programs that have become firmly established, in either the first or the second rank.

IV. New and promising programs, some of which are potentially of the first rank.

V-a, V-b. Marginal programs—i.e., either marginal in resources relative to the intentions of the program, being thus in serious need of strengthening, or marginal in relation to the over-all needs of the field.

VI. Inadequate programs.

In estimating over-all quality I have combined three sorts of considerations:

First, I have drawn on quite objective data reflecting several important measures of quality: library resources, including not only the extent and quality of holdings, but especially the rate of expenditure for maintaining or developing a research collection; the ability and willingness to be selective in the admission of doctoral students; the proportion of students in full-time study, including both resident study prior to the dissertation and the preparation of the dissertation; and the amount of support available for students. (See above, especially Section 1.)

Second, I have considered the faculty resources available in relation to the kind and scope of doctoral studies proposed, with reference also to the clarity and definition of fields of study offered and the relatively traditional or novel character of the program. My evaluation here has also been supplemented by a judgment concerning faculty quality, an admittedly subjective judgment but one informed by extensive visitation of institutions and review of documents and questionnaires. (See above, Section 2, also Chapter 4, and Part IV below.)

Finally, I have taken into important account the actual or potential relation to a university of the first or second rank. For this purpose, I have drawn particularly, though not exclusively, on the 1969 Roose and Andersen ratings of graduate programs (1970), specifically the ratings of the following departments in the humanities and the social sciences: classics, English, philosophy, anthropology, history, and sociology. Since it is not possible to carry on doctoral studies in religion of the highest quality except in relation to a strong university, this consideration is of special significance.[21] (See also Chapters 3 and 4.)

[21] The following classification in relation to related university strengths is instructive:
(1) These programs are related to universities with three or more of the six specified departments rated in the 1969 Roose-Anderson summary as "strong or distinguished": Brandeis, Brown, Chicago, Columbia, Graduate Theological Union (with University of California, Berkeley), Harvard, Johns Hopkins, Northwestern, Pennsylvania, Princeton Seminary, Princeton University, Stanford, Union Seminary (N.Y.), Wisconsin, and Yale.
(2) These programs are related to universities with three or more of the six specified departments rated in the 1969 survey as "good": Duke, Iowa, New York University.
(3) These programs are related to universities with three or more of the six depart-

The groupings that follow, I repeat, are not to be understood as qualitative rankings per se. Distinctions are also made in relation to age and size of the programs, in order to avoid direct comparison of the older programs with the new and promising ones. There are significant variations in quality, over-all and in special fields, within each group. All those in the first four groups are to be considered as adequate, strong, or distinguished. None, however, is beyond the possibility of improvement, and I have, therefore, offered a number of specific indications of needs and weaknesses in the interest of suggesting how the quality of graduate instruction can be improved.[22]

I. *Older and Established Programs of the First Rank*
    Chicago
    Columbia
    Duke
    Harvard
    Princeton Seminary
    Union Seminary (N.Y.)
    Vanderbilt
    Yale

All these schools belong to the oligopoly or grandfather institutions in religious studies. Each has awarded over a hundred doctorates in the past twenty years. Each draws on the combined resources of a strong theological faculty and a university of the first or second rank (though the patterns of relation between the theological faculty and doctoral programs are quite different; see above, Chapter 3). These are all institutions with strong libraries, with more than 60 percent of the doctoral students in full-time study, and with a proven record of selectivity in admissions. (For distinctions to be drawn within these areas see above, especially Section 1.) In relation to the objective indices, Chicago, Columbia-Union, Harvard, and Yale rank above Duke, Princeton Seminary, and

ments rated as "adequate": Boston, Case Western Reserve, Claremont, Emory, Fordham, Notre Dame, Pittsburgh, Southern California, Syracuse, Vanderbilt.

It should be noted that Canadian institutions were not rated in the Roose-Anderson report. Nor is it to be supposed that the ratings of the United States institutions are inerrant. But they represent informed opinion and cannot be simply disregarded.

It is also noteworthy that the recent proposed revision of accreditation standards in the American Association of Theological Schools makes even stronger the former position that the absence of a university relation compromises the quality of teaching and research doctoral programs.

[22] Ten institutions are not mentioned in the listings, for varying reasons. Brigham Young, Dominican, and Iliff appear to be phasing out their doctoral programs. For differing reasons they should be encouraged to do so. The Johns Hopkins program in Near Eastern studies seems to be moving away from emphasis on ancient Near East religion. St. Mary's University and Seminary, Baltimore, has apparently not moved to the implementation of its proposed Ph.D. program, and I would not encourage the institution to do so. Insufficient data were available to formulate a responsible judgment concerning the following programs: Laval, Montreal, New York University, St. Paul, and Yeshiva.

Vanderbilt; but all these institutions are definitely stronger than those in Group II.

The primary question to be raised for these schools is whether their programs are too large even for their considerable resources, both in numbers of students and in field distribution. Most of these doctoral programs are already engaged in reduction in size, and some are reducing the number of fields covered (notably Princeton Seminary). Chicago needs to be concerned about the attrition rate, Columbia and Princeton Seminary about the high proportion of students writing dissertations *in absentia*. While Columbia has major strengths in the Union Seminary faculty and in collateral departments in the university, the faculty resources in the department need to be expanded.

II. *Older and Established Programs of the Second Rank*
    Boston
    Catholic University (S.T.D.)
    Hartford
    Hebrew Union
    Iowa
    Jewish Theological
    Northwestern-Garrett
    Southern Baptist

All these programs have been in existence for more than twenty years (though in the case of Jewish Theological, only the D.H.L.), and all except Iowa are based in a theological faculty. All may be counted as good or at least adequate, though all rank lower than Group I on the objective indices, including library resources, and each has special needs.

Most of these institutions will be well advised to be more disciplined in numbers of doctoral students (Boston, Hartford, Iowa, and Northwestern-Garrett have expanded greatly in size since 1954, without a corresponding increase in resources). Catholic University has special needs in faculty stability, in freedom from ecclesiastical control, and in closer relation to the university as a whole. Hartford has an interesting diversity in faculty strengths and has been experimental in program, although it has so far lacked the possibility of a relation with a university. With the exception of Hartford and perhaps Iowa, all these programs are relatively traditional in the fields of study proposed. Hebrew Union, Jewish Theological, and Southern Baptist have also lacked a relation to a major university. For Jewish Theological, the possibility is plainly at hand, but this is not the case for either Hebrew Union or Southern Baptist in their present locations. Hebrew Union has been distinctive as a place in which both Jewish and non-Jewish students have engaged in biblical and Judaic studies. Jewish Theological has been more obviously oriented to the religious community, and its doctoral programs have been less disciplined and less clearly oriented toward research and teaching, although it is without question a major center for certain areas of Jewish studies. Southern Baptist has been the most highly disciplined of the Baptist Th.D. programs (for example, in selectivity of students and in insisting on full-time work) and has made serious attempts to assure breadth in faculty training by not allowing participation in doctoral instruction until after a period of study at another kind of institution. Iowa needs a substantially stronger commitment to the development of library resources and care in the areas chosen for non-Western religious studies. With respect to the Northwestern-Garrett programs, it may be asked whether closer relations with the university are perhaps desirable.

III. *New Programs That Are Firmly Established*
    Brandeis
    Claremont
    Emory
    McGill
    Princeton University

These are programs established after 1950. All have granted fifteen or more Ph.D. degrees. All have been relatively traditional in the design of the programs. Of the five, Princeton is clearly established in the first rank according to all the objective indices and has been the most rigorously disciplined. The others compete at least with schools in Group II. Claremont and Emory need to be concerned about overexpansion, and all except Princeton about part-time study, particularly at the dissertation stage.

IV. *New and Promising Programs, Some of Which Are Potentially of the First Rank*
    Brown
    Graduate Theological Union
    McMaster
    Marquette
    Notre Dame
    Pennsylvania
    Southern Methodist
    Stanford
    Syracuse
    The Toronto Group
    Wisconsin

All but two of these programs have come into being since 1960. Brown is included, although occasional religion doctorates have been granted for a long time, because its present department has developed less rapidly than the institutions identified in Group III above. Also the program at Emmanuel in Toronto goes back to 1939, but the Toronto schools should here be considered as a whole, in view of the newly reshaped Toronto Graduate School of Theological Studies and the new program at the University of St. Michael's College. The resources of those institutions and the promise of their programs depend on the further development of relations with the University of Toronto, which has both strong library resources and important cognate departments. The program of religious studies at the University of Ottawa might also be a candidate for inclusion in this category, in terms of the direction of its development, but insufficient evidence is available to formulate a definite judgment.

It is noteworthy that of the eleven programs listed, all but three (Graduate Theological Union, Southern Methodist, and the Toronto group) are efforts to develop doctoral studies without reliance on theological faculty resources.

All these programs have some marks of distinctiveness that have been noted earlier; they also have important needs. Six of the programs draw on the resources of universities of the first rank: Brown, GTU (Ph.D. in relation to University of California, Berkeley), Pennsylvania, Stanford, the Toronto group, and Wisconsin. Brown has been small and selective, though traditional in its areas of study, and it is much in need of greater library support. The GTU has over-expanded, but holds promise of distinction through relation with the University of California. Pennsylvania has a small core of faculty in the department and needs care in defining its fields of concentration, but it is developing a distinctive and disciplined program with extensive relations to strong collateral departments, notably in anthropology, philosophy, and oriental studies. Stanford has begun a small and imaginative experiment emphasizing humanistic disciplines, though the library resources need much strengthening. Wisconsin has offered only Buddhist studies, though the future is somewhat in question because of the untimely death of the principal figure in that program.

Notre Dame and Syracuse are also located in universities with strength in some related departments. Notre Dame has been traditional in the areas of emphasis, with the exception of the field of liturgics, but has been quite disciplined in its growth and program structure, and it has undertaken in an important way to improve the library. Syracuse has attempted to formulate some distinctly different directions of study, though the program will be improved with greater focus and discipline, and especially with the enhancing of library resources, which are very weak.

McMaster, Marquette, and Southern Methodist all lack the base of a university of recognized strength at the graduate level. Southern Methodist, however, has a strong core of theological faculty and a good record of selectivity of students and support for full-time study; there is moreover the prospect of further resources. McMaster has attempted a distinctive mix of cross-cultural study and has provided excellent support for students, though it may have expanded too rapidly and is in need of greater strength in library. Marquette, though quite traditional in its foci and weak in language and library resources, has been relatively controlled in size and efficient in operation.

V-a. *Programs That Are Marginal in Resources in Relation to Intentions*
     Catholic University (Ph.D.)
     Drew
     Fordham
     Southern California
     Temple
     University of California, Santa Barbara

"Marginal" here means that substantial reforms or improvements are needed if the program is to be viable. Most of these programs are low in selectivity (except for Southern California) and are heavily populated by part-time students (except for Santa Barbara). Library resources are at best moderate to weak.

Both Fordham and Temple have expanded beyond all reason and with low selectivity. Fordham has been traditional in orientation, though also attempting work in non-Western religions without a sufficient supporting base in the university. Temple, with a core of good faculty, has been quite undisciplined and unfocused both in areas of study and in programs; serious efforts toward discipline and focus have been undertaken since 1970, but supporting resources in collateral departments and especially library have been poor.

The Catholic University Ph.D. program needs further to distinguish itself from the old religious education doctorate and to define its goals more sharply and to review its requirements and resources, particularly in relation to the School of Theology.

Southern California has attempted a unique focus on a single area, social ethics, in relation to the general university interest in urban studies. The School of Religion faculty resources and the library, however, are in need of further strengthening. The University of California, Santa Barbara, program has only begun and would be helped particularly by much stronger library and cognate department resources.

Drew once possessed a strong theological faculty and a dynamic doctoral program, but since the resignation of a large number of that faculty in the late 1960's, it is doubtful whether it has been wise for the university to reenter doctoral studies in religion.

V-b. *Marginal in Respect of Need*
    Chicago Theological
    Concordia
    Fuller
    General
    Lutheran (Chicago)
    Pittsburgh
    St. Louis
    Seabury-Western
    Union (Va.)

The programs grouped above are noted as marginal, not because there are not in each case significant competencies for graduate work in at least one or more areas, but because throughout they duplicate fields of study amply represented in major institutions; because (with the exception of Pittsburgh, where the relation is not developed) they exist without relation to a strong university; because they are largely addenda to seminary curricula; and because they tend to be populated largely by part-time students (with the exception of Fuller). In some cases, strictly confessional interests may justify the continuation of the programs. Chicago Theological has sought to define distinctive foci for study, but serious questions must be raised about the development of two competing doctoral programs (Chicago Theological and Chicago Lutheran) immediately adjacent to the largest doctoral program in the country—even if this be a result of the insularity of the university.

VI. *Inadequate Programs*
     Aquinas Institute
     Baylor
     Case Western Reserve
     Dallas
     Dropsie
     Grace
     New Orleans Baptist
     Rice
     Southwestern Baptist

Although competent faculty are present in these institutions, the question must be raised whether any of them is at present capable of offering doctoral studies of high quality. Aquinas earlier proposed to build on a relation with the University of Iowa, but that has not proved feasible, and the resources available in faculty and library of the three participating seminaries are simply insufficient. Those schools would be well advised to concentrate on professional degree training. Baylor lacks cognate strengths in the university and has essentially replicated a Th.D. program without the practical theology but with serious denominational circumscription. Case Western Reserve and Rice have too tiny a faculty base in religious studies, and too little possibility of drawing on cognate departments, plus serious library problems.[23] Dropsie has a distinguished history, but by 1970-1971 had been reduced to about three full-time faculty and a very high proportion of part-time students; the library holdings could usefully contribute to the program of some other institution. Dallas and Grace have served special clienteles, notably the Bible colleges, but in respect, for example, of library and faculty resources to make possible full-time study in distinction from the seminary program, they do not at all appear to have the potentiality for doctoral education of high academic quality.

In contrast to most of the other institutions listed here, Southwestern and New Orleans Baptist have been among the larger producers of doctoral degrees. But that fact is itself indicative of the need for radical surgery, since the programs have not in fact proved to be mainly directed toward research and teaching, but are extensively pursued by pastors on a part-time basis. Both libraries are weak in foreign language holdings.

CONCLUDING NOTE

Two major qualifications must be made again with respect to all the above groupings of institutions. First, the classifications have not been made in relation

[23] Case Western Reserve has now ceased to admit Ph.D. students.

to special fields of study and therefore conceal important differences in the fields offered and in the quality of work. These general estimates must therefore all be viewed in relation to the spectrum of subfields actually offered (see Chapter 11) and to specific strengths and weaknesses. In a review by special fields, particularly if made without relation to the age or size of the programs, quite different groupings would emerge. For example, in certain areas of Jewish studies, Brandeis might move ahead of any of the old established programs, and not all the "grandfather institutions" would appear high on the lists for philosophy of religion or for the study of Asian religions.

Second, a summary rating made in 1980 will almost certainly result in different overall evaluations, if only because of the chronological distinctions made in groups I-IV. One may expect and hope that the list of schools unquestionably in the first rank will include not only grandfather institutions, but also several of the newer programs.

6

The Numbers Game

1. 1984

What are the needs for faculty in religion and theology? In discussing this question I shall make use of the model developed by Allan Cartter, projecting the college age population, total college enrollments, faculty sizes and needs through 1990 on the basis of 1970 census figures and other data.[1] The birthrate statistics for the 1960's show that the college age group (eighteen through twenty-one) will continue to increase until 1980 and will then decline at least until 1988, when it may be expected to rise again at least slightly. Cartter concludes that the total college enrollments will increase until 1982 and will then also begin to decline. This conclusion assumes that the percentage of high school graduates entering college will continue to increase from approximately 54 percent in 1965 (and 62 percent in 1970) to a maximum of 70 percent in 1985, and that it will then stabilize. This seems a reasonable maximum, even allowing for continuing expansion of community colleges and an increase in state and federal support for higher education.

On these assumptions, Cartter makes the projections shown in Table 6-1 of the new faculty needed with doctoral degrees. Note that the faculty replacement rate is calculated at approximately 2 percent, in accord with the conclusions reached by Cartter in his now famous 1966 article "The Supply of and Demand for College Teachers." Also, he has assumed that slightly less than 50 percent of the total new faculty will have the doctorate.

a. Any attempt to relate such general projections specifically to the field of religion is hazardous in the extreme because of the impossibility of projecting with confidence what the religion enrollment patterns will be. As is shown later (Chapter 9, Figure 9-3) enrollments in religion courses in Protestant-related institutions have increased over the past fifteen years, but at a somewhat slower rate than total enrollments in those institutions. Religion enrollments in Roman Catholic institutions have actually declined significantly since 1964.

[1] The basic data are published in Cartter (1971), pp. 132-140.

97

TABLE 6-1*

FACULTY (THOUSANDS) NEEDED TO MAINTAIN PRESENT QUALITY OF INSTRUCTIONAL STAFF 1960-1990

Year	Student Enrollments			Total Full-Time Faculty	Faculty Needed			
	Full-Time Equivalent	Change (2-year Average)	Change %		For Replacements	For Expansion	Total	New (with Ph.D.)
				Actual				
1960	2913	145	5.0	169	3.4	7.0	10.4	4.6
1961	3173	117	3.7	177	3.5	8.0	11.5	5.1
1962	3411	249	7.3	190	3.8	13.0	16.8	7.3
1963	3639	233	6.4	202	4.0	12.0	16.0	7.0
1964	4030	310	7.7	220	4.4	18.0	22.4	9.9
1965	4564	463	10.1	233	4.6	13.0	17.6	7.7
1966	4936	453	9.2	245	4.9	12.0	16.9	7.4
1967	5380	428	7.6	261	5.2	16.3	21.5	9.5
1968	5810	437	7.5	279	5.6	17.5	23.1	10.2

				Projected				
1969	6064	342	5.7	292	5.8	13.6	19.4	8.5
1970	6303	247	3.9	302	6.0	10.0	16.0	7.0
1971	6755	450	6.7	320	6.3	18.0	24.3	12.0
1972	7115	406	5.7	336	6.6	16.2	22.8	10.0
1973	7489	367	4.9	351	7.0	14.7	21.7	9.4
1974	7831	358	4.6	365	7.2	14.3	21.5	9.3
1975	8197	354	4.3	380	7.5	14.2	21.7	9.4
1976	8525	346	4.1	394	7.8	14.1	21.9	9.5
1977	8799	301	3.4	406	8.0	12.0	20.0	8.8
1978	9050	263	2.9	417	8.2	10.5	18.7	8.2
1979	9324	262	2.8	427	8.4	10.5	18.9	8.3
1980	9537	245	2.5	437	8.6	9.8	18.4	8.1
1981	9705	190	2.0	445	8.8	7.6	16.4	7.2
1982	9834	148	1.5	451	8.9	5.9	14.8	6.5
1983	9746	20	0.2	452	9.0	0.8	9.8	4.3
1984	9514	-160	-1.7	446	8.8	-6.4	2.2	1.0
1985	9228	-259	-2.8	436	8.6	-10.4	-1.8	-1.0
1986	8862	-326	-3.7	423	8.4	-13.0	-4.6	-2.0
1987	8639	-294	-3.4	411	8.1	-11.8	-3.7	-1.6
1988	8541	-161	-1.9	405	8.0	-6.4	1.6	0.7
1989	8545	2	0.0	405	8.0	0.1	8.1	3.2
1990	8674	65	0.8	408	8.1	2.6	10.7	4.7

*Reprinted by permission from *Science*, Vol. 172 (April 9, 1971), p. 134

On the other hand, enrollments in private nonsectarian institutions have increased considerably more rapidly than total enrollments, and enrollments in public institutions have grown three times as fast as over-all public college enrollments.

What kind of game, then, shall we play? Shall we assume that these contrasting tendencies will balance each other and that the total growth in religion enrollments (and thus faculty) will approximately parallel the total expansion in colleges generally, as seems to have been the case for the past decade as a whole? Or shall we assume, since the development of religion programs in the public sector has only begun (with 30 percent of the institutions presently having a program, and nearly half of those established between 1965 and 1970), and since the great bulk of the future expansion in college enrollment generally will come in the public sector, that religion enrollments may reasonably be expected to increase at a more rapid rate than college enrollments generally?

We may be able to assume relative stability in both total enrollments and religion enrollments and faculty in church-related institutions. They have reached the saturation point in the establishment of religion programs (93 percent of all church-related schools have programs), and it is possible that the effects of the reduction or elimination of religion course requirements have already been reflected in religion enrollments. Yet this is a major variable, since in absolute numbers the church-related institutions enroll by far most of the students in religion courses; any significant further decline in the proportions of students studying religion in these schools will greatly reduce the demand. (This will also heighten the flooding of the market by the large numbers of Catholics seeking to teach in non-Catholic institutions.)

Some modest further religion enrollment increase might be expected in private nonsectarian institutions, with the establishment of religion programs in some of the institutions not now having such organized studies (about half have programs), even though the total enrollments in private institutions may not increase significantly. And given a continued growth in public institutions, it is not unreasonable to suppose that religion enrollments will continue at least for a time to increase more rapidly than total enrollments, though certainly not as dramatically as in the period 1965–1970 (Chapter 9, Table 9–7).

And what if the other departments in the humanities that have abandoned their concern with the larger human questions, thus encouraging the trend to religious studies, were to reclaim their traditional vocation?

It would be foolhardy to predict a firm rate of increase for religion enrollments specifically. I strongly suspect that it will *not* be the same as college enrollments generally, but either lower or higher, depending on which of the opposing variables proves to dominate. But for the sake of illustrating the problem I shall play two games and make two projections, one assuming that religion enrollment and faculty increases do parallel the total college enrollment and faculty patterns as projected by Cartter, and the other making the egregious assumption that religion enrollments and faculties will increase at a rate of 50 percent greater than the over-all expansion.

b. Some other assumptions can be made with reasonable confidence. Theological school faculties will probably not increase in size and will perhaps decline. The most recent available figures from the American Association of Theological Schools show 2,374 full-time faculty members in 106 member schools and 72 associate member schools. Many of these are in small institutions that may well merge or close. We may therefore reasonably project a continuing need for replacement for theological school faculties, but not an expansion.

The proportion of faculty in religion and theology programs trained abroad will probably decrease somewhat, since most of those presently teaching with foreign degrees are in Roman Catholic institutions where the traditional patterns of supply are changing most rapidly. This, however, is a factor that we may reasonably ignore.

The question to what extent university graduate programs, master's or doctoral, will be used for professional preparation of clergy need not be taken into consideration. Should the movement develop extensively to use such programs for substantial portions of professional preparation, graduate enrollments will increase, though by corresponding reduction in theological school enrollments. This does not, however, bear on the need for doctorates for teaching in college, university, or seminary—and several denominations now report a surplus of clergy.

Any projections we make concerning the need for religion faculty also involve uncertainties respecting the number of persons teaching religion courses in institutions that have no organized program of religious studies and/or teaching in other departments. As to the former, no reliable information is available—and the two categories overlap considerably. But in relation to the problem of supply and demand, I believe it reasonable to assume that the number of religion doctoral recipients who enter teaching in other departments of colleges and universities will be balanced by the number of doctoral recipients from other fields who are employed in organized religion programs. In other words, transfers in and out will here be approximately equal (Table 9-16 in Chapter 9 shows that approximately 7 percent of the faculty in religion programs were trained in other departments).

c. How many faculty are there presently in religion programs? For the purpose of projections, I estimate a 1967–1970 total of 4,500. In the 768 institutions about whose programs we have information, there are 4,515 total faculty. Slightly over 22 percent are part-time, and if we count each of these 1,000 as half-time, the full-time equivalent is 4,000. For the additional 105 programs we may estimate a maximum of 500 faculty members, thus a total full-time equivalent of 4,500.

Approximately 60 percent of all present religion faculty hold an earned doctorate. The present quality would be maintained or improved if 60 percent of new faculty hold the doctorate, since many faculty receive the doctorate after beginning full-time teaching. This percentage can thus reasonably be used in estimating the number of new faculty needed with the doctorate. (Note that Cartter's projections assumed less than 50 percent of new faculty holding a doctorate—the present proportion of doctorate-holding faculty being estimated at 65 percent in universities, 44 percent in four-year colleges, and 15 percent in two-year colleges.)

d. We shall be on quite safe ground if we assume that the replacement rate in the field of religion is no more than 2 percent at least through the 1980's. Transfers to other employment from teaching need not be taken into account since the rate of transfer in is likely to be greater than that of transfer out. Most important here is the age distribution of present religion faculty, as shown in Table 6–2.

TABLE 6–2
AGE DISTRIBUTION OF FACULTY
IN UNDERGRADUATE RELIGION PROGRAMS
1969–1970

	Number of Faculty	%
30 and under	375	10.0
31 to 40	1,455	38.7
41 to 50	1,088	28.9
51 to 60	593	15.7
61 and over	251	6.7
	3,762	100.0

Based on reports from 633 institutions.

The critical element here is the relatively young age of religion faculty. Only 22.5 percent, as of 1969–1970, were over fifty years of age. Assuming an average retirement age of sixty-seven, not more than 1.3 percent will be lost through retirement per year for the next seventeen years. Losses from death will increase the rate, but by no more than 0.7 percent per year. Beginning in the late 1980's the replacement rate will begin to rise, to 3, 4, and perhaps 5 percent. But for the next decade and a half, we are fully justified in assuming a maximum replacement rate of 2 percent per year.

e. Finally, we need to estimate the "production" of doctorates in religion and theology. If the pattern of increase that characterized the decade 1960–1970 continues, we shall have production of the order indicated in Figure 6–1. I assume here that the number of Th.D.'s will not increase significantly and that the number of Ph.D.'s will continue to grow at approximately the same rate as in the past decade (this is a quite conservative estimate because the great increase in graduate study in religion has come since 1965), but tapering off to a peak in 1984—the year in which the number of faculty needed for expansion (either in religion or in college faculties generally) becomes a negative number.

FIGURE 6-1

EARNED DOCTORATES IN RELIGION AND THEOLOGY

Projected to 1990

Ph.D. and Th.D./S.T.D./D.H.L.

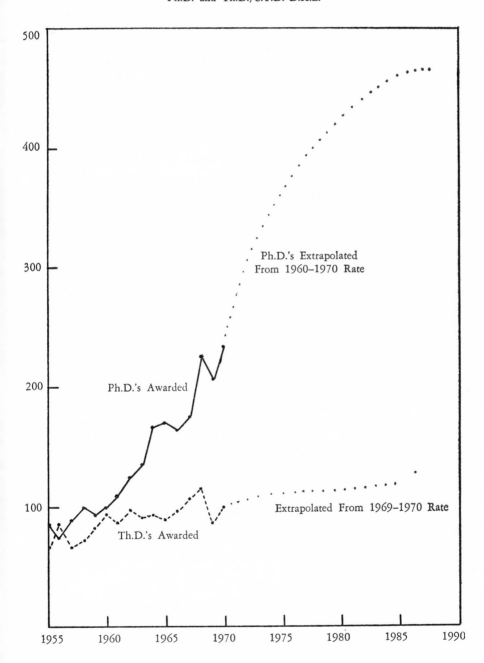

f. Putting all these uncertainties together, but excluding for the moment the replacement of faculty in theological schools, Tables 6–3a and 6–3b project the numbers of new religion faculty needed with the doctoral degree (paralleling Cartter's projection of all United States expansion in full-time faculty). Table 6–3a assumes the same rate of expansion in religion as in college enrollments generally. Table 6–3b assumes a 50 percent more rapid increase in religion than in college enrollments of faculty generally, at least through the peak enrollment year 1982.

The pattern is evident. Even on what I believe to be an egregiously optimistic assumption of further expansion in the field of religious studies, a continuation of the expansion in doctoral studies that has taken place in the 1960's, particularly in the latter half of the decade, will mean a rapidly growing surplus in the number of degree recipients available for teaching over the number of positions available.[2] Almost twice as many students are now receiving doctorates in religion as can be reasonably expected to find teaching positions in colleges and universities. (The actual experience of 1970 and 1971 suggests that the estimates of need in our tabulation for those years are actually inflated.) Even on the most optimistic assumptions that religion will claim a greater role in the undergraduate scene, the situation will become worse in the next decade. And what if religion should claim only a declining share of the market—that is, grow at a rate of only 75 percent of college expansion generally? Any way we look at it, given the present rate of expansion in graduate study, the ratio of supply to demand could grow within a dozen years to three to one, four to one, or even five to one.

---

[2] I have omitted from these tabulations the replacement needs for theological faculties, but even if one assumes that the total number of theological faculty members will not increase from the present 2,400, and that the replacement rate might be 3 percent and that two-thirds of all new faculty would hold the doctorate, this would account for only an additional 50 faculty members needed per year.

TABLE 6-3a

PROJECTED RELIGION FACULTY NEEDED, 1970-1990

ASSUMING SAME RATE OF EXPANSION AS FOR COLLEGE AND UNIVERSITY FACULTY GENERALLY

Year	All U.S. Full-Time Faculty (000's)	Religion Faculty (U.S. and Canada)				New Faculty Needed with Doctorates	Religion Doctorates Awarded*
		Full-Time Faculty	Faculty for Expansion	Faculty Replacements	Total New Faculty		
1969	292	4,500		90			300
1970	302	4,650	150	93	243	146	330
1	320	4,925	275	99	374	224	350
2	336	5,175	250	104	354	212	370
3	351	5,400	225	108	333	200	390
4	365	5,625	225	112	337	202	410
5	380	5,850	225	117	342	205	430
6	394	6,075	225	122	347	208	450
7	406	6,250	175	125	300	180	470
8	417	6,425	175	129	304	182	490
9	427	6,575	150	132	282	169	510
1980	437	6,700	125	134	259	156	530
1	445	6,825	125	136	261	157	540
2	451	6,925	100	138	238	143	550
3	452	6,975	50	140	190	114	555
4	446	6,875	-100	138	38	23	560
5	436	6,700	-175	134	-41	-25	560
6	423	6,500	-200	130	-170	-102	560
7	411	6,325	-175	126	-49	-30	560
8	405	6,250	-75	125	50	30	560
9	405	6,250	—	125	125	75	560
1990	408	6,300	50	126	176	106	560

*Projections of doctorates awarded includes only those from programs designed to prepare for teaching and research.

TABLE 6–3b

PROJECTED RELIGION FACULTY NEEDED, 1970–1990

ASSUMING 50 PERCENT GREATER EXPANSION THAN COLLEGES GENERALLY

Year	All U.S. Full-Time Faculty (000's)	Religion Faculty (U.S. and Canada) Full-Time Faculty	Faculty for Expansion	Faculty Replacements	Total New Faculty	New Faculty Needed with Doctorates	Religion Awarded* Doctorates
1969	292	4,500		90			300
1970	302	4,725		95	320	182	330
1	320	5,140	225	103	518	311	350
2	336	5,515	415	110	485	291	370
3	351	5,855	375	117	457	274	390
4	365	6,195	340	124	464	278	410
5	380	6,535	340	131	471	283	430
6	394	6,875	340	138	478	287	450
7	406	7,155	280	143	423	254	470
8	417	7,415	260	148	408	245	490
9	427	7,640	225	153	378	227	510
1980	437	7,830	190	157	347	208	530
1	445	8,020	190	160	350	210	540
2	451	8,170	150	163	313	188	550
3	452	8,245	75	165	240	144	555
4	446	8,095	-150	162	12	7	560
5	436	7,845	-250	157	-93	-56	560
6	423	7,545	-300	151	-149	-89	560
7	411	7,285	-260	146	-114	-68	560
8	405	7,135	-150	143	-7	-4	560
9	405	7,135	—	143	143	86	560
1990	408	7,210	75	144	219	131	560

*Projections of doctorates awarded includes only those from programs designed to prepare for teaching research.

2. How to Reduce and Grow at the Same Time

I do not expect that the situation projected for the latter half of the 1980's will actually come to pass. The crisis will not be as bad as 1984 suggests. Social policy is not likely to permit the extensive closing of colleges and the unemployment of college teachers that the projected decline in enrollments for the latter half of the 1980's would involve. Some way will be found to keep faculty employed and institutional facilities used. At the same time, the difficulty in finding teaching positions will diminish the attraction of doctoral studies. That effect is already evident. In other words, there will be constriction in teaching and research programs in graduate study in religion, whether we like it or no. The question is simply whether this reduction can be planned or guided in any intelligent manner or whether it will take place only as a result of the forces of the market place. What should such planning entail? Three points seem obvious.

a. There is still room and need for expansion of religious studies programs at the undergraduate level, especially in public institutions. Only 30 percent of the public four-year colleges had organized programs of religious studies in 1970, and there is evidence that the programs in the larger public institutions are understaffed relative to their enrollments (see Chapter 9, Sections 1 and 3). If the scholarly study of religion is an important feature of higher education, efforts ought still to be made to extend that study into institutions in which it is not now represented except in a peripheral and inadequate way, both in the expansion of existing programs and in the founding of new ones. Whether such new starts will occur is, of course, greatly dependent on the budgetary decisions of legislators and the judgments of university administrators concerning priorities.

The major expansion in public education, however, will not occur on the mother campuses of state institutions. Most of the growth for the future is projected for regional campuses and for community and junior colleges, where curricula are not likely to be elaborate and (except in the case of church-related junior colleges) where religion is not likely to be dealt with in any special program of study. Yet the present patterns of doctoral education in religion are not such as appropriately to prepare teachers for these institutions, where religion is studied not in advanced or specialized courses, or in an undergraduate major, but largely at the introductory level and as part of humanities and social sciences courses considered as general education. The two-year institutions have not unreasonably looked askance at Ph.D.'s applying for faculty positions. For such schools, programs at the master's level or Doctor of Arts study oriented toward teaching rather than research and specialization may be more adequate training grounds, and it may be desirable for large numbers of Ph.D. aspirants to be redirected into such programs.

b. Reduction at the doctoral level, I have said, will occur, though one cannot as yet see that there has been any concerted move to retrench. A partial review of admissions to religion doctoral programs for the fall of 1970 showed that some seventeen institutions had reduced the size of their entering classes by significant amounts, but that another thirteen institutions had increased. In these thirty institutions taken altogether, the net decrease in new doctoral enrollments from 1969 to 1970 was only 3 percent.

What are responsible directions for reduction? In view of our entire analysis, particularly in Chapter 5, the appropriate lines of action can be briefly stated. These relate both to total numbers of students and to the numbers of institutions engaged in doctoral instruction.

(1) A supply of Ph.D. and Th.D/S.T.D./D.H.L. recipients fully adequate for any presently identifiable needs would be assured if the doctoral religion student population were reduced by at least a third. This would provide for all foreseeable faculty needs and also produce highly trained scholars for numerous other vocational opportunities. If properly planned, such a reduction would also improve the quality of graduate study in religion immensely.

But any over-all reduction needs to be ordered with respect to particular areas of redundancy and of need.

The primary areas of redundancy, as judged by present concentrations of graduate study and by the major directions of development at the undergraduate level (see Chapter 9), are the traditional seminary triad: Bible, the history of Christianity, and theology, though the situation in theology is clouded because of the fluid nature of the field. This is not at all to question the continuing value of these areas. They will and should play a major role in religious studies. But readjustment is in order.

I have earlier raised the question whether there is justification for sixty separate doctoral programs in biblical studies. This must be emphasized in relation both to the quality of programs and to the sheer numbers of students. It is true that the proportion of biblical specialists in undergraduate faculties in religion (about 22 percent—see Chapter 9) and among theological school faculties is not much different from the proportions of present doctoral students in the area (about 22 percent) and the proportion of doctorates awarded in the past five years (23 percent) (see Chapters 11 and 13). But it is evident that the role of biblical studies is declining relatively at the undergraduate level, partly because of the abandonment of former requirements in church-related institutions and partly because of the broadening of the scope of religious studies and the adoption of new modes of introduction to religion. Even if one were to make the assumption of no decline in numbers of faculty needed, it would appear that *all* the persons now teaching Bible in college programs and in theological schools could be replaced by new doctoral recipients in the next fifteen to twenty years—not counting any contribution from other sources, such as from departments of Near Eastern languages or classics or from outside the Western Hemisphere.[3]

---

[3] I am estimating generously a maximum of some 2,000 biblical faculty (we know of 804 in the 633 undergraduate religion programs about which we have precise information, and there are another 600 to 700 at most in the theological schools). Given the present doctoral student population in religion, one may project the award of at least 100 doctorates a year in biblical studies.

In the history of Christianity and Christian thought there has already been a significant decline over the past twenty years (see Chapter 13, Table 13–1), but still some 18 percent of the present doctoral students are specializing in this broad area, whereas only 12 percent of the faculty in religion programs work in the area. (Some subfields, such as medieval studies and nineteenth-century religious thought, are nevertheless poorly represented.)

In Christian theological studies, the proportion of present doctoral students (12 percent) also approximates the proportion teaching in the area (13 percent), though an outward movement is indicated by the fact that considerably fewer persons are now teaching in this field than were trained in it (see Chapter 9, Table 9–16, and also Chapter 13 on the internal development of the field). One may also note that in Roman Catholic theological studies there is a particular imbalance because of the large numbers of Catholic scholars seeking employment in non-Catholic institutions.

What are the fields of doctoral study in which reduction in numbers is *less* desirable? In relation to the changing patterns of study and to the declared intentions of undergraduate departments for expansion and replacement, as well as to the subfields where the most interesting developments are occurring, the areas of need appear to include the following: the religious traditions of Asia, particularly of East and Southeast Asia; the religions of nonliterate peoples; Islam; Jewish studies undertaken in the context of the broader study of religion, rather than as primarily ethnically oriented programs; Afro-American religion; the study of religion and society, including especially sociology of religion and "religion and culture"; and the new religious or quasi-religious phenomena. To this list may perhaps be added ethics (particularly ethics and society) and contemporary religious thought, both of which reflect continuing growing interest in the broad theological area.

(2) Responsible directions of consolidation in respect of institutions have already been suggested in Chapter 5 and need not be repeated here in detail. Most of the larger doctoral programs should be reduced in size, some of them drastically, and in the number of subdisciplines covered. Such actions will greatly enhance the quality of graduate studies.

Of the present sixty-nine doctoral programs in the United States and Canada, between a quarter and a third could well be phased out and the able students encouraged to continue in the quality programs elsewhere. As noted in Chapter 5 (Section 4), some twenty-five of the present programs have to be judged as inadequate or marginal, and there are an additional four that are apparently (and wisely) withdrawing from doctoral studies. It would be a great disservice both to the field and to higher education generally if retrenchment in the strong centers were simply to result in expansion in the weak institutions.

c. What I have just said does not, however, exclude the desirability of the establishment of a strictly limited number of additional doctoral programs in institutions of high quality, particularly in the public sector, but only after the most careful consultation with other institutions and with responsible scholarly groups. In our examination of resources, the names of the University of Toronto and the University of California, Berkeley, have frequently cropped up as centers of distinctive major strength. Such institutions should be encouraged to develop modest and disciplined doctoral programs, building also on existing connections with the adjacent strong theological faculties and their programs. (The University of California, Berkeley, still lacks a significant base in undergraduate studies; Toronto is further advanced.)

Plans for new doctoral programs, either preliminary or relatively well developed, have in recent years been made at a number of other institutions.[4] With respect to all these and to possible projections elsewhere, it should be emphasized strongly that for the coming decades, institutional quality and responsibility will not be measured by the amount of expansion into doctoral studies, but by restraint and by creativity in the development of other modes for utilizing faculty competence and for meeting the legitimate need for stimulus sometimes provided by teaching advanced students. The day when the development of a doctoral program could be judged the natural and inevitable end result of a first-class department of religious studies has come to an end.

----

[4] For example, Ph.D. projections at Boston College (in conjunction with Andover Newton Theological School); Indiana University; Pennsylvania State University; Rutgers University; University of Virginia; Wesleyan University; and University of Windsor. In spite of the fact that each of these has claimed to be distinctive in resources and program, I see no good reason why any of them should be encouraged to proceed now. Indiana, Rutgers, and Wesleyan have already reconsidered.

PART III

CONTEXTS

7

Origins

By Harold Remus

The course of advanced education in religion in America may be divided into five main periods. Only in the last three, beginning in the last quarter of the nineteenth century, does there emerge graduate education as it is known today. But some of the foundations were laid much earlier, and their disclosure makes intelligible many of the distinctive configurations of graduate education in religion in the second half of the twentieth century.

1. THE COLONIAL PERIOD

Prior to the American Revolution advanced or specialized education in religion meant the training of the clergy and took place in several ways.

First, clergy were educated in Europe. The early Puritan divines in New England and the first Presbyterian ministers in the Middle Colonies came from the British Isles, but by the end of the colonial period both the Congregationalists and the Presbyterians were training most of their ministers in this country. Other groups, however—the Anglicans, the Lutherans, the German and Dutch Reformed, the Roman Catholics—still looked to Europe for their clergy.

Second, ministers were educated in colleges established, like Yale, "to propagate in this Wilderness, the blessed Reformed, Protestant Religion."[1] The founders of Yale and of other colonial colleges shared the Harvard founders' dread of "leaving an illiterate ministry." The Harvard fathers were determined that their sons in the ministry should not lapse into the ways of those who repudiated a learned ministry as inimical to religion. This conflict between "letters and spirit" has persisted throughout the course of advanced education in religion in America, paralleling and sometimes heightening an anti-intellectualist strain in American culture generally.

The prospective minister who was able to attend one of the available colleges did not begin concentrated study of theology until after completing the four years of undergraduate work, during which time he sat alongside future magistrates and merchants and acquired much the same classical learning (including

---

[1] The first Roman Catholic school in the United States was not inaugurated until after the Revolution (Georgetown Academy, 1789).

113

study of the Christian religion) as they. Thereupon he commenced reading in theology, with a faculty member, perhaps while serving as a tutor in the college, after three years of which he would present himself for ordination. Though doctorates in theology had been granted in Europe since the Middle Ages, graduate education in religion in America did not lead to such a degree. In 1692, Harvard had indeed conferred on Increase Mather the title of Doctor of Sacred Theology, the first doctorate awarded in America and regarded as earned rather than merely honorary, though Increase was president of the school at the time. (See the discussion in G. H. Williams, 1954, "An Excursus.") His son Cotton used it as an occasion to vindicate the act and to defend a learned ministry, arguing that as doctorates in theology had been granted in the Old World, so now also in the New.[2] But his statement that it was the "first and sole instance of such a thing done in the whole English America"[3] was prophetic of the course of events for two centuries.

A third, very common means for young men to acquire the specialized education in religion necessary for the ministry was to read under the tutelage of a clergyman, either after or in place of college.[4] The certification of men apprenticed in this way varied with the ecclesiastical body. Records from the day show that candidates might be required to pass tests in theology and in the learned languages, submit a thesis, and preach a sermon. The fear of an illiterate ministry is illustrated in the action taken by the first American presbytery requiring a layman who had been preaching—a common phenomenon—to desist and turn his energies to study under established ministers, a process that took him four years.[5]

2. PROFESSIONAL AND CONFESSIONAL EDUCATION, 1776-1876

Independence meant that for some churches, especially those that had supported the losing side in the Revolution, the supply of clergy receiving their professional training in Europe diminished or ceased, at least for a time. But the old ways of educating native clergy were also proving inadequate. The system whereby the prospective minister read theology under an established pastor and observed his practice had obvious difficulties. The pastor busy with

---

[2] At issue was whether Harvard had the right to confer degrees when it had not been granted express permission to do so. Increase Mather contended that Harvard stood "in prophetic—i.e., doctoral—succession by way of the Genevan Academy with the school of the prophets under Elijah, from whom the mantle of teaching authority passed from 'president' to 'president' " (Williams, p. 309). Increase was here drawing on the medieval and Reformation traditions which interpreted Jesus and the great personalities of the Old Testament—all the way back to Adam—as *doctores*, i.e., teachers and prophets, and Elijah's mantle as the Old Testament equivalent of the doctor's gown. See Williams, pp. 313–350.

[3] *Magnalia Christi Americana*, Book 4, Part 1, para. 9. The statutes of Harvard College which Cotton transcribes in para. 8 outline the requirements for earning the Doctor of Divinity degree.

[4] For a winsome description of this system in Connecticut, see Bainton, 1957, Chapter 5.

[5] In Armstrong *et al.*, 1956, pp. 18–19.

his own study, with sermon preparation, and with instruction had little time left for his apprentice. The pastor's library was also usually meager. The future minister doing his reading under a professor at a college was often little better off, since the professor's primary obligation was to undergraduate education. At the same time the second Great Awakening and the population moving westward created a demand for more ministers. "In theology, as in law and medicine, the time was ripe for formal graduate study to take the place of the system of apprentice training."[6]

In the colleges the graduate study of religion gradually came to be distinct, though not separate from the rest of the school. At Harvard, beginning in 1811, special courses were designed expressly for divinity students, and certain professors were designated to teach them (in addition to their undergraduate courses), until in 1819 the divinity school became a separate administrative unit. At Yale the divinity school came into being (1822) after fifteen ministerial students petitioned for recognition as a special group that would receive special instruction. A new professorship in theology was established, and several members of the college faculty were appointed to divinity instruction. Andover Seminary was established in 1808,[7] followed by Princeton (1811), Union in Virginia (1812), Bangor (1816), General (1817), Auburn (1818), Newton (1825), Lutheran in Gettysburg (1826), Hartford (1834), Union in New York (1836), and still others.

Roman Catholic development of higher education generally and of advanced education in religion specifically lagged behind Protestant efforts. In the colonial period strictures on religious freedom kept Catholics from founding their own schools. After American independence was won, Catholic efforts to educate native clergy paralleled Protestant efforts, with some distinctive differences.[8]

The Council of Trent had specified a seminary in every diocese or at least in contiguous dioceses. The first Catholic seminary in the United States was established in 1791, St. Mary's in Baltimore, conducted by one of the pioneer orders in seminary education, the French Sulpicians. Other dioceses were not so fortunate in securing the services of an order, and many diocesan seminaries had their start when the bishop began training candidates in his own residence.[9] By 1868, fifty Roman Catholic seminaries had been established, with an enrollment of 913 (Ellis, 1967, p. 85). With the Roman Catholic population at four

[6] Conrad Wright, in Williams, 1954, p. 22. A brief treatment of the rise of Protestant seminaries is given in Sweet, 1937.

[7] This is generally taken as the beginning of the Protestant seminary movement in the United States, though other seminaries, such as New Brunswick, trace their origins to an earlier date. See Sweet, 1937, pp. 263–264, and Brown, 1934, pp. 75–76.

[8] Ellis, 1967, pp. 1–172, offers a recent and concise history of Roman Catholic seminary education and cites many older works.

[9] For example, St. Charles Borremeo in Overbrook (Philadelphia) (*St. Charles Seminary*, 1943, p. 12); St. John's in Brighton (Boston) (Sexton and Riley, 1945, pp. 24 ff.).

and a half million, the church had to continue to depend on European clergy. In addition, some American youth were sent to Canada to study, or to the American Colleges established in Rome and Louvain in the 1850's. In the latter, the education was connected with the great university center there. In the United States, however, seminaries were generally isolated from other institutions of higher learning.

In the dominant Protestant culture as well the movement to establish seminaries was in part a movement away from the ethos of the colleges and the education they offered. The time after the Revolution was one both apathetic and hostile to religion. The assertion by a student at the College of New Jersey (Princeton) that only two members of the student body professed Christianity at this former hotbed of religious zeal is echoed in other contemporary accounts of college life. The proportion of graduating seniors who chose to study for the ministry declined steadily over the years. The old orthodoxies were subjected to attack with weapons from the arsenal of Thomas Paine and Ethan Allen, the English Deists, the French *philosophes,* and German critical philosophy. Since the colleges were not able to supply candidates for the ministry, other schools were established that would.

The seminary movement was also confessionally motivated. Seminaries proliferated in the nineteenth century partly out of rivalry, not only between denominations but within them as well, with the localism and sectionalism that spawned so many colleges sometimes serving a catalytic function here too. When a professed Unitarian was elected professor of theology at Harvard in 1805, a counterseminary was established at Andover three years later, with strict confessional standards laid on the faculty. Harvard's insistence that no doctrinal assent would be required of its faculty amounted to an act of Unitarian confessionalism. To the south, Hartford Seminary was founded as a counterpoise to Yale, and the Lutheran seminary in Philadelphia to the one in Gettysburg. At Princeton Seminary, Charles Hodge maintained that no one was a Christian in general, but was "either an Episcopalian or a Methodist, a Presbyterian or an Independent, an Arminian or a Calvinist" (cited in Hudson, 1965, p. 166). The price of staunch confessionalism, however, was repeated involvement of Princeton Seminary, and many others as well, in the incessant doctoral controversies of the nineteenth century, with consequent strain on academic energies and resources.

Alongside the seminaries existed colleges that prepared men for ministry in Protestant churches that disavowed separate, graduate education in religion for their clergy, and the Methodist church's system of training its ministers while serving churches. All these methods of education in religion went far to fulfill the primary purpose for which they had been established: the preparation of ministers and domestic and foreign missionaries. The apprentice system would not have been able to supply the quantity needed or equal the quality of instruction in the seminaries and church colleges, uneven as this was. And it left much to be desired. The times were not propitious for quality in education, of whatever sort. The settlers struggling for survival on the frontiers generally had neither the financial resources (including tax money) nor the education of the Massachusetts Bay Puritans who planted Harvard in the wilderness. The dispute over slavery and the civil warfare at mid-century took priority over the task of education. Moreover, the war split many of the churches, which were the founders and sustainers of seminaries and private colleges.

Whatever the reasons, in retrospect one can see that the institutions committed to advanced or graduate education in religion lacked the elements that have come to be regarded as requisite to graduate study.

First, there was the relatively large number of these institutions, with consequent small size and inadequate resources. Between 1820 and 1831 eleven Protestant seminaries were established, between 1839 and 1869 thirty-seven more, and between 1869 and 1914 another thirty-six (Brown, 1934, pp. 79–82). As late as 1914, Anson Phelps Stokes noted that only a fourth of the Protestant seminaries of that day were able to meet the test of sufficient library resources (10,000 volumes), physical plant ($100,000 valuation), and endowment ($250,000 minimum) (Stokes, 1914, p. 5). Several had but one professor, and some reported total annual incomes as low as $550.[10] The many published histories of the seminaries are an almost unrelieved account of mere struggle for survival. Hopes of the founders were high, but all too often the cost of quality education went even higher.[11] For Roman Catholic institutions financial support from abroad often preceded or supplemented local resources, but the fact that in 1900 there were 109 seminaries enrolling fewer than 5,000 secular and regular clergy candidates indicates a situation parallel to that in Protestantism (Ellis, 1967, pp. 86, 89 ff.).

Second, the majority of seminaries were situated apart from centers of learning, often in out-of-the-way places largely cut off from the intellectual currents of the day. Stokes counted at most 40 Protestant seminaries, out of 182, with such academic connections, formal or informal. In 1924, when the continent was far more urban than in the nineteenth century, 42 percent of the Protestant seminaries and theological colleges in the United States and Canada were located in towns of less than 20,000 population, though seminaries in the cities were apt to draw more students (see Kelly, 1924, pp. 26 f., 155). In American Roman Catholicism there was only one significant effort in the nineteenth century to integrate the training of priests with a university, albeit a feeble one, and it came to an abrupt end.[12] Most of the Catholic seminaries were situated in small towns or rural settings.

[10] Figures for 1920–1921 are found in the first comprehensive study of American seminaries, the Kelly report of 1924. According to that report, 42 percent of the 123 (out of 131) United States Protestant seminaries reporting on faculty had less than five full-time professors on their staff.
[11] The second president of a church college founded at the end of the nineteenth century outlined detailed plans for awarding the B.D., Ph.D., and S.T.D. But financial worries, inadequate library, and lack of accreditation marked the school's history, and the doctor's degrees were, fortunately, never awarded.
[12] The University of St. Mary of the Lake, Chicago. See Ellis, 1967, pp. 161–162.

Third, the professors called to labor in such circumstances were overworked and underpaid. Some were men of considerable powers and with academic background comparable to that of the best college professors of the day. Alongside their teaching they were able to produce respectable works of scholarship. Others brought to the task only the education acquired in colleges or seminaries as ill equipped and poorly staffed as those in which they themselves taught.

Fourth, many of the students, even at the old, established schools, came without college degrees,[13] and time that might have been devoted to graduate education in religion had to be given over to collegiate instruction.

It is not until the next period that graduate education of high quality would develop, in religion as well as in other fields.

3. THE BEGINNINGS OF DOCTORAL STUDY AND DOCTORAL PROGRAMS, 1876-1918

In 1861 the first Ph.D. awarded in the United States was granted by Yale College.[14] By 1871 twenty had been awarded, and in the next fifteen years three times this number were conferred. Other schools followed suit, so that by 1900 the university as a center of research offering graduate education in a multiplicity of fields had assumed the lead in higher education, displacing the college of 25 years previous with its traditional classical curriculum and unearned master's degrees. It is in this period concluding with the end of World War I that the first doctoral degrees in the area of religion were awarded and the first doctoral programs specifically in the field of religion were established.

Divinity schools connected with universities were at first content to have their students or graduates pursue doctoral studies in various departments of the university graduate school such as philology or philosophy. Their dissertations covered subjects like many of those treated in doctoral programs in religion today; upon receipt of the Ph.D. they often went on to teach religion in colleges or seminaries. Thus of 419 Ph.D.'s awarded at Harvard from 1896 to 1908, 36 were in the areas of Semitic philology, biblical and patristic Greek, philosophy of religion, metaphysics, ethics, and theology, with thesis titles such as "The Forty-second and Forty-third Psalms," "The Yezidis, or Devil Worshippers: Their Sacred Book and Traditions," and "The Ground of Moral Obligation."[15] So also at Yale, where thesis titles included "The Text of the First Book of Kings," "The Priesthood in Israel," and (by a women student)

---

[13] See Kelly, 1924, pp. 175–176; and May, 1934, III, 67–70, who indicates that the situation in law and medical schools was comparable. At Harvard Divinity School in the years 1868–1871, the percentage of students entering with the B.A. ranged from 14 to 26; the medical and law schools were also in a state of neglect (Sidney Ahlstrom, in Williams, 1954, p. 92 and note 38). After Catholic University opened at the end of the century, the rector found it necessary to deal with the problem of seminary graduates who had to do remedial work before proceeding to the S.T.B. curriculum (Ellis, 1967, p. 102).

[14] Chittendon, 1928, I, 88–89, 127.

[15] *Annual Reports of the President and Treasurer of Harvard College*, 1893–94 (pp. 103-105), 1907-08 (pp. 132 f., 139-141).

"The Dependence of the Concept of Duty on Faith in God" (*Yale Pot-Pourri*, 1898, p. 116).

The last decades of the nineteenth century were a critical period for American religion because of the impact of Darwinian thought, the historical study of the Bible, comparative study of religions, and other new knowledge. It was divinity schools like those we have been considering, located in centers of learning, which gave a hearing to new thought and were ready to try the new methods in research that had drawn American students in all fields to German universities and had revolutionized the study of religion and theology there. German theology and methods were introduced in Harvard Divinity School in the early decades of the nineteenth century, and with the revitalization of the school under President Eliot after 1880 the faculty, most of whom had studied in Germany, were committed to historical scholarship. At Yale, too, philological and historical criticism won an early foothold and gradually gained ascendancy. When William Rainey Harper, who received his Ph.D. from Yale in 1875, was called to the presidency of the new University of Chicago, he worried that he might not be permitted to teach the Bible as he had been accustomed to at Yale—a fear that proved groundless. He and the faculty he assembled were committed to the new methods and ideals of research, and the university's benefactor was determined to keep it free from denominational restrictions on learning (although the Divinity School was viewed by Rockefeller as a Baptist institution and subject to denominational regulation).[16]

The new academic disciplines emerging at the end of the nineteenth century also affected the way religion was studied in these centers of learning. Comparative religions was honored with departmental status at the new University of Chicago, and at Harvard under George Foot Moore it developed from a subsection of systematic theology into an independent discipline.[17] The social and psychological approaches to religion are reflected in thesis titles like "Japanese Phallicism" (Chicago, 1894) or "Semitic Phallicism" (Harvard, 1908), "Historical Illustrations of the Psychology of Religious Belief" (Harvard, 1905), and "A Consideration of Prayer from the Standpoint of Social Psychology" (Chicago, 1908). Religion scholarship itself occasionally led to new disciplines in the university, as when Francis Peabody's courses in social ethics in Harvard Divinity School resulted in establishment of the university's Department of

---

[16] A Chicago student's account of Harper's teaching, insisting on independent examination of the sources and use of scholarly literature in several languages, is given in Storr, 1966, pp. 161–62. See also pp. 197 f. The number of American Ph.D.'s on the original faculty outnumbered those from German schools (*ibid.*, p. 76). Among those teaching religion were holders of the Ph.D. from Yale and Leipzig (*Quarterly Calendar of the University of Chicago*, Vol. I, No. 1 [June, 1892], pp. 4 ff.).

[17] William Fenn, in Morison, 1930, p. 470. John H. Barrows at the University of Chicago reported in 1894 that "in six of the leading American institutions, comparative religion has found a place" and predicted that "one of the inevitable effects . . . will be the rewriting of Christian theology . . . under the guiding principle of evolution, and in the light of these comparative studies" (*Quarterly Calendar*, Vol. III, No. 3, [November, 1894], pp. 5-6).

Social Ethics in 1906.[18] The bulk of graduate study in religion, then as now, however, was in the areas of Bible, history of Christianity, and theology.

The period of early graduate education was a time of movement on the part of at least some seminaries back to closer association with the university. Andover rejoined Harvard Divinity School, Union relocated near Columbia, the Baptist seminary in Chicago was included in the new university, and Yale Divinity School was reorganized for a time (1914–1920) as the Yale School of Religion. One of the chief architects of the reorganization proclaimed that "the century of partial distrust which led to the segregation of ministerial training from the thought-world of the university has come to a close" (Bacon, 1914, p. 50). As early as 1913 Garrett announced that by arrangement with Northwestern its students could pursue a Ph.D. program at the latter.[19] At Yale the School of Religion was to train not only ministers but other workers in religion, including college teachers, and it was to employ university methods and disciplines in doing so. The aim of offering education in religion other than or beyond the professional kind received fuller recognition when in 1920 a Department of Religion was established in the Graduate School to offer the Ph.D. in philosophy of religion (with the Philosophy Department) and, as an exclusive charge, in "Historical and Contemporary Religion," with specializations in "Comparative Religion, Christian Origins, Biblical Theology, History of Doctrine, Contemporary Theology and Theological Ethics, and the Psychology and Philosophy of Religion."[20] The program was jointly administered and taught by Divinity School and Graduate School faculty. In addition divinity students could continue, as in the past, to pursue a Ph.D. program in the Graduate School in departments such as Philosophy or Semitic and Biblical Languages. A pattern of joint Divinity School and Graduate School administration of doctoral programs of religion is still common today and persisted at Yale until 1963 (see Chapter 3, above).

At Harvard the "pact" with the Graduate School whereby divinity students could work toward the Ph.D. was felt, in the words of the Divinity School dean, to be an "anomaly by which students registered in one department of the university become candidates for degrees administered by another." In 1914 the university authorized the Divinity School to grant the Th.D., and in the next two years five were awarded. Predicting that the new program would reduce the number of divinity students in Ph.D. programs, the dean acknowledged that in "exceptional cases" some students "may properly prefer to stand for the more widely recognized degrees of A.M. and Ph.D. . . ."[21] Twenty years later, however,

[18] James Ford, in Morison, 1930, p. 223. The department title was suggested by William James.

[19] *Garrett Biblical Institute Bulletin*, Vol. I, No. 2 (March, 1913), p. 22.

[20] Macintosh, 1922, p. 128; see further *Yale Divinity Quarterly*, XVI (1919–1920), 133. To avoid confusion with the new Department of Religion, the School of Religion resumed its former name.

[21] Report of Dean Fenn, in *Annual Reports of the President and Treasurer of Harvard College 1913–14*, p. 120.

a desire for a Ph.D. in religion by persons who wished to teach religion courses in colleges and universities led to establishment of such a degree in the history and philosophy of religion in the Graduate School, and in 1941 new arrangements were worked out between the Graduate and the Divinity schools to enable students in the latter to work toward the Ph.D.

In addition to the Th.D. at Harvard, ecclesiastical doctoral programs were instituted under church auspices at several other institutions in this period.

Southern Baptist Theological Seminary in Louisville had been in existence thirty-three years when its Th.D. program was inaugurated in 1892. The first four doctorates were awarded two years later, and five in the next year.[22] The faculty numbered six at the time, and the historian of the school, wondering at their "daring and audacity" in establishing in the school thirteen departments of specialized studies in addition to the regular theological curriculum, observed, "This large program of studies was no doubt far too extensive for their number or the resources of the Seminary" (Mueller, 1959, pp. 117-118). Resources were further strained by controversy over the doctrinal stands of two of the professors accused of questioning traditional views, resulting in the resignation of both professors.

The Th.D. program at Union Seminary in New York was established about the same time as the one at Harvard, but the first degree was not granted until 1924 and then not again until 1930.[23] The usual factors enumerated as essential to quality graduate education were present at Union: adequate financial resources, good library, eminent faculty, and location in or near a top-rank university or center of learning. By this time Union had established its freedom from denominational control and had weathered the severe controversies in the Presbyterian church over the relation between traditional doctrinal formulations and new knowledge and methods, so that its long tradition of a learned ministry and faculty was able to assert itself in full strength.

A strong desire to elevate the quality of Roman Catholic higher education in the United States and to increase the church's leadership in the intellectual life of the country led, after years of travail, to the opening of Catholic University of America in 1889 as an exclusively graduate school of theology with the right to confer the doctoral degree (see Ellis, 1946, and 1956, pp. 430–433). Six of the original faculty of ten were European-born and -trained; three of the Americans were converts (Herbermann, 1889). Not until 1895 were the first S.T.D.'s awarded, and on the eve of World War I only nine had been conferred.[24] Some of the forty Ph.D.'s granted by other faculties in this period were in the field of

---

[22] Between 1894 and 1918 four doctorates a year were awarded on the average. (Based on Crismon, 1962.)

[23] *Union Theological Seminary Bulletin* (July, 1924), p. 33, and 1925-1930.

[24] *Catholic University of America Year Book 1914-15*, p. 47 (reporting on degrees from 1889 to 1913).

Bible and religion,[25] however, so that the situation was similar to that at Harvard when the Th.D. was established alongside the Ph.D. In the years since, many students at Catholic University have pursued Ph.D. study in the area of religion in various departments of the Graduate School.[26] The present Department of Religion and Religious Education in the Graduate School dates its origins to the 1930s, the Ph.D. program having been established in 1940.

Like many Protestant theological schools, Catholic University felt the effects of tensions in the church. John J. Keane, the first rector, was persuaded not to hire an eminent biologist suspected of harboring erroneous views on the relation between religion and evolution, and seven years later Keane himself was peremptorily dismissed as rector by Leo XIII.[27] At the height of the Modernist controversy the Old Testament scholar Henry Poels, who like Crawford Toy at Louisville thirty years earlier could not bring himself to accept traditional views of the Pentateuch, was dismissed. In their debate about Roman Catholic intellectual life in America, Roman Catholic scholars have in recent years assessed the baleful effects of these and similar actions on the quality of graduate education in their schools.[28]

By 1880 the tiny Jewish population of the American colonies—about 1,200 Jews and five religious communities at the end of the colonial period—had swelled to a quarter of a million with 270 synagogues, and twenty years later to a million with 1,000 synagogues.[29] Until well into the nineteenth century synagogal and communal affairs were handled by the laity, who might engage a cantor to read, preach, and teach. Intricate questions of the law were referred to the learned rabbis of London or Amsterdam. When synagogues became more numerous and some were able to provide for a rabbi, they sent to Europe. When the stream of immigration became a flood, however, the Jewish communities, like other American denominations, had to give attention to the necessity of training a native clergy. The first permanent rabbinic school, Hebrew Union College, was established in 1875 and graduated its first rabbis in 1883. Three years later Jewish Theological Seminary was founded by representatives of Historical (Conservative) Judaism. The strong impetus given to Orthodoxy

[25] Thesis titles included "St. Francis as a Social Reformer" (1904), "The Meaning and Purpose of the Ten Extraordinary Points in the Pentateuch" (1904), and "The Problem of Evil" (1911) (*ibid.*, 1905–06, 1912–13).

[26] See the volumes (originally Ph.D. theses) in the various series published by the university: "Studies in American Church History," "Patristic Studies," "Studies in Medieval History," *et al.*

[27] See most recently the discussion by John T. Ellis, in McCluskey, 1970, pp. 213-215, 229–230, 243–244.

[28] A convenient anthology of the debate is Christ and Sherry, 1961, which includes excerpts from one of the key essays, Ellis, 1955. A post-Vatican II discussion, with application to the Catholic university, is the symposium edited by Neil G. McCluskey, 1970. Valuable historical background and application to theological education are contained in Ellis, 1967.

[29] Gaustad, 1962, pp. 144–145. The statistics are given variously by different authorities A concise account of Jewish religious life and institutions in the United States is Davis, 1960.

by immigrants from Eastern Europe resulted in the establishment in 1897 of the school for the study of Torah and the training of rabbis that eventually developed into Yeshiva University (Klaperman, 1969, pp. 48 ff.).

The Jewish scholarship that developed in the United States in the second half of the nineteenth century was pursued by rabbis of European origin and training.[30] With the establishment of the seminaries and of Semitics chairs in universities, a tradition of native American scholarship began to develop, but, like religion scholarship generally, always in contact with Europe. Solomon Schechter, brought from Europe as president of the reorganized Jewish Theological Seminary in 1902, enlarged the existing faculty with other eminent European scholars and in 1905 instituted a D.H.L. program, with the first two degrees awarded in 1907 and seven more by the end of World War I.[31] Dropsie College was chartered in 1907 as a graduate, research institution with the authority to confer the Ph.D. in Hebrew and cognate literature and in rabbinic learning. The first Ph.D. was granted in 1912, and the recipient, Bernard Revel, became the president and shaping force of the Orthodox school (Yeshiva) in New York. Proof that Jewish scholarship was taking root in this country was the succession of professors by their pupils and the publication of scholarly works such as *The Jewish Encyclopedia.*

Semitics chairs or departments were established in a number of America's foremost universities in the late nineteenth century: Columbia, Johns Hopkins, Harvard, Pennsylvania, Chicago. The incumbents of these chairs were sometimes Christian scholars (for example, Crawford Toy and David Lyon at Harvard), but many were Jewish: Richard Gottheil at Columbia, Cyrus Adler at Johns Hopkins (the first to receive the Ph.D. in Semitics there), Morris Jastrow at Pennsylvania, and Emil G. Hirsch at Chicago. As Arnold Band observes (1966, p. 6), "Personal commitment to some aspect of contemporary Jewish life is not a requisite for teaching Judaic studies, but since extensive familiarity with difficult sources is crucial for professional competence, it is only natural that the qualified candidates for posts would be men who had studied these sources before their graduate training, and these are likely to be Jews." And although, as Band notes, these scholars "are often considered semitists, . . . they all did some work in rabbinic literature."[32] Others worked in biblical studies (Elbogen, 1943–1944, p. 52). The titles of graduate courses in these Semitics programs sound much like those in doctoral programs in religion today,[33] the methods were those of modern scholarship, with stress on historical understanding, and the Ph.D.'s thus trained often went on to teach religion courses in colleges or to appointments in seminaries. An important event for the development of Judaic

[30] A survey of American Jewish scholarship up to 1943 is Elbogen, 1943–1944.
[31] Adler, 1939, pp. 10–11; Israel Davidson, in Adler, p. 80; Jewish Theological Seminary of America, *Register*, 1966-69, p. 57.
[32] Band, 1966, p. 6. For appointments in rabbinics see Elbogen, 1943–1944, p. 52.
[33] See, for example, David G. Lyon, in Morison, 1930, pp. 232-233.

studies in their own right was the appointment at Harvard in 1915 of Harry A. Wolfson as instructor in the Semitics department and then, in 1926, as the first Nathan Littauer Professor of Jewish Literature and Philosophy.

4. BETWEEN THE WARS

To some who lived through the period after World War I it seemed a return of the skepticism and disdain for religion that marked the years after the American Revolution. A later observer has termed it "the American religious depression" (Handy, 1968). For those engaged in education and concerned about religion, the great fact confronting them seemed to be the separation of the two. The period is marked, therefore, by a number of attempts to overcome the separation, on both the graduate and the undergraduate levels. Serious efforts were also made to build on the foundations for graduate education in religion laid prior to the war. A sense that the war had attenuated the cord attaching American religion scholarship to Europe, especially Germany, strengthened the conviction that native scholarship should and could be more productive in its own right. At the same time, the winds of neo-orthodoxy that began to blow from the Continent in the twenties proved to be a revivifying force in Protestantism.

Of the various attempts to establish the teaching of religion at state universities the most successful, and the only one to develop a doctoral program in this period, was the School of Religion founded in the twenties at the University of Iowa.[34] An important factor in its success was a sympathetic administration and faculty. The faculty of the school were hired with a view both to academic competence and to confession—Protestant, Catholic, Jew—and were paid by the denominational constituencies. After foundation grants expired, the university assumed the school's administrative cost, and over the years it has increasingly contributed to the payment of faculty salaries. After a decade of operation undergraduate enrollment was over 600, and at the end of another ten years it had risen to over 2,000. Graduate work was also pursued, and in the school's first twenty-five years thirteen Ph.D.'s were awarded.[35]

Whereas the School of Religion was organized on the principles of cooperation of university and religious communities (with equal representation for the three major faiths) and was active in campus religious life, the plan drawn up at Princeton University in 1935 called for a program administered and funded exclusively by the university and clearly distinct from campus religious activities.[36] It was the mixture of the study and the practice of religion "which bred a suspicion that has in the end driven the study [of religion] from an independent place in the curriculum. . . ."[37] The religion professor was to be a person

[34] See Bach, 1952; Lampe, 1963.
[35] On the movement to establish schools of religion on or near state campuses see Bach, 1952, and the early statements by Foster, 1921, 1922.
[36] See the summary in Michaelsen, 1965, pp. 137 ff.
[37] *Report of the Special Committee of the Faculty on Religious Education*, 1935; quoted in Michaelsen, 1965, p. 137.

trained specifically in the field and was to employ the historical method, while not neglecting discussion of the issues. The first incumbent was appointed in 1940, and, with flourishing enrollments, a department was established in 1946, and finally in 1955 a Ph.D. program, preparation for which was said to be the equivalent of "that required for the Bachelor's Degree in the Department of Religion at Princeton."[38]

With the establishment of Ph.D. programs in religion at state and private universities, accepting an undergraduate major in religion as optional preparation in place of a seminary degree, a new pattern in graduate education in religion was established. Meanwhile, older patterns persisted and developed further. The Yale Ph.D. program established just after World War I has already been noted. In 1923 the Columbia-Union Ph.D. program was announced,[39] and prior to American entry into World War II the Harvard, Duke, and Catholic University Ph.D. programs. In addition at least eight Th.D. or S.T.D. programs were inaugurated in the United States before the war came to an end (see Chapter 12, Table 12–1). Degree production at fourteen schools offering the Th.D., S.T.D., and Ph.D. averaged almost fifty a year in the decade 1927–1936.[40] The time was ripe for evaluation and standarization. The Protestant seminaries, from which came the great majority of doctoral candidates, had in the twenties not yet worked out an accreditation system for their schools. The nomenclature for the first theological degree was confused and designated diverse curricula and widely varying entrance and graduation requirements. Little concerted thought had been given to questions of faculty, financial, and library resources. There were complaints about the quality of graduate students. The dean of Harvard Divinity School noted in 1924 that those enrolled with the intent of becoming college and seminary teachers were "serious and competent" and pursued clearly defined courses of study. "It is a matter of common knowledge, however, that the graduate classes in all theological seminaries tend to be peopled by another class of men, mainly ministers, who are devoting to casual and inconsequential study time which would be much better spent in the discharge of professional duties, or who are seeking in these schools possible doorways out of their present profession."[41]

The needed evaluation came from the Conference of Theological Seminaries which had been formed in 1918 and in the mid-twenties inaugurated a major self-study that included doctoral programs (Ph.D. as well as Th.D.) in its

[38] Quoted in Ramsey, 1962, p. 297, who gives a description of the graduate program. See also the descriptions and discussions of other graduate programs in MacGregor, 1962; Michaelsen, 1962; Beach, 1963; and Martin, 1963.

[39] *Union Theological Seminary Bulletin* (May, 1923), p. 13.

[40] American Association of Theological Schools, *Bulletin*, XII (1938), 30–31. These were schools accredited by the Conference of Theological Seminaries of the United States and Canada or its successor the AATS.

[41] Willard L. Sperry, in *Annual Reports of the President and Treasurer of Harvard College 1923-24*, pp. 174–175.

purview.[42] Many of the issues raised by the study and in the ensuing discussion have a familiar ring. F. C. Grant observed that seminaries were divided on the content of the B.D. curriculum. In "the old-fashioned Divinity School . . . 'The Christian Tradition' provided the subject matter. . . ." In "the modern university 'School of Religion' [as some theological schools were then called] . . . the curriculum is designed, apparently, to provide the approach to a 'scientific' study of religion in general, its history, psychology, philosophy, its literature, its organization and practices" (AATS, *Bulletin*, IX [1934], 43). Most seminaries fell somewhere in between. The study found that several seminaries not connected with universities were offering the Ph.D., but even in those that had such connections, said William Adams Brown, "it cannot be said that all of them are using their opportunity to the full. Too many still regard their graduate work as an addendum to an already fully developed curriculum and leave the individual professor to discharge his part of the responsibility of developing it as he will" (Brown, 1934, p. 210). Moreover, too few doctoral programs "have a definite policy designed to attract a particular group of students and to present them with a particular kind of help. At no point is an understanding between seminaries more needed so that needless competition may be avoided and the field chosen or assigned be cultivated to the full" (*ibid.*). Brown also lamented "meticulous research in some field of little general interest or importance" and "the highly specialized departmental system which separates things that belong together and tends to produce men who know much in a narrow field rather than men who see things in the large and in the whole" (*ibid.*). Reporting on libraries, Raymond P. Morris noted some good ones, but reported that one theological school had eighty-nine students studying for the Ph.D. in theology, sociology, history, and education with only $1,500 available annually for book and periodical facilities (in May, 1934, III, 181).

From the study emerged a statement on degree nomenclature and standards which was adopted by the Conference in 1932.[43] The Th.D. was to be the degree awarded at seminaries not associated with a university, and the level of achievement represented was to be "equivalent to that which is required in earning a Ph.D. degree in a standard university. . . ." Such seminaries were discouraged from granting the Ph.D. At seminaries that cooperated with universities in Ph.D. programs, the degree was to be conferred by the university. In its list of accredited schools the Conference (later reconstituted as the American Association of Theological Schools) annually or biannually noted the schools with doctoral programs or resources that did not conform in some way with the standards. The recommendations had some effect,[44] but in 1942 a much

---

[42] The results were published in four volumes: Brown, 1934; Mark A. May, 1934 (2 vols.); May and Shuttleworth (1934).

[43] See AATS, *Bulletin*, VIII (1932), 15, and subsequent issues.

[44] Southern Baptist Theological Seminary, for instance, which had established a Ph.D. program in 1928 to supply Southern Baptist colleges and universities with religion teachers, reinstituted its Th.D. program ten years later (Mueller, 1959, p. 215).

longer statement of standards for ecclesiastical doctor's degrees was adopted by the AATS (*Bulletin*, XV, 65-67), spelling out guidelines for admissions and examinations, for purpose, nature, and length of doctoral programs, and for library resources and quality of faculty.

The issues raised by the study's report on faculty research also have a familiar sound (see Brown, 1934, pp. 214-216). Larger institutions and those connected with universities had productive faculties. At least three schools—Chicago, Union in New York, and Yale—reported full-time research professors. Despite the existence by this time of a number of learned societies and professional organizations in the field of religion, Professor Brown saw a pressing need for more coordination of research and for "some central body which can serve as a clearing house of opinion, and which, when agreement has been reached, can secure the cooperation of the scholars whose assistance is essential." Only partially, at best, had there been realized at the end of the period the hope voiced by A. C. McGiffert at Union at the beginning: "Our opportunity is unmatched. Unhampered by a State church, with complete freedom from political control in religious affairs, acquainted by long study with all that other countries have done, we are better fitted than England or France, or even Germany herself, to do important theological work if we will but give ourselves to it."[45]

5. POST-WORLD WAR II

The period following World War II was the time of greatest numerical growth in graduate education in religion, as the present study has abundantly documented. The growth was related, quite naturally, to expansion and change in the study of religion at the undergraduate level. Since these developments and the present nature of graduate study in religion are treated extensively elsewhere in this volume, only brief comments are needed here.

The increase in undergraduate departments of religion in colleges and universities and of Ph.D. programs to train scholars to teach in such programs went far to overcome the separation between religion and higher education that troubled many in the twenties and thirties. Efforts to establish the teaching of religion at state universities proceeded steadily, amid much discussion and influenced by court decisions.[46] Once they were on the campus, religion teachers became acutely self-conscious about their presence there, and much effort was expended to justify it and the study of religion as an academic discipline.[47] A forum for this discussion was provided by the National Association of Biblical Instructors, whose change in name in 1962 to the American Academy of Religion was symptomatic. The Council on Graduate Studies in Religion, organized in 1947 with a membership composed of schools granting a Ph.D. in religion,

---

[45] Inaugural address as president, *Union Theological Seminary Bulletin* (July, 1918), p. 34.

[46] See *Religion in the Public Schools*, 1964; Michaelsen, 1964, 1965, 1970; McLean, 1967; Spivey, 1968.

[47] Samples of the discussion are Michaelsen, 1964 (New Haven); Hartzell and Sasscer, 1967; and McLean, 1967. An extended treatment is given in Holbrook, 1963.

met annually to discuss common problems and to issue occasional recommendations regarding standards.

A major change in the constitution and workings of the Society of Biblical Literature in 1969 has moved it toward the type of coordinating agency for scholarly research, in the area of Bible and cognate areas, that William Adams Brown hoped for in the 1930's. Another significant development has been the closer relations between the various professional and learned societies in the field of religion in the 1960's, with Roman Catholic organizations especially collaborating in the post-Vatican II period. The Council on the Study of Religion organized in 1969, comprising in its membership seven societies, seeks to serve as the kind of central clearing house that Brown envisaged (see Welch, 1970).

In this period the quality of Catholic biblical scholarship came to be acknowledged by even the most Protestant scholars. Vatican II has produced a considerable change in the way religion and theology are studied in the Roman Catholic doctoral programs, with names like Rahner, Lonergan, and Teilhard de Chardin figuring as prominently as Aquinas.

Protestant scholarship profited in the thirties and forties from the forced emigration of a number of continental scholars and in the forties and fifties was an importer of European scholarship and scholars and an exporter of graduate students to Germany and Switzerland especially. The balance of trade began to right itself in the sixties, with works by American scholars, even younger ones, being deemed worthy of German translation. Laments about the dearth of first-rate scholarship in some areas continued to be voiced, however (e.g., Ramsey, 1961, 1964).

The destruction of the traditional centers of learning in Europe before and during World War II made it necessary for the Jewish community in America to put forth greater and special efforts to train its own scholars. At Jewish Theological Seminary the number of D.H.L. degrees granted rose from eleven in the 1930's to fourteen in the 1940's, and then to forty-eight in the 1950's. A Ph.D. degree was also instituted in the 1960's.[48] Dropsie College (now University), which had granted twenty-three Ph.D's in the 1930's and twenty-four in the 1940's, conferred fifty-one in the 1950's.[49] The Orthodox seminary in New York which in the 1920's had become a college and then finally Yeshiva University inaugurated a D.H.L. program, which in 1970 was discontinued in favor of the Ph.D. Hebrew Union College instituted a Ph.D. program in the late 1940's. In addition, university Ph.D. programs in Judaic studies increased.[50] In 1966 Arnold Band reported such programs in at least twenty-two universities. Over 80 percent of the professors in Band's study had received their graduate training in the United States. Many of these scholars, he notes, were teaching in

[48] Jewish Theological Seminary of America, *Register*, 1966–69, pp. 57–58.
[49] Dropsie University, *Bulletin*, 1970-72, pp. 66–78.
[50] "Judaic studies" is used in the broad sense employed by Band, 1966, p. 5: "the discipline which deals with the historical experiences, in the intellectual, religious, and social spheres, of the Jewish people in all centuries and countries."

departments of religion—"a sign of our times: religion is studied as a historical phenomenon in these departments, and not as a truth to be propagated."[51]

Yet the story of graduate education in religion in the 1960s and 1970s is not finally to be told in confessional or even in ecumenical terms, but rather more and more in relation to common scholarly endeavors cutting across and even independent of the lines of religious traditions. Looking back, one can see that the styles of the most recent period recall patterns that began to be urged early in the century, but may only now be coming closer to embodiment.

6. CANADA

Several distinct patterns of advanced education in religion have evolved in Canada, reflecting linguistic, cultural, and religious divisions in the country. In French-speaking Canada, institutions established for the training of clergy led to universities in which the study of religion was integral from the beginning. In the English-speaking sphere the status and locus of advanced religion study were settled only after conflicting denominational claims had been resolved. In recent decades such education has been reconceived as an academic discipline, along lines similar to those in the United States.[52]

As in the English colonies to the south, the desire to train a native clergy for New France led to establishment of a seminary in Quebec by Bishop Laval in 1663, and in Montreal by the Sulpician order not long after. Both seminaries reached a considerable size and trained thousands of priests, many from the United States or for missionary service there. The Quebec seminary was the mother of both Laval University in Quebec and the University of Montreal. From the beginning the seminary was associated with the College of the Jesuits established in 1635, first as an elementary school, but then developing into a classical college on the French model. At Laval's urging, the Jesuit fathers added theology to their curriculum, and the students in Laval's Grand Séminaire received their theological training in the college. The students in the pretheological institution (Petit Séminaire) he established in 1668 likewise attended classes in the college. After the British conquest in 1759 the seminary took over the college's work. Bishop Laval had wisely provided the seminary with lands and other income so that it was able to finance both classical and theological training, and when the first national council of the Canadian Catholic church in 1851 called for the establishment of a Catholic university, the seminary provided both the means and the men to bring it into being soon thereafter. The superior of the seminary was *de jure* the rector of the university, which was modeled after

[51] Band, 1966, pp. 14, 15, 12. More information on Judaic studies programs will be forthcoming in the study presently being conducted by Dr. Paul Ritterband of Columbia University under the auspices of the National Foundation for Jewish Culture.

[52] H. H. Walsh's history of Canadian Christianity (1956) gives attention to the development of religion study, relating it to political and social as well as religious factors. Glimpses of religion education in New France are found in *The Jesuit Relations*. Roy, 1930, provides further documentation on French-speaking Canada; secondary studies include Rochemonteix, 1895-96; Scott, 1926; Maurault, 1940; and Vachon, 1963.

130   ORIGINS

Catholic universities in Europe, especially Louvain. Further ties with the Continent were established through the scholarships granted to future professors to complete their education at Paris, Rome, or Louvain.

A faculty of theology was one of the four faculties in the new university, and graduate degrees in theology were announced. Until 1866, however, only one of the five chairs envisaged for the faculty was filled. In the early years of the university, students who had earned the master's or licentiate were eligible for the doctorate, which required preparation and defense of a dissertation.[53] No degrees seem to have been awarded under this plan,[54] and in 1868–1869 the requirements were changed (though they remained the same in the faculty of arts). Now the doctoral candidate, after first acquiring the bachelor's and licentiate in theology, was awarded the degree about a year or so after the licentiate if he successfully passed certain exams (*Annuaire* for 1868–1869, p. 47). These requirements remained substantially the same until well on into the present century.[55]

In the branch of the University of Laval established in Montreal in 1876, a faculty of theology was included. Though affiliated with Laval, the faculty also had ties with the Sulpician seminary in Montreal. In 1925, after Montreal had been granted independent status, the faculty of theology was canonically established. It now offers both the civil and canonical doctorates (Ph.D. and D.Th.).

The present Toronto Graduate School of Theological Studies is a cooperative venture of five denominational colleges at a public university that developed, after long struggle, out of a denominational institution: King's College.[56] King's status as an Anglican institution with an Anglican professor of divinity, but receiving public funds, had been conferred by a British government smarting from the loss of the thirteen colonies, in the hope that an established church would foster loyalty to the crown. This privileged status was not left unchallenged by other denominations. However, a recommendation that divinity chairs be established on a confessional basis was not taken up by them, and a government commission in 1839 adjudged it academically unfeasible: ". . . it would be wholly subversive of the order of an University, to have within it, chairs for the Professors of different Denominations of Religion" (see Alexander, 1906, p. 188). Finally, in the middle of the nineteenth century King's was reconstituted as a public provincial university with affiliated denominational colleges. Some of the

[53] See *Annuaire de l'Université-Laval* for 1859-1860 (pp. 29-31) and for 1862-1863 (pp. 49-51).
[54] Those listed by the university for the years 1852-1870 are degrees granted by other schools but recognized by Laval (see, e.g., *Annuaire* for 1894-1895, p. 64).
[55] See the *Annuaires* for 1894-1895, pp. 136-37; 1914-1915, p. 48; 1923-1924, p. 219. Cumulative lists of licentiate and doctoral degrees awarded each year are found in the *Annuaires*.
[56] See the histories of the University of Toronto by Alexander, 1906, and Wallace, 1927, and those of the federated colleges.

weaknesses of this system were remedied toward the end of the nineteenth century in a federation scheme which enrolled more denominational colleges with theological faculties. Some of the federating colleges taught only theology and left arts to the University College, while others taught both theology and arts. Emmanuel College inaugurated a Th.D. program in 1939. In 1944 it and three of the other colleges moved toward closer cooperation at the graduate level by instituting the Toronto Graduate School of Theological Studies, which offered initially a common course of studies leading to the M.Th. and then, in 1961, one leading to the Th.D. The degrees themselves are conferred by the colleges. The present constituency includes Emmanuel College (United Church of Canada), Knox, (Presbyterian), St. Michael's (Roman Catholic), and Trinity and Wycliffe (both Anglican).

An example of cooperative graduate study in religion at a private nondenominational school is the Faculty of Divinity (since 1970 the Faculty of Religious Studies) at McGill University.[57] McGill's origins were at least as stormy as those of the University of Toronto, and again a crucial issue was whether one church—the Anglican—would be permitted a privileged position. In endowing the future university, James McGill, though a professing Anglican, had said nothing about the teaching of religion, and the royal charter, while calling for "the Education of Youth in the principles of true religion," had not specified which religion was to be taught. In defending the proposed sole right of the Church of England to teach and practice its doctrines in the college, though exempting non-Anglicans from such instruction or worship, the Governors of the school in 1843 stated: "We do not believe that there is, rationally speaking, a choice between the two alternatives, of omitting wholly to establish any system of religious instruction and public worship in the College, or of providing for it by placing the Institution in strict and acknowledged connection with some one recognised form of doctrine" (see Macmillan, 1921, p. 148). But the British government interpreted the silence of the testator and the charter's failure to specify further the "true religion" to indicate "a design that Christianity should be taught, not in any single or exclusive form, but in any and every form in which its great fundamental truths and precepts could be imparted to the students . . ." (ibid., p. 199). In time, four theological colleges—Congregational, Presbyterian, Methodist, and Anglican—came to be affiliated with the university. In 1912 these formed a cooperative Divinity School, in which the colleges cooperated in instruction but continued to confer their own degrees. The arrangement led to the formation in 1948 of an ecumenical Faculty of Divinity that trained ministers for the Anglican church and the United Church of Canada. The university made the faculty appointments and conferred the degrees, including, after 1952, the Ph.D. A by-product was the creation of the Institute of Islamic Studies in 1952.

The clustering and cooperation of Canadian theological colleges and the

[57] See the histories of McGill by Macmillan, 1921, and MacLennan, 1960, and those of the affiliated colleges, especially Howard, 1963, pp. 77-84; the Brief to the Royal Commission, 1961, pp. 36-38, contains a sketch of the Faculty of Divinity.

association of most with a university stand in contrast to what was generally
the situation in the United States, and on occasion they have been held up as
a model for religious studies in America.[58] However, the Canadian churches
have known their share of denominational rivalry and intradenominational
strife, and these were sometimes reflected, as in the United States, in the
founding of competing theological schools. Some schools, even older ones,
remained extremely small, and connection with a university was no assurance
of quality.[59]

In the last decade of the nineteenth century the Anglican church in eastern
Canada sought to improve the quality of advanced education in religion by
establishing a Board of Examiners for the degrees of B.D. and D.D. (see
Howard, 1963, p. 43). The future of graduate education in religion, however,
lay in the university centers, and here the patterns and issues have not been dis-
similar from those in the United States. Ph.D's were awarded at Toronto and
McGill from the beginning of the century, and some were in the area of religion, with dissertation titles such as "The Mythical Serpents of Hebrew Literature" (in the Semitics department at Toronto in 1902[60]) and "The Ethics and
Religious Theories of Bishop Butler" (Toronto, 1903). Before graduate work
could be offered expressly in religion, however, resistance to the study of religion in public universities or in private, nondenominational institutions had
to be overcome. The arguments mounted in favor of such study recall those
familiar from the American scene (see, for instance, Wevers, 1956; Conway,
1959; Grant, 1968). The President's Committee on the School of Graduate
Studies at the University of Toronto reported in 1965 that the legislative clauses
bearing on the teaching of religion in the university had had a "hypnotic
effect," deterring the establishment of a Ph.D. program in religious studies
when the resources for such a program were at hand. The clauses were "designed
to avoid a situation in which academic credit might depend on a profession of
faith in religion. In the opinion of this Committee, they cannot be interpreted
as prohibiting the academic study of religion, at least at the graduate level."[61]

Although no Ph.D. program has been established in the university as yet,
the Institute of Christian Thought at St. Michael's College in the university
system was established in 1969 to offer the M.A. and Ph.D. to students without
professional theological training. Students in the program must also enroll
for courses in the Pontifical Institute of Medieval Studies. Religion is being

[58] Foster, "Canadian Theological Colleges and American Schools of Religion," 1922.

[59] See most recently Feilding's survey, 1966, of Protestant theological colleges. On the
Roman Catholic side, see Allen, 1968 (English-speaking Canada), and Langevin, 1968
(French-speaking Canada).

[60] Hebrew had been taught in King's College, for theological students, and in 1864 became a part also of the B.A. curriculum of the university; other Near Eastern languages
were added over the years, and a department of oriental languages (later renamed Semitic
languages) was formed. See Alexander, 1906, p. 88.

[61] University of Toronto, 1965, p. 41-42.

studied at the undergraduate level in the university through the Combined Department of Religious Studies established in 1968 and composed of the departments of religious studies in St. Michael's, Trinity, and Victoria Colleges. The department also draws on representatives from Erindale College, from Near Eastern Studies in University College, and from Islamic Studies and Near Eastern Studies in the Faculty of Arts and Sciences and collaborates with the Ad Hoc Committee for Judaic Studies. It pluralistic approach is typical of other such departments established in Canada in the 1950's and 1960's.

In the mid-1960's Ph.D. programs were established in religious studies departments unconnected with faculties of theology at McMaster University and the University of Ottawa. The latter's former Ph.D. and D.Th. programs are now offered by St. Paul University, which is federated with Ottawa and assumed the latter's civil and pontifical charters in 1965; at that time Ottawa was constituted as a provincial university and a Department of Religious Studies was established to offer a Ph.D. independently of St. Paul.

In 1955 the first issue of the *Canadian Journal of Theology* noted that indigenous scholars and scholarship were still largely desiderata ("Theological Scholarship," 1955; Cragg, 1955). When the *Journal* ceased publication in 1970 to give way to a periodical entitled, significantly, *Studies in Religion*, the editor remarked on the changed situation. Whereas in the early 1950's "most Canadian theologians were still working on the periphery of the world of higher education" and the study of religion was virtually excluded from the major universities (except in the Province of Quebec), "in 1970 a Canadian university which fails to provide for religious studies, Christian and non-Christian, invites the criticism that its curriculum is anachronistic and inadequate." The linguistic and denominational barriers of the fifties, observed the editor, were giving way to a "wider community of theological and religious scholarship" (Fairweather, 1970).

8

Graduate Education in Religion in Europe

INTRODUCTION

The following statements have been prepared by five distinguished European scholars, so that graduate studies in religion in the United States and Canada could be set in the context of current practices and tendencies in that part of the world to which American scholarship in religion and theology has historically been most closely related. (Unfortunately, it was simply not feasible to try to cover the entire European scene.)

As the authors make clear, none of these statements is intended to be an inclusive account—and for reasons of space we asked the writers to be brief. No attempt was made to impose a common framework for the reports. Rather we tried to interpret to our contributors the nature of the present study and left them free to sketch those aspects of the educational program in their countries that might be useful for American readers. The result is a healthy diversity in approach and emphasis. Thus Professor Hoens stresses mainly history of religions study in Dutch universities, and Professor Colpe treats particularly the problematic of German theological studies.[1] Common to all, however, is attention to the connection of religion study with professional ministerial training, a matter of special interest also in the United States.

Since 1969 Carsten Colpe has been Professor of Iranian Philology in the Free University of Berlin. He is at the same time lecturer in the Kirchliche Hochschule in Berlin and visiting professor for the general history of religions in the theological faculty in Göttingen. From Göttingen he received both the Ph.D. degree in philosophy and Semitic and Iranian philology (1955) and the Th.D. degree in Old and New Testament and Systematic Theology (1960). Prior to assuming his present position he taught history of religions and New Testament in Hamburg, Yale, and Göttingen. His publications include *Die religionsgeschichtliche Schule: Darstellung und Kritik ihres Bildes vom gnostischen Erlösermythus* (1961) and the important article on "Son of Man" in

[1] All the essays except the one by Professor Ninian Smart have been translated and/or edited for English style, and Professor Colpe's statement has been abbreviated somewhat.

134

Kittel's *Theologisches Wörterbuch zum Neuen Testament*. He has also contributed to the encyclopedia *Religion in Geschichte und Gegenwart* and to the Pauly-Wissowa *Real-Encyclopädie der classischen Altertumswissenschaft* and is an editor of the new *Reallexikon für Antike und Christentum*.

Jean George Heintz, Maître de conférences in the areas of biblical archéology and Semitic philology at the University of Strasbourg, France, has had a varied educational background. From the Faculty of Protestant Theology at Strasbourg he received the licentiate degree in theology, and from the Faculty of Letters and Humanities at the same university he received the licentiate in letters. In 1964 he was granted a diploma by the Center for Oriental Studies at the University of Geneva, which also awarded him the university prize. After further research and study at the École Biblique in Jerusalem, in 1968 he was awarded the doctorate in religious sciences with a dissertation on the "prophetic" letters of the royal archives of Mari in relation to the Old Testament. In the same year he was appointed assistant in the Protestant faculty in Strasbourg and was elected to membership in the Société Ernest Renan. In addition to his duties in Strasbourg he teaches at the École du Louvre in Paris, in the area of Semitic epigraphy. His publications include contributions to the *Dictionnaire des Symboles* and Kittel's *Theologisches Wörterbuch zum Neuen Testament*.

Since 1947 Dirk Jan Hoens has been on the faculty of the University of Utrecht, where he also began the study of theology, history of religions, and oriental languages and received the theological degrees. His study for the ecclesiastical examination was conducted at the University of Leiden. First appointed as Assistant Professor for Hebrew and Arabic, Dr. Hoens later became Associate Professor and (1960) Professor of Living Religions. His doctoral dissertation, *Śānti I. A Contribution to Ancient Indian Religious Terminology* (1951), was honored with the coveted Mallinckrodt Prize. Other writings include *Sarvodaya: Een modern voorbeeld van het absorptievermogen van het Hindoeisme* (1961) and "Initiation in Later Hinduism according to Tantric Texts," in C. J. Bleeker (ed.), *Initiation* (1964).

Per Erik Persson is Professor of Systematic Theology at the University of Lund, where he also did his graduate work. His doctoral dissertation on Thomas Aquinas, *Sacra Doctrina* (1957), evoked much interest on its publication and has now been translated into English. Some of his subsequent works have also dealt with Roman Catholicism: *Romerskt och Evangeliskt* (1959; E.T., *Roman and Evangelical*) and *Kyrkans Ämbete* (1961), a detailed study of the Protestant and Roman Catholic ministry in biblical and historical perspective. His most recent publication deals with the concept of God, *Att Tolka Gud i Dag* (1971). Persson has served as visiting professor in the United States and is a member of the Faith and Order Commission of the World Council of Churches.

Ninian Smart is Professor of Religious Studies at the University of Lancaster, the first university in the United Kingdom to set up a department of religion. He has taught at universities in Wales, London, and India and, in this country, at Princeton, Yale, and Wisconsin. It was while serving in the

British Army Intelligence in 1945 that he learned Chinese, at the University of London. After military service in Ceylon, he matriculated at Oxford, where he did his graduate work in philosophy of religion. His interest in Eastern culture led to the study of Sanskrit and Pali, and his first book, *Reason and Faiths* (1958), related the philosophy and history of religions. His publications include *World Religions: A Dialogue* (1960), *Doctrine and Argument in Indian Philosophy* (1964), *Philosophers and Religious Truth* (1964), *Secular Education and the Logic of Religion* (1968), *The Yogi and the Devotee* (1968), and the *Philosophy of Religion* (1970).

1. THE TEACHING OF THE HISTORY OF RELIGIONS AND OF THE
THEOLOGICAL SCIENCES IN FRANCE

By J. G. Heintz

Introduction

The teaching of the religious sciences in France draws on two sources which the tensions between the history of ideas and the history of beliefs have often placed in antithesis. The first, of a theological nature, is related to the rich Christian tradition of which the monastic culture of the Middle Ages and the humanism of the Reformation constitute the fundamental streams. The second, of a rationalistic bent and more recent, has brought a critical and often polemical perspective into a realm that until then had been the preserve of theologians. At the same time, by refusing to acknowledge Christianity's claims to preeminence, it has widened the perspectives of this realm in order to lay the foundations of a true "science of religions."

Though the distinction between these two traditions still retains its importance from a methodological standpoint, such a dichotomous presentation of the religious sciences in France would not give an accurate account of the present trend in education research, for the advance in strictly philological and historical methods has steadily brought these two traditions closer together on the basis of scientific criteria alone.

A glance at the history of this science in France confirms this impression. After the creation of a chair in the history of religions at the Collège de France in 1880 and after the organization of the Section of Religious Sciences at the École pratique des Hautes Études (Fifth Section, Sorbonne) in 1886, there followed the establishment of such chairs in the Protestant and Roman Catholic faculties in the University of Strasbourg and, subsequently, at the Catholic institutions in Paris, Lille, Lyons, and Toulouse. In view of the present diversity of aims and methodologies in the history of religions, it would, of course, be futile to seek to prove the absolute convergence of the two streams of tradition mentioned above. However, the community of teaching and of research which characterizes them in certain cases—if only at the level of an "ideal type"—must at least be noted.

In order to give an objective presentation of the possibilities for study in the *sciences des religions* in France, we shall provide brief characterizations of the various institutions which, as presently constituted,[1] offer work in this area. However, various distinctions need to be kept in mind.

The first concerns the status of the institution. Whereas the strictly university institutions are under the jurisdiction of the Ministry of National Education and have the power to confer official degrees, other institutions owe their existence to private initiative, chiefly, as regards the science of religions, on the part of one or more churches. Hence their title, "Facultés libres."

The second distinction, which in part overlaps the first, concerns the aims of these institutions. Whereas the public (*officiel*) institutions have as their primary aim instruction of the university type, attuned to, and if possible correlated with, the other university faculties, the private (*libre*) institutions usually have a more limited aim, that of training priests or pastors for the church that provides their support. These two kinds of education, public university and private confessional, are not necessarily mutually exclusive, and we emphasize that one cannot make a priori value judgments about either.

The university degrees and diplomas conferred are either official (that is, public, or "state") or private, according to our first distinction, and array themselves as follows (presupposed is the secondary school diploma, which is usually granted when the student is seventeen or eighteen):

the licentiate or master's (4 to 5 years of study);
the doctorate of the "third cycle" of studies, i.e., the *doctorat de spécialité* (e.g., *doctorat ès-sciences religieuses*), awarded after two more years of study and the defense of a dissertation;
the university doctorate, a degree generally taken by advanced foreign students;
the state doctorate (e.g., *ès-Lettres, en Théologie*, etc.), awarded generally to French citizens after the defense of a dissertation.

Before choosing an institution the student is well advised to inquire about the scientific and cultural environment and especially whether or not there are centers of studies and research in related fields. As indicated in the list below, it is essentially two cities which offer these advantages: Paris, the capital, and Strasbourg, where the university and private institutions offer extensive resources in the sciences of religion.

a. University Institutions (National Education)

1. Paris

In the capital there are two renowned institutions of higher learning which, though not directly under the jurisdiction of the university, constitute the fundamental scientific locus of the science of religions in France:

a. At the Collège de France the chair of history of religions, established in 1880, is a perfect example of this kind of independent education and original research. The chair has been occupied by Albert Réville (1880–1906), Jean

---

[1] These are institutions under the jurisdiction of the Ministry of National Education and operating within the framework of the law governing higher education (cf. *Journal Officiel*, November 12, 1968).

Réville (1907–1908), Alfred Loisy (1909–1932), Jean Baruzi (1933–1951), and H. C. Puech (since 1952). The Collège does not confer degrees or diplomas, but is an exceptional place to pursue individual research or studies leading to the doctorate. (For further information see the *Annuaire du Collège de France,* published annually [pp. 5–19, "Introduction"], or *Revue de l'Enseignement Supérieur,* 1962, No. 2, pp. 1–50.)

b. Founded in 1868, the École pratique des Hautes Études in 1886 added a fifth section, "Sciences religieuses," which offers a spectrum of study unique in the nation as regards the study of living and historical religions. (See further the *Annuaire de l'École pratique des Hautes Études,* Sect. 5, Sciences religieuses, LXXVII [1969–1970], 5–28; and the volume published at the school's centennial, *Problèmes et méthodes d'Histoire des Religions,* 1968.)

c. The Université de Paris (Sorbonne). While the two preceding institutions offer opportunity for specialized education and basic research, the various sections of the Département des Sciences humaines at the University of Paris are authorized to grant official degrees and diplomas. Thanks to the large number and the specializations of the different institutes, schools (like the School of Oriental Languages and so on), and research groups[2] affiliated with it, the university offers facilities for every sort of graduate education and research.

In addition to the sessions of the Académie des Inscriptions et Belles-Lettres at the Institut de France, which are often concerned with the study of religion, mention should also be made of the existence of many learned societies, such as the Société Ernest Renan, founded in 1919 for the development of "studies in the history of religions and in religious philosophies" (Art. 1 of the statutes). The Society publishes an *Annuaire* and the *Bulletin de la Société Ernest Renan,* which appears annually as a supplement to the *Revue de l'Histoire des Religions* and contains the proceedings of its meetings.

2. Strasbourg

The Université des Sciences Humaines de Strasbourg accommodates a number of education and research units whose principal interest is the study of religion.

a. The Faculté de Théologie Protestante, successor of the Académie that was founded in 1538 and remains associated with the memory of John Calvin and Martin Bucer, devotes itself to education in the main theological disciplines and ancillary fields: history of religions, Old and New Testament, history of Christianity, systematic and practical theology, and musicology. In these different disciplines the faculty grants the licentiate and the doctorate of the third cycle as well as the university and state doctorates. A program of research, "of the third cycle" and lasting two years, prepares students for that doctorate; a large percentage of those presently in the program are foreign students. The research work of the faculty profits from many specialized centers, such as the

---

[2] For example, the Groupe de sociologie des religions, a detailed report of which is given in *Archives de Sociologie des Religions,* XXVIII (1969), 1–92.

Centre d'Études et de pratique pédagogique, the Centre d'analyse et de documentation patristiques, and the Centre de sociologie du protestantisme. Faculty research is reported in the *Revue d'Histoire et de Philosophie religieuses* and in two exegetical and theological series, the "Cahiers" and the "Études d'Histoire de Philosophie religieuses." (On the history of the faculty, see Jacob, 1962. A *Bibliographie des sciences théologiques*, compiled by the professorial staff, will soon be published in its journal *Revue d'Histoire et de Philosophie religieuses*.)

b. The Faculté de Théologie Catholique, established in 1902, offers instruction in the same disciplines as the Protestant faculty, but from the Roman Catholic perspective. The faculty is also authorized to grant the same degrees. The vitality of this institution is attested by the existence of its Institut de Droit canonique, its Centre de recherche et de documentation des Institutions chrétiennes, and its Centre de pédagogie religieuse, and the publication of the *Revue des sciences religieuses* (the official organ of the faculty), the *Revue du Moyen Age latin*, and the *Revue de Droit canonique*. (See further *Mémorial du Cinquantenaire [1919–1969] de la Faculté de Théologie Catholique* [de l'Université de Strasbourg], 1970.)

c. The Centre de recherches d'Histoire des Religions completes this ensemble of institutions—a unique setup in the French university system. Standing in close academic relationship with the Faculty of Letters in the university and with the two theological faculties of the university, the center is a unique establishment in France for religious studies and, more particularly, for the study of the origins and development of Christianity.[3]

Each year the Centre organizes an international scholarly colloquium devoted to one of the subdisciplines in the history of religions. The proceedings are published in the series "Bibliothèque des Centres d'études supérieures spécialisés." The director, Professor Marcel Simon, was recently elected president of the International Association for the History of Religions at its thirteenth congress, in Stockholm, in August, 1970.

b. Private Institutions

As their principal purpose is the training of clergy, these institutions are presented here according to their church affiliation.

1. *Roman Catholic*

a. Although not founded until 1875, the Institut Catholique de Paris is in fact the heir of a long history dating back to the tradition of religious thought at the ancient Sorbonne of the thirteenth century. As a private institution of higher education and research, it comprises many faculties, institutes, and schools, of which only a small part is of importance here, above all the Faculté de Théologie, which is authorized by the Holy See to grant degrees in theology, canon law, and scholastic philosophy.

[3] Outside the university but connected with it is the Lutheran World Federation's Centre d'Études Oecuméniques in Strasbourg, which publishes a series entitled "Oecumenica."

At the end of a long (six-year) or short (two-year) period of study in the classical theological disciplines, students are eligible for the licentiate in theology. Those who go on to study for the doctorate must prepare a dissertation under the direction of a professor of the faculty and participate in various research projects and seminars. (The annual supplement to the fourth number of the *Nouvelles de l'Institut Catholique de Paris* supplies further information on the school.)

Since 1968 there has been a division of biblical studies that is jointly operated and staffed by the Faculty of Theology and the School of Ancient Oriental Languages; here the student may prepare for an advanced degree in biblical studies. (See further the *Mémorial du Cinquantenaire [1919–1964] de l'École des Langues Orientales Anciennes de L'Institut Catholique de Paris*, in the series "Travaux de l'Institut Catholique de Paris," Vol. X [1964].)

The many faculties and institutes in the Institut offer opportunities for specialized study. In addition to those already mentioned, there are the Faculty of Canon Law (founded in 1880) and the Institutes of Social Studies (1923), of Liturgical Music (1923), of Pastoral Catechetics (1950), of Religious Studies (1947), of Spirituality (1947), of Liturgy (1956), and of Pedagogy (1969). Two recently created institutes are a witness to the reality of this community of learning and research that has manifested itself increasingly since the Second Vatican Council: the Institut de Science et de Théologie des religions, which was established in 1967 under the direction of Cardinal Daniélou and is dedicated particularly to missiology; and the Institut supérieur d'Études oecuméniques, established in 1967 in collaboration with several of the non-Catholic institutions mentioned below (Section B,4).

The Instituts catholiques outside Paris—at Lille, Lyons, Angers, and Toulouse —are organized along the same lines as the Paris Institut and grant the same degrees. However, their resources for specialized study and research are more limited. In each of these it is especially the faculty of theology that provides the opportunity for the study of religion from a Catholic perspective.

At Lyons the Jesuit Faculté de Théologie is restricted to members of that order. It edits the series "Théologie" (78 volumes to date) and the journal *Recherches de Science religieuse*. The Dominican Faculté de Théologie at the "Saulchoir," near Paris, is likewise restricted to members of that order. In other university centers outside Paris, courses for lay Catholics offer an introduction to the academic study of religion; among others, the Institut des sciences religieuses in Nancy.

2. Protestant Faculties

a. The Faculté libre de Théologie protestante de Paris enrolls students with a secondary school diploma (or the equivalent) who intend, for the most part, to prepare themselves for a pastoral ministry. The licentiate in theology is conferred after four years of study. The school also enrolls auditors and foreign students, who thus have access also to the numerous possibilities for study in the public and private institutions in the metropolitan area.

b. The Faculté libre de théologie protestante de Montpellier is under the jurisdiction of the Reformed churches of France. Established in 1598, its history has been as turbulent as that of the churches that founded it. After many years in Montauban, it was transferred to Montpellier in 1920, following the promulgation of the law separating church and state. The Faculty enrolls students from a variety of confessional and national backgrounds and of every shade of opinion, as long as they possess the necessary academic qualifications. It grants the same kind of diploma as the Protestant Faculty in Paris. It also confers a doctorate "à titre étranger," which is awarded to foreigners after defending a dissertation and offering evidence of a certain level of cultural and theological knowledge. The Faculty is responsible for the publication of the journal *Études Théologiques et Religieuses.*

c. The Faculté libre de Théologie de Vaux-sur-Seine, founded in 1965, seeks to provide theological training that is both of high quality and spiritual in nature.

3. Orthodoxy

The study of Orthodoxy from a confessional perspective is provided in France by the Institut de Théologie orthodoxe Saint-Serge in Paris, which was established in 1925. The courses are offered in Russian or French and are restricted to students of the Orthodox faith who are studying for the licentiate, master's, or doctoral degrees. However, non-Orthodox students are admitted as auditors.

4. Institutes of Ecumenical Studies

The Institut supérieur d'Études oecuméniques was established in 1967 within the framework of the Institut catholique de Paris as an outgrowth of the ecumenical movement and of the Second Vatican Council. It brings together Roman Catholic, Orthodox, Protestant, and Anglican professors who, for the most part, also teach in the faculties mentioned above (A,2,a, and B,2,a–c, as well as the Lutheran Centre in Strasbourg and the Ecumenical Institute in Bossey, near Geneva). Most recently, a section named Connaissance du Judaisme has been added to the Institut; in many ways it foreshadows graduate education in religion of tomorrow.

This very brief presentation is at least an attempt to give as faithful a picture as possible of the study of religion at the scientific and university levels in France at the present time (1970).[4] It is scarcely possible to discern a unified structure for this study and even less to discover a generally acknowledged trend in research. This prohibits us—or spares us—from offering statistical data. Through these various institutions and educational programs appear the tensions of history and of thought in the Western world, in which religion remains a controversial reality and, at times, is experienced as a revelation.

---

[4] Outside of France, but at least partially under the jurisdiction of the official educational system (through the Académie des Inscriptions et Belles Lettres de l'Institut de France), is the École Biblique et Archéologique française in Jerusalem, which offers specialized instruction and basic research, in the land of the Bible.

2. THE PATTERN OF GRADUATE STUDIES IN RELIGION IN GERMANY:
   TRADITIONS, CHANGES, AND PROBLEMS

By Carsten Colpe

It is hazardous to attempt a succinct description of graduate education in religion in Germany, especially since it is apt to be cited abroad as authoritative. What is presented here really has little in common with such education in North America, and if one makes point-for-point distinctions—with respect to the concept of religion, the structure of secondary and higher education, courses, examinations, and the like—one runs the risk of setting up a scale for comparing what is not really comparable. Moreover, the attempts made since 1965 to reform the study of theology, the student revolution beginning in 1967, and the recurrent attempts to orient the study of theology along Anglo-Saxon lines have led to so many changes that one really can no longer describe theological studies in Germany in terms of official programs or regulations or even by reference simply to what has been customary. On the other hand, the situation is changing so much from year to year and from place to place that it is impossible as yet, especially for a single individual, to gather the details up into a brief, reliable summary. Finally, the interplay between the traditional and the changing means that this reporter cannot avoid introducing his personal views of the problems and his own proposals for their solution (hence, for balance, the bibliographical note at the end). Our discussion will alternate between presenting the traditional and the changing, and the attendant problems, but will focus especially on what appears to be of greatest significance for the future, whether that is what has proved itself in the past, or is beginning to crystallize as the result of changes, or is only emerging as a problem.

a. In Germany 95 percent of what Americans call studies in religion is included in the study of theology in preparation for the ministry, the priesthood, or the teaching of religion in public schools. "Graduate studies" begin on entrance into the university, immediately after the final secondary school examinations. Although American students are more mature from the standpoint of human experience, German students are more advanced intellectually. Over the years the two groups grow more alike as each acquires the characteristics of the other. Because much of the course material that in America constitutes graduate work in religion is taught in Germany in the kind of secondary school now commonly called the *Gymnasium*, something must be said about this kind of school—first, with respect to Protestant theology.

In Germany, Latin, Greek, and Hebrew are still generally accounted prerequisites for beginning the study of theology, since one must be able to read in the original the Old Testament, the New Testament, and the Greek fathers to Cyril of Alexandria, the Latin fathers from Tertullian to Augustine, as well as the Latin texts of the Scholastics, the Reformers, the Protestant confessional writings, and the documents of Protestant orthodoxy. Here the Protestant principle of fidelity to the text of scripture obviously has been extended to include other sources as well. The appropriation of the biblical witness alone would fail to take account of two thousand years of historical change, and the mere reproduction of the biblical assertions without reflection on the interpretation of God's word in history would today signify an anachronism whereby the church is isolated in a world of its own, quite removed from reality. The difference between this and the Roman Catholic esteem for tradition is that for Protestantism the norm remains the Bible and does not pass over into tradition. This calls for a critical Protestant position over against tradition, for the cultivation of analytical methods, and for investigation of the non-exegetical origins of the interpretations that have emerged in the church's history. For all these reasons, there can be no objection to critical study of the written sources and the mastery of the languages that unlock them; indeed, they are deserving of recognition as denoting a versatility of thought and knowledge comparable to that in other fields of study.

This is what makes the humanistic *Gymnasium*—in which Latin is taught for nine years, Greek and Hebrew optionally for the last three years—the most proper pretheological education. The humanism that this kind of school seeks to inculcate must be seen in the context of what German learned circles regard as the ideal education—the mathematical-scientific, logical-grammatical, and historical-dialogical contemporization of Graeco-Roman antiquity. In *Der Streit des Philanthropinismus und des Humanismus in der Theorie des Erziehungsunterrichts unserer Zeit* (1808), Bavarian philosopher F. J. Niethammer said that the Greek logos raised man from a state of raw nature to that of a thinking being, thereby establishing his humanity. This logos, incarnate in Christ, was the principle of human education and thus the cornerstone of the humanism which in the *Gymnasium* promotes the humanity of its students, whereas the *Aufklärung*, with its preference for industry, business, and material gain, was directed to man's animal nature. One sees in this description essential characteristics of that intellectual movement which arose in Italy during the Renaissance, spread to surrounding countries, and especially in Germany entered into a productive symbiosis with the Reformation. After 1870 the designation "humanism" was fittingly applied to this movement as well.

This humanism, like that of the *Gymnasium*, had to value the written text most highly of all the sources of knowledge capable of contributing to the shaping of humanity in the classical mold. The humanist's almost fetishistic reverence for the written text and the Protestant theologian's fidelity to scripture were in fact continually converging: earthly education and the ways of attaining divine salvation supported each other most happily, even to the point of coalescence. Accordingly both philologians and theologians reacted and still react similarly to all attempts to cast doubt upon the legitimacy of this way or these ways. The dismay of the philologian who becomes defensive if someone, with the aid of the sounds of actual speech, questions the sole validity of the letters or even the sentences of his written text is not so very different from the dismay of the theologian who is asked to believe that direct "inspiration" tells just as much about the will of God as does obedience to scripture.

Thus both educational tradition and church doctrine led in a similar way to certain principles for pretheological education. In practice this meant that a son or (after World War II) a daughter whom good fortune or parental foresight had destined for the ministry entered a humanistic *Gymnasium* at the age of ten, where he got his Latin, Greek, and Hebrew "down pat," so that when he received his diploma he could immediately begin the study of theology proper. Admission to the first theological examination requires a minimum of eight semesters of study beyond the *Gymnasium* if Greek was included in the examination for the earlier diploma and seven if Hebrew was also included. At least six of these semesters must be taken in a faculty of Protestant theology in a state university.

At present (1971) such faculties are found in the following universities in the German Federal Republic: Marburg, Heidelberg, Kiel, Goettingen, Erlangen, Tuebingen, Bonn, Muenster, Mainz, Hamburg, Bochum, and Munich; in the German Democrat Republic: Griefswald, Rostock, Leipzig, Jena, Halle, Berlin (now East Berlin).[1] Study at one of the *Kirchliche Hochschulen* (Bethel bei Bielefeld, Wuppertal, West Berlin, and Neuendettelsau) is also recognized. These schools were set up after the Third Confessional Synod of the German Evangelical Church (1935) as rival institutions to those corrupted by National Socialism. Following World War II they continued as full-fledged church-related theological schools alongside the theology programs offered in the state universities. Of the *Kirchliche Hochschulen* the one in West Berlin is empowered to confer the doctorate and has recently been granted the authority to certify qualification for university lecturing; it therefore has equal standing with a university theological faculty.

The classic course of study, which for lack of anything better (that is, more up to date) is still highly recommended and surprisingly often followed, runs much along the following lines. In the first third of the student's career, proseminars in New Testament, Old Testament, and church history must be completed; in the second third, the major seminars in the same fields, plus those in systematic theology; in the last third, the proseminars and major seminars in practical theology (homiletics, catechetics, liturgics, and pastoral care) and again in systematic theology, along with review work in the exegetical and historical fields. To all this the student should add, as much as possible, the lecture courses. For a number of years after the war the major lecture courses (*Hauptvorlesungen*) met four hours a week. Now that more books are available to students and the typical "one way" lecture method has been replaced more and more by study and discussion groups, the lecture courses have commonly been reduced to three hours a week. The first lecture courses the student is expected to attend in biblical studies are exegetical, on various books of the Bible. Then are supposed to follow those that bear the misleading title "Introduction" to the Old or New Testament; in fact these are an extensive literary

---

[1] In each list chronological order of establishment is followed. The Protestant faculties at Bochum and Munich are post-World War II. After World Wars I and II Strasbourg became French; after World War II Koenigsberg and Breslau were lost to Germany and Giessen was closed (although it is supposed to be reopened).

history of scripture presupposing intensive exegetical study of the most important biblical writings. The capstone of these lecture courses is the one dealing with the "theology" of the Old or New Testament. In the Old Testament field the "History of Israel" is also highly regarded as the major and standard lecture course; its counterpart in New Testament—a history of primitive Christianity or of the apostolic age—generally lays the foundation for lecture courses in church history.

The latter are traditionally divided into four periods: ancient, medieval, Reformation and Counter Reformation, and modern. Here, too, a hierarchy of values has established itself. At the top is the history of the Reformation (particularly the young Luther and his times), then the ancient church, with emphasis on the first two centuries and Augustine, then medieval, and finally, modern. Until the student protest movement, the neglect of the modern period and the present had its undoubted parallels in the fields of general history and literature. In this respect theology was relatively more progressive in that occasionally—though hardly out of interest in the modern period as such—one treated a contemporary theme, the *Kirchenkampf* of 1933–1945.

Systematic theology, for which the student is prepared to some extent by study of the theology of the Reformers in his church history lectures or seminars, deals with its materials in a variety of ways, mostly under the heading of Dogmatics I and II and ethics. Although drawing chiefly on history, lecture courses in symbolics and the history of Protestant theology subserve the interests of systematics. The lecture subjects vary more than in the exegetical courses. Of late, philosophy of religion subjects are becoming increasingly prominent.

The position of practical theology in the theological course of study has always been problematic, and for precisely this reason it is offered in a greater (and often more interesting) variety of ways. The subjects of the lecture courses are generally less standardized and cover everything connected with the life of the church, from worship, administration of the sacraments, perquisites, pastoral care, teaching, and polity to a theology or critique of these subjects, from a development of current practices purely on the basis of church tradition to the justification of their Christian character in ongoing debate with "secular" social, psychological, and pedagogical counterparts.

Until recently the recommendation that students should do work in fields other than the five classical theological disciplines has been more theory than practice. Among the fields recommended, philosophy stands at the top of the list—and here again as classical a subject or author as possible, or an approach applicable to philosophy of religion, and in addition some variety of existentialist philosophy, whose description of man's "fallenness" can most correlatively be contrasted with the Christian gospel. Universities vary in the status of studies in domestic and foreign missions and, connected with the latter, of *Religionswissenschaft* (about which more will be said later). Then follow, on perhaps equal terms, literature and art—less the methodology of these disciplines and not necessarily connected with Christian or religious themes, though these are naturally held in favor. The natural sciences were and are scarcely counted necessary. Psychology and the social sciences are viewed with great distrust and are likely to be accepted only under pressure of student demands; cybernetics and systems or communications theory are little, if at all, regarded as relevant for theology.

A more or less basic treatment of theological subjects takes four years, and the attempts to lengthen this span seem both justifiable and understandable. The student in greatest difficulty, however, is the one who must "catch up" in the ancient languages before he can even begin the study of theology. He must work to bring himself up to the level of the graduate of the humanistic *Gymnasium*. Everywhere carefully planned programs are offered to enable such a student to meet (in one to three semesters) the requirements for a language which he lacks. But these crash language programs work at most for only 50 percent of the students. For the others several semesters more are required. After the language examinations follow semesters during which the student does not have to concentrate on languages, the so-called languageless semesters—a quite absurd expression, since these ought to be the semesters in which one can wield the languages as working tools. Therein lies an unconscious justification for the question raised repeatedly by students learning languages as well as by others: Why must one first be educated as a humanist if one wants only to proclaim the gospel? The many attempts at curricular reform repeatedly begin with this problem without ever arriving at a convincing solution.

During the student's career a quarter- or half-year's employment in some nonacademic, practical work (like factory, farm, hospital, social work, school, and so on) is desired or required. Nowadays, when interest in and concern with social realities is not only more eagerly sought after but also better grounded theoretically, such work must be considered a part of graduate studies. Many students take a semester's leave of absence; others do this work during vacation. Occasionally this requirement coincides with employment undertaken by a student to finance his education (though such cases are less frequent because of improvements in the scholarship system). Certification of such work is required before a student may take his first examination and must be presented along with his academic credentials. Up until recently the first examination was administered to candidates by a special commission appointed by their respective territorial churches. The commission always included a professor from a theological faculty located in the territory of that church. The theology faculties themselves administered the first examination to candidates who did not intend to enter the service of the church or were, for a particular reason, assigned by the territorial church to a faculty for examination. Only in the recent past has the candidate been given the choice of examination by the church or by a faculty of theology. Thus, the examination requirements, which previously had varied throughout Germany because of the distinctive characteristics and peculiarities of the several territorial churches and the universities, have gradually become more uniform.

The first examination is followed by about two years of further study in various areas of practical theology, along with work in a congregation or a school, after which time examinations for ordination (the "Second Exam") are administered by the churches.

The student who works toward a doctor's degree in theology does so before the first examination or after beginning his professional career as pastor or teacher. His major field must be one of the five classical theological disciplines, with minors in two to four of the others. The requirement is the preparation of a dissertation, followed by a rigorous oral examination. Certification for teaching in a university requires, in addition to the doctorate, the preparation of another scholarly dissertation (the *Habilitationsschrift*); a lecture before the faculty, followed by a defense of the same; and a trial public lecture.

b. In recent years increased attention has been given to the training of teachers of religion for the *Gymnasien* and other schools. In years past this kind of training had the nickname "narrow gauge theology," because the lack of a special program necessitated the omission of some of the courses of the full theology curriculum in order to make room for other subjects that would have to be taught in a *Gymnasium* (such as science and modern languages). *De facto,* however, students preparing to teach religion must deal in the same measure with theological questions as those who go on to be pastors, and in addition, they must apply what they have learned to the particular requirements and tasks of schoolteaching. The distinctive nature of this training of teachers is increasingly recognized, first, because school pupils do not ask the teacher (as parishioners ask their pastor) only about the validity of the Christian tradition but also about the validity of non-Christian traditions and philosophies and about secular religions; and, second, because there is an acknowledged need for a program of instruction in religion which can measure up to that for other subjects. To meet this need, university faculties of theology and *Kirchliche Hochschulen* have increasingly had to make special provisions for future teachers of religion. These students do not have to learn Hebrew (thus they need special Old Testament courses), and instead of the full Greek program they take special abbreviated courses that by-pass classical Greek and lead directly to the *koine*. The courses in the five classical theological disciplines are also no longer simply selections from the total theological program, but are adapted and provided to meet the specific needs of religion teachers, among which the need for at least an introduction to general *Religionswissenschaft* has proven especially urgent.

c. We may touch briefly on the differences in the education of candidates for the Roman Catholic priesthood, since the basic structures are much the same as for Protestants. From the outset Roman Catholic training is more directly supervised by the church. Candidates come not only from state-operated *Gymnasien* but also from those operated by the church and attended by students who decided at an early age to study for the priesthood. A distinctive, liturgically regulated communal life flourishes in the latter. From secondary school graduation to ordination involves at least twelve semesters of theological study. The first four semesters are devoted chiefly to the study of scholastic philosophy and various philosophical problems that arise out of it and conclude with the so-called philosophical examination (*Philosophicum*). Catholic priests are more extensively trained in philosophy than Protestant ministers, though in biblical studies, including the ancient languages, Protestants have the advantage, for to the Catholic theologian the study of doctrine, including its history, is traditionally of primary importance. Recently, however, the study of scripture has been stressed more than before, and thus, alongside Latin, there is increasing study of the biblical languages. One generally starts the language courses after the *Philosophicum*. The other differences, especially the greater diversity of systematic disciplines (basic theology, moral theology, apologetics) in Catholicism, need not be taken up here.

There are faculties of Roman Catholic theology at the Universities of Bonn, Freiburg, Munich, Muenster, Tuebingen, Wuerzburg, Mainz, and Bochum (up to the end of World War II there was also one at Breslau, and an academy at Braunsberg in East Prussia). Philosophical-theological *Hochschulen* are located in Bamberg, Dillingen, Freising, Passau, and Regensburg. After each of the first three years in the priesthood Roman Catholics must take an examination, then one final major examination before being assigned to a parish. After that priests take part in retreats which provide not only spiritual deepening and renewal but continuing education as well.

d. Now we turn to the approximately 5 percent of graduate studies in religion not included in the regular study of theology. In the problematic nature of these studies Germany may well be unique among countries in which theology and religious studies are pursued. In the United States it is increasingly taken for granted that every university and college will have a department of religion which includes non-Western studies. As far as France, England, the Netherlands, and Scandinavia are concerned, one need only glance at the *Annuaire* (Vols. 77–78, 1969–1970, 1970–1971) of the École pratique des Hautes Études to see what a wealth of religious studies are available in those countries. Three Italian (Rome, Messina, Trent) and five Swiss (Basel, Geneva, Lausanne, Zurich, and Bern) universities have chairs in the history of religions. The small number of such chairs in Italy reflects the unfavorable disposition of the Roman Catholic tradition to such studies, whereas the number of Swiss chairs is striking in light of the size of that country.

In Germany, however, such chairs are found only in Berlin,[2] Bonn, Leipzig, Marburg, Erlangen, and Goettingen (in the order of their founding). In these universities there are no departments with staffs of professors, researchers, and a number of students enrolled, but simply a single professor and a lecturer (*Dozent*) or assistant, occasionally both, in addition to a small library. Naturally, in the course of their work in particular cultures, representatives of certain theological, ethnological, philosophical, or philological-historical subdisciplines often give attention to the religion of those cultures and develop the ramifications in terms of the history of religions and *Religionswissenschaft* and offer

---

[2] Since 1910. After the division of the university into the Free University and Humboldt University this chair was continued in both, the latter based in the philosophy of religion.

courses based on their findings, thereby continuing a tradition in vogue since the Enlightenment. At present the study of religion is occasionally combined with other disciplines, both taught by one person. In the philosophy faculties, the combination is usually with oriental studies; in Protestant theological faculties, usually with exegetics (particularly Old Testament) or missiology, less often with systematic theology; and in Catholic theological faculties, generally with apologetics or missiology. The students usually take their examinations, which open the way to a career, in one of these disciplines. The doctoral degree is also conferred in one of these disciplines, even though the dissertation topic is in the area of religion. Even where there is a chair in the history of religions, one is well advised to devote oneself to *Religionswissenschaft* only when one is securely established in one of the major disciplines cited above and, if possible, has taken an examination also in that discipline. Recently, in place of such an examination, one may take a master's degree in religious studies (for which there is no state examination), which corresponds to the Anglo-Saxon master's degree. By and large, however, specialization in religious studies, whether in a non-Christian religion or in a comparative-phenomenological area, is pursued through the writing of a thesis under the umbrella of one of the major disciplines. Thus, there are clergymen, *Gymnasium* and *Hochschule* teachers, and persons in other professions, as well as university professors, who hold a doctorate in religious studies. However, even those who teach in this area were frequently trained in another. There are no special career possibilities as such for persons trained in religious studies.

The reason for these peculiar arrangements for training in religious studies is the German penchant for principle. Instead of doing pragmatically what appeared to be necessary, one reflected on whether the need was legitimate, and if so, whether the present experts could meet it. Thus the representatives of the humanities looked to the theologians for assistance, and the latter regarded *Religionswissenschaft* as a cultural study which was in principle not their concern. To justify this position liberal theologians pointed out that they were already engaged with religion in that they were studying Christianity, and dialectical theologians pointed out that the object of their study was the word of God, not man-made religion. Where teaching posts for history of religions were nevertheless created, there followed the long and arduous task of determining whether they should be assigned to the faculty of theology or philosophy. The literature produced on this question will amuse the non-German reader, especially when he learns that the final decision was *not* made exclusively on the basis of such theoretical considerations, but rather in terms of the particular candidate, the available funds, and the like. The teaching posts for religious studies, then, are in one of these two faculties and occasionally are even shifted from one to the other. Moreover, both kinds of doctorates are conferred in religious studies: Dr. theol. or Dr. phil. (along with the major subject there are two minors, one of which is, if possible, philosophical-historical). For a short time after World War II Marburg offered the degree of Dr. scient. rel., but only a few such degrees were conferred, and after a short time, in view of the kind of theoretical considerations sketched above, the degree was discontinued.

It seems clear that a number of problems connected with these studies, as well as the *Religionswissenschaftler's* flair for pseudo versatility in many disciplines, must disappear as soon as a new division and definition of the humanities can be decided on. Their present structure, inherited from the turn of the nineteenth century, is in any case creaking in all the joints. The problematical pattern of graduate studies in religion is therefore closely bound up with the tasks of reform in higher education in general, which result on the one hand from the inadequacy of the self-contained bodies of knowledge in the traditional academic disciplines and, on the other hand, from the necessity of making the latter relevant to a changed social situation beset by gigantic problems. With respect to the situation in Germany, the reform of graduate studies in religion has two aspects: (1) the reform of theological studies in a narrower sense; (2) the conceptualizing and justification of religious studies in a wider sense within and/or outside the study of theology. Both aspects were recognized and were being given some attention before the student revolution.

e. Information about the reform efforts and their results is relatively accessible (see bibliographical note); thus little needs to be said about them here. The reform of theological study calls for more attention to pedagogy, psychology, the social sciences, church law, ecumenics, and even *Religionswissenschaft,* the latter not only in connection with missiology but apart from it as well. This calls for a reduction of the material to be covered in the classical theological subjects and, concomitantly, the development of new methods for practical learning. This entails a restructuring of studies, with new divisions (such as basic, major, and graduate studies), more frequent written and oral examinations, more and smaller seminars, and fewer lecture courses. Also envisaged are more opportunities for the training of religion teachers in faculties other than theology (as up to now, for instance, in Frankfurt and Saarbruecken). That would give recognition to such study as having a value of its own and free it from the onus of being just a stepsister. The significance in this respect of the study of non-Christian religions has already been discussed. The related necessity of studying sociology and psychology of religion has been recognized of late even in fields which have nothing to do with the education of pastors or teachers. In Cologne, for example, sociological research has increasingly stressed sociology of religion, with its own theoretical rationale and freed from indentured service to ecclesiastical sociology on the one hand and to Marxist critique of religion on the other.

These examples illustrate that more is involved in reform than a reordering of course content and sequence. The question of social relevance which was posed by the repeated efforts to establish methodologically specific learning goals has also changed the images of the professions and thus led to frequent new attempts to restore an educational unity between theory and practice. With that the division of the classical educational programs, including theology, into study and practice (for example, as student teacher or intern) loses its meaning, and the classical concept of education as simply transmitting knowledge loses its function. In place of the latter comes the idea of learning through research.

The content of this research comes into being less by the ideally complete mastery of a given body of knowledge and more in reference to specific projects, and in one's profession is not basically different than in research and study. A consequence of these insights and changes is that those with a higher education are more pervious to each other, not only as individuals, but as a group, to nonacademics and workers. This could have a variety of consequences for graduate study in religion, some of which can already be seen. For example, our world, historically speaking, is secularized, and yet innumerable social subsystems repeatedly take on religious dimensions, however one may define religion. The dialectic of secularization is thus a phenomenon for religion scholarship; yet it cannot be isolated as such, but rather permeates at least the premises of almost all fields of knowledge and asserts itself at every stage of a path in which theory (including research in religion) and practice, one's study and one's profession, are intertwined.

These are some of the problems of reform, and the student revolution is seeing to it that they are not forgotten. There is need for a separate study of how—under, alongside, and against—the "theology of the study of theology" there could develop in a number of quarters another theory whose opposition to the official views attains an intensity and consistency not found in any other disciplines in the German *Hochschulen*. Even the most revolutionary student of English literature or of mathematics—however much he may urge different methods, new themes, and a concept of vocation more oriented to social change or revolution—still wants to study what now, and occasionally earlier as well, deserves the name of English literature or of mathematics. But there are students of theology who say that they would not have matriculated for the study of theology except that in this way one can exert pressure at that place where society is most vulnerable to overthrow, namely, the church. Or they pass off as theology something quite different from what one otherwise understands by the term.

Whatever the particular nuances, it is presumably generally agreed that theology is grounded in continual, radical reference to the original datum of Christian faith, the revelation of God in Jesus Christ, and that as a discipline theology has as its object of investigation its own premises. Further, in fidelity to the church and its confession, on the one hand, and in critical tension with them, on the other, theology reflects on the word entrusted to the church, both interpreting it and spelling out its present applications in an ongoing debate with the world and its organs of opinion.

In contrast, what many a revolutionary student understands by theology is something like this: The indulgence of the natural sexual drive would imperil the existing power structure, for a sexually uninhibited person admits of no restraints in other areas of his life. Therefore the ordinance of private property was invented and supplied with sanctions: the sexually omnipotent father figure who inherits and bequeaths property; monogamy (or at least monandry) by which the father guarantees the biological descent of his heirs and controls their number; the superego by which external authority is interiorized. From the superego developed belief in God, and capitalistic society allotted to the church the task of inculcating such belief. By providing metaphysical sanctions for sexual morality, the church exploits the neurotic structure of sexually inhibited mankind, thus concealing the church's social, political, and economic function and disarming rational critique. The task of theology is to unmask the church's true role, and the study of theology sets students free from all sexual and social restraints so that they may in turn free others from their enslavement. If professors of theology do not seek the same goals for students, the study of theology must be organized without, and if necessary against, them. To this end strikes, campus takeovers, and psychological measures against authoritative representatives of the theology of the ruling class (for in truth that is the ruling theology) are to be employed to get free classroom space and financial aid, with which may be purchased, *inter alia*, an adequate supply of texts basic to the study of theology so conceived. These consist of writings of Marx, Engels, Freud, T. Reick, Fromm, and above all Wilhelm Reich.

The students can actually illustrate from their own lives and from an impressive body of pamphlets and tracts how the application of sexual and other repression led to the origins of religious piety as a psychic disposition. There is no point in suppressing or manipulating such student movements, even though they probably are not strong enough to command much attention. They call for changes based on student motivations which theology and *Religionswissenschaft* have not acknowledged as yet, but must acknowledge if they want to retain their credibility. The needed reform may be achieved through existing institutions or methods or with the aid of new ones, but old and new must be flexible enough to be used in various combinations to meet new and unexpected needs and problems that may arise. One may expect that even within a few years graduate studies in Germany, including those in religion, will look quite different than they do today.

BIBLIOGRAPHICAL NOTE

Paul Wernle. *Einführung in das theologische Studium*. 3rd, rev. ed. 1921. Probably the best treatment of the period before World War I.
Martin Doerne, editor. *Grundriss des Theologiestudiums*. 3 vols. 1948–1952. Represents the period between the wars and immediately thereafter.
Walter Baetke. *Aufgabe und Struktur der Religionswissenschaft*. Part 3, pp. 206–228. An excellent statement of the distinctive character of *Religionswissenschaft* vis-à-vis theology.
Wolfgang Hermann and Gerd Lautner. *Theologiestudium: Entwurf einer Reform*. 1965. Articulates the growing discontent of students and offers proposals for reform.
H. E. Hess and H. E. Tödt, editors. *Reform der theologischen Ausbildung*. 7 vols. to date. 1967 ff. Essays by students, professors, church officials, and others.
Carsten Colpe. "Bemerkungen zu Adolf von Harnacks Einschätzung der Disziplin 'Allgemeine Religionsgeschichte,'" *Neue Zeitschrift für Systematische Theologie und Religionsphilosophie*, VI (1964), 51-69; "Die Funktion religionsgeschichtlicher Studien in der evangelischen Theologie," *Verkündigung und Forschung*, XIII (1968), 1–12. The difficulties Germans experience with respect to *Religionswissenschaft* and an attempt to stake out a legitimate theological position for the discipline.

G. Lanczkowski. *Religionswissenschaft als Problem und Aufgabe*. 1965. Parallels the preceding, but focusing on the problem of the exclusiveness of Christianity. Kurt Rudolph: "Die Problematik der Religionswissenschaft als akademisches Lehrfach," *Kairos*, XI (1967), 22–42. Points to theological adulteration of *Religionswissenschaft*. Both Lanczowski and Rudolph cite extensively from earlier writers from Scandinavia, Western Europe, and English-speaking countries, including an article by J. M. Kitagawa (*Journal of the American Academy of Religion*, XXXVI [1968], 191–202) which is well known in Europe and has helped to demonstrate that both here and in the United States the problems are beginning to be assessed in the same way and that in both places the solution seems equally remote.

3. GRADUATE WORK IN RELIGION AND THEOLOGY IN BRITISH UNIVERSITIES[1]

By Ninian Smart

Over twenty universities in the United Kingdom have faculties or departments of theology or religious studies and the like. Where there are faculties, as in Oxford, Cambridge, London, ancient Scottish universities, and elsewhere, there is usually some church connection, and traditionally a large number of of those reading degrees have been ordinands. Departments of theology or religious studies exist in a number of secular universities, such as Birmingham, Leeds, Lancaster, Exeter, and so on. Occasionally, as in Glasgow and Aberdeen, there are a faculty of theology and a department in the faculty of arts. The wide variety of arrangements means that in order to discuss postgraduate studies in the United Kingdom, some disentangling of types of graduate work and of the rather confused nomenclature of degrees is necessary.

First, there are research degrees (the years typically needed to complete these are given in brackets), such as the Ph.D. [3+], M.Litt. or M.Phil. [2], and M.A. [1+]. Some cases of the B.D. (as at Birmingham, Oxford, and Cambridge) are essentially research degrees. Second, there are graduate degrees by course work and short dissertation: the M.Th. [1+] and M.A. [1]; and others by course work wholly—typically in specialized diplomas—for example, the Diploma in Pastoral Studies [1]. Third, there are postgraduate degrees which are essentially second first degrees in type, notably the B.D. as traditionally taken in Scottish universities (though some are now introducing B.D. as a first degree). The Diploma in Theology at Birmingham also has this character, being in substance a shortened version of the B.A. in Theology. Such second first degree-type courses are normally designed for ordinands and are most typically found where there are theological colleges, either as part of the university or closely associated with it. However, since these are in essence like first degrees, I shall not further consider them here, as an anatomy of them would more probably belong to a description of first degree syllabuses (see my article, Smart, 1970).

The variety of institutions means a variety of ethos. However, until relatively recently the predominant investment in theology and religion was in biblical

[1] The present note is not intended to be comprehensive. Also curricula and institutions are changing all the time in the United Kingdom universities and thus it is not even easy to guarantee continued accuracy. I have made some use of the article by Burge (1965) and of statistical material collected by my colleague Dr. E. J. Sharpe.

studies, patristics, and church history. The concept of the department of religion, as in the American style, is quite recent, and most universities which have departments of theology or biblical studies do rather little work in such fields as the comparative study of religion, sociology of religion, or even often philosophy of religion.

The M.A./M.Th. type of degree, mainly by course work, is designed typically to supplement work undertaken in the first degree and to encourage more specialization. This type of degree has become more popular in recent years, and there is some evidence of a trend toward the relatively underdeveloped fields mentioned above—partly because those who teach in schools or colleges of education need a knowledge of these fields, partly because of some dissatisfaction among both educationalists and students with traditionalist emphases. The specialized diplomas mentioned earlier tend to cater for ordinands or already ordained persons, usually on an ecumenical basis.

Regarding research degrees, it needs to be pointed out that quite a lot of work on religion is done outside theology/religious studies departments/faculties. Perhaps as much as 20 percent of research theses concerned with religion listed by ASLIB (Association of Special Libraries and Information Bureau, 3 Belgrave Square, London, S.W.1.) in the last few years are completed outside theology/religious studies. For example, there has been a notable growth of work in the sociology of religion. Much of this has concerned the study of sects, partly because of the influence of Brian Wilson at Oxford and of David Martin at the London School of Economics. (See Martin, 1968, 1969, 1970.) On the other hand, almost nothing has been done in the psychology of religion, apart from a fairly flourishing investment in developmental psychology, especially that of Piaget, as applied to religious education (probably the most up-to-date bibliography in this field and one which describes a lot of Ph.D. and similar work is Lupton, 1970).

Within the theology/religious studies departments/faculties, there has been a considerable growth in research theses since Burge's survey of higher degrees completed between 1952 and 1962 (Burge, 1965). During that period the universities with the largest graduate schools in religion/theology were Edinburgh, Oxford, London, and Cambridge. However, at least three other universities in England now have moderately strong graduate schools, which have developed in the last few years, namely, Leeds, Birmingham, and Lancaster. Glasgow, Aberdeen, and St. Andrews in Scotland also traditionally have a reasonable number of Ph.D. students. Nearly all the universities with theology/religious studies have some research students. The fact that some of the major civic universities (together with Lancaster, the only new university which has a fairly large department—Sussex and Kent have three people each teaching the subject) have an interest in the history of religions other than Christianity and to some extent in sociology of religion means that there is some shift from the pattern of postgraduate studies evident in 1952 to 1962.

Then, as Burge's analysis shows, the strongest investment, as far as research theses went, was in biblical studies, church history, and theological thought, with an astonishing number—over 20 percent—of all Ph.D. theses being biographical ("The Life and Times of . . ."). In addition to increased work in the history of non-Christian religions and in phenomenology and sociology of religion, there is also much more being done than before in philosophy of religion. In the period after the war until the early 1960's, very few theses indeed were written in philosophy of religion. The reason was partly to do with the biblical and ancient historical emphasis of many department and faculties; partly to do with the gap between continental theology and linguistic analysis as practiced in Britain; and partly because of a relative lack of interest in philosophy departments in this field. Thus, one can detect a shift in the pattern of graduate work which reflects shifts, too, in undergraduate curricula. It is worth noting in this connection that an increasing number of those who engage in postgraduate work in religion have no formal ecclesiastical connection. This may accelerate the changes mentioned because of the fact that the candidate is the most important factor determining the area of study, as we shall see in a moment.

Because in secular universities the assumption has been that theology is more or less identifiable with Christian theology (on the whole Anglican and Protestant), there has been until recently relatively little concern with Jewish and Roman Catholic studies. It is rare in departments of theology/religious studies to find Jews or Catholics teaching. This is one of a number of ways in which the pattern of studies and of research is still influenced somewhat, though much less so than previously, by the ecclesiastical tradition in the United Kingdom.

Evidence appears to show that the topics of research theses in most cases result directly from choices made by the candidates. That is, there is relatively little pressure to gear reseach to the interests of the supervisor or of the department or of some group in the department. In this respect postgraduate research in religion and theology differs considerably from the pattern in the sciences and to some extent the social sciences. There is a problem here, for it may well mean that important areas of investigation are left underdeveloped. The principle of the candidate's choice is, of course, a good one in many respects, but it certainly may combine with patterns of curriculum in slowing down the development of important new areas of research.

It is also noteworthy that a considerable amount of research conducted for degrees is done at a part-time basis. It is not possible to arrive at accurate statistics, but perhaps as many as 40 percent of those registered for graduate work in religion/theology are part-time. There is a considerable wastage among such candidates. They tend to be teachers, parsons, and lecturers in colleges of education and have difficulty in maintaining the time and tempo for research in the circumstances of their full-time jobs. Nevertheless, it is often stimulating for the individuals concerned to be carrying on with higher degree work. One reason for the number of part-time people is that in general there is a strong drive toward graduate work in a situation where there is very little finance for full-time graduate students. Although universities may have some studentships and occasionally employ such devices as tutorial fellowships (involving some teaching) to help people who wish to take Ph.D.'s and so forth, the vast majority of graduate students in the United Kingdom are supported directly by the state. Typically they have studentships provided by the Department of Education and Science (the old Ministry of Education); the competition for studentships in the humanities is great. Only rarely is it possible for a postgraduate course in religion/theology to be recognized by the Social Science Research Council. It is true that a number of educational institutions, such as colleges of education, are often willing to second people for a year; but the bulk of graduate students doing research require, of course, a longer period. The difficulty of obtaining finance is indicated by the fact that at Lancaster, for example, graduate applicants to the Department of Religious Studies number about one hundred per annum, of whom at least 90 percent could be admitted, from the point of view of their having adequate qualifications—normally an upper second-class honors degree or its equivalent; but of these only about 15 percent succeed in gaining finance for further study, and some of this is provided by private savings. The restriction of finance in the United Kingdom, together with other factors, is one reason why quite a high proportion of graduate students (for instance, in Edinburgh, Oxford, Cambridge, and Lancaster) are from overseas. Other factors are Commonwealth arrangements—thus some Commonwealth universities second lecturers to do Buddhist, Islamic, and other studies in the United Kingdom— and also the fact that the cost of living and of fees remains relatively cheap in the United Kingdom compared with the United States and Canada. Some universities, notably Edinburgh, maintain continuing contact with the continent of Europe, notably Germany—although it must be said that both for the linguistic reasons and other reasons, there is much less exchange of a postgraduate kind between departments of religion/theology in the United Kingdom and institutions in Europe than might seem desirable.

The regulations of different universities vary considerably, so that in some universities one cannot proceed to a higher degree in theology unless one has a first degree in that subject. This occasionally can lead to serious problems; I recall, for instance, that the Board of Studies in Theology at the University of London refused admission to a brilliant Israeli student who had in fact studied Jewish and Islamic literature and theology, on the grounds that he did not have a first degree in theology (that is, Christian). Regulations have altered since that time at London. On the other hand, most departments of theology/religious studies would accept people with first degrees in other subjects, such as history, where they are appropriate to the projected research. To some extent also, the M.A. degrees by course work serve as bridges from other disciplines into religion/theology. The possibility of such crossings over is, of course, in fact logical because the divisions between departments are often quite artificial (the British practice in this matter is a good deal more rigid and problem-creating than the United States practice). There is certainly a strong trend at present for those who have done work in sociology, history, and philosopy to wish to do work on religion at the postgraduate stage. This is quite a desirable trend, in that such candidates are well equipped in method, and this is important if fields such as philosophy of religion and the sociology of religion are not to be treated in a somewhat amateurish fashion. The trend also, it may be noted, runs parallel to the interest in religious matters displayed among undergraduates where religion is not treated dogmatically or from a narrowly ecclesiastical point of view.

The moves can go in the opposite direction also. Thus, at the undergraduate level it is not usually feasible for people to tackle the relevant languages in the history of religions. Undergraduate courses on Islam and Buddhist history, for example, do not normally require Arabic, Sanskrit, Pali, and so on. However, a person with a good training in religious studies can proceed fruitfully to learn an appropriate language at the graduate level and to study in a more specialized institution such as the School of Oriental and African Studies in London.

Although the United Kingdom is a small country, it remains notoriously difficult to discover fully information about what is happening in the subject. There is as yet no coordinating body, such as exists in America, and there is little in the way of a common strategy in regard to the development of religion/theology. Thus, although the quality of British graduate work in the subject is fairly high, not enough is done to exploit the results of research and to exchange relevant information. As for the future, it is to be hoped that some moves can be made in this direction and that somebody may get around to codifying the information about research work and more general graduate studies in the United Kingdom. What appears certain is that the volume of graduate work will continue to increase and that there will be greater investment in modern studies and in what may be generally called the "scientific study of religion."

4. THE STUDY OF RELIGION IN DUTCH UNIVERSITIES

By D. J. Hoens[1]

Religion is studied in the faculties of theology, arts, and social sciences at six universities in the Netherlands. Four of these universities are state schools (Leiden, Groningen, Utrecht, and Amsterdam), one is Protestant (the Free University of Amsterdam), and one is Roman Catholic (Nijmegen). Much of the work in the history of religions and the phenomenology of religion in the Netherlands has been done by scholars in the faculties of theology in the four state universities. Here, too, the prospective ministers of the Dutch Reformed, Lutheran, Remonstrant, and Mennonite churches have traditionally received their theological training, which includes study not only of their own religion but of others as well and of religion as a phenomenon. Thus for the *candidatus* degree (comparable to the American B.D.) students take three years

[1] Many colleagues have provided information for this report, but I am especially indebted to J. Platvoet and J. D. J. Waardenburg, who collaborated in the writing. The report does not pretend to be exhaustive. Since programs in several universities are presently in flux, some of the information may be dated when it appears. The following provide further information: Van Proosdij, 1970; Schreuder, 1970; Waardenburg, 1971–1972.

of courses in history of religions and phenomenology of religion and must pass examinations in these areas.

Dutch universities offer two graduate degrees: that of the *doctoral examination*, which is taken at least two years after the *candidatus* examination, and the *doctor's degree*, for which no special courses are required, but a dissertation suitable for publication is prepared. Since the time when the study of religion (*Religionswissenschaft*) was introduced as a distinct discipline in the theological faculties, a distinction has been made between such study and theology proper. Our report deals primarily with *Religionswissenschaft*.

Graduate students in religion generally study in faculties of theology, but some are found in the arts or social science faculties where they are enrolled in departments such as oriental languages, literature, and culture, or sociology or psychology of religion. A number of graduate students in the theology faculties also take courses in the arts and social science faculties that treat various aspects of religion. Work in the social sciences has become increasingly important, especially in the study of living religions. Students who specialize in a particular religion have heavy language requirements. Those who specialize in phenomenology of religion devote more attention to methodology, but must also be able to use the sources of at least one religion in the original language. Undergraduate preparation includes courses in the history of living and ancient religions, in phenomenology of religion, and perhaps in cultural anthropology, psychology of religion, and so forth. A look at some of the salient or distinctive features of graduate programs in religion in the several universities will illustrate some of these general remarks.

a. The theological faculty of the University of Leiden has pioneered in giving recognition to new disciplines. In 1876, the first chair in the history of religions in the Netherlands was established in this faculty. The first incumbent was the noted scholar G. P. Tiele. In 1948 the professorship was divided into the areas of living religions and religions of antiquity. (The same division has been made in the Universities of Utrecht and Amsterdam.) In 1946, the first Dutch chair in sociology of religion was constituted in this faculty, and in 1953 the first Dutch appointment was made in psychology of religion.

Doctoral students in the theological faculty who specialize in a particular religion are required to master the necessary languages (Sanskrit, Arabic, and the like). Those who concentrate on religions of nonliterate people prepare by doing work in cultural anthropology. In the arts faculty the university has long offered programs in oriental and African languages, literatures, and cultures, and the religious aspects of non-Western cultures may be studied in these programs. There are chairs in Egyptology, ancient Mesopotamian studies, Chinese and Japanese studies, Islamics, Buddhology, and Asian and Southeast Asian (Indonesian) languages, literature, and history. In the social sciences faculty, religion may be studied in the context of cultural anthropology and of sociology of the non-Western world. There are chairs for regional studies of Southeast Asia, Africa, and Latin America.

b. At the University of Groningen the study of religion in the theological faculty is defined as a cultural study, and much attention is paid to the development of the social sciences. The university's recently created Institute of Iconography is distinctive. In the doctoral program in the theological faculty, students study two classical or oriental languages, or one such language along with cultural anthropology, plus methodology and phenomenology of religion. For students planning to teach in religious or secondary schools the university offers a special graduate program in *Religionswissenschaft*, with history of religions as a minor.

c. Doctoral programs in the faculty of theology at the University of Utrecht are of two types: one for students who intend to pursue careers in scholarship and the other for students who are preparing to teach religion in secondary schools or for mission work.

In the first type students who specialize in a particular religion spend three years in language study and take seminars in which the sources are read in the original languages and seminars in phenomenology of religion. Students specializing in phenomenology of religion have a two-year seminar in the subject and another in a research topic in the field. They must be able to work with the original sources of one religion.

Students in the second type of program participate in seminars on phenomenology of religion, on special research topics, and on topics approached from the perspectives of several disciplines (see below). Literature on methodology and sociology and psychology of religion is also studied.

Sociology and psychology of religion have recently been added to the study of religion in the faculty of theology. The integration of these fields in the *candidatus* program for history of religions and phenomenology of religion is in preparation.

The doctoral student may also study religion outside the theological faculty. The Oriental Institute in the arts faculty offers programs in Indian history and culture, including religion. The languages necessary for studying Hinduism and Buddhism are also offered in the institute. In the social sciences faculty a chair in cultural anthropology has been established, and the student may here study anthropology of religion.

An interesting feature of the doctoral programs in religion at Utrecht is the interdisciplinary seminars. One that is offered, on the position of women in Islam, brings together professors and students of sociology, Arabic, and history of religions. Another, on Geo Widengren's *Religionsphänomenologie*, includes representatives from theology, cultural anthropology, and sociology. Other seminar topics include the sociology of religion of Peter Berger, religious community, and relationships between Muslim and non-Muslim communities.

d. Given the University of Amsterdam's location in a large city, the theological faculty not unexpectedly pays close attention to the social sciences and applies sociological method especially to the study of living religions. A special feature of the doctoral program is the seminar in analysis of myth using the method of structural anthropology.

In the arts faculty one of the professors from the theological faculty offers a course in Buddhism. Egyptian religion is studied in Egyptology courses and the religions of South Asia and Southeast Asia in courses on the languages, literatures, history, and culture of these regions. Religious texts are read in Arabic courses offered in the Institute for the Modern Near East.

An exchange program with the faculty of theology at the Free University of Amsterdam enables graduate students in the two schools to enroll for courses in the other school. Students in the Roman Catholic theological school in Amsterdam receive instruction in psychology and sociology of religion in their own institution, but take courses in the history of religions and phenomenology of religion in the faculty of theology at the University of Amsterdam.

e. At the Free University of Amsterdam an Institute for the Study of Religion was established in 1971, in which the faculties of theology, arts, and social sciences collaborate. Special attention is paid to the encounter of Christianity with other religions and to the problem of dialogue with them. The faculty of theology at this Protestant university has adopted the methods of study of the state universities. This means, *inter alia*, that the history of religions and phenomenology of religion are independent disciplines and required of all theology students, whereas formerly these were subjects treated in courses in natural theology, philosophy, or mission.

Although other possibilities are open, the graduate programs in the theological faculty generally are of three types: (1) *Religionswissenschaft* as the main field, (2) missiology as the main field with *Religionswissenschaft* as a minor, (3) systematic theology and philosophy as the main field with *Religionswissenschaft* as a minor.

f. In the Roman Catholic study of religion a number of changes have taken place in recent years. The various seminaries in the country have been consolidated into four theological schools ("Theologische Hogescholen"). As in the Free University of Amsterdam, the pattern of study in these is now like that in the state universities. In the University of Nijmegen the graduate programs in religion are characterized by interdisciplinary work. Students in the faculty of theology are encouraged to combine the historical and philological approaches with those of the social sciences. And in the faculty of social sciences the sociological approaches to religion are set in the wider context of the sociology of culture and must be combined with the study of the history of religions and of the history of culture. Psychology of religion is studied in conjunction with the psychology of culture, which is a comparative study of the cultural conditions of both individual and mass psychological phenomena in Western and non-Western societies.

In the faculty of theology the traditional program has included history of religions (specifically Indian religions and Islam), phenomenology of religion, philosophy of religion, theology of religion, and theological hermeneutics. The student may specialize either in history of religions or in phenomenology and philosophy of religion. In 1969, however, a new kind of program was inaugurated in which students do group research on selected topics. In the 1969–1970 academic year, for example, the group applied Lévi-Strauss's structural analysis of myth to Ceylonese folk tales. In 1970–1971 they studied the relation between Hinayana Buddhism and "popular religion" in Ceylon. The application of the methods of structural and social anthropology to the study of Ceylonese religion has necessitated reflection on problems of methodology and philosophy of religion, especially since the group intends to apply these methods in the field work it plans to undertake. In addition to their cooperative work the students in this new program take courses in the traditional program noted above. The group will prepare a joint research paper as one of the requirements for their degree.

In the graduate programs in sociology and psychology, in the faculty of social sciences, empirical study of religion plays an important role. Students in the sociology program who specialize in the sociology of culture and religion or the sociology of church and religion do field research in these areas, alongside their course work in psychology of culture and religion and history of culture and religion. Students in the psychology program who concentrate in psychology of culture and religion likewise do field research alongside seminars and workshops.

In the theology (as distinct from religion) graduate programs in the faculty of theology, students are required to take courses in *Religionswissenschaft*, in the sociology or psychology of religion, and so on. Students in liturgy, for instance, study religious rites from the perspectives of the history of religions and phenomenology of religion. Those in systematic theology, moral theology, and ecumenics do work in the psychology of religion, and those in missiology take courses in sociology and psychology of religion.

5. GRADUATE EDUCATION IN RELIGION IN THE SCANDINAVIAN COUNTRIES

By Per Erik Persson

Some features of graduate education in religion are common to all the Scandinavian countries. In all of them such education is connected primarily with the theological faculties of state universities: Copenhagen and Aarhus in Denmark, Helsinki and Turku in Finland, Oslo in Norway, and Lund and Uppsala in Sweden. Degree nomenclature is also uniform, the "Candidate of Theology" (in Sweden "teol. kand.—examen," in Denmark and Norway "cand. teol.—examen") designating the degree required as a basis of graduate study, and "Doctor of Theology" (in Sweden "teol. dr.," in Denmark and Norway "dr. teol.") designating the highest degree. These purely external similarities apart, there are wide differences in the degree programs. Only in Finland and Sweden does one find an organized program of graduate education after the "teol. kand.—examen." In Denmark and Norway there are no courses or specific seminars for students working for the "dr. teol." degree, the rationale being that the scholarly training required for higher degrees is attainable only through individual, independent achievement.

Though the point of departure for graduate studies in each of these countries is the Candidate of Theology degree, even this does not denote exactly the same thing. In Sweden, following the latest curriculum revision (1969), the candidate certificate means that the student has normally studied in the theological faculty about four years. In Finland somewhat more time may be required. In Denmark and Norway, however, the student may spend six years or more meeting the minimum requirements. The shorter period of time in Sweden results primarily from reduction of requirements in biblical languages in comparison with the other countries.

There are also differences regarding the subjects studied in the undergraduate program. All the faculties mentioned have Old Testament and New Testament exegesis, church history, dogmatics (sometimes combined with symbolics), and ethics (usually combined with philosophy of religion); but in Sweden and Finland history of religions (including psychology of religion) and practical theology are also part of the studies leading to the candidate degree, whereas in Denmark and Norway they are not (history of religions can be studied only in the humanities faculties).

In all the Scandinavian countries history of religions (or comparative religions), dealing almost exclusively with non-Christian religions, can be studied on both the undergraduate and the graduate levels in most of the humanities faculties. At the undergraduate level it is combined with electives in other disciplines (such as language, philosophy, history, political science, and the like) for the degree of "fil. cand.—examen." What is said in the following paragraphs about study for a doctorate in theology applies also to graduate education in religion in the humanities with the difference that the degree awarded is the Doctor of Philosophy (in Sweden, "fil. dr.," in Denmark and Norway, "dr. phil.").

The title "Candidate of Theology" does not in itself say very much about the student's degree of preparation for graduate education. Great variations are possible. If a Danish or Norwegian theological student intends to do further research in some field in the range of the theological discipline, he—or she— usually starts doing some of the research already before completing the examination for the candidate degree. Every student is required to specialize in one of the traditional theological disciplines, but not all will attain a real scholarly level. If such is his intention, the time of study for the candidate is prolonged, sometimes up to eight or nine years. In Sweden and Finland, too, there may be great differences between students who all have the degree of Candidate of Theology. Within the various theological fields the student can choose among three different levels of study. The first usually gives an all-round orientation in a field, such as New Testament exegesis. The second and third levels require in addition more advanced and specialized knowledge, with the third including also a research paper of scholarly quality. The student who chooses the third level in one of the fields has to give about half a year or more than is normally required. In principle the student is free to try for honors ("Third Level") in all the fields of study, in which case his studies are prolonged accordingly.

The student who intends to go on to graduate study must receive Third Level honors in the field in which he plans to do his work.

Since 1955 the Danish faculties of theology have been offering another graduate degree in addition to the Doctor of Theology, namely, the Licentiate of Theology, which is open to highly qualified recipients of the candidate degree. The requirements are a thesis, which does not have to be printed, and a public lecture in the faculty of theology. The time spent in study is estimated at two years or more. During the fifteen years since the inauguration of the degree, almost no one has taken it, however, probably because it does not lead to anything: in Denmark a Doctor of Theology is entitled to give lectures and seminars in the faculty, whereas the Licentiate is not. The student who plans on an academic career goes directly for the doctor's degree. The same may be said with regard to Norway. The very few licentiate degrees that have been granted have usually gone to students whose dissertations had not been accepted for the doctor's degree.

Quite a number of students in Denmark have started careers through another Danish institution, the annual competition for the "gold medal of the university." The competition is open to students under thirty, who within the year write a research paper, usually not longer than two hundred pages, addressed to problems formulated by the theological faculty. A very good paper is awarded a gold medal or with mention in the annual of the university, which is looked upon as a great honor.

A Danish or Norwegian student planning to study for a doctorate in theology receives little or no guidance from his professors. He may receive a scholarship, but he is supposed to work on his own. Often he chooses to study in another country. When he has completed his dissertation and considers himself ready, he sends the thesis to the faculty, where a committee is appointed to judge its quality. If it is not approved, this is communicated only to the author. A thesis that is passed is printed and then debated at a public defense, two of the professors from the examining committee acting as opponents. In Norway, prior to the defense the candidate must also give two public lectures in the faculty, one on a subject chosen by the faculty and the other on a theme of his own choosing. At the annual university festival the candidate is then named Doctor of Theology, which carries with it the privilege of lecturing in the faculty if he so desires.

In contrast to Denmark and Norway, in Finland and Sweden we find planned and supervised programs of graduate education in the theological faculties. The basic pattern in both countries is the same, but in Sweden a quite new system was introduced in 1969. The old system consisted of two steps, the Licentiate of Theology and the Doctorate of Theology. This is still the system in effect in Finland. In Sweden it will continue alongside the new system until July 1, 1971, for the licentiate, and July, 1974, for the doctorate. We shall describe this two-step system first.

The licentiate in Sweden and Finland is both a terminal degree and a step on the way to the doctorate. (In this and other respects it differs from the Danish licentiate degree discussed earlier.) In order to be allowed to study for the licentiate degree in a certain field the student must receive his Candidate of Theology degree with Third Level honors in that field. If he plans to study in the exegetical disciplines he must also demonstrate First Level knowledge of the Greek or Semitic languages, adjudged according to the standards of the faculty of linguistics. Further requirements are, in all disciplines, the reading of a comprehensive list of scientific literature, on which the student is examined by the professor in several oral examinations, and in writing of a research paper of some hundred pages. (In the Finnish faculties the examination includes two different theological disciplines, one of which is then the principal area in which the research paper is written, whereas in Sweden the student studies only one such discipline.) The completed research paper is mimeographed (rather than printed) and is rated by the professor in the field on a scale from two to three, where three is top grade. The oral examination on the literature is rated in the same way. During the whole period of study, which usually lasts at least three years, the student is required to take active part in seminars held by the professor. In these seminars, drafts (or portions) of research papers are subjected to discussion and criticism similar to that given doctoral dissertations. The whole time the professor also gives personal advice and guidance to the student in his research.

A student may, if he wishes, conclude his graduate education with the licentiate. This is the degree required, for instance, for teachers in religion in the gymnasium (something between high school and college) of the Swedish school system. The student who has received his licentiate but wishes to earn the doctorate proceeds to the writing of the doctoral dissertation. Depending on the subject and other circumstances, this will usually take another two to four years. Often the dissertation is an elaboration of the paper for the licentiate degree, treating the subject in greater depth. Parts of the dissertation in progress are usually discussed in the seminars mentioned above, where the participants try to find the weak points, the idea being that the work is thus improved and the finished product will be better than if the author were left totally on his own, as in Denmark, for example. Of course, the student is himself ultimately responsible for his work. When it is finished it is printed and publicly defended, a lecturer in the faculty usually serving as one of the opponents. The dissertation is not rated by the professor alone this time, but by the faculty as a whole, on a scale from one to three. The degree is awarded at a graduation ceremony at the end of the academic year where the new doctor of theology receives his hat, ring, and diploma as tokens of his new status. Only the best dissertations give their authors the right to lecture in the faculty, an authorization that is recognized by the title "Docent."

This type of graduate program guarantees a highly qualified doctorate. Its weakness has been that it has taken perhaps too much time—the two steps together some seven or eight years of hard work. If the student has had to do other work alongside his research in order to support himself and his family, even more time was required, and the student did not receive the degree until he was in or beyond middle age.

This and other reasons are behind the radical reform of the programs of graduate education in all faculties of the Swedish universities that was instituted in July of 1969. The requirements with regard to the basic candidate degree are the same as before the reform, but the course of subsequent graduate study has been remarkably changed. The licentiate degree has been totally abolished and a new pattern introduced that combines elements from the two earlier steps in the old system. If the student devotes full time to working for the doctor's degree he will, under this new plan, acquire it in four years instead of seven or eight. This means that the amount of work is more than was demanded for the licentiate degree in the old system, but far less than was necessary for the old doctorate. From the old program leading to the licentiate the new system has taken over the mastery of a comprehensive biblography; this is supposed to take one and a half to two years and is tested, as previously, in oral examinations. The remainder of the four years is given to work on the dissertation, which is intended to be less voluminous than those written under the old system (some 160 printed pages are paid for by the university against 320 pages formerly). Quality does not always follow quantity, and a smaller work can offer a very good specimen of research. The new system retains the public defense of the dissertation against an opponent appointed by the faculty. However, the rating assigned to the dissertation is now given, not by the faculty as a whole, but by the student's professor and examiner, and there is no gradation in ratings, only passed and not passed.

Another characteristic of the new system is that the amount of instruction has increased. Now not only drafts and portions of theses are discussed in seminars, but difficult parts of the literature in the field as well. Special courses in methodological problems of the disciplines are also offered, and heavy emphasis is laid on the guidance of the individual student.

In 1970, a Finnish government committee proposed a graduate program for all faculties along the same general lines of the new Swedish system of 1969. As of this writing (January, 1971) it was uncertain if and when the program would be introduced in the universities.

9

Undergraduate Studies: Growth and Redirection, 1950-1970

Of decisive importance for the state and prospects of any kind of graduate education in religion is the remarkable development and transformation of undergraduate religion programs since World War II. In spite of the useful body of literature that has appeared to describe and interpret these changes, no comprehensive account has been given.[1] Thus for the present study, without attempting to duplicate the earlier works, we undertook an inclusive survey of the undergraduate scene in order to have at hand relatively complete and reliable information.

As noted earlier (Preface), from a population of 1,311 accredited four-year institutions of higher learning in the United States and Canada, 873 organized programs or departments of religion have been identified as existing in 1969–1970. To all of these programs, a seventeen-page questionnaire (based on a pre-pilot and a pilot study) was sent in the spring of 1970. By May 4, 1970, 592 questionnaires (68 percent) had been returned, and this date was taken as the cutoff point for initial computer processing. Of these responses, 404 indicated an undergraduate major or combined major in religion (for convenience referred to below as a "full program"), whereas 188 reported that no major in religion was offered. More detailed studies, bearing particularly on structure and curriculum, were made of the 404 full programs than of the partial programs.

Eventually, 654 responses (75 percent) to the main questionnaire were received and some of our studies, particularly relating to faculty characteristics, were made of this whole group. In addition, 114 replies were received to a brief follow-up questionnaire sent to all those who did not return the main question-

[1] See the Bibliography, notably the following: Holbrook, 1963; Ramsey, 1965; Michaelsen, 1964 (New Haven) and 1965; Hartzell and Sasscer, 1967; McLean, 1967; Spivey, 1968; and Ramsey and Wilson, 1970. Michaelsen's 1965 study provides particularly useful detailed information on the history and character of religion programs in ten major universities.

naire, and information from these responses has been used in a few summary
tabulations.[2]

1. THE PRESENT SCENE

How far has the "quiet revolution" gone? By 1969-1970, nearly all the accredited four-year institutions of higher learning in the United States and Canada were offering courses in religion. As we noted, approximately two-thirds of those schools had established a special program of religious studies. And of the 873 with a program or department, about two-thirds offered an undergraduate major in religion.[3] The two factors most highly associated with the presence of a religion program are religious affiliation and institutional quality.

a. Religion Programs and Institutional Affiliation

Religious affiliation is plainly the most important factor accounting for the presence of departments of religious studies, though the study of religion is also significantly, even if not yet massively, established in public higher education. Figure 9–1 shows the proportions of public, private nonsectarian, Roman Catholic, and Protestant colleges and universities with a religion program in 1969–1970 (either full or partial).

It is not surprising that the vast majority of both Protestant and Roman Catholic institutions have programs in religious studies. These emerged first in church-related institutions. What is striking is that by the end of the 1960's almost half of the private nonsectarian schools and 30 percent of the public institutions had some formal program for the study of religion.[4]

[2] The distribution by religious affiliation, by size, and by geographical location of the respondents to the main questionnaire was closely parallel to that of the whole population (873) of institutions initially reporting a program. Thus no important sources of bias seem to be present in the 25 percent nonresponse.
  Since several categories of response have been used in tabulations, we shall, where important, identify them in the tables as follows:
  Data Base A = the screening questionnaire identfying 873 programs among the 1,311 four-year institutions.
  Data Base B = the 404 full programs responding by May 4, 1970.
  Data Base C = all 654 programs responding to the main questionnaire.
  Data Base D = the 114 schools returning the brief follow-up questionnaire.
[3] I am here extrapolating (*a*) from the fact that of 768 schools from which we have definite information concerning the type of program, 532 offer an undergraduate major, and (*b*) from evidence that the general character of the nonreporting institutions is like that of the 768.
  For comparison, it may be noted that according to a listing undertaken in 1971 by the American Philosophical Association, there were between 850 and 900 institutions in the United States and Canada with either a philosophy department or at least one faculty member teaching philosophy full-time.
[4] To this we may add that of 311 junior colleges responding to the screening questionnaire, only 65 reported no offerings in religion. A special program in religion was reported by 137, and various courses by another 109.

FIGURE 9–1

PERCENTAGES OF FOUR-YEAR INSTITUTIONS, UNITED STATES AND
CANADA, WITH RELIGION PROGRAMS, 1969-1970

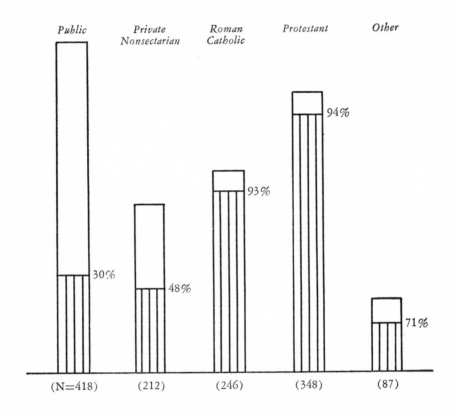

NOTES: The column labeled "other" includes not only institutions with other religious
affiliations but also 33 schools whose affiliation was not reported.

Data Base A (1,311 institutions)

As might be expected, religion programs are more likely to be found in liberal arts colleges than in teachers colleges or technical schools. Programs are also more numerous in geographical areas where church-related institutions are most concentrated. Nevertheless, such programs are more the norm than the exception in virtually all parts of the United States and Canada. In the United States the percentage of institutions having a religion program is highest in the North Central region (74 percent), followed by the South Atlantic (68 percent), Extra-Continental United States (67 percent), Middle Atlantic and South Central (62 percent each), Pacific (57 percent), Canada (53 percent), New England and Mountain (46 percent each).

The distribution of undergraduate religion programs by size of institution can be summarized as follows, in Table 9–1. Again, the variation is probably not in-

TABLE 9–1

SIZE OF INSTITUTION IN RELATION TO RELIGIOUS STUDIES PROGRAMS

Number of Undergraduates	*Percentage of Institutions With Program* %
750 or fewer	70
751–1,250	76
1,251-2,750	64
Over 2,750	50
	(Data Base A)
	(N=1,287)

dependent of religious affiliation, since the public universities tend to be the largest.

Religious affiliation of an institution is in a somewhat different way a factor in determining whether a religion program includes an undergraduate major. For the 812 institutions with a program in 1969–1970, where religious affiliation was reported, Table 9–2 shows the distribution of types of programs.

TABLE 9–2

TYPE OF RELIGION PROGRAM BY INSTITUTIONAL AFFILIATION

	Public %	*Private NonSect.* %	*Roman Catholic* %	*Protestant* %	*Other** %
Undergraduate Major	35	62	39	81	84
No Major	59	30	44	11	8
No Information on Type	6	8	17	8	8
	100	100	100	100	100
No. of Institutions	(127)	(103)	(230)	(326)	(26)

*Mostly religiously oriented schools, including Jewish and nondenominational Protestant. (Data Bases A, C, D.)

Important variations are evident in this distribution. The high incidence of religion programs in Protestant-related institutions is paralleled by the high proportion with an undergraduate major. In Roman Catholic institutions, however, religion programs have been largely of a service character, often with religion requirements. Only a minority of Roman Catholic institutions offer a religion major, and, as we shall see, this is a recent innovation for many of them. Undergraduate instruction in religion in the Catholic liberal arts colleges has been offered traditionally to provide basic grounding in religious teaching for the laity. Extended studies in religion and theology were carried on largely in special seminaries directed to the training of clergy and members of the religious orders. Also it was traditionally assumed that philosophical studies might most properly come at the undergraduate level, with theological studies being developed in subsequent education.

Private nonsectarian institutions, in the establishment of religion programs, have moved rapidly to make them parallel to the undergraduate majors offered in other departments, though on the whole the establishment of religion programs in private nonsectarian schools has come later than in religiously related institutions. Likewise, public institutions have been the most recent to establish religion programs and have thus been still slower in moving to the establishment of a major.

b. Religion Programs and Institutional Quality

Second to religious affiliation, *the presence of a religion program is most strongly associated with the academic quality of the institution*; the higher the quality, the greater the likelihood of there being a program in religion. This appears from two comparative studies we have made, one using Cass and Birnbaum's ratings of institutions according to selectivity in admissions (in relation to 1,240 of the institutions in our population), and the other using the resource index score developed by George Nash in his description of 1,444 four-year institutions.[5]

[5] Cass and Birnbaum, 1969; Nash, 1969.

(*a*) The Cass and Birnbaum index categorizes colleges as "selective," very selective," "very (+) selective," "highly selective," and "among the most selective in the country." These categories, according to the authors, are "based on statistical and other factual information: the percentage of applicants selected by the college, the average test scores of recent freshmen classes, the ranking of recent freshmen in their high school classes, and other related data that measure the scholastic potential of the student body." Some institutions of widely acknowledged high quality are not given a ranking because information was not made available. Plainly the Cass and Birnbaum index is not intended as a total measure of academic quality or educational accomplishment. But equally plainly it is an important index, since the scholastic capability of students is a major determinant of the nature and quality of educational experience.

(*b*) Nash describes the resource index score in the following way: "Although it takes into account a number of resources that might be presumed to be useful in imparting an education, it tells us nothing about the academic level of the students or the job actually done by the college. . . . Schools that score high on the index are colleges of high prestige: Amherst, Princeton, Stanford, Vassar, Yale and so forth. Colleges generally regarded as being low prestige do not usually score high on the resource index and conversely highly regarded colleges do not often score low . . . .

"The five items included in the resource index are the following:
"1. The proportion of faculty holding the doctorate
"2. The faculty-student ratio

Table 9–3 shows the percentages of institutions having various types of under-graduate programs in religion in relation to the ratings of selectivity in their admission of undergraduates. It is evident that the more selective institutions are more likely to have undergraduate religion programs: 79 percent of the schools in the top selectivity groups have a religion program, whereas only 57 percent of the unrated schools do so. Further, there appears to be a strong correlation between selectivity and the likelihood of having a full program of religious studies as compared with a partial program. This general correlation with selectivity is also related, of course, to the lower incidence of religion programs in public institutions, which are less likely to be rated as selective than are private institutions.

TABLE 9–3

COLLEGE PROGRAMS IN RELIGION IN RELATION TO SELECTIVITY
IN ADMISSION OF UNDERGRADUATES

	Most Selective Very Selective Highly Selective	Selective	Not Rated
	%	%	%
Schools With Full Program	45	33	24
Schools With Partial Program	12	17	14
Program Not Specified*	22	22	19
Total Schools With Religion Program	79	72	57
Schools With No Program	21	28	43
	100	100	100
	(N=246)	(N=263)	(N=731)

*I.e., these institutions did not respond to the main questionnaire.

"3. The total educational and general income per student
"4. The number of library volumes per student
"5. The total number of volumes in the library.
"Each of the institutions was assigned a separate decile score from one to ten on each of the five items on the index. The following procedure was used. The colleges were ranked from the highest to the lowest on number of library books per student. The 115 colleges in the top decile each had more than 123 books per student. The number of books in each library was based on the figure from the Office of Education. All students, graduate and undergraduate, full and part-time, were included in the denominator. Those colleges in the 9th decile have between 84.5 and 122.9 books per student. The 112 colleges in the lowest decile each had less than 18.3 books per student. The colleges in the top decile were given 10 points—those in the lowest decile one point. The same procedure was repeated for each of the other four items. . . .
"The range of colleges on the resource index is from a low of 5 to a high of 50. The distribution of 1,444 colleges and universities is as follows:
"1) Thirteen percent scored 40 or above. For the purpose of this analysis they are considered high resource index score colleges.
"2) Twenty-six percent fall between 30 and 39 and they have been classified as having an upper-middle resource index score.
"3) Forty percent of the colleges are classified as having lower-middle resource index scores because their scores range from 20 to 29.

A comparable, even stronger result emerges when Nash's resource index is used as a measure of institutional quality. Table 9–4 shows the relation between scores on the resource index and the presence or absence of a program of religious studies for all 834 institutions that appear in Nash's list and ours.

TABLE 9–4

RELIGION PROGRAMS IN RELATION TO THE
RESOURCE INDEX SCORES OF INSTITUTIONS

Type of Program		Resource Index Scores		
	High	Upper Middle	Lower Middle	Low
	%	%	%	%
Full Program	53	40	28	19
Partial Program	6	13	15	16
Program Not Specified	26	22	28	14
	—	—	—	—
Total With Program	85	75	71	49
No Program	15	25	29	51
	—	—	—	—
	100	100	100	100
	(N=177)	(N=218)	(N=327)	(N=172)

Higher rankings on the resource index score are strongly correlated with the likelihood of having an undergraduate religion program. Furthermore, high rankings are correlated with presence of a full program in contrast to a partial program. It is not surprising, of course, that institutions with high rankings on the resource index score are more likely to have organized programs of religious studies, since institutions with greater resources are able to support more kinds of academic programs. This qualification having been made, however, the conclusion may be properly drawn from both the resource index scores and the selectivity ratings that programs for the academic study of religion have received a notable degree of recognition among the colleges and universities of highest quality.

2. PATTERNS OF EXPANSION

a. Establishment of Religion Programs

How shall we date the origins of religion programs? At least three indices are useful: the date of the first full-time faculty appointment in religion, the time of initial establishment of a specific program of study, and the date of the organization of the present structure of the department or program. Of the first two of these, the former is probably a more important indicator of institutional commitment to a program. Hence to plot the chronology of program development, in-

"4) Twenty-one percent of the colleges were classified as having low resource index scores because they scored between the minimum of 5 and 19."

While the index does not necessarily describe the situation at any individual institution, it is an index of resources in relation to size of school, i.e., per student, and is thus one genuine measure of quality. Of the 1,311 schools on our list, 834 were included in Nash's list with ratings. The over-all distribution of the 834 schools among the four categories parallels almost exactly the distribution in the Nash sample.

formation was sought particularly on the date of the first full-time appointment
and on the origin of the present structure.

Table 9–5 shows the relation between religious affiliation of an institution and
the period of the first full-time appointment in institutions with a full program.
(Such information was recorded for only 280 of the 404 full program institutions
in Data Base B.)

TABLE 9–5

INSTITUTIONAL AFFILIATION IN RELATION TO THE
TIME OF FIRST FULL-TIME FACULTY APPOINTMENT IN RELIGION

(By Percent of Institutions With Full Programs, 1969–1970)

Year of First Full-Time Appointment in Religion	*Institutional Affiliation*			
	Public	*Private* Nonsectarian	Catholic	Protestant
	%	%	%	%
Before 1909	3	26	13	47
1909–1940	7	18	49	34
Since 1940	90	56	38	19
	100	100	100	100
	(N=29)	(N=50)	(N=55)	(N=146)

Protestant-related institutions were the first to have full-time faculty in religion, almost half having made their first full-time appointment before 1909.
Roman Catholic institutions came next (most of them were later in establishment), with half the Catholic schools making their first full-time appointments
between 1909 and 1940. Fifty percent of the private nonsectarian institutions
and 90 percent of the public institutions have made their first full-time appointment since 1940.

The development of religion programs in public institutions is even more recent than Table 9–5 shows. A fuller account of the public sector is given in Figure 9–2, based on information available from 96 of the 127 four-year public
institutions in the United States and Canada having religion programs in 1970.
(These include both full and partial programs.) Figure 9–2 shows the cumulative growth and dramatically exhibits the explosive nature of the expansion during the past decade. The date of origin is calculated either from the time of the
first full-time appointment or the establishment of the program, whichever was
earlier. As noted earlier in this report, a major turning point in the development
in the public sector, though by no means the whole explanation, was the United
States Supreme Court decision in the Schempp case (1963).

b. Enrollment Growth

It has been widely held that undergraduate enrollments in religion have increased at a much more rapid pace than enrollments in other areas of study in
the post-World War II era. In order to test this assumption we sought information on total undergraduate enrollments and enrollments in religion courses for

FIGURE 9-2

DATES OF ORIGIN OF RELIGION PROGRAMS
IN 96 FOUR-YEAR PUBLIC INSTITUTIONS

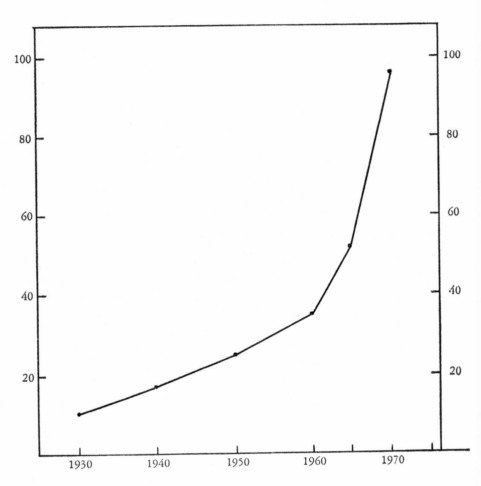

NOTES. Programs established 1930 or earlier: 10 (especially in Southern universities)

1931 – 40	7
1941 – 50	8
1951 – 60	10
1961 – 65	17
1966 – 70	44

This summary includes both full and partial programs.

the fall terms in 1954, 1959, 1964, and 1969. The state of college and university enrollment records, together with the human failings of questionnaire respondents, makes information of this sort notoriously difficult to obtain. We have, however, apparently reliable data for the fifteen-year period on a representative group of 167 Roman Catholic, Protestant-related, and private nonsectarian institutions, plus a further body of information on 38 public institutions for the period 1964–1969.

The patterns of increase reveal strikingly divergent trends in different kinds of schools. These divergencies are shown in Table 9–6 and Figure 9–3, which compare enrollments in undergraduate religion courses with total undergraduate student bodies for the fifteen-year period 1954–1969 in Roman Catholic, Protestant-related, and private nonsectarian institutions. (Public institutions are left aside for the moment, since religion course enrollment data prior to 1964 are too scanty to be useful.)

TABLE 9–6

ENROLLMENTS IN UNDERGRADUATE RELIGION COURSES
IN RELATION TO TOTAL UNDERGRADUATE STUDENT BODIES
FALL TERMS 1954–1969

	1954	1959	1964	1969	Increase 1954–1969
A. *104 Protestant-related Institutions*					%
Number of Undergraduates ____	78,250	94,933	117,467	137,932	75
Religion Course Enrollments ____	25,704	30,915	37,232	39,438	53
Ratio of Religion Enrollments To Total Student Body _____	33%	32.6%	32%	29%	
B. *36 Roman Catholic Institutions*					%
Number of Undergraduates ____	33,173	41,048	52,510	60,265	82
Religion Course Enrollments ____	22,767	29,886	33,649	29,915	31
Ratio of Religion Enrollments To Total Student Body _____	69%	73%	64%	50%	
C. *27 Private Nonsectarian Institutions*					%
Number of Undergraduates ____	52,001	58,301	67,254	77,098	48
Religion Course Enrollments ____	3,798	4,986	5,871	8,523	124
Ratio of Religion Enrollments To Total Student Body _____	7%	8.6%	8.7%	11%	

Table 9–6 also shows the approximate ratios of the numbers of students taking religion courses to the total student body at the different times. These are only approximate, since the figures for religion enrollments represent registrations in courses, and some individual students will be counted twice or more. On the other hand, the numbers of religion majors are in most instances relatively small, the great majority of undergraduates studying religion taking only one course at a time. In any case the differences among the types of institutions are clearly revealed (and the comparison of rates of change is not affected). Vastly larger

FIGURE 9-3

RELATIVE RATES OF GROWTH: TOTAL UNDERGRADUATE ENROLLMENTS
COMPARED WITH REGISTRATIONS IN RELIGION COURSES

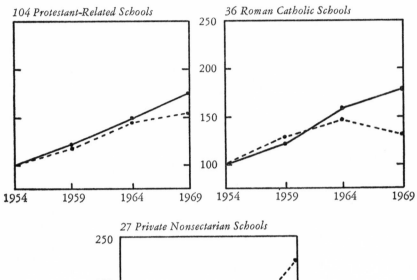

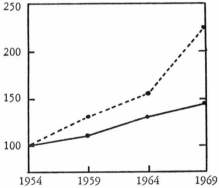

NOTES. Base year 1954 = 100.
●————● Total number of undergraduates.
●– – – –● Total registrations in undergraduate religion courses.

proportions of the undergraduates in the church-related institutions are at any given time enrolled in religion courses, due perhaps in large part to religion requirements. In private nonsectarian institutions, the proportion is much smaller, though it is still striking that by 1969 approximately one out of every nine or ten students in these twenty-seven institutions was taking a course in religion.

Figure 9–3 presents more graphically the same relative rate of growth of registrations in religion courses compared with total undergraduate enrollments, using 1954 as the base year ($=100$).

The patterns of change in the different types of institutions are radically different. In *Protestant-related* institutions, registrations in religion courses have increased over the whole period, but at a slower rate than the total student bodies, especially between 1964 and 1969. In *Roman Catholic* institutions, religion course registrations increased slightly more rapidly during the first five-year period, then more slowly than the total undergraduate student bodies between 1959 and 1964, and then dropped absolutely in the last five-year period, to a total almost exactly equal to that of 1959.

In other words, for both kinds of religiously oriented institutions, registrations in religion courses have declined relative to the total growth of the institutions. One explanation for these relative declines is plain: the elimination or drastic reduction of religion requirements, particularly in many Roman Catholic institutions after the Second Vatican Council. For example, in 1959, twenty-two of the thirty-six Roman Catholic institutions showed 90-100 percent of the student body enrolled in religion courses and another nine had over 50 percent, whereas a decade later only six enrolled 90-100 percent and only five others enrolled 50 percent or more. Several dropped from 100 percent to less than 20 percent of the student body enrolled in religion courses.[6]

It is equally important, however, to note that in spite of the reduction of requirements, religion enrollments have often continued to climb. Even the overall decline in Roman Catholic colleges between 1965 and 1969 is relatively modest compared to the sharp decrease in enrollments in some language courses in the two years between 1968 and 1970, following the extensive elimination of requirements in foreign languages.[7]

[6] Altogether we have records of 172 institutions that have abandoned or reduced requirements in religion (compared with 218 that have maintained a constant requirement, 19 that have increased, and 242 that have never had any requirement).

[7] A survey of foreign language enrollments at 153 institutions, reported in the *Chronicle of Higher Education*, January 11, 1971, p. 3, showed the following changes:

Language	1968	1970	% Change
French	33,547	28,492	−15.1
German	15,717	13,553	−13.7
Italian	2,312	2,476	7.1
Russian	3,279	2,407	−26.6
Spanish	29,523	28,784	− 2.5
Latin	3,881	2,669	−31.4
Greek	1,479	1,152	−22.1
Other	1,705	2,091	22.6

Both Tables 9-6 and Figure 9-3 also show, however, that in *private nonsectarian* institutions the enrollments in religion courses have increased much more rapidly than the total student bodies, particularly between 1954 and 1959, and again even more between 1964 and 1969. During the former five-year period, religion course registrations grew over twice as rapidly as the total student population; then during the third five-year period religion course enrollments grew three times as rapidly as the student bodies as a whole.

Here we begin to see that the relative growth of undergraduate religion enrollments is a phenomenon especially of private nonsectarian and public education and that it is to be particularly located in the period since 1964.

Table 9-7 documents this growth with respect to four-year public institutions in the United States and Canada. The increase in religion course enrollments has been nearly triple that of the increase in total undergraduate population. The proportion of students taking religion courses remains smaller than in private nonsectarian institutions, but has increased relatively more rapidly between 1964 and 1969. (Compare Table 9-6).

TABLE 9–7

ENROLLMENTS IN UNDERGRADUATE RELIGION COURSES
IN RELATION TO TOTAL UNDERGRADUATE STUDENT BODIES
1964–1969

25 Public Institutions With Religion Programs Established Prior to 1964*

	Fall 1964	Fall 1969	Increase
Total Number of Undergraduates	169,300	262,900	55%
Religion Course Enrollments	5,697	14,373	150%
Ratio of Religion Enrollments To Total Student Body	3.4%	5.5%	

*Of these twenty-five institutions, twenty showed an increase in the proportion of students enrolled in religion courses, two declined (Michigan State and East Texas State), and three remained the same (though two of these, Iowa and Western Michigan, already enrolled 10 percent and 9 percent of the undergraduates, respectively). An additional thirteen public institutions, with programs established after 1964, reported 6,151 students enrolled in religion courses in the fall term, 1969 (3.9 percent of their total undergraduate enrollment of 158,627).

Related changes have taken place in the numbers of undergraduate religion majors graduated between 1964 and 1969. Although for all types of schools, the number of majors has increased, the most rapid growth is to be found in the public and in the Roman Catholic institutions. The increase in public institutions is, of course, directly related to the establishment of programs and the rapidly increasing registrations in religion. The sharp increase in Roman Catholic colleges, in spite of the decline in religion course enrollments, reflects the transformation of undergraduate religion departments. General service programs, with several courses required of all or many students, often with no undergraduate major offered, have been changed into elective programs parallel to other departments and majors. While in all types of institutions, religion departments tend to be service departments, with the bulk of their enrollments coming in a few courses from students who take an elective or two out of general interest, it is also evident that the undergraduate major in religion has become a live option for undergraduates in every type of institutions.

What are the reasons for the rapid growth in religion enrollments in public and in private nonsectarian institutions? No extensive studies are available, but the few samplings that have been made, along with the informal reports of religion faculty, indicate that this is not a function of a resurgence of religion in any ordinary sense. Most students taking religion courses report themselves as being moderately or casually religious, although many of these are in some state of revolt against their religious backgrounds and welcome the possibility of a serious study of religion free from authoritarian pressures. It is noteworthy that the major expansion of religious studies in public institutions has coincided with a decline in institutional religion.

"Intellectual curiosity" is by far the dominant reason students give for enrolling in religion courses, according to informal polls conducted at the University of California, Santa Barbara, and at the University of Iowa (Michaelsen in McLean, 1967). The third and fourth most frequently cited reasons[8] were the search for meaning in life and desire to learn more about one's own religious tradition. All three of these motivations are related to the serious-minded and deeply troubled character of the undergraduate generation of the 1960's and 1970's. To these students, religion courses seem to provide an opportunity to study questions of morality and meaning, to deal with "real issues" rather than with only a highly technical skill or language. In some instances the role formerly played by philosophy and literature has been assumed by the study of religion.[9]

c. Growth in Faculty

Has faculty expansion kept pace with the increases in undergraduate religion

[8] The second most common reason was the need to meet an academic requirement. The large "Religion in Human Culture" course at Iowa counted toward a general education requirement.

[9] Spivey, 1968, gives this account: "Two comments about the reason why students study religion are in order. First, in the rapidly changing world where traditional values and institutions, such as the church and the home, are losing their influence, then it is natural that the university should become a place where values, meaning, and purpose are both questioned and pursued. Moreover, the educational model adopted by much of the university avoids the 'big questions' in the interest of solving littler ones. The scientific model, which stresses precision and exactness, has invaded such traditionally humanistic areas of study as literature and philosophy so that often the only place where students can ask and ponder the 'big questions' is the religion department—'Now that philosophy has become analytical and literature courses are often technical, courses in religion offer a privileged neutral opportunity for studies in the comparative interpretation of basic human values like freedom, love, justice, and openness.' [Michael Novak, "Christianity Renewed or Slowly Abandoned?", *Daedalus* (Winter, 1967), p. 259.] A second, related comment is that the study of religion thrives best when religious life falters. When the church and synagogue are weak, then religion study will be strong because people will be questioning and thinking about traditional religious roots. There is, then, some basis for concluding that today's students are primarily motivated to study religion for academic reasons because when they are done, they are likely to be no more committed than before; yet they will have a better understanding of the nature of commitment."

enrollments? The answer is mixed. Table 9-8 shows that since 1954 growth of faculty in religion programs has been most rapid, as might be expected, in public and private nonsectarian colleges and universities. Religion faculties in church-related institutions have expanded more slowly.

TABLE 9–8
RATES OF FACULTY GROWTH (FTE) IN RELIGION PROGRAMS
IN 423 COLLEGES AND UNIVERSITIES, 1954–1969
(By Affiliation of Institutions)
(Base Year 1954=100)

Type of Institution	Fall 1954	Fall 1959	Fall 1964	Fall 1969	(Total FTE 1969)
Public (N=37)	100	123	178	260	(174.0)
Private Nonsectarian (N=72)	100	121	146	183	(361.0)
Protestant-related (N=205)	100	116	142	165	(949.5)
Roman Catholic (N=90)	100	120	136	155	(611.5)
Other (N=19)	100	111	134	172	(106.0)

NOTE. Data Base C. Of the 654 schools, 423 reported religion faculty sizes for 1954 and following. These include both "full" and "partial" programs. In this sample, both public and Roman Catholic institutions are underrepresented, relative to their proportions in the universe of institutions presently having religion programs. Compare Figure 9–1. Public colleges are underrepresented because of the relatively recent origin of many of their programs (thus no faculty figures could be given for 1954). Roman Catholic colleges are underrepresented because of a lower response rate.

Even though the sample of institutions in Table 9-8 is larger than those in Tables 9-6 and 9-7, the rates of growth in religion faculties may usefully be compared with the rates of increase in undergraduate religion enrollments presented in those tables. It is noteworthy that Roman Catholic religion faculties have continued to increase, even though enrollments in religion courses actually fell between 1964 and 1969. Religion faculty in Protestant-related institutions seem to have grown at a slightly more rapid rate than religion enrollments in those institutions.

In both public and private nonsectarian institutions, however, it appears that faculty expansion has not kept pace with the increase in undergraduate religion enrollments, particularly during the period 1964-1969. In private nonsectarian institutions, religion course enrollments increased by 45 percent between 1964 and 1969, while the number of faculty increased only 25 percent. In public institutions, religion enrollments increased by 150 percent, whereas Table 9-8 shows an increase in religion faculty of only 50 percent between 1964 and 1969.[10] A review of the present sizes of religion faculties in relation to enrollments shows that the day is almost past for the department of one or two faculty members, often part-time and nearly always expected to teach all aspects of religious

[10] This comparison may actually understate the disparity somewhat, since a study of faculty expansion simply in those public institutions for which religion enrollment data, 1964–1969, are available indicates an increase in religion faculty of only 46 percent, compared with the 150 percent increase in religion course registrations. (See also Table 9-10, below.)

studies. This is especially true for institutions offering a major. Information from 430 such schools indicates that while 42 had only two faculty members and 4 somehow managed with only one, 69 of the departments had more than ten members on the staff and the largest had thirty-six. Yet relative to enrollments, religion faculties remain modest in size, with the median number of faculty for full-program departments being 5.7 (for partial programs the median was 4.2). Table 9-9 indicates the over-all distribution of department sizes for 633 schools in relation to the types of program.

TABLE 9–9

RELIGION FACULTY SIZE IN RELATION TO TYPES OF PROGRAMS

FALL, 1969

Number of Faculty	*Numbers of Schools*			
	Full *Program*	*Partial* *Program*	*Not* *Classified*	*Total*
More than 20	13	1	0	14
16–20	16	2	1	19
13–15	16	2	3	21
11–12	24	5	2	31
9–10	28	11	1	40
8	26	10	0	36
7	28	12	1	41
6	49	8	2	59
5	51	16	1	68
4	80	29	5	114
3	53	29	0	82
2	42	29	2	73
1	4	28	3	35
Total:	430	182	21	633

(Data Base C)

An inspection of the student-faculty ratios make clear that there is a deterioration with increase in size. Table 9-10 shows the range in the number of students registered in religion courses per faculty member, the mean average, and the ratio in the median institutions for 227 institutions from which appropriate data were available. The ratios are calculated from total undergraduate registration in religion courses for the fall term 1969, in relation to full-time faculty equivalents (each part-time faculty member being counted as one-half). The ratios do not, of course, indicate class sizes, since each full-time faculty member presumably was teaching two or three or perhaps more classes. But they do indicate the average number of students in religion courses for which each faculty member was responsible. The very small departments (those with fewer than 125 students) should perhaps be ignored in this comparison, since these often represent either new programs or very small institutions. But it is important to note that the average faculty member in institutions with religion enrollments greater than 1,020 was teaching twice as many students as his counterpart in departments with enrollments between 125 and 252. Over-all, as enrollment increases, so does the ratio of students to faculty. It also appears that instructors in public institutions,

TABLE 9–10
RATIOS OF ENROLLMENT TO FACULTY IN RELIGION DEPARTMENTS,
FALL 1969

Departmental Enrollments	Range	Student/Faculty Ratios Mean	Median
Over 1,020			
Public (N=10)	54–300	118	147
Private (N=2)	102–162	142	
Catholic (N=11)	91–356	138	112
Protestant (N=9)	96–550	132	136
509–1,020			
Public (N=12)	83–278	126	118
Private (N=8)	29–191	71	86
Catholic (N=10)	71–214	94	86
Protestant (N=12)	70–183	109	129
253–508			
Public (N=11)	53–210	101	105
Private (N=16)	20–230	75	84
Catholic (N=8)	37-143	74	76
Protestant (N=48)	45-257	85	82
125–252			
Public (N=9)	51–111	62	67
Private (N=13)	38–100	60	57
Catholic (N=8)	26–111	52	53
Protestant (N=40)	21–189	62	66
0–124			
Public (N=10)	9–200	32	34
Private (N=10)	8–77	31	30
Catholic (N=5)	6–75	17	33
Protestant (N=19)	8–94	28	26

particularly in the middle enrollment ranges, have heavier student loads than their colleagues in other types of institutions.[11] Again, this reflects in part that faculty expansion in public institutions has not kept pace with increasing enrollments.

3. THE SHAPE OF DEPARTMENTS

Although undergraduate programs have not infrequently been started as interdepartmental majors, they have regularly moved to the status of separate departments or combined departments (most commonly with philosophy), or other distinct administrative and budgetary units. Among the institutions with an undergraduate religion major, 60 percent report having an independent department of religion, religious studies, or theology. Another 32 percent have a combined department of religion and some other discipline (usually religion and philosophy). Surprisingly, only 1 percent of the programs are organized as inter-

[11] With the exception of Protestant schools in the 509–1,020 religion enrollment range.

departmental. The others are offered in schools of religion in the college or university or in Bible colleges.[12]

An important structural consequence of the modest size of departments is a heavy involvement of religion faculty in administrative responsibilities, since one in five religion faculty members serves as chairman or director of the department or program in religion. (Data Base C = 654 programs.) Another fifth of the faculty, however, are involved in other major administrative responsibilities, either as chairman or director of another department in the college, or of undergraduate or graduate religion programs, or as the chairman or director of another undergraduate or graduate program, or as a general college administrator (7 percent of the faculty were reported as having general administrative responsibilities). Only slightly over half of all religion faculty have no administrative responsibilities.

The great majority of faculty members in all religion programs have full-time academic appointments: 81 percent of those in full programs, 69 percent of those in partial programs. For the full-time appointees the dominant pattern is that of appointment full time in a religion department (with over half the total faculty in this category). Joint appointments in religion and philosophy is the next most common pattern (12 percent in the full programs). A smaller number hold joint appointments with divinity school and graduate theological departments (7 percent). A sprinkling (about 2 percent each) hold joint appointments with history, social science departments, and language departments. Among the part-time faculty in full religion programs, nearly a quarter also serve as college chaplains and a slightly larger proportion serve as campus ministers, parish ministers, or perform other outside ministerial duties. The older common combination of teaching with college chaplaincy or outside ministry continues to be somewhat more prominent in institutions with partial programs.

4. FACULTY PROFILE[13]

a. Age

As Table 9-11 makes clear, *the relative ages of religion faculties dropped sharply during the 1960's*, a consequence doubtless both of the rapid over-all expansion of undergraduate education in the United States and of the recent development of many religion programs.

---

[12] These percentages refer to the 390 institutions which reported their organizational form, out of the 404 full-program schools in Data Base B. Only one institution reported that its undergraduate major was offered by a school of religion adjacent to the university, its work being accredited by the university. Such schools of religion are still fairly common, but they rarely offer undergraduate majors; hence they do not appear in this analysis.

[13] The following interpretations are based on a study of 3,809 faculty members in 633 institutions (with both full and partial programs). For each faculty member in the program, information was sought relating to: highest academic degree, highest "ecclesiastical" or professional earned degree, name of institution granting the highest degree, ordination, employment status in the college, administrative duties, academic rank, age, present area of specialization, area of graduate training, and prior affiliation. Of the 3,809 members studied, 2,858 were teaching in programs with an undergraduate major, 815 in partial programs, and the rest in unspecified programs.

184   UNDERGRADUATE STUDIES

TABLE 9–11
AGES OF RELIGION FACULTY, 1970 AND 1963

	1970		1963 (U.S.)	
Age	No.	%	Age	%
Under 21	3	*		
21–30	372	10	Under 30	4
31–40	1,455	39	30–39	31
41–50	1,088	29	40–49	26
51–60	593	16	50–59	28
Over 60	251	7	60 and Over	11
	3,762	101		100
				(N=2,148)

*Smaller than 0.1 percent. The 1970 data are from responses of 633 institutions to our questionnaires, the 1963 data from Silverman and Metz, 1970, p. 48.

The median age for all faculty in religion programs in 1970 was just over 40 —a figure that compares with the national United States average of slightly under forty in four-year institutions. The median age of religion faculty would probably be lower except for the traditional pattern of graduate instruction, which has included a professional degree program plus the doctoral program and has thus resulted in later entry into college teaching than in other departments in the humanities and social sciences. There are only slight variations in age ranges among types of institutions and programs, except that religion faculty in Canadian programs are definitely younger, with 58 percent of the faculty being forty or under.

b. Educational Background

The percentage of religion faculty with earned doctorates appears to be comparable to that in the higher-quality four-year college and university faculties generally (Table 9-12). Precisely parallel information for all college faculties is not available, but preliminary reports from the recent Carnegie Commission survey show the following approximate percentages of holders of the Ph.D. or other doctorate (not including the first professional medical degree or the Ed.D., but counting the Doctor of Arts or equivalent).

TABLE 9–12
PERCENTAGE OF DOCTORATES AMONG UNIVERSITY AND
FOUR-YEAR COLLEGE FACULTY 1969–1970

Percent of Doctorates

Universities
High Quality 62.0
Medium Quality 62.3
Low Quality 53.0
Four-Year Colleges
High Quality 59.5
Medium Quality 44.5
Low Quality 33.5

The earned degree status of all religion faculty (full- and part-time) in 633 institutions (both full and partial programs) is indicated in Table 9-13.

TABLE 9-13

EARNED DEGREES OF RELIGION FACULTY

Highest Earned Academic Degree	%
Ph.D.	44
M.A.	26
M.S.	2
B.A.	15
B.S.	3
None	10
	100
	(N=3,409)

Highest Earned Ecclesiastical Degree	%
S.T.D./Th.D./D.H.L.	25
M.S.T./S.T.M./Th.M.	11
Licentiate in Theology (Lic. Th.)	9
B.D./S.T.B./M.H.L.	29
M.A. in Religious Education	3
None	23
	100
	(N=3,078)

NOTE. In the case of both kinds of degrees the proportion of doctorates is higher for full-program religion faculty members than for partial-program faculty.

In order to get a true picture of the total proportion of earned doctorates, one must combine the Ph.D.'s with the "ecclesiastical" doctorates (Th.D./S.T.D./ D.H.L.). Of the 2,648 faculty members for whom information concerning *both* civil and ecclesiastical degrees is available, 1,109 hold the Ph.D., and 536 hold the Th.D., S.T.D., or D.H.L. (of whom 58, or 11 percent, also hold the Ph.D.). Thus for this population, which includes all types of four-year institutions and part-time as well as full-time faculty, the proportion holding at least one earned doctorate is at least 60 percent.[14]

With respect to the *Ph.D.* only, not unexpected patterns of distribution appear. The proportion of Ph.D. holders rises sharply with the selectivity of the institution; thus, from 35 percent in institutions rated "selective" to 65 percent in those rated "most selective." Among types of schools, public institutions have the highest proportion of Ph.D.'s (63 percent of their faculty), followed by private non-sectarian schools (55 percent) and Protestant-related institutions (54 percent). Catholic institutions have the lowest proportion of Ph.D.'s (24 percent), many

[14] The proportion in our total population is probably somewhat higher, since we know of 1,490 Ph.D holders and 753 faculty with an S.T.D., Th.D., or D.H.L. Assuming that no more than 11 percent of the latter also hold Ph.D's, and taking the larger number of faculty for which we have degree information (3,409 cases), it appears that approximately 63 percent of all faculty in these religion programs have an earned doctoral degree.

of the faculty holding S.T.D.'s. There is also a correlation between the size of the institution and the proportion of Ph.D.'s: the smaller the institution, the lower the proportion. Also, full-program institutions have a higher proportion of Ph.D.'s (46 percent) than partial-program faculties (34 percent).

Religion faculty have received their graduate training from a wide range of institutions, with a heavy concentration, however, in the traditional centers of theological study. The more than 3,300 faculty members for whom we have such information have received their graduate degrees from a total of 632 institutions. The major sources of highest earned degrees are indicated by rank order in Table 9-14. Those who have received their advanced training abroad studied mostly in Roman Catholic institutions (62 percent). Correlatively, nearly a third of the

TABLE 9-14

SOURCES OF HIGHEST DEGREES

Of 3,329 Faculty Members Teaching in Undergraduate Programs at 633 Colleges and Universities in the United States and Canada*

American and Canadian Institutions	Number	Percent
Yale University	176	5.29
University of Chicago	141	4.24
Catholic University of America	131	3.94
Harvard University	121	3.63
Boston University	103	3.09
Columbia University	95	2.85
Duke University	72	2.16
Union Theological Seminary	66	1.98
Drew University	57	1.71
Vanderbilt University	52	1.57
Fordham University	51	1.53
Princeton Theological Seminary	50	1.50
Southwestern Baptist Theological Seminary	46	1.38
Marquette University	42	1.26
Southern Baptist Theological Seminary	40	1.20
Princeton University	38	1.14
University of Southern California	37	1.11
Dallas Theological Seminary	37	1.11
Hebrew Union College	35	1.05
University of Ottawa	34	1.02
Concordia Seminary	33	0.99
University of Iowa	32	0.96
New York University	31	0.93
University of Notre Dame	31	0.93
Woodstock College	28	0.84
Northwestern University	25	0.75
Emory University	22	0.66
University of Pittsburgh	21	0.63
Claremont Graduate School	20	0.60
Saint Louis University	20	0.60
	1,687	
Others (464 Institutions)	1,148	34.48
	2,835	

Foreign Institutions

Gregorian University (Rome)	97	2.92
University of Edinburgh	30	0.90
Oxford University	25	0.75
Angelicum (Rome)	23	0.69
Fribourg	18	0.54
Louvain	16	0.48
	209	
Other Foreign Institutions (132)	285	8.56
	494	
	3,329	99.97

* For those faculty not holding an earned doctorate, the source of the highest professional degree was recorded.

faculty in Roman Catholic institutions received their highest training abroad as compared with 11 percent of the faculty in the public institutions, 12 percent in private nonsectarian institutions, and slightly over 7 percent for all other institutions. Slightly under 10 percent each of the foreign degree recipients are found in public and private nonsectarian institutions.

c. Ordination

In view of the close historical connection of undergraduate religion programs with church-related institutions, it is not surprising that the *majority of faculty are ordained* (70.9 percent of the 3,744 faculty members for whom information is available). The proportion seems to be very slightly higher in full programs than in partial programs (but see the qualifications below concerning faculty in Roman Catholic institutions). The proportion is somewhat lower among faculty who hold the Ph.D.; of these, 64 percent have been ordained.[15]

Among the analytic variables used in our study of undergraduate religion faculty, it is only program structure, selectivity, and religious affiliation of institution that show significant variations in the proportion of ordained faculty. "Schools of religion," either within or adjacent to universities, have the highest percentage of ordained faculty (82 percent and 95 percent, respectively) whereas interdepartmental programs have the lowest (42 percent)—though each of these two groups accounts for only 3 percent of all religion faculty. Departments and combined departments (such as religion and philosophy) are close to the over-all average (with 71 percent and 75 percent respectively). In the "most selective" institutions only 50 percent of the faculty are ordained (75 out of 151 faculty members), whereas in schools in the other selectivity categories the proportion of ordained faculty is close to the over-all average.

[15] This high over-all proportion of faculty who have been ordained correlates with the proportion of faculty holding a professional or ecclesiastical degree; of those faculty on whom definite information is available concerning both types of degrees (2,648 cases), 73 percent have at least one professional degree (S.T.D., Th.D., D.H.L., M.S.T., S.T.M., Th.M., Licentiate in Theology, B.D., S.T.B., M.H.L., M.A. in Rel. Ed.).

Religious affiliation of the institution is naturally the most important variable, with by far the lowest proportion of ordained faculty in programs in public non-sectarian institutions and the highest proportion in conservative Protestant institutions, as shown in Table 9-15. The proportion in private nonsectarian institutions (64 percent) is surprisingly large.

TABLE 9-15
PROPORTION OF FACULTY ORDAINED
IN RELATION TO RELIGIOUS AFFILIATION OF INSTITUTION

	Total No. of Faculty	% Ordained
Public	220	15
Private, nonsectarian	417	64
Roman Catholic	1,178	68*
Other	145	73
Jewish	38	74
Liberal Protestant	688	77
Conservative Protestant	613	83

* The percentage figure for Roman Catholic institutions may be misleading since a number of faculty members are nuns or members of religious orders who are not ordained to the priesthood.

d. Prior Affiliation

Faculty members have come to their present posts in about equal proportions from employment in another academic institution (34 percent) or from study in another institution (29 percent) or from nonacademic employment (27 percent). Again, the most important differentiating factor is the religious affiliation of the institution. Conservative and liberal Protestant institutions, along with those not classified, have a considerably higher proportion of faculty who have come to their present positions from nonacademic employment (45 percent, 33 percent, and 41 percent, respectively—as compared with a range of 17 percent to 21 percent for other types of institutions). Presumably these are faculty members who have come from parish responsibilities. Jewish institutions have an unusually high proportion (26 percent as against 1 percent to 6 percent for all other types) of faculty members who have come directly into their present teaching responsibilities from study in the same institution. Public institutions have the highest incidence of faculty who have come into the program from another department of the college (15 percent, as compared with the over-all average of 6 percent).

e. Fields of Specialization

Among the most important characteristics of undergraduate programs in religion are those disclosed by the varying competencies of the faculty. We asked two questions in this connection: what is the *present* primary area of specialization, and what was the field of graduate training of each member of the faculty? One choice was to be made in each case from a list of thirty-three fields. The list was deliberately skewed toward much finer distinctions in the area of Christian studies, since it was plain that the majority of faculty would be included here.

Table 9-16 indicates the distribution of faculty by fields, with the rank order being determined by the *present* primary area of specialization.

TABLE 9–16

FIELDS OF SPECIALIZATION OF RELIGION FACULTY

	Present Specialization		Primary Area of Graduate Training	
	No.	%	No.	%
Systematic Theology/Dogmatic Theology	476	13.0	612	17.7
New Testament	475	13.0	436	12.6
Old Testament	328	9.0	251	7.2
Ethics/Moral Theology/Social Ethics	298	8.1	192	5.6
History of Christian Thought/Theology	246	6.7	279	8.1
History of Christianity/Church History	191	5.2	200	5.8
Philosophy of Religion	190	5.2	172	5.0
History of Religions/Comparative Religion/Phenomenology of Religion	168	4.6	95	2.7
Religious Education	159	4.3	180	5.2
Philosophy	141	3.8	163	4.7
Judaica/Jewish History/Hebraic Studies	131	3.6	110	3.2
Religion and Literature/Theology and Culture	103	2.8	56	1.6
Religions of the East	72	2.0	33	1.0
Religion in America	72	2.0	53	1.5
Pastoral Theology/Homiletics	64	1.7	67	1.9
Sociology of Religion	57	1.6	41	1.2
Psychology of Religion	52	1.4	46	1.3
Ancient Near Eastern Religion	41	1.1	40	1.2
Liturgy	38	1.0	31	0.9
History	32	0.9	61	1.8
Literature	25	0.7	28	0.8
Sociology	22	0.6	26	0.8
Buddhism	22	0.6	14	0.4
Hinduism	21	0.6	17	0.5
Islam	18	0.5	13	0.4
Chinese Religion	14	0.4	10	0.3
Linguistics	14	0.4	18	0.5
Psychology	14	0.4	30	0.9
Education	13	0.4	44	1.3
Classics	12	0.3	21	0.6
Anthropology	11	0.3	11	0.3
Primitive Religion	7	0.2	2	0.0
Other	134	3.7	110	3.2
	3,661	100.1	3,462	100.2

It is evident from this distribution that the faculty resources are massively concentrated in the area of Christian studies, particularly theology and the history of Christian thought, the history of Christianity, biblical studies, and ethics. Furthermore, the general distribution among the several fields has not changed much between the graduate specializations and the present primary fields of activity. Equally important, however, are some noteworthy gains and losses in particular fields and changes between faculty members' areas of graduate training and their present specializations. A further analysis of the data in Table 9-16 shows that for the most part individuals have continued to work primarily within their fields of graduate specialization; specifically, in most of the fields cited, between 75 percent and 85 percent of the persons trained in the field are now specializing in it. Major exceptions, however, are found in the following fields: systematic theology, with only 63 percent of those with graduate specialization in this area being still considered as concentrating in it; the history of Christian thought, also with 63 percent; religion and literature and/or theology of culture, with only 55 percent; and pastoral theology, with 60 percent.

In systematic or dogmatic theology especially, there has been a large net loss: of 612 persons trained in the field, only 387 are identified as still specializing in it. These faculty have moved into a variety of areas, notably into ethics, but also significantly into theology and literature, biblical studies, history of Christian thought, and history of religions. The movement into theology from other areas has been small.

The most volatile field has been religion and literature/theology of culture— admittedly a loosely defined area. As we noted, only 55 percent of the persons with this as their primary graduate training field are still concentrating mainly in it, yet the area has had a relatively large gain in personnel. The consequence is that only a third of those now working primarily in the field have this identified as their area of graduate specialization.

Along with religion and literature, the fields with the largest gains, relative to the numbers with graduate specialization in the field, are: history of religions, religions of the East, and ethics. Of these, only in ethics can more than half of the present faculty be identified with graduate specialization in the same field.

We have from this study no information on the extent to which faculty transferring into new areas have received postgraduate training in them, though we know that in many instances this is the case. One factor in the movement is doubtless the frequent requirement on religion teachers, particularly in small departments, to work in areas beyond those in which they were specifically trained. More significant, we have one more clear indication of the growing importance, on the one hand, of the history of religions and religions of the East and, on the other hand, of ethics and "religion and culture." We also see in the whole spectrum of specializations those areas that are relatively weak in faculty resources (see also Table 9–18, below, describing the desired patterns of faculty expansion).

5. WHAT IS TAUGHT?

The patterns of faculty specialization are obviously related to the spectrum of the undergraduate curricula. Table 9–17 summarizes data from 358 institutions with an undergraduate religion major, indicating the total numbers of courses in each area offered by the whole group of institutions and the percentages of institutions of each type offering at least one course in the course areas designated.

Table 9–17 shows both the continuing heavy concentration on Christian studies in the undergraduate curriculum and at the same time a considerable variety. It is not surprising that in every type of institution, including public, Old and New Testament are the most widely represented courses. This category includes

TABLE 9–17

TYPES OF UNDERGRADUATE RELIGION COURSES OFFERED*

Percent of Institutions Offering
One or More Courses in the Area

Course Area or Title	Total No. Courses Offered	Public (N=36) %	Private Nonsect. (N=61) %	Roman Catholic (N=66) %	Protestant (N=195) %
Introduction to Religion	360	61	39	36	38
Old Testament or New Testament	1,368	72	85	74	76
History of Christianity or Christian Thought	531	33	49	36	78
Systematic Theology	307	29	26	51	31
Roman Catholicism	157	18	20	52	33
Protestantism	67	8	5	40	5
Eastern Orthodoxy	20	6	2	11	1
Judaism	146	39	30	30	16
Ethics	332	58	44	62	54
Contemp. Religious Problems/Thought	369	64	46	42	51
Philosophy of Religion	176	47	44	23	42
World Religions/History of Religions	279	45	49	35	61
Religions of the East (combined)	101	42	21	18	15
A Specific Eastern Religion	143	36	21	8	5
Islam	30	18	11	5	4
Primitive Religion	48	14	5	17	6
Religion and Society	83	30	11	12	14
Sociology of Religion	53	22	11	11	8
Psychology of Religion	74	25	13	15	17
Religion in America	179	42	46	23	34
Afro-American/Black Religion	34	8	10	6	6
Religion and Culture	90	39	15	11	13
Religion and Literature	81	36	16	18	14

* Summary based on reports from 358 institutions of the 404 in Data Base B. Each institution was asked to report how many courses were offered in 1969-1970 in each of the specified areas, counting each course only once, and assigning it to the area most appropriate. The column "Total No. Courses Offered" gives the combined total for all the schools. The percent columns show what percent of the institutions offered one or more courses of the types specified. Thirty-three institutions of various other religious affiliations have not been included in this tabulation.

specialized courses in the Old and New Testaments, hence the large total number of courses offered; but it does not include general introductions to Bible, which are offered in many of the institutions not having specific courses in Old Testament or New Testament.

The focus on Christian studies may also be partly represented in the wide frequency of courses on ethics and on contemporary religious problems or thought—though in both instances we also see evidence of the growing interest in problem-oriented courses. The history of Christianity or of Christian thought is widely represented in private nonsectarian as well as in church-related institutions. The percentage of Roman Catholic institutions offering such study appears to be low, 36 percent, but this is counterbalanced by the high incidence of courses in Roman Catholicism and in Protestantism. Similarly, the relatively low incidence of philosophy of religion courses in Roman Catholic institutions is counterbalanced by the much higher proportion of systematic or dogmatic theological studies.

The study of non-Western religions is obviously commonly represented in the form of a single course in world religions (or comparative religions or history of religions). Relatively little is offered in specialized and presumably advanced courses in religions of the East, either as a whole or individually, such as Hinduism, Buddhism, or Chinese or Japanese religions. Except for public institutions, only a fifth or fewer of the schools offer courses devoted specifically to religions of the East. Roman Catholic institutions have evidently been the slowest to introduce even survey courses in world religions, with only 35 percent having such a course.

Courses in the development of American religion have made their way quietly, though again more slowly in Roman Catholic schools, and the study of Afro-American or black religion has begun to appear.

Studies in Judaism are moderately well represented, except in Protestant institutions. It is astonishing, however, that so little is done with Islam (or, in the Christian orbit, with Eastern Orthodoxy).

Public institutions are also shown in Table 9–17 to have markedly different curricula from those in other types of schools. Public universities and colleges have most extensively devised special introductions to religion. They are as likely to offer courses in Judaism as in the history of Christianity or Christian thought (though the systematic study of Christian theology is also significantly represented in these institutions). It is in the public sector that the study of Eastern religions, both in summary form and in specific courses in the Eastern traditions, is most widely represented. Public institutions are also twice as likely as the other types to have courses in religion and society, in sociology of religions, in religion and culture, and in religion and literature.

6. IN SUM: THE CONTINUING REVOLUTION

If we turn now from the statistical survey of the immediate past and present and draw on other sorts of evidence, what are the principal directions of change emerging in undergraduate religious studies? I would group these into five categories.

a. Changing Goals in Undergraduate Religious Studies

A new conception of the purpose of the study of religion is evident in the rapid growth of programs in the independent and public colleges and universities. These are pluralistic in faculty, they have no intent to prepare students for clerical careers, and they eschew both evangelistic and pastoral goals. But comparable changes are going on in church-related institutions. In part, these are associated with the increasing secularization of private colleges. But even in institutions seeking to maintain close ties to the religious communities, the departments of "Theology" or "Religious Education" or "Bible," with their former confessional and/or professional orientation, are being transformed into programs that are at least transconfessional or ecumenical or pluralistic. Important differences do remain, of course. Religion department chairmen in colleges associated with Roman Catholicism or with conservative Protestant denominations, when asked to describe the aims of their programs, assign a relatively high importance to developing church leadership and commitment to a particular religious tradition, whereas chairmen in public and private nonsectarian institutions reject these goals.

Yet these differences should not be exaggerated. Plainly the direction of movement in programs in church-related institutions has been away from circumscription by the particular interests of the specific religious community, even though with considerable struggle, and toward a more inclusive view of religious phenomena. On the other hand, teachers in undergraduate programs in public and private nonsectarian institutions show signs of drawing back from the exaggerated postures of disinterested objectivity (or utter neutrality, or disinterested irreverence) which have led to fears of acknowledging any kind of commitment and to failure to teach students any principles of criticism for assessing commitments. The mere laying out of one fact after another, without any concern whatever for the norms and structures of meaning in religious phenomena, has been brought under severe attack by students who are more concerned with wisdom than with technical competence and who come to the study of religion because it necessarily involves the questions of priorities in life. Hence in nearly all types of programs we have surveyed, "development of concern for values" and "giving a sympathetic understanding of a wide range of religious traditions and cultures" rank equal in importance with "providing factual and analytical understanding."

b. Toward Eastern Religions

I have suggested that the attention presently given to non-Western religious traditions in undergraduate curricula may be called "tokenism," since half of the undergraduate programs give a nod in the direction of Eastern religions, but very few offer detailed work. On the other hand, 80 percent of the institutions offer courses in both Old and New Testament. This is not necessarily more Western-oriented than college curricula generally. European history and American history have tended to dominate the work of history departments, and I would not wish to reject the argument that the Western religious traditions have a certain claim to prominence in our educational scheme.

But obviously one of the strongest concerns in undergraduate religion programs in their study of religious traditions is to move further beyond the orbit of Judaism and Christianity. Table 9–18, compiled from responses to the question, "In what fields, in order of priority, would you consider it most desirable to make replacements or additional faculty appointments in the next three years?" indicates the overwhelming priority of the history of religions among the desired areas of expansion in undergraduate programs—though it also suggests that this will be more in the form of generalists who must be responsible for broad ranges of world religions than for specialists in Eastern religions, Islam, or the like.

TABLE 9–18*
PRIORITIES FOR NEW FACULTY APPOINTMENTS

Area of Specialization	First Priority	Second Priority	Third Priority
History of Religions/Comparative Religion/ Phenomenology of Religion	64	29	21
Religions of the East	18	13	9
Chinese Religion	3	3	4
Buddhism	3	0	1
Hinduism	1	2	1
Islam	10	9	2
Primitive Religions	2	2	4
Judaica/Jewish History/Hebraic Studies	11	14	16
Ancient Near Eastern Religion	3	2	3
Old Testament	19	20	16
New Testament	23	25	15
History of Christianity/Church History	14	18	13
History of Christian Thought/Theology	11	15	12
Systematic Theology/Dogmatic Theology	11	10	11
Philosophy of Religion	12	15	8
Philosophy	28	4	7
Ethics/Moral Theology/Social Ethics	25	26	20
Sociology of Religion	9	13	15
Religion and Literature/Theology and Culture	19	24	17
Anthropology	3	4	3
Religion in America	4	9	2
Psychology of Religion	2	10	10
Psychology	0	2	1
Pastoral Theology/Homiletics	2	5	1
Religious Education	13	4	5
Liturgy	0	3	0
History	0	3	2
Classics	1	1	0
Sociology	4	2	2
Linguistics	1	0	3
Education	1	1	0
Literature	0	0	0
Others	15	13	15
	(N=332)	(N=301)	(N=239)

* Based on responses from the 404 "full program" institutions whose reports were tabulated in detail (Data Base B).

A similar pattern of pressures is evident in the reports of course areas in which enrollments have had to be restricted because of lack of faculty. Table 9–19 shows the distribution of the course areas in which a total of 160 institutions reported having to restrict enrollments in one or more courses.

c. Toward Interdepartmental Studies

Another pattern of outward movement in religious studies has been toward interdepartmental alliances and interdisciplinary studies in both the humanities and the social sciences. Whereas formerly the special connections were likely to

TABLE 9-19

ENROLLMENT RESTRICTIONS DUE TO LACK OF FACULTY

Course Areas	Number of Institutions Restricting Enrollment
World Religions/History of Religions/Comparative Religions	44
New Testament	28
Introduction to Religion	27
Old Testament/Hebrew Bible	24
Ethics	22
Religions of the East	19
Contemporary Religious Thought/Problems	16
Islam	15
Religion in America	14
Philosophy of Religion	13
Buddhism	12
Judaism/Jewish Thought/Hebraic Studies	12
Chinese and Japanese Religions	11
Afro-American or Black Religions	11
Sociology of Religion	11
Introduction to Bible	10
Psychology of Religion	10
Religion and Literature	10
Religion and Culture	9
Hinduism	8
Ancient Near Eastern	8
African Religion	8
Systematic Theology/Dogmatic Theology	8
Religion and Society	8
Protestantism	7
Judaism and Christianity	6
History of Christian Thought/History of Theology	6
Eastern Orthodoxy	6
Primitive Religion	5
History of Christianity/Church History	4
Roman Catholicism/Catholic Theology	4
Phenomenology of Religion	4
Other	4
Methodology for the Study of Religion	2
Religious Education	1
Church Music	1

be with philosophy, history, and classics, attempts are growing to build on closer associations with anthropology, sociology, and psychology, with Asian and other regional studies, and with English, art, and music. Thus the direct involvement of the study of religion in a broad range of other "disciplines" is made manifest.

The interdisciplinary concept of religious studies has also led to various attempts to organize programs entirely on this basis, but those have usually limped along because they have no organizing core (the University of Michigan undergraduate program is a useful illustration: see Michaelsen, 1965), and we have already noted the low incidence of such program structures.

More important have been the attempts to work outward from within a program focused on the study of religion through the continuing establishment of relevant connections. The pattern is dramatically illustrated in a recent proposal for the development of a department of religious studies in a public institution. Beginning with two senior faculty in the areas of philosophical theology (including the history of Western religious thought) and of Hellenistic language and literature (with concentration on New Testament studies), the design of the program calls for additional appointments in the following order, with the interdepartmental connections indicated: a scholar in one oriental language and religious tradition, overlapping with the present staff and perhaps jointly appointed with the history department; a specialist in ethics and/or aesthetics; a colleague trained in American history and letters, again in connection with the history department; a joint appointment with English in religion and literature; a second person in biblical studies with special competence in ancient Near East and Old Testament; a colleague with a second oriental language and a second oriental tradition; a specialist in linguistics; a colleague in nineteenth-century European religious history and tradition, to complement the American specialization; a specialist in Graeco-Roman religions, with training in classics; a Judaic scholar; and finally a specialist in religion and the arts, working in conjunction with the school of fine arts. This grand scheme envisages the development of graduate as well as undergraduate studies, but the principles are symbolic of wide tendencies at the undergraduate level.

d. Enlarging the Concept of Religion

There are strong tendencies toward the expansion of work in phenomenological and comparative studies, to complement (and to some extent to replace) the traditional concentrations on religious ideas and scriptures and on the religious traditions per se. The movement is especially strong in the direction of social studies. This means only in part the tradition of formal sociological analysis. More broadly it means concern with the many expressions of both overt and covert religious phenomena and impulses in all aspects of culture: the "civil religion in America," as Bellah calls it; the myth and folklore of popular culture; the religious dimensions of the new youth subcultures; the manifestations of the holy and the sacred in the theatre, in art, and in literature (so that Camus and D. H. Lawrence are almost as likely to appear on reading lists as Augustine and Barth); the religious themes of alienation and reconciliation in the work of presumably antireligious thinkers like Nietzsche, Marx, and Freud; the quasi or *de facto* religious phenomena in the political and social realm (like National Socialism), and so on.

In many ways, religion programs are seeking to provide "an expanded consciousness of the religious phenomena in our culture" (Slater). This occurs in special courses with titles like "Theology and Culture" and "Religion and Literature." It appears in programs that seek to abandon entirely the traditional organization around religious traditions (Judaism, Catholicism, Protestantism, Islam, Hinduism, Buddhism, and so on) and to focus instead on problems, themes, and religious expressions that emerge in widely varying ways. The intent is to go beyond both the old-fashioned "comparative religions" (exemplified at its best by

George Foot Moore's classic *History of Religions*, 1913, 1919) and the newer
"ecumenical encounter," which is judged to be more appropriate to the interests
of theological seminaries than to those of college or university. Consider, for example, such course titles as these from a proposed new curriculum: "The World,
the City of God and the Problem of Justice", "Redemption and Freedom: Faith
or Satori?" Here as well as in the introduction to religion in this institution a
deliberate attempt is being made to cut across historical periods and to bring material from East and West together.

A similar thrust appears in the growing number of introductions to the study
of religion, attempting to ask anew the question, "What is the best place to
begin?" Formerly, the Bible held unquestioned dominance as the basis for further
work in religion. That hegemony is rapidly being ended.

No single pattern of approach to religious studies is yet taking the place of the
Bible. Rather, three interrelated kinds of courses seem to be prominent. Some
represent a survey approach to world religions. A second group focuses on the
phenomenological approach: an attempt to analyze the nature of religious experience and the idea of the holy. A third group emphasizes the role of religion
in contemporary culture. The distinctions between these types are not sharp. Many
of the "comparative religion" introductions use one or more religious traditions
as a basis for examining phenomena common to all religions: ritual, discipline,
myth and symbol, internal reform, communal structures and the like. Others unite
traditional studies with contemporary religious phenomena and problems. One
interesting proposal focuses intensively on four topics: religion and society; scripture, tradition, and change; religious experience and its communication; and
problems of religious diversity—drawing in every case on a wide range of religious traditions. A great deal of interesting experimentation is going on, and no
one can confidently predict what the dominant pattern of approach is likely to be,
if indeed there is to be one.

e. The Undergraduate Major

The diversity and fluidity that prevail in the new attempt to define appropriate
approaches to the study of religion have their parallels in changing conceptions
of the undergraduate major. In an earlier day undergraduate religion majors in
church-related institutions largely served one of two purposes: undergraduate-
level professional preparation for careers in religious education or other kinds of
church service, or professional studies leading to subsequent seminary education.
The latter, of course, was true primarily for Protestant institutions, since training
for the Roman Catholic priesthood was carried out in separate college-level seminaries rather than in Catholic liberal arts colleges (this is reflected in the responses to our questionnaire concerning the purposes of the undergraduate major
in the somewhat lower proportion of Roman Catholic respondents who said their
program was concerned with the preparation for church leadership; the traditional
purposes in the Catholic institutions have been, through the pattern of required
courses, the education and spiritual nourishment of the laity). Except in the most
conservative institutions, both of these purposes have declined greatly in importance. The suitability of the undergraduate major in religion as preseminary edu-

cation was for a period seriously questioned by the leaders in theological education
—partly because of the earlier poor quality of much undergraduate instruction in
religion, partly because of the judgment that the best preseminary training was
a broad liberal arts education, including philosophy, history, literature, social science, and language, with the specialized studies in Bible and theology to come at
the graduate level only.

These former purposes have not altogether vanished, of course, and indeed
with the improvement in quality of undergraduate religion programs and the
broadening of their scope it is argued that religion is at least as liberalizing a
major as any other and that it is quite artificial to postpone beginning studies in
the field of religion until after college. Increasingly important, however, are defi-
nitions of the religion major as (*a*) one mode among others of general liberal
arts education in the humanities and social sciences, and (*b*) preparation for graduate (not professional) studies in religion leading to careers in teaching (see also
Holbrook, 1963, Chapter 2). To this one may add the role of the undergraduate
major as preparation for secondary school teachers, to man the growing number
of high school courses in religion.

These contrasting new interpretations, which themselves exist in tension with
the older conceptions, point to a present lack of cohesion—even a disorder—in
undergraduate religious studies. One further example of that has been the abandonment so far of all efforts to devise a Graduate Record Examination in the field
of religion, even though negotiations have been undertaken several times in the
past fifteen years. Attempts were dropped partly because of uncertainty concerning the numbers of students who might be expected to take such an exam, but
equally because of the difficulty of defining the proper foci and allowing for all
the varieties of undergraduate programs.

It is certainly not to be assumed that the primary purpose of the undergraduate
major in religion should be preparation for graduate studies. On the contrary,
this should doubtless be of secondary importance. Yet with respect to any undergraduate concentration, the question must be raised of how it provides a disciplined and developing understanding of the subject matter. The danger of many
of the attempts to define a religion major as the epitome of liberal arts education,
or as essentially interdisciplinary in character, is that they result in a merely hap-
hazard collection of interesting courses, in which none finally builds on any other
and it is impossible to say at the end in what the student has begun to be genuinely competent. (Note again the frequent absence of prerequisites for religion
courses.)

Yet there are other tendencies that may be leading toward consensus as to the
appropriate constituents of a coherent and disciplined undergraduate program of
study. Three kinds of ingredients appear to be of special prominence. First, some
area of concentration in the field is essential—and the range of possibilities for
such specialization must be broadened to include the Eastern religious traditions,
primitive religions, and the more comprehensive understanding of religious phenomena that we referred to earlier. Second, a responsible pattern of study cannot
be limited simply to one religious tradition, but must include serious attention to

two or more, preferably from diverse cultural traditions. Third, there must be serious and extensive attention to the questions of general theory and method in the interpretation of religion, including historical, philosophical, literary, phenomenological, psychological, and sociological perspectives and styles of approach. It is not evident that any complete agreement has been reached on the necessity for these ingredients, and certainly not on their appropriate relation to one another. A wide variety of permutations is possible. But these elements are recurring with sufficient frequency in the reorganization of undergraduate programs that we may at least conjecture that they will provide much of the shape for the growth of the next decade.

PART IV

DEMOGRAPHY AND DESCRIPTION

10

The Doctoral Student

The "typical" doctoral student in religion—Protestant, Catholic, or Jew—still reflects the origins of graduate education in religion in professional ministerial training and the continuing ties between the two types of education. After majoring in one of the humanities in college, he spent three years in seminary. Either there or while employed afterward as a minister, the attraction of academic life and the desire to pursue the study of religion more intensively than was possible in the seminary led to the decision to enroll in a doctoral program, probably at a university connected with a theological faculty. His field of study is apt to be one familiar to him from seminary—Bible, theology, or history of Christianity—although he may be at pains to redefine the way these are studied. Most of his fellow students will be male and, like himself, older than the graduate students in other disciplines. Along the way to graduate school he will have married and acquired family responsibilities, unless he is in the Roman Catholic priesthood. Financing his graduate studies is therefore a cause of frequent anxiety, despite scholarship aid he may receive, and he finds it necessary to seek outside employment, frequently as a minister in a local church. Even if he is not employed in a church, he attends regularly and identifies with one of the established denominations. However, his commitment to scholarship and his vocational goal set him apart from his seminary classmates who entered on the ministry as a lifetime career. After receipt of his degree he hopes for a teaching position that will permit him to pursue his scholarship further.

There is another kind of student, however, who is seen increasingly in doctoral programs in religion. He—or she—is under thirty and entered graduate school directly after college. If he is married, he is not apt to have dependents. This, the stipend he receives, and his spouse's income make it possible for him to study full time. In college his major was religion, and he is attracted to the study of non-Christian religions, even though he grew up in one of the traditional American denominations and still identifies with them in some way—but not to the extent of frequent attendance at worship. Because he does not have as many outside responsibilities as the first type of student, he is apt to spend more time on the campus and to see faculty and fellow students frequently. Like the other type, he looks forward to a career of teaching and research.

203

The pages that follow present data underlying these two sketches and seek to characterize doctoral students in religion more fully.

1. DEMOGRAPHY

In the 1967–1970 academic year there were over 3,000 students in 75 doctoral programs in religion at 69 schools in the United States and Canada. Questionnaires were sent to students in all but five of the schools. Returns were received from almost two-thirds (1,965) of the students.[1]

a. Three-fourths of the respondents were enrolled in Ph.D. programs at 45 institutions, the remainder in Th.D., S.T.D., and D.H.L. programs at 22 institutions.[2] The greater number of Ph.D. students is not merely a function of the greater number, and thus greater accessibility, of such programs. Nor is it simply the result of differentiation between Ph.D. and Th.D. programs by fields of study; as yet there is little to distinguish the two kinds of programs, except in the area of non-Christian religions, where the Ph.D. given in the university context clearly predominates (see Chapter 11). The reasons for the preponderance of Ph.D. students would seem to lie in other directions. The great majority of the students want to teach, and they widely believe that the Ph.D. has greater salability in the academic marketplace. Many also seek a less seminary-oriented atmosphere, one more pluralistic and with the wider range of educational opportunities and other experiences that a university offers.

b. Most religion doctoral students have earned a professional degree. The ratio of professional to nonprofessional degree holders in 1969–1970 was virtually the same (74 percent) as among undergraduate teachers of religion in that year (73 percent) (see Chapter 9). For the Th.D. student, of course, a seminary degree is normally a prerequisite for doctoral study. But students with professional degrees are also clearly in the majority (66 percent) among respondents studying for the Ph.D. There is some evidence, however, that the situation is changing. Table 10–1 shows that in the last year for which we have data (and the one least likely to be affected, as it happens, by the draft) the percent of students entering *without* a professional degree is higher than in previous years. The change is most evident in the percent of students entering with a bachelor's degree only; that is, directly from college.

---

[1] Further details of the distribution and return of the questionnaires are given in the Preface. Three schools—Dallas, Rice, and Southwestern Baptist—received an early form of the questionnaire with fewer questions than the final form. This is noted, where necessary, in reporting the data.

[2] The students are distributed as follows:

Ph.D.	75%	(N=1,476)
Th.D.	22%	(N=439)
S.T.D.	2%	(N=47)
D.H.L.	0.2%	(N=3)

On the degree nomenclature see Chapter 3. For convenience our discussion designates Th.D., S.T.D., and D.H.L. programs and students simply as "Th.D."

TABLE 10-1

PERCENT OF Ph.D. STUDENTS IN RELIGION (1969-1970),
ACCORDING TO PRIOR PROFESSIONAL DEGREE (OR THE EQUIVALENT)

Year of Entrance Into Doctoral Program	Holding B.A. Only	Holding B.A. and M.A. Only	Total Without Prof. Degree	Total With Prof. Degree
	%	%	%	%
1969 (N=329)	22	19	41	59
1968 (N=360)	13	18	31	69
1967 (N=260)	13	22	35	65
1966 (N=226)	14	21	35	65
1965 (N=130)	15	22	37	63
1964 and Before (N=168)	7	15	22	78

Among Ph.D. students the distinction between those with professional degrees and those without illuminates a number of differences between the two groups and will be encountered frequently in the pages that follow.

Ph.D. students holding a professional degree are concentrated in universities connected with theological faculties (Table 10-2). These nineteen schools include those with the oldest and some of the largest and most productive Ph.D. programs in religion. Nearly half the students *without* professional degrees are also enrolled in these schools, but they are outnumbered by students with professional degrees by almost three to one. The two types of students are almost equal in representation in the twenty-one universities not associated with theological faculties. (See Chapter 12, Table 12-11, for a listing of percentages of professional degree holders in individual institutions.)

TABLE 10-2

DISTRIBUTION OF Ph.D. STUDENTS IN RELIGION (1969-1970)
WITH AND WITHOUT PROFESSIONAL DEGREES
AMONG VARIOUS TYPES OF SCHOOLS

	No Professional Degree	With Professional Degree
Universities Connected With Theological Faculties (19 Schools)	227	606
Universities Not Connected With Theological Faculties (21 Schools)	256	283
Independent Schools of Religion or Theology (4 Schools)	17	80

c. Doctoral students in religion are considerably older than doctoral students in the humanities generally, but the gap seems to be narrowing. In the Carnegie Commission Study of 1969–1970,[3] 64 percent of doctoral students in the humanities were found to be under thirty. By contrast, 62 percent of the doctoral students responding to our questionnaire were thirty or over, with 13 perecnt of

[3] Data on doctoral students in the humanities have been supplied by the Carnegie Commission on Higher Education, which, since 1969, in cooperation with the American Council on Education, has been conducting a survey of students and faculty in American colleges and universities. (See Preface.)

these being forty or older. The median age of the respondents is 32.0. The slight difference in median age between students studying for the Ph.D. (31.6) and the Th.D. (33.7 years) (Table 10–3) is attributable to the fact that the Ph.D. category includes a significant percentage of students who did not acquire a professional degree before undertaking doctoral study. The median age for such students (28.2) is about that of doctoral students in the humanities (27.9), according to the Carnegie returns, but contrasts with a median age of 32.7 for Ph.D. students in religion who hold the professional degree.

TABLE 10–3

MEDIAN AGES OF DOCTORAL STUDENTS IN RELIGION (1969–1970)

Ph.D. (N=1,453) -- 31.6
    No Professional Degree (495) ------------------------------- 28.2
      B.A. Only (211) --- 25.0
      B.A. and M.A. (284) -------------------------------------- 31.0
    With Professional Degree (958) ------------------------------- 32.7
Th.D. (N=357) -- 33.7

d. Men outnumber women nine to one in doctoral programs in religion, although the proportion of women is increasing slightly. This ratio is comparable to that among recent recipients of doctorates in the physical and social sciences and (in the humanities) in philosophy.[4] Once again respondents with and without professional degrees are quite distinct. Ninety-seven percent of the Th.D. students (virtually all of whom hold professional degrees) are men, as are 98 percent of the Ph.D. students with professional degrees. However, only 66 percent of the Ph.D. students without professional degrees are male (see Table 10–4). The ratio of men to women among students twenty-five and under who do not hold a professional degree (70/30) is exactly the same as among doctoral students in the humanities generally, according to the Carnegie returns. If students without professional degrees are on the increase among Ph.D. students in religion, as seems to be the case, the percentage of women will increase, though probably never to the ratio obtaining among Ph.D. students in the humanities generally. This is because students with professional degrees will continue to constitute a significant percentage of the doctoral population in the religion area, and among these students another factor is operative, namely, the continuing preponderance of men (for cultural and sometimes religious reasons) among seminary students and in the ranks of the clergy.

e. Age and celibacy requirements are the important variables in the marital status of our respondents. Since doctoral students in religion are older than graduate students generally, a higher percentage are married (69 percent, as compared with 60 percent of the humanities doctoral students in the Carnegie sample). Most students with professional degrees are, as we have noted, older than

[4] *Earned Degrees Conferred: 1967–68,* Part A, p. 8, Table 4. According to these figures (from the Office of Education), the ratio of men to women among doctoral recipients in religion is even higher: 95/5.

TABLE 10–4

RATIOS OF MEN TO WOMEN AMONG DOCTORAL STUDENTS
IN RELIGION (1969–1970), BY AGE AND PRIOR PROFESSIONAL TRAINING

	Ph.D.				*Th.D./S.T.D./-*
	No Professional Degree			*With*	*D.H.L.*
	25 and		30 and	*Professional*	
	Under	26–27	Older	Totals	*Degree*	
	%	%	%	%	%	%
Men	70	76	54	66	98	97
Women	30	24	46*	34	2	3
	100	100	100	100	100	100
	(N=148)	(N=165)	(N=182)	(N=495)	(N=959)	(N=489)

* The increase in the ratio of women in the uppermost age bracket is attributable primarily to the greater percentage of Roman Catholic sisters in that bracket (76 percent of the 42 sisters responding to the questionnaire).

students without such degrees, and accordingly 78 percent of the Th.D. respondents and 75 percent of the Ph.D. respondents with professional degrees reported they were married. Among male Ph.D. students without professional degrees, only 50 percent of those twenty-five or below are married, as compared with 71 percent of those twenty-six to twenty-nine, and 76 percent of those thirty or older. On the other hand, the percentage of married male students with professional degrees declines with age because Roman Catholic priests, 91 percent of whom are thirty or older, constitute almost a fifth of the students holding such degrees.

Among women Ph.D. respondents single women make up the largest group, almost three-fourths of the total. A third of these are Roman Catholic sisters, of whom two-thirds are enrolled in Catholic schools; most are older and decided while employed, generally as teachers, to undertake doctoral study, for which their orders provide financial support. Almost two-thirds of the other single women are under thirty years of age and decided while still in school—seminary, graduate school, or (usually) college—to undertake doctoral study. The women Ph.D. respondents who are married tend to be older. A few are housewives and women who decided while employed outside the home to do graduate work, but most (over two-thirds) are women who decided while in school (usually college) to undertake doctoral study.

f. Students from outside the United States and Canada constitute 7 percent of the respondents; they are about equally represented among Ph.D. and Th.D. students.[5] Virtually all are men; over half are from Third World countries; 82 percent have professional degrees and are thirty years of age or older.

[5] The percentages among our respondents are virtually the same as those reported independently by the directors of graduate study for the entire doctoral student population in religion. According to United States Office of Education statistics for 1965, foreign students constituted 8 percent of all graduate students (*The Academic and Financial Status of Graduate Students, Spring 1965*, p. 8, Table 2); in the Carnegie study they constituted 6 percent of doctoral students in the humanities.

Americans of minority backgrounds are as poorly represented among doctoral students in religion (3 percent, as reported by directors of graduate study) as they are among graduate students generally (4 percent).[6] They were even more poorly represented among our respondents (only 1 percent); therefore, little can be said about them.

2. ACADEMIC BACKGROUND

In the humanities generally, the majority of graduate students enter their degree programs immediately after receipt of the baccalaureate degree: 60 percent according to the United States Office of Education (*Academic and Financial Status of Graduate Students, Spring 1965*, p. 37, Table 23). Religion doctoral students as a whole do not conform to this pattern, since three-fourths first complete a theological degree. Most of this group decided to undertake advanced study while in seminary or while employed (in all likelihood as ministers)[7]— see Table 10–5 (cols. 3 and 4).

TABLE 10–5

WHEN DOCTORAL STUDENTS IN RELIGION (1969–1970)
DECIDED TO UNDERTAKE DOCTORAL STUDY

	Ph.D.			Th.D./
	No Professional Degree		*With Professional Degree*	*S.T.D./ D.H.L.*
	B.A. Only	*B.A. and M.A.*		
	%	%	%	%
In High School	3	1	2	2
In College	62	27	15	12
In Seminary	10	11	43	40
In Graduate School	5	14	1	1
While Employed	13	42	37	43
Other	7	5	3	3
	100	100	101	101
	(N=210)	(N=279)	(N=951)	(N=355)

For doctoral students in religion who hold only the collegiate baccalaureate degree, the pattern of decision and entry is more like that of graduate students generally. Sixty-two percent decided while in college to pursue doctoral study in religion (Table 10–5, col. 1), and of these the majority (68 percent) entered

[6] According to the Carnegie study, reporting on doctoral students in the humanities, and the United States Office of Education, reporting on graduate students generally (*The Academic and Financial Status of Graduate Students, Spring 1965*, p. 8, Table 2). The Lilly Endowment Study of seminarians likewise reported a percentage of 4 percent (Bridston and Culver, 1965, p. 218, Table 26).

[7] Seventy-seven percent of the Ph.D. respondents with professional degrees are ordained and 51 percent of those who reported outside employment were working as ministers; 79 percent of the Th.D. respondents are ordained and 61 percent of those employed were working as ministers.

their doctoral programs immediately after receipt of the bachelor's degree. From Table 10–5 (cols. 1 and 2) it is also apparent that a number of students dropped out of seminary in order to begin doctoral studies and that religion programs attracted some graduate students enrolled in other disciplines. As Table 10–6 shows, the great majority of doctoral students in religion did their undergraduate work in one of the humanities, with philosophy and religion being the most common majors, followed by history and English. There were no significant differences in undergraduate majors between students in Ph.D. and in Th.D. programs, or between those with and without a professional degree.

TABLE 10–6

UNDERGRADUATE MAJORS OF RELIGION DOCTORAL STUDENTS
(1969–1970)

	%
Philosophy	22
Religion*	19
History	14
English	12
Social Sciences	11
Natural Sciences	7
Classics	5
Foreign Languages and Literature	3
Other	8
(N=1,723)	101

* Includes religion, theology, Bible, philosophy of religion, *et al.*

There has been, however, an interesting change in the proportion of religion majors among Ph.D. students not holding a professional degree. As shown in Table 10–7, among these students there is a marked increase in religion majors with decrease in age. No such pattern is evident among students holding professional degrees. The increase in religion majors in the nonprofessional degree

TABLE 10–7

INCREASE OF UNDERGRADUATE RELIGION MAJORS AMONG PH.D. STUDENTS IN RELIGION NOT HOLDING A PROFESSIONAL DEGREE
(1969–1970)

Age Group		With Undergrad. Religion Major	With Other Undergrad. Major
25 and Under	(N=146)	31%	69%
26 – 27	(N=88)	23%	77%
28 – 29	(N=73)	16%	84%
30 – 34	(N=80)	14%	86%
35 – 39	(N=49)	14%	86%
40 and Over	(N=47)	4%	96%
	(N=483)	(N=98)	(N=385)

group obviously reflects both the general growth of undergraduate religion major programs (see Chapter 9) and the changing basis for doctoral study. Religion graduate students are becoming more like students in other fields, relying on their undergraduate years to prepare them for advanced academic work. At the same time, partly because of the extent to which religion is studied in other undergraduate departments, it may be expected that graduate study in religion will continue to attract significant proportions of students who have majored in philosophy, literature, and the social sciences.[8]

Little can be said with respect to objective measures of the ability of our respondents in relation to other doctoral students, since response was so poor to the questionnaire item asking for scores on the verbal aptitude section of the Graduate Record Examination. The scores reported covered the spectrum, from below 500 to over 800, in every age group. Without overestimating the importance of GRE scores, it would not be too much to suggest that a generally higher cutoff point for admission to doctoral programs at some schools would serve to improve the quality of the doctoral student population there and overall.[9]

3. PROGRESSION IN STUDY

Among all respondents, 62 percent considered themselves full-time students. The highest proportion of full-time students is found among Ph.D. students without professional degrees (71 percent), and the lowest among Th.D. students (51 percent). Table 10–8 shows the overall distribution of full-time and part-time study by types of students and status.

Some differences in academic progress appear between students enrolled in

TABLE 10–8

ENROLLMENT STATUS OF DOCTORAL STUDENTS IN RELIGION (1969–1970)

	Ph.D.		Th.D./
	Without Professional Degree	With Professional Degree	S.T.D./ D.H.L.
Full-time			
Course Work and Exam Preparation	60	46	33
Dissertation	11	17	18
Part-time			
Course Work and Exam Preparation	8	9	14
Dissertation in Residence	4	7	6
Dissertation in absentia	12	17	25
Other	5	5	4
	100	101	100
	(N=504)	(N=966)	(N=488)

[8] Thus one cannot assume that the 385 students in Table 10–7 who had neither a professional degree nor an undergraduate religion major had not had extensive work in religion before beginning doctoral study. Included in this figure also are students with master's degrees in religion and some who began seminary study and changed to a doctoral program without completing the professional degree.

[9] One institution, for which scores were available for the whole of its considerable doctoral population, had 45 percent of its students below the 500 mark and another third below 550.

programs requiring only one set of examinations (field or general or comprehensive exams) prior to the dissertation and those in programs requiring two
sets.[10]

Of the students with *two sets* of examinations, about a third of the Ph.D. candidates had taken the first set by the end of their first year of study. By the end
of the second year this proportion had risen to about 60 percent. Among Th.D.
respondents, on the other hand, almost 90 percent passed the first set in the first
year. If the first set of examinations was intended to serve as a qualifying or
screening device, therefore, it was for a good number of students coming later in
their programs than the faculty perhaps hoped or intended it would. Ph.D. students with professional degrees seemed to have an advantage when it came to
taking the first set of examinations: about two-thirds had passed them within
two years, as compared with about half of those without professional degrees.[11]

Among students with *one set* of examinations, a fourth had passed within the
first two years. By the end of the third year, the proportion had risen to about
half. There were virtually no differences between Ph.D. and Th.D. students in
the rates of progress through the examinations. However, again Ph.D. students
with professional degrees proceeded to the examinations more quickly than those
without such degrees. By the end of the first two years in the program 29 percent of the former had passed their examinations, as compared with 15 percent
of the latter. By the end of three years the respective proportions were 53
percent and 37 percent.

It would seem that Ph.D. students in programs with two sets of examinations
proceed somewhat more slowly through both sets than those required to take
only one set. By the end of their third year 34 percent of the Ph.D. students with
two sets of examinations had taken both sets, while 47 percent of those with one
set had passed their examination within that time. Among Th.D. students, however, the rates were very much the same among the two groups: 44 percent of
those with two sets had passed both by the end of the third year as compared with
48 percent of those with one set. It is noteworthy that among all types of students, less than half had completed their examinations within three years.

How soon do the modern languages generally required in graduate programs
become functional tools for doctoral students in religion? During the course of
their first year of study, 42 percent of the respondents had passed both language
examinations. During the second year the proportion was still less than two-

---

[10] Respondents were asked to indicate whether they had one or two sets of exams prior to
the dissertation and at what point(s) in their programs these had been passed. About 20
percent of the responses were incomplete or confused and have been disregarded. Also excluded from consideration as to rate of progress are students who were still in their first
year of study and hence in the winter and spring of 1970 would generally have had no opportunity to sit for these examinations. Of the usable responses, about half were from students in programs with one set of exams.

[11] A greater percentage of Ph.D. students without professional degrees who are engaged
in course work and exam preparation were full-time than were their counterparts with professional degrees; that is, their enrollment status should have given them an edge.

thirds,[12] suggesting that despite the recommendations of the Council on Graduate Studies in Religion a large number of students are not ready to use these languages while doing the bulk of their course work and preparation for general examinations.[13] In general, the day-to-day use of the languages which makes them functional, before or after the langage examinations, appears to be slighted. Only rarely (as in the theology field at Notre Dame) are the language examinations complemented by courses requiring all reading in French and German.

4. FINANCIAL SUPPORT

About two-thirds of all respondents were receiving financial aid of some kind —tuition grants, fellowship stipends, assistantships, and so on, including grants from outside sources (see also Chapter 5, above). However, a fourth of the Ph.D. and half of the Th.D. respondents receiving aid held only tuition grants, and many of these involved only partial tuition remission. Cash stipends were received by 48 percent of the Ph.D. students and 34 percent of the Th.D. students. The proportion of Ph.D. students receiving stipends compares favorably with the 46 percent of humanities graduate students who receive stipends; the Th.D. proportion is less favorable.[14] Outside sources of aid were mainly foundations (notably in Kent, Danforth, and Woodrow Wilson fellowship programs) and religious communities (especially among Roman Catholic students).[15] Altogether, only 20 percent of Ph.D. students and 12 percent of Th.D. students received any financial aid from outside sources.

That the levels of financial support are inadequate for religion doctoral students is shown by the proportion who are forced to seek outside employment. Among Ph.D. respondents receiving financial aid of any sort (including tuition grants), 42 percent were employed outside their institutions, about half as ministers and another third in teaching. Among Th.D. respondents receiving aid,

[12] These percentages are based on reports from about three-fourths of the respondents; 12 percent did not respond to the question on language examinations or gave incomplete responses; another 11 percent reported that examinations were not required.

[13] The importance of modern languages to graduate study varies from one field to another, and the percentages cited are in part a reflection of the value accorded languages by faculty and students in the various fields. Some programs now allow students working in certain areas to substitute courses in statistical method for one of the languages.

[14] See *The Academic and Financial Status of Graduate Students, Spring 1965*, p. 26. About half of the graduate students in the social and behavorial sciences received stipends (*ibid.*) (These data are exclusive of tuition grants and include master's as well as doctoral candidates.)

[15] Except for the small number of history of religion students who require certain languages at one time considered important by the federal government, religion students generally do not receive government stipends. See the Office of Education data in *The Academic and Financial Status of Graduate Students, Spring 1965*, p. 28. While the Office's data on religion students are based on very limited returns (only 300 students, from 15 schools) and present a more optimistic picture of the stipends received by graduate students in religion (61 percent of the sample reporting such aid), its report that none of these students received federal government aid is close to the truth. They were the only graduate students in all fields covered by the survey who did not report such aid. In the 1970–1971 academic year even the stipends available for the history of religion students mentioned were reduced.

the proportion employed was even higher—over two-thirds—with about the same percent employed as ministers. Even many "full-time" students in residence have outside employment. Over half the full-time Ph.D. students replying to the question reported such employment, with 40 percent of those employed putting in over 15 hours a week. Three-fourths of the full-time Th.D. respondents reported outside employment, with 37 percent of those employed working over 15 hours a week.

These statistics are not unexpected in view of the personal situation of doctoral students in religion, the majority of whom are married and, being older, have acquired family and other responsibilities. Such students will probably continue to be in the majority for some time to come. With their professional theological degrees they often have employment opportunities that doctoral students generally do not have. But such jobs are not well paying and with their ill-defined hours and responsibilities often encroach on study time. Extensive outside employment is in any case not a satisfactory answer to the problem of financial support if one is concerned about quality and efficiency of graduate education. The percentage of religion students receiving foundation grants will probably not increase, and it is likely that the few government stipends once granted religion students will decline, even should the field of religion receive fuller recognition as a university discipline. On the students' institutions themselves, it seems, will fall the main responsibility for more adequate financial support, if full-time study continues to be the norm. In a period of economic stringency, that will entail limiting the number of applicants admitted to those who can be adequately supported through the length of their programs—though at the same time it may be desirable to make more explicit provision for viable patterns of part-time and interrupted study.

5. Religion and the Study of Religion

In what ways is religion—in the ordinary sense of adherence and observance—important for the doctoral student in the field of religion?

Virtually all respondents stand in one of the main religious traditions of the West, Judaism or Christianity, all but 5 percent identifying themselves, at least nominally, with one of the established religious groups in America (see Table 10–9). Overwhelmingly they are Christian, even the majority of students who devote themselves to the study of non-Christian religions retaining at least nominal identification with one of the Christian bodies. In their religious preferences doctoral students in religion are closer to the United States population as a whole than they are to other doctoral students in the humanities. Of the latter, only 62 percent indicated a religious preference of any sort, according to the Carnegie study, whereas among the general population the proportion is about 96 percent.[16]

---

[16] United States Bureau of the Census, *Current Population Reports (1958)*, pp. 1, 6, reporting on responses to the question, "What is your religion?" Our comparisons are with United States data since only 4 percent of our respondents were enrolled in Canadian schools, and even some of these were United States citizens.

TABLE 10-9

RELIGIOUS PREFERENCES OF DOCTORAL STUDENTS IN RELIGION
(1969-1970)

	%
Baptist	4.5*
Baptist (Southern)	4.8*
Episcopalian	4.6
Latter-day Saints (Mormon)	0.7
Lutheran	5.2
Lutheran (Missouri)	2.0
Methodist	11.9
Presbyterian	11.0
Roman Catholic	26.8
Society of Friends (Quaker)	0.9
Unitarian-Universalist	0.5
United Church of Christ	4.3
Jewish	4.3†
Buddhist (N=9)	0.5
Hindu (N=1)	—
Muslim	0.0
No Preference	5.1
None of the Above	12.8
(N=1,795)	99.9

* Baptist students are probably underrepresented in this sample because the religious affiliation question was not asked of students at Dallas, Rice, and Southwestern Baptist (with a total of 148 students).

†Jewish students are somewhat underrepresented because of a lower response rate from students in Jewish studies programs, but not enough to alter the over-all percentage significantly.

The distribution of religion doctoral students among the various denominations is reasonably close to that of the general population, though strictly comparable data are not available—the Census Bureau's data on religious preference are a dozen years old and offer insufficient detail on denominations, while the denominational statistics in the *Yearbook of American Churches* (1970) report church membership rather than religious preference and, in a number of important cases, exclude children.[17]

Since all but a handful of respondents indicated a preference for one of the Jewish or Christian traditions, in which communal religious observance is central, participation in public worship services may be taken as one indication of their commitment to these traditions. All but 11 percent of the students participated weekly or almost weekly in public worship when they were growing up, and over three-fourths still continue to do so. The difference between students

[17] In the table the 12.8 percent who indicated that none of the options on the questionnaire fit their cases belong, for the most part, to some of the smaller Protestant denominations or dissociate themselves from denominational labels, but not from Christianity as such. Their pattern of attendance at public worship, past and present, whether taken as a whole or grouped by prior professional training or by ordination status, is virtually the same as that for the Ph.D. and Th.D. respondents generally.

with and without professional degrees appears here again. A much larger proportion of those with professional degrees participate in worship weekly or nearly so (89 percent among the Th.D. and 81 percent among the Ph.D.) than of those without such degrees (58 percent).[18] Frequency of participation increases with age among the two groups, but the marked differences between them persists even so (Table 10–10).[19]

TABLE 10–10

PERCENTAGE OF DOCTORAL STUDENTS IN RELIGION (1969–1970)
WHO WORSHIP WEEKLY OR NEARLY SO,
BY AGE GROUPS AND PRIOR PROFESSIONAL TRAINING

	25 and Younger %	26–27 %	28–29 %	30–34 %	35–39 %	40 and Older %
Ph.D. Students With No Professional Degree (N=486)	47	48	59	67	69	82
	(69)	(43)	(43)	(53)	(33)	(41)
Students With Professional Degree Ph.D. (N=950)	65	74	70	81	87	91
	(15)	(93)	(99)	(269)	(181)	(106)
Th.D. (N=355)	72	80	85	86	95	92
	(5)	(20)	(40)	(113)	(69)	(65)

(Numbers in Parentheses Indicate Numbers of Persons)

Almost a fourth of the students without professional degrees indicate a frequency of public worship ranging from a few times a year to never. By contrast, almost two-thirds of the humanities doctoral students in the Carnegie study participate in religious services with this degree of frequency (or infrequency). Thus, however much students without professional degrees may diverge in this respect from the remaining doctoral students in religion, the majority are still quite distinct from humanities doctoral students generally.

It has been argued that for the scholar and teacher of religion the academic pursuit of his subject is itself a form of religious ritual (Sloyan, 1969; on the Jewish side, cf. Klaperman, 1969, p. 34). Most of the students interviewed stated that the study of religion was in some way a personal quest, undertaken in part out of religious concern. Though some voiced the common complaint that graduate school separates work and experience, the academic life and the rest of life, they felt a life of teaching and scholarship was the best way to exercise their combined intellectual and religious concerns.

Neither in the questionnaires nor in interviews were students asked explicitly about personal beliefs. Such questions would doubtless have demonstrated that persons trained to think critically about religion fall on the heterodox end of the

[18] The two groups differ hardly at all in frequency of worship in childhood, about 90 percent having participated weekly or nearly so.
[19] Students with professional degrees who are employed as ministers naturally worship more frequently than those not so employed, but even when not employed as ministers they participate more frequently than do students without professional degrees.

orthodoxy scales that researchers commonly construct. In the interviews, however, certain attitudes toward belief became evident. In their professors, students
said, they expected commitment, but they usually did not judge this by particular
beliefs. Their own commitment to teaching and their future students they might
term "religious," but in some general sense such as being "for" the students and
contributing to their growth as persons through the enlargement of thought and
experience that the study of religion can afford. They observed that their own
beliefs would inevitably affect their scholarship or teaching, both positively and
negatively, but that this was not peculiar to the field of religion. Commitment
to a narrow belief system, however, would very likely impair one's work as a
scholar or teacher since it was apt to be a species of ignorance and of limited experience.[20] Belief conflicts were reported at some schools, with students objecting
to a professor too doctrinaire in either upholding or rejecting traditional views;
but that, too, is not peculiar to the field of religion.

One may venture the prediction that the majority of religion graduate students
will continue to come from and to identify themselves in some way with the established religious communities and to participate to some degree in their life.
In increasing measure, however, especially with a greater influx of students without professional degrees, there will be students alienated from these communities
and/or holding themselves aloof from conventional forms of piety.[21] Among
these, but also to a degree among the other students as well, forms of religious
expression may well be sought that comport more with their own study of religion, for which non-Christian religions and contemporary psychology, mysticism,
and agnosticism may be as important as the classical traditions of the West.

6. STUDENT ASSESSMENT AND CONCERNS

Religion doctoral students do not seem to differ much from doctoral students
in the humanities generally in their assessments of their programs.[22]

The great majority (84 percent) said they were basically satisfied with the
education they were getting, even though most of these had some reservations
to express. Students gave high ratings to the academic achievements of their
faculty (somewhat higher than to the academic ability of fellow graduate stu-

[20] These observations may be taken as fairly representative of most of the students at the
schools where interviews were conducted and, presumably, of a large number of doctoral
students in religion, but probably not of those at the few schools serving constituencies
for whom certain distinguishing beliefs are especially important. A few students interviewed defined religious commitment in quite specific terms and saw a close link between
belief and scholarship or teaching, at least in certain areas such as theology.

[21] A small subgroup among the respondents on the religious preference and worship
questions may be symptomatic. These are the 91 (5 percent, who reported no religious
preference. Virtually all (96 percent) are Ph.D. students. Of these, two-thirds do not
hold professional degrees and are under thirty; 79 percent participate in worship from
several times a year to never, even though three-fourths of the 79 percent attended church
or synagogue weekly or almost weekly as children and some attended parochial schools as
well.

[22] For comparison with other graduate students in the humanities our questionnaires included questions taken from the Carnegie Commission study, asking students to rate their
program, faculty, and fellow students.

dents). They thought the faculty were generally accessible and interested in graduate students, and they reported good relations with fellow students. The general intellectual environment was rated good to excellent. The quality and variety of classroom instruction and course offerings received lower ratings, however.

The only significant variation from responses of humanities doctoral students as a whole comes at the point of the judgment that exciting developments are taking place in the field—91 percent of the religion students believe this to be true, as against 72 percent of humanities doctoral students generally.

Such generalizations are fundamentally uninteresting, however, because of the differences they conceal between institutions and among individual students. The mediocre student getting a mediocre education in a mediocre institution is just as likely to find it good as the excellent student getting an excellent education in a first-class institution. The creative minority and the merely unhappy are lumped together among the dissatisfied. From student interviews, for example, it is evident that morale is much higher in some institutions than in others and that a number of particular concerns are being articulated.[23]

The basic concern of students to proceed with dispatch through their education was expressed in a variety of desiderata, such as greater flexibility in course requirements, or more careful and explicit guidelines on examinations. There were frequent complaints about too few graduate-level course offerings, or of graduate seminars that were too large or populated by too many college or seminary undergraduates. Students reported that faculty members were usually accessible, and some felt that these individual contacts sufficed to deal with student grievances. At most of the schools visited, however, there were or had been organized efforts for change. Occasionally those involved such matters as content and ordering of courses, faculty appointments, and admittances to the doctoral program. More commonly the changes concerned essentially administrative matters—degree requirements, course and examination procedures, awarding of financial aid—again those items that might expedite progress through the program. The faculties were reported as generally responsive to such overtures, and in some cases had themselves initiated conversation and change, although at more than one school certain retirements and personnel changes were prerequisite to positive faculty response. Where changes had been effected, resulting in a greater student voice in departmental decisions, morale was reported to be higher than before.

The relation between faculty and students was variously assessed. Some students seem content with the *Doktor-Vater* image of the professor. Most resent it, mildly or fiercely, partly because they bring to graduate study a different model of education and of human relations in general, and partly because they feel the authoritarian structure is not productive of first-rate scholars and teachers. Students well along in their twenties, or even older, are apt to be less than happy if

---

[23] At each of the seven schools visited, interviews were conducted with a group of students (or two groups when there was more than one doctoral program) and, except at Princeton University, with individual students. Participants in both kinds of interview were selected at random from the roster of doctoral students.

expected to play a filial role in graduate school, especially when undergraduates on the campus are achieving a greater say in their education. But the younger graduate students are likely to feel much the same, for many have had schooling that placed a premium on independence. In interviews they were apt to say that what they looked for most in a graduate professor was the encouraging of independence and originality.

Students generally hold their faculty in high regard as scholars and recognize that heavy demands on their time often make it difficult for them to devote more attention to graduate students. But students want particularly to be respected as individuals. This means having their work taken seriously enough to receive evaluation more frequently than once a semester and comment more substantial than a mere grade. Students want occasional assurance that the faculty is committed to seeing them through, and if not, they would like to be told as much. There are noticeable differences between schools or departments where students felt the faculty stood behind them from the beginning and those where they were left with little guidance or wondering just when they could count on faculty support—after creditable seminar performances? After passing of exams? Or not until the dissertation was completed and successfully defended?

How to achieve technical competence while retaining the originality and creativity that are vital to undergraduate teaching as well as to good scholarship was a problem felt keenly by many students. Those at one school noted that the doctoral programs there were designed to train the handful of elite students who would succeed their professors in the university. The program did little to prepare the rest for the kind of teaching they would be doing in liberal arts colleges. Many would have agreed with the junior faculty member who wrote that

> most people who receive Ph.D.'s in religion and have the capacity for technical research and writing are incapable of thinking in larger intellectual terms, or if they are capable, they are not interested in doing so because they have been so completely brainwashed by their graduate education. The system squeezes out whatever originality may once have been present, and the scholar winds up answering questions that no serious thinker ever asked or that no one should have asked.

At most schools where students were interviewed, however, there were some who felt that their faculty and their programs gave them full rein to pursue significant problems and in a way that wedded personal and professional concerns.

Another fundamental issue for many students is the way in which the field of religion is to be defined (see above, Chapter 2). A number of students at universities connected with theological faculties were sensitive to the way seminary categories still define the field. Students at most schools were also eager to pursue the study of religion in relation to other disciplines, and many were doing so. Interdisciplinary work was seen not only as aiding in a fuller understanding of religion but also as providing another avenue of access to undergraduates, many of whom are familiar with the methods of the social and behavioral sciences especially. In some instances interdisciplinary work was a requirement of the doctoral program, and faculty were often reported to be doing such work themselves. However, some students doubt whether faculty trained in more traditional modes will be able to move from these toward an approach to religion that is genuinely inclusive of non-Christian religions, past or present, and of other academic disciplines. At one school students felt the cleft between themselves and the faculty so keenly on this point that they organized and conducted their own seminars. The concern of a number of students, especially at the prestige schools, to broaden and redefine the traditional disciplines in the field of religion will doubtless have its effect in the coming decade and may even unsettle the presently placid meetings of the professional societies, as it has in other fields.

II

The Fields of Study:
An Overview

Changes in the direction of graduate education in religion are discussed at several places elsewhere in this report. In order to provide a context for viewing those changes and to give some relatively simple overview of a large and complex area, we set out here in summary form an accounting of the principal fields of study in relation to the sixty-nine institutions offering doctoral studies in religion.

The diversity of graduate religious studies makes simple description almost impossible. This is in part due to the breadth of the field and its intersections with other disciplines. It is also due to the radical variations in the ways in which institutions define their programs. Descriptions range from very precise identifications of fields of specialization offered (like biblical archaeology, medieval Judaism) to listings of broad areas (such as historical studies, biblical studies, religions of India), to no specification at all (with programs being individually tailored to faculty competence and student interest), to such categories as "cultural history of various religious traditions." Considerable differences occur in names for the same area of study. The designations "history of religions," "comparative religions," and "world religions" constitute one of the major illustrations of this diversity. Sometimes these categories are used to include the religions of the Far East, Islam, and primitive religions, as well as phenomenology of religion; sometimes the latter areas are distinguished in addition or alternatively. Comparable ambiguities occur in the identification of such fields as "ethics and society," "social ethics," "religion and society," and "sociology of religion."

The confusions here are in part the result of the casualness and freedom with which catalogue and brochure descriptions are written. They are also a function of some attempts to define new areas of study, in which consistency has not yet been achieved. Even in these areas, however, it may be asked whether something more nearly approximating uniformity of designation might be achieved without sacrifice of the freedom to experiment and to cross the traditional lines of division. (A complete list of the fields of specialization offered by the sixty-nine institutions studied, with all the terminological variance, would occupy fifteen pages!)

For analyzing the areas of specialization of students presently in doctoral study and the fields in which dissertations were written 1965–1969 (see also Chapter 13), we have developed a list of fifty-one categories organized so as to take reasonable account of the distribution of specialties and the variety in nomenclature. The full list is given below in Table 11–3. In order to relate the field distributions to institutions in any comprehensible graphic fashion, it is necessary both (1) to collapse the number of fields and (2) to group the institutions according to some important pattern of classification.

(1) The fifty-one categories have been collapsed into fourteen areas. "History of religions," for example, includes programs described as comparative religions or world religions, also phenomenology of religion. "Far Eastern religions" include all specific programs in Eastern religions, such as Buddhism or religions of China. The nature of the studies carried on requires that ethics (including Christian or theological ethics and moral theology) be distinguished from "ethics and society" and "social ethics," as well as sociology of religion, all of which have been grouped under the heading of religion and society. Pastoral theology and psychology, however, has been classified not under practical and applied theology, but with religion and psychology, since programs in these two areas are in fact frequently indistinguishable.

(2) The institutions are here grouped in five types:

> Type I includes the Ph.D. programs offered in universities independently of theological faculties.

> Type II includes the Ph.D. programs offered through university theological faculties or combined university-seminary faculties.

> Type III includes the Ph.D. programs offered by independent schools of religion or theology.

> Type IV includes the Th.D., S.T.D., and D.H.L. programs offered by independent theological schools.

> Type V includes the Th.D. and S.T.D. programs offered by theological schools that are integrally related to a university (the AATS classification has been used in identifying theological school programs that are so related).

Within these parameters, Table 11–1 displays a complete account of areas of doctoral specialization offered in 1969–1970 by the sixty-nine institutions studied. These are the fields of specialization announced by the institutions (though we have occasionally had to interpret published accounts by information gained in interviews). The chart reveals both the high concentration of programs in certain areas and important differences among the types of institutions. The traditional trivium—Bible, history of Christianity and Christian thought, and theological studies—is heavily represented in all types of institutions. The study of non-Western religions (or history of religions) appears almost entirely in the university and university-related programs. Doctoral work in practical theology, on the contrary, is offered, with one exception, only in the seminary-based programs and mainly in the independent theological schools. Studies in philosophy of religion, in religion and society, and in ethics are prominent especially in the university-seminary combinations (Types II and V). Theology and culture programs have developed only in the Ph.D. institutions (except for the GTU Th.D., which, however, is given in a university context).

It is apparent from Table 11-1 which institutions propose to offer a wide variety of fields, which have concentrated on only a few or even one, and which do not specify particular fields. (See Chapters 4 and 5.)

TABLE 11-1a

AREAS OF DOCTORAL SPECIALIZATION OFFERED

Ph.D. Type I	History of Religions	Far Eastern Religions	Islamic Studies	Near Eastern Religions (Ancient)	Judaic Studies	Biblical Studies	Historical Studies (Christian)	Theological Studies (Christian)	Philosophy of Religion	Ethics	Religion and Society	Theology & Culture, Arts	Religion & Psychology	Practical Theology
Baylor	—	—	—	—	—	X	X	X	—	—	—	—	—	—
Brandeis	—	—	X	X	S	X	—	—	—	—	—	—	—	—
Brigham Young	Programs in Abeyance													
Brown	—	—	—	X	X	*	—	—	—	—	—	—	—	—
Calif., UCSB	Unspecified													
Case W. R.	—	—	—	—	—	X	X	—	—	—	—	—	—	—
Catholic U.	X	—	—	—	—	X	S	—	—	—	—	—	—	X
Fordham	X	—	—	—	—	X	X	X	—	—	—	—	—	—
Iowa	X	S	—	—	X	X	X	X	—	X	—	—	X	—
J. Hopkins	—	—	X	X	—	—	—	—	—	—	—	—	—	—
McMaster	—	S	—	X	—	—	*	—	—	—	X	—	—	—
Marquette	—	—	—	—	—	X	X	X	—	—	—	—	—	—
New York U.	—	—	—	—	X	—	—	—	—	—	—	—	—	—
Notre Dame	—	—	—	—	—	X	—	X	—	—	—	—	—	†
Ottawa	X	—	—	X	X	X	X	X	—	—	—	—	X	—
Pennsylvania	X	S	X	—	X	X	S	—	X	—	—	—	—	—
Princeton	X	—	—	—	—	—	X	—	X	X	—	—	—	—
Rice	—	—	—	—	—	X	—	—	X	X	—	—	X	—
Southern Cal.	—	—	—	—	—	—	—	—	—	—	—	X	—	—
Stanford	—	X	—	X	—	X	S*	—	—	—	—	—	—	—
Syracuse	—	—	—	—	—	X	X	X	X	—	X	X	X	—
Temple	X	—	—	—	—	X	X	—	—	—	—	—	X	—
Wisconsin	—	S	—	—	—	—	—	—	—	—	—	—	—	—

* Brown, McMaster, and Stanford specify "Western Religious Thought."

† Notre Dame offers liturgical studies (historically oriented) and is beginning pastoral theology.

S=only special fields in the area are offered.

TABLE 11–1b

AREAS OF DOCTORAL SPECIALIZATION OFFERED

Ph.D.	History of Religions	Far Eastern Religions	Islamic Studies	Near Eastern Religions (Ancient)	Judaic Studies	Biblical Studies	Historical Studies (Christian)	Theological Studies (Christian)	Philosophy of Religion	Ethics	Religion and Society	Theology & Culture, Arts	Religion & Psychology	Practical Theology
Type II														
Boston	—	—	—	—	—	X	X	X	—	—	X	—	X	—
Chicago	X	—	—	—	—	X	X	X	—	—	X	X	X	—
Claremont	X	—	—	—	—	X	X	X	—	—	X	X	—	—
Columbia	X	X	—	X	X	X	X	—	X	X	X	—	—	—
Drew	—	—	—	—	—	X	X	X	X	X	X	X	—	—
Duke	—	—	—	—	—	X	X	X	—	—	—	—	—	—
Emory	—	—	—	—	—	X	X	X	—	—	X	—	—	—
GTU	—	—	—	—	—	X	X	X	—	—	X	X	X	—
Harvard (Rel. & NEL)	X	—	—	X	X	X	X	X	X	X	X	—	—	—
McGill	X	—	X	—	—	X	X	—	*	X	—	—	—	—
Montreal	—	—	—	—	—	X	—	X	—	—	—	—	—	X
Northwestern	X	—	—	—	—	X	X	X	X	X	X	—	X	X
Pittsburgh	—	—	—	—	—	X	X	X	—	X	—	—	—	—
St. Louis	—	—	—	—	—	X	X	—	—	—	—	—	—	—
St. Michael's	—	—	—	—	—	X	X	X	X	X	—	—	—	—
SMU	—	—	—	—	—	—	S	X	X	X	—	—	—	—
Vanderbilt	—	—	—	—	—	X	X	X	—	X	X	—	—	—
Yale	X	—	—	—	—	X	X	X	X	X	—	—	—	—
Yeshiva	—	—	—	—	X	X	—	—	—	—	—	—	—	—
Type III														
Aquinas	—	—	—	—	—	—	—	X	—	—	—	—	—	—
Dropsie	X	—	X	X	X	X	—	—	—	—	—	—	—	—
Hartford	X	—	X	—	—	X	X	X	X	—	—	X	X	—
Hebrew Union	—	—	—	—	X	X	—	—	—	—	—	—	—	—
Jewish Theol.	—	—	—	—	X	X	—	—	—	—	—	—	—	—
St. Mary's	—	—	—	—	—	X	X	X	—	X	—	—	—	—

* McGill offers "Philosophy and Psychology of Religion."
S=only special fields in the area are offered.

TABLE 11–1c

AREAS OF DOCTORAL SPECIALIZATION OFFERED

Th.D./S.T.D./- D.H.L. Type IV	History of Religions	Far Eastern Religions	Islamic Studies	Near Eastern Religions (Ancient)	Judaic Studies	Biblical Studies	Historical Studies (Christian)	Theological Studies (Christian)	Philosophy of Religion	Ethics	Religion and Society	Theology & Culture, Arts	Religion & Psychology	Practical Theology
Chicago T.S.	—	—	—	—	—	S	S	—	—	—	S	—	—	—
Concordia Sem.	—	—	—	—	—	X	X	X	—	—	—	—	—	X
Dallas T.S.	—	—	—	—	—	X	X	X	—	—	—	—	—	X
Dominican	—	—	—	—	—	X	X	X	—	—	—	—	—	X
Fuller	—	—	—	—	—	X	X	X	—	—	—	—	—	—
General T.S.	—	—	—	—	—	X	X	X	—	X	—	—	—	X
Grace T.S.	—	—	—	—	—	X	—	X	—	—	—	—	—	—
GTU	—	—	—	—	—	X	X	X	—	—	—	X	—	X
Iliff	—	—	—	—	—	X	X	X	—	—	—	—	X	—
Jewish Theol.	—	—	—	—	X	X	—	—	—	—	—	—	—	—
Lutheran (Chi.)	—	—	—	—	—	X	X	X	—	—	—	—	—	—
New Orleans	—	—	—	—	—	X	X	X	—	X	—	—	X	X
Princeton Sem.	X	—	—	—	—	X	X	X	X	X	X	—	—	X
Seabury-West.	—	—	—	—	—	X	X	X	—	X	—	—	—	—
S. Baptist	—	—	—	—	—	X	X	X	X	X	X	—	X	X
S.W. Baptist	—	—	—	—	—	X	X	X	X	X	—	—	—	X
Union, N.Y.	—	—	—	—	—	X	X	X	—	—	—	—	—	X
Union, Va.	—	—	—	—	—	X	X	X	—	—	—	—	—	X
Type V														
Catholic U.	—	—	—	—	—	X	—	X	—	X	—	—	—	—
Harvard (Th.D.)	X	—	—	—	—	X	X	X	—	X	—	—	—	X
Laval	—	—	—	—	—	X	—	X	—	X	—	—	—	—
Montreal	—	—	—	—	—	X	—	X	—	—	—	—	—	X
St. Paul	—	—	—	—	—	—	—	X	—	—	—	—	—	—
Toronto	—	—	—	—	—	X	X	X	X	X	—	—	—	X

S=only special fields in the area are offered.

With the fields designated by the institutions it is useful to compare the reports from 1969–1970 doctoral students concerning their areas of specialization. Table 11–2 thus displays the distribution of student responses, using the same groupings of schools and fields.

About sixty percent of all 1969–1970 doctoral students are accounted for in this tabulation. In some institutions the proportion is considerably less, and in those cases particularly the distribution by fields needs to be viewed with caution (see Chapter 12, Table 12–9, for total 1969–1970 doctoral student enrollment in each institution). In some instances, notably Southwestern Baptist, "no response" indicates that usable information was not received. In most cases, however, the tabulation appears to give a reasonable indication of the proportions of students pursuing their studies in the several areas.

It is important to note here that the categories "history of religions" and "Far Eastern religions" are not discrete, but overlap greatly; student responses characteristically tended to identify specializations, even though such specializations are not formally announced by the institutions. Even apart from this, however, significant differences appear between institutions in which students are working within the announced areas of concentration and schools in which students report

TABLE 11–2a

DISTRIBUTION OF DOCTORAL STUDENTS BY AREAS OF SPECIALIZATION
1969–1970

Ph.D. Type I	History of Religions	Far Eastern Religions	Islamic Studies	Near Eastern Religions (Ancient)	Judaic Studies	Biblical Studies	Historical Studies (Christian)	Theological Studies (Christian)	Philosophy of Religion	Ethics	Religion and Society	Theology & Culture, Arts	Religion & Psychology	Practical Theology	Total*
Baylor	1	—	—	—	1	10	7	1	—	2	—	1	—	—	23
Brandeis	—	—	—	2	19	6	—	—	—	—	—	—	—	—	27
Brigham Young	1	—	—	—	—	—	5	1	—	—	—	—	—	3	10
Brown	—	—	—	—	5	2	4	—	2	1	—	1	—	—	15
Calif., UCSB	—	—	—	—	—	—	1	—	—	—	—	—	—	—	1
Case W. R.	—	—	—	—	—	4	1	—	—	—	—	—	—	—	5
Catholic U.	2	—	—	—	—	2	7	6	2	4	1	—	1	12	37
Fordham	6	4	—	—	—	10	16	27	9	2	—	1	1	—	76
Iowa	1	6	—	—	—	10	26	3	—	6	—	1	2	—	55
J. Hopkins	—	—	—	—	—	—	—	—	—	—	—	—	—	—	NR
McMaster	—	7	—	2	—	2	5	—	1	—	1	—	—	—	18
Marquette	—	—	—	—	—	8	5	12	—	—	1	1	1	—	28
New York U.	—	—	—	—	—	—	—	—	—	—	—	—	—	—	NR
Notre Dame	—	—	—	—	—	9	5	8	2	—	—	—	—	10	34
Ottawa	—	—	—	—	—	—	—	—	—	—	—	—	—	—	NR
Pennsylvania	—	4	—	—	—	5	9	—	6	—	—	—	—	—	24
Princeton	—	4	—	—	—	2	7	1	5	2	—	1	—	—	22
Rice	—	—	—	—	—	4	—	3	2	—	—	—	—	1	10
Southern Cal.	—	—	—	—	—	—	—	—	—	—	8	—	—	—	8
Stanford	—	—	—	—	1	—	1	—	2	—	—	—	—	—	4
Syracuse	—	2	—	—	—	—	2	—	2	—	1	8	1	—	16
Temple	12†	4	1	—	1	4	18	4	10	6	2	6	4	—	72
Wisconsin	—	9	—	—	—	—	—	—	—	—	—	—	—	—	9
Totals	23	40	1	4	27	78	119	66	43	23	14	20	10	26	494

* The "Total" column indicates the number of codable responses from the graduate student questionnaires.

† Including one in primitive religions.

a considerably wider or narrower spectrum of specializations than announced. Such discrepancies are in part to be accounted for by the variations in the way institutions describe the fields of specialization, in part by lack of discipline in allowing students to work in areas for which the institution is not truly equipped.

TABLE 11–2b

DISTRIBUTION OF DOCTORAL STUDENTS BY AREAS OF SPECIALIZATION
1969–1970

Ph.D. Type II	History of Religions	Far Eastern Religions	Islamic Studies	Near Eastern Religions (Ancient)	Judaic Studies	Biblical Studies	Historical Studies (Christian)	Theological Studies (Christian)	Philosophy of Religion	Ethics	Religion and Society	Theology & Culture, Arts	Religion & Psychology	Practical Theology	Total*
Boston	—	—	—	—	—	9	5	4	1	—	16	—	6	8	49
Chicago	13†	9	1	—	—	23	23	12	13	2	25	19	21	—	161
Claremont	1	3	—	1	—	19	5	2	14	1	8	2	—	1	57
Columbia	—	7	—	—	2	3	4	—	16	1	6	—	1	—	40
Drew	—	—	—	—	—	4	5	9	7	7	5	4	4	—	45
Duke	—	1	—	—	—	17	15	4	—	6	2	3	—	—	48
Emory	—	—	—	—	—	17	14	6	3	6	7	8	—	—	61
GTU	—	—	—	—	—	6	5	1	15	1	13	5	5	5	56
Harvard (Rel. & NEL)	3	6	2	6	—	20	6	4	—	1	8	—	1	—	57
McGill	—	—	—	—	—	4	4	1	4	1	—	—	—	1	15
Montreal	—	—	—	—	—	1	—	1	—	—	—	—	—	—	2
Northwestern	—	—	—	—	—	8	6	5	5	1	2	1	12	3	43
Pittsburgh	—	—	—	—	—	1	2	—	—	—	—	—	—	—	3
St. Louis	—	—	—	—	—	4	10		—	—	—	—	—	1	15
St. Michael's	—	—	—	—	—	1	3	3	2	—	—	1	—	—	10
SMU	—	—	—	—	—	—	5	3	3	2	—	—	—	—	13
Vanderbilt	—	—	—	—	—	18	14	4	2	5	2	—	—	—	45
Yale	1	1	1	—	1	20	23	8	15	8	2	—	—	—	80
Yeshiva	—	—	—	1	5	1	—	—	—	—	—	—	—	—	7
Total	18	27	4	8	8	176	149	67	100	42	96	43	50	19	807

Type III															
Aquinas	—	—	—	—	1	3	2	12	1	1	1	1	—	2	24
Dropsie	3	—	—	5	5	1	—	—	—	—	—	—	—	—	14
Hartford	1	5	6	—	—	6	4	1	1	—	1	—	3	—	28
Hebrew Union	—	—	—	1	9	13	—	—	—	—	—	—	—	—	23
JTS	—	—	—	—	—	—	—	—	—	—	—	—	—	—	NR
St. Mary's	—	—	—	—	—	—	—	—	—	—	—	—	—	—	NR
Total	4	5	6	6	15	23	6	13	2	1	2	1	3	2	89

* The number of codable responses from the graduate student questionnaires.
† Including two in primitive religions.

TABLE 11–2c

DISTRIBUTION OF DOCTORAL STUDENTS BY AREAS OF SPECIALIZATION
1969–1970

Th.D./S.T.D./-D.H.L. Type IV	History of Religions	Far Eastern Religions	Islamic Studies	Near Eastern Religions (Ancient)	Judaic Studies	Biblical Studies	Historical Studies (Christian)	Theological Studies (Christian)	Philosophy of Religion	Ethics	Religion and Society	Theology & Culture, Arts	Religion & Psychology	Practical Theology	Total*
Chicago T.S.	—	—	—	—	—	—	1	—	—	—	3	2	—	—	6
Concordia Sem.	—	—	—	—	—	8	—	3	—	—	—	—	—	4	15
Dallas T.S.	—	—	—	—	—	7	—	3	—	—	—	—	—	3	13
Dominican	—	—	—	—	—	—	4	—	—	—	—	—	—	—	4
Fuller	—	—	—	—	—	3	1	1	—	—	—	—	—	—	5
General T.S.	—	—	—	—	—	1	1	—	—	1	—	—	—	1	4
Grace T.S.	—	—	—	—	—	9	—	9	—	1	—	—	—	—	19
GTU	—	—	—	—	—	15	7	2	6	1	1	1	4	3	40
Iliff	—	—	—	—	—	2	—	2	1	—	—	—	2	—	7
JTS	—	—	—	—	1	—	—	1	—	—	—	—	—	—	2
Lutheran (Chi.)	—	—	—	—	—	6	1	4	1	2	—	—	—	—	14
New Orleans	—	—	—	—	—	14	5	—	—	—	—	—	1	5	25
Princeton Sem.	—	2	—	—	—	19	13	8	2	1	6	—	7	12	70
Seabury-West.	—	—	—	—	—	—	—	—	—	—	—	—	—	—	NR
S. Baptist	—	—	—	—	—	21	5	5	1	4	1	1	2	1	41
S.W. Baptist	—	—	—	—	—	—	—	—	—	—	—	—	—	—	NR
Union, N.Y.	—	—	—	—	—	12	6	2	3	3	4	—	2	4	36
Union, Va.	—	—	—	—	—	2	—	1	—	—	—	—	—	—	3
Total	—	2	—	—	1	119	44	41	14	13	15	4	18	33	304
Type V															
Catholic U.	—	—	—	—	—	4	1	7	1	4	—	—	2	3	22
Harvard (Th.D.)	—	1	—	—	—	8	1	—	—	1	—	—	1	2	14
Laval	—	—	—	—	—	—	—	—	—	—	—	—	—	—	NR
Montreal	1	—	—	—	—	—	—	1	—	—	—	—	—	1	3
St. Paul (D.Th. and Ph.D.	1	—	—	—	—	1	3	5	—	—	—	—	—	1	11
Toronto GSTS	—	—	—	—	—	4	3	4	1	—	1	—	—	—	13
Total	2	1	—	—	—	17	8	17	2	5	1	—	3	7	63

* The number of codable responses from the graduate student questionnaires.

The highly condensed classification of fields of specialization in Table 11–2 conceals many important distinctions in these areas. It does not show, for example, the relatively high incidence of the study of American religion, in the general heading of "historical studies," at several institutions (as at Chicago,

Emory, Iowa, Vanderbilt, and Yale). This defect can be partially remedied, though not with respect to individual schools, by a more detailed tabulation of student specializations in relation to the entire list of categories used for coding both graduate student questionnaires and the 1965–1969 dissertation topics. Table 11–3 displays the distribution of all student respondents by degree types (Ph.D., Th.D./S.T.D./D.H.L.). The field list involves some overlapping of subfields, as a result of the effort to take into account the variations in program description, but clearly shows the heavy concentrations in a few areas and the small numbers of students in others (see also Chapter 13).

TABLE 11–3

FIELDS OF SPECIALIZATION OF DOCTORAL STUDENTS IN RELIGION
1969–1970

| | *Number of Students* | | |
	Ph.D.	*Th.D. S.T.D. D.H.L.*	*% Total*
History of Religion(s)	22	—	1.2
Comparative Religion(s)	12	1	0.7
World Religions	3	1	0.2
Far Eastern Religions	3	1	0.2
Religions of India ("South Asian")	41	0	2.2
Buddhism	20	1	1.1
Religions of China	7	1	0.4
Religions of Japan	—	—	0.0
Primitive Religions	4	—	0.2
Phenomenology of Religion	3	—	0.2
Judaic Studies	21	1	1.2
Jewish History	9	—	0.5
Jewish Religious Thought	4	—	0.2
Rabbinic, Talmudic Studies	8	—	0.4
Medieval and Modern Judaism	10	—	0.5
Ancient Near Eastern Religions (including language and literature)	16	—	0.9
Modern Near Eastern Studies	2	—	0.1
Islamic Studies	11	—	0.6
Biblical Studies, Bible, Sacred Scripture, Biblical Literature, Biblical Archaeology, Biblical Theology	31	12	2.3
Old Testament	92	40	7.2
New Testament	137	82	11.9
Christian Origins/Early Christianity	17	3	1.1

TABLE 11-3 (continued)

FIELDS OF SPECIALIZATION OF DOCTORAL STUDENTS IN RELIGION
1969-1970

	Number of Students		
		Th.D.	
		S.T.D.	*%*
	Ph.D.	*D.H.L.*	*Total*
Historical Studies (Christian)	9	—	0.5
History of Christianity, Church History	37	9	2.5
Historical Theology, History of Christian Thought	29	4	1.8
Patristics	19	6	1.4
Medieval Period	6	—	0.3
Reformation (English and Continental)	27	6	1.8
Protestant Thought (including denominational studies)	16	2	1.0
Roman Catholic Thought or Studies	10	2	0.7
American Religion or Thought	84	13	5.3
Modern Christian Thought	39	7	2.5
Theological Studies, Theology, Christian Theology	67	32	5.4
Systematic Theology	78	24	5.5
Ecumenical Studies	7	—	0.4
Philosophy of Religion, Philosophical Theology	141	15	8.5
Philosophy and Psychology of Religion	5	—	0.3
Ethics, Christian Ethics, Theological Ethics	60	14	4.0
Moral Theology	5	4	0.5
Ethics and Society, Social Ethics	52	11	3.4
Religion and Society	41	4	2.4
Sociology of Religion	20	2	1.2
Theology and Culture	18	4	1.2
Religion and the Arts	46	1	2.6
Religion and Psychology	37	2	2.1
Practical Theology	5	13	1.0
Preaching/Homiletics	1	8	0.5
Liturgical Studies	14	3	0.9
Pastoral Theology and Psychology	28	16	2.4
Religious Education (includes "Theology and Education" at GTU)	26	11	2.0
Missions and Evangelism	2	2	0.2
NR and Uncodable	67	13	4.3
	1,469	371*	99.9

* Th.D. column does not include Southwestern Baptist.

12

Demography

1. The Growth of Doctoral Studies in Religion, 1950–1970

Of the present fifty-two religion Ph.D programs in the United States and Canada, two-thirds have come into being since World War II. Twenty of these were established in the 1960's, and by 1969–1970 they enrolled more than a quarter of the Ph.D. students in religion. Six Th.D. programs also had their origin in the 1960's, though on the whole the Th.D., S.T.D., and D.H.L. programs have grown much less.

The following tables, 12–1 through 12–5, exhibit the patterns of expansion in programs, degrees awarded, and graduate enrollment.

Table 12–1 shows the chronology of establishment of doctoral study in religion and theology by decades since 1930, with the specific date of program origin or award of the first degree, insofar as information was supplied by directors of graduate study. In a few cases, occasional doctorates were awarded earlier by some of the institutions, but the dates given indicate continuous existence of a doctoral program.

TABLE 12-1

DATES OF ESTABLISHMENT OF DOCTORAL PROGRAMS
IN RELIGION AND THEOLOGY

Before 1930

Institution	Degree	Year	Institution	Degree	Year
Boston	Ph.D.		Iowa	Ph.D.	1929
	& Th.D.	1874	Jewish Theological	D.H.L.	1902
Brown	Ph.D.	1896	Johns Hopkins	Ph.D.	1876?
Catholic U.	S.T.D.	1889	Montreal	Th.D.	1878
Chicago	Ph.D.	1892	New Orleans	Th.D.	1923
Dallas	Th.D.	1926	Northwestern	Ph.D.	1925
Dropsie	Ph.D.	1909	Southern Baptist	Th.D.	1892
General Theological	Th.D.	1926	Southwestern Baptist	Th.D.	1908
Hartford	Ph.D.	1895	Union (N.Y.)	Th.D.	1917
Harvard	Th.D.	1915	Union (Va.)	Th.D.	1929
Iliff	Th.D.	1928	Yale	Ph.D.	1869

230

TABLE 12-1—(Continued)

1931-1940

Institution	Degree	Year	Institution	Degree	Year
Catholic U.	Ph.D.	1940	Harvard (Rel.)	Ph.D.	1934
Duke	Ph.D.	1936	Princeton Theological	Th.D.	1940
Emmanuel	Th.D.	1939			

1941-1950

Institution	Degree	Year	Institution	Degree	Year
Columbia	Ph.D.	1946	Hebrew Union	Ph.D.	1947
Concordia	Th.D.	1944	Lutheran (Chicago)	S.T.D.	1946
Dominican	S.T.D.	1941	USC	Ph.D.	1941
Grace Theological	Th.D.	1944	Vanderbilt	Ph.D.	1948

1951-1960

Institution	Degree	Year	Institution	Degree	Year
Aquinas	Ph.D.	1952	McGill	Ph.D.	1952
Brandeis	Ph.D.	1953	Montreal	Ph.D.	1958
Claremont	Ph.D.	1959	Ottawa	Ph.D.	1960
Drew	Ph.D.	1955	Princeton U.	Ph.D.	1955
Emory	Ph.D.	1958	Yeshiva	Ph.D.	1958
Jewish Theological	Ph.D.	1958			

1961-1970

Institution	Degree	Year	Institution	Degree	Year
Baylor	Ph.D.	1966	Pennsylvania	Ph.D.	1962
Brigham Young	Ph.D.	1961	Pittsburgh	Ph.D.	1967
U. Cal., S.B.	Ph.D.	1969	Rice	Ph.D.	1968
Case Western	Ph.D.	1961	St. Louis	Ph.D.	1969
Chicago Theological	D.Th.	1966	St. Mary's	Ph.D.	1969
Fordham	Ph.D.	1967	St. Michael's	Ph.D.	1966
Fuller	Th.D.	1968	Seabury-Western	Th.D.	1967
GTU	Th.D.	1962	SMU	Ph.D.	1965
GTU	Ph.D.	1964	Stanford	Ph.D.	1968
Knox	Th.D.	1965	Syracuse	Ph.D.	1964
Marquette	Ph.D.	1963	Temple	Ph.D.	1961
McMaster	Ph.D.	1965	Trinity	Th.D.	1961
NYU	Ph.D.	1961	Wisconsin	Ph.D.	1961
Notre Dame	Ph.D.	1961			

Table 12–2 charts the increase in teaching and research doctorates awarded in religion and theology between 1952 and 1970. Since the *Review of Religion* supplement of 1954 provides a listing of the 569 Ph.D. dissertations completed in religion programs from 1940 through 1952, the latter year was chosen as the first year for reporting.

TABLE 12-2

RELIGION DOCTORAL DEGREES AWARDED, 1952-1969*

Year		Ph.D.	Th.D./S.T.D./D.H.L.	Total
1952		78	71	149
1953		72	87	159
1954		82	80	162
1955		88	67	155
1956		75	87	162
1957		90	67	157
1958		99	74	173
1959		93	82	175
1960		101	95	196
1961		110	88	198
1962		125	98	223
1963		137	92	229
1964		169	93	262
1965		171	90	261
1966		166	97	263
1967		178	106	284
1968		227	115	342
1969		208	88	296
1970	(est.)	(235)	(100)	(335)

* Figures are incomplete or missing for Johns Hopkins, Harvard Near Eastern Languages and Literatures, New York University, Pittsburgh, Union (Va.), Wisconsin, Knox, Laval, Ottawa, St. Paul, and Trinity.

Table 12–3 compares the expansion in doctoral degree production in religion with that in selected other fields and with the total for the United States, as compiled by the American Council of Education. The totals for religion are greater than those reported from our own study, since our tabulations include only degrees from teaching and research programs. However, the comparative growth rates reliably indicate that doctoral degree production did not expand as rapidly between 1952 and 1969 as in any of the other individual fields noted, nor as rapidly as total doctoral degree production.

Table 12–4 shows the expansion of doctoral enrollments in selected institutions from 1959 to 1969, comparing the expansion in enrollment in those established programs for which reliable enrollment data are available for 1959 and subsequent years with the expansion in the programs established in the two following five-year intervals. Although the older Ph.D. programs increased in enrollment by approximately 50 percent, most of the expansion came in the newly established institutions. The Th.D. programs did not increase significantly, with the exception of the Th.D. at the Graduate Theological Union.

TABLE 12-3

UNITED STATES DOCTORAL DEGREE PRODUCTION*

1952-1953 to 1968-1969

Year	Total Doctorates	Reli- gion	His- tory	Philos- ophy	Eng- lish	Sociol.	Foreign Lang.	Bio- chem.
1952-53	*	222	301	107	328	157	165	142
1953-54	8,996	226	355	103	356	184	184	145
1954-55	8,840	210	310	84	341	167	152	147
1955-56	8,903	217	274	82	382	170	196	146
1956-57	8,756	246	333	85	350	134	164	123
1957-58	8,942	290	313	102	333	150	149	149
1958-59	9,360	264	342	100	373	157	170	139
1959-60	9,829	276	366	137	397	161	174	165
1960-61	10,575	238	389	146	400	184	195	187
1961-62	11,622	282	360	123	486	173	198	183
1962-63	12,822	276	402	134	516	208	199	212
1963-64	14,490	306	533	137	556	198	277	264
1964-65	16,467	331	600	144	689	230	312	290
1965-66	18,239	333	628	203	699	244	365	315
1966-67	20,621	312	691	249	848	327	450	331
1967-68	23,091	401	726	278	977	367	521	442
1968-69	25,100	346	871	287	1,151	430	581	471

* Source: ACE *Fact Book*, 1970, pp. 70.228 ff. No total given for 1952-53.

TABLE 12-4

ENROLLMENT GROWTH IN DOCTORAL PROGRAMS IN RELIGION,
UNITED STATES AND CANADA, 1959-1969*

	Fall 1959	Fall 1964	Fall 1969
Ph.D.			
18 programs est. before 1959	744	900	1,111
7 programs est. 1959-64	0	193	504
9 programs est. 1964-69	0	0	184
Total	744	1,093	1,799
Th.D./S.T.D./D.H.L.			
14 programs est. before 1959	528	470	519
1 program est. 1959-64 (GTU)	0	17	64
3 programs est. 1964-69	0	0	19
Total	528	487	602

* Based on reports from 50 institutions, providing appropriate data for 52 programs. Major omissions from the older programs include Catholic University, Claremont, Columbia, and Jewish Theological.

Table 12–5 compares expansion in enrollment for advanced degrees in religion with growth in other fields (the numbers include master's as well as doctoral-level students, but not first professional degree students). Of particular significance is the relatively small expansion between 1960 and 1964 in graduate study in religion and the great expansion in the following four-year period. In percentages, religion expanded more rapidly between 1964 and 1968 than any other field. Only anthropology approximated this rate of expansion.

TABLE 12-5

ENROLLMENT FOR ADVANCED DEGREES
by Field of Study, 1960–1968*

	1960	1962	1964	1966	1968
HUMANITIES	37,185	46,031	60,191	75,484	95,082
English and Journalism	13,463	16,873	22,661	27,499	32,296
Philosophy	2,258	2,684	3,450	4,153	4,931
Religion	5,314	5,447	6,111	7,383	12,620
SOCIAL SCIENCES	63,700	75,152	105,549	124,773	152,308
Anthropology	1,006	1,338	1,871	2,684	3,678
History	9,170	10,671	14,565	17,533	20,247
Sociology	3,277	3,924	5,345	6,688	8,682
BIOLOGICAL SCIENCES	29,864	34,107	43,015	50,299	62,367
PHYSICAL SCIENCES	37,477	42,712	52,287	56,441	63,884

* Source: ACE *Fact Book*, 1970, pp. 70.38–39.

2. COMPARATIVE INSTITUTIONAL DATA

Degrees Awarded; Length of Time in Study; First Employment of Doctorate Recipients; Current Enrollments; Full- and Part-Time Study; Proportions of Ph.D. Students holding Professional Degrees.

The tables that follow are drawn from three sources: reports from departmental and graduate chairmen concerning the numbers of degrees awarded each year between 1952 and 1969 and the fall term 1969 total enrollment in the doctoral programs; chairmen's reports on all degree recipients from 1965 through 1969; and questionnaires sent to all identifiable doctoral students in the sixty-nine institutions involved in the study.

The reports on the numbers of degrees awarded and the current enrollments are complete with the exceptions indicated in each instance. From the reports on individual degree recipients, we include here only information bearing on length of time in study and first employment of the recipient. (Patterns of dissertation study as disclosed by these reports are dealt with in Chapter 13.) Statistics here are less complete, because of unavailability of information, particularly with respect to the first employment of doctoral recipients. As noted earlier (Preface), the over-all response rate for the graduate student questionnaire was approximately two-thirds, with institutional response rates varying from 100 percent to 0 percent. As a rule we have taken a response rate of 60 percent or more from students in a given institution as sufficient for providing a reliable picture. Tables 12–6a and 12–6b show the total numbers of doctoral degrees awarded between 1952 and 1969 and between 1965 and 1969—indicating the high de-

TABLE 12-6a

EARNED DOCTORATES IN RELIGION AND THEOLOGY 1952-1969

Ph.D.

	1952-1969	1965-1969
Yale University	308	97
Boston University	288	89
University of Chicago	254*	93
Columbia University	167	41
Duke University	158	59
Harvard University	126	53
Drew University	123	79
Vanderbilt University	108	42
Dropsie University	90	23
University of Southern California	85	12
Northwestern U./Garrett Theological Seminary	66	38
Hartford Seminary Foundation	64	25
University of Iowa	59	37
Princeton University	44	23
Emory University	43	31
Hebrew Union College	42	17
Claremont Graduate School	38	29
Catholic University of America	38†	20
Temple University	24	22
Marquette University	17	17
Yeshiva University	16	11
University of Ottawa	†	15
Brandeis University	†	11
McGill University	15	8
Brigham Young University	10	8
Brown University	7	4
Case Western Reserve University	7	7
University of Wisconsin	5†	5
Aquinas Institute	5	4
Fordham University	5	5
University of Pennsylvania	4	4
Graduate Theological Union	4	4
University of St. Michael's College	4	4
Jewish Theological Seminary	2	2
Syracuse University	1	1
McMaster University	1	1

* Including Divinity School (230) and New Testament and Early Christian Literature (24).

† Incomplete data.

NOTES. No degrees awarded yet: Baylor, University of California (Santa Barbara), Notre Dame, Rice, St. Louis, St. Mary's, Southern Methodist, and Stanford. No reports: Johns Hopkins, New York, Laval, and Pittsburgh.

gree of concentration in a few schools in the past and the relative changes that
have taken place, in the latter half of the 1960's, in the proportions of degrees
awarded. Compare Tables 12–1 (dates of program establishment) and 12–9
(fall term 1969 doctoral enrollments).

TABLE 12-6b

EARNED DOCTORATES IN RELIGION AND THEOLOGY 1952-1969

Th.D./S.T.D./D.H.L.

	1952-1969	1965-1969
Southwestern Baptist Theological Seminary	266	75
Southern Baptist Theological Seminary	256	46
Princeton Theological Seminary	156	56
New Orleans Baptist Theological Seminary	155	47
Catholic University of America	148	45
Union Theological Seminary, New York	138	53
Dallas Theological Seminary	123	43
Iliff School of Theology	79	18
Harvard University	78	48
Jewish Theological Seminary	62	14
Concordia Seminary	49	20
University of Montreal	41	7
Emmanuel College (Toronto)	27	12
General Theological Seminary	20	5
Grace Theological Seminary	15	12
St. Paul University (Ottawa)	*	9
Lutheran School of Theology, Chicago	14	3
Dominican House of Studies	12	5
Graduate Theological Union	6	6
Seabury-Western Theological Seminary	1	1

* Incomplete data.
NOTES. No degrees awarded yet: Chicago Theological, Fuller.
No reports: Union (Va.), Knox, Trinity.

Tables 12–7a and 12–7b report the comparative lengths of time in study (elapsed time) for all institutions from which information is available. (For over-all averages and relation to other fields of study, see Chapter 5.)

TABLE 12-7a

LENGTH OF TIME IN STUDY*

Doctoral Recipients 1965-1969

Ph.D.

Name of School	Number of Degrees Awarded†		Years in Program		
			Median	Minimum	Maximum
Boston	83	(56)	6	2	21
Brandeis	11	(5)	7	4	9
Brown	4	(3)	6	5	9
Case Western Reserve	7	(7)	8	6	16
Catholic	20	(20)	3.5	1	7
Claremont	31	(24)	4.5	2	10
Columbia	41	(41)	8	2	21
Drew	80	(79)	6	3	21
Duke	52	(52)	4	2	14
Emory	30	(30)	4.5	3	9
Fordham	7	(7)	3	2	4
Graduate Theological	4	(4)	4	3	4
Harvard	61	(60)	7	3	14
Hebrew Union	17	(16)	4.5	3	13
Iowa	35	(33)	5	2	18
Marquette	17	(17)	4	2	6
McGill	8	(8)	3	2	8
Northwestern-Garrett	35	(35)	5	2	16
Pennsylvania	4	(4)	4	4	6
Princeton	23	(23)	5	3	12
St. Michael's	5	(5)	9	4	17
Temple	22	(22)	5	3	7
Vanderbilt	33	(33)	7	3	18
Yale	93	(72)	5	2	10

*Time span is calculated from entrance into doctoral program at institution conferring degree.

†Numbers in parentheses indicate number of recipients for whom length of time has been reported.

NOTES. Listed are only schools reporting a time span for three or more degree recipients. Major institutions for which no figures were available: Chicago, Hartford.

Fractional medians are used in cases where the students divided exactly evenly between the next smaller and the next larger number of years.

TABLE 12-7b

LENGTH OF TIME IN STUDY*

Doctoral Recipients 1965-1969

Th.D./S.T.D.

Name of School	Number of Degrees Awarded†		Years in Program		
			Median	Minimum	Maximum
Concordia	19	(19)	5	2	11
Dallas	20	(20)	4	3	11
Dominican (S.T.D.)	5	(5)	8	3	13
Emmanuel	12	(12)	8	2	11
General	4	(4)	7	6	9
Grace	11	(11)	5	3	6
Graduate Theological	6	(6)	5	3	6
Harvard	40	(39)	7	4	13
Iliff	17	(17)	5	2	15
New Orleans	47	(46)	6	2	13
Princeton Theological	43	(41)	6	3	13
Southern Baptist	46	(46)	4	3	8
Southwestern Baptist	75	(75)	6	3	12
Union (N.Y.)	53	(52)	6	3	21
Union (Va.)	17	(17)	4	2	7

* Time span is calculated from entrance into doctoral program at institution conferring degree.

† Numbers in parentheses indicate number of recipients for whom length of time was reported.

NOTES. Listed are only schools reporting a time span for three or more degree recipients. Major institutions for which no figures were available: Catholic University.

Tables 12–8a and 12–8b show the kind of first employment of doctoral recipients as reported by the institutions for doctoral recipients about whom such information is available. The number of degrees awarded, as shown in these tables, may vary slightly from those reported in Tables 12–6a and 12–6b, since the total number of individual reports on degree recipients did not always correspond exactly with the summary report of degrees awarded.

Table 12–9 shows the total fall term 1969 enrollments in doctoral programs in all the institutions involved in the study.

Table 12–10 shows for each institution the proportion of students in full-time residence study (including course work, examination preparation, and dissertation writing).

Table 12–11 reports, for the Ph.D. programs, the proportions of doctoral student respondents holding a professional degree or the equivalent. (The professional degree is normally a prerequisite for admission to Th.D./S.T.D./D.H.L. study.)

TABLE 12–8a

FIRST EMPLOYMENT OF DOCTORAL RECIPIENTS

Ph.D.

	Degrees Granted 1965–69	Teaching in College or University	Teaching in Seminary	Teaching Unspecified	Priesthood, Ministry, Rabbinate	Other	NR
Aquinas	2	1	0	0	0	0	1
Brigham Young	8	0	8	0	0	0	0
Brown	4	4	0	0	0	0	0
Case Western Reserve	7	6	0	0	1	0	0
Catholic University	20	9	1	0	0	1	9
Claremont	31	21	4	1	1	1	3
Columbia	41	19	2	0	0	1	19
Drew	80	44	10	6	17	1	2
Duke	52	37	8	0	1	6	0
Emory	30	19	5	3	1	2	0
Fordham	7	1	0	0	0	0	6
Graduate Theological	4	3	0	0	0	1	0
Harvard (Rel.)	61	40	6	4	9	2	0
Hebrew Union	17	6	0	3	5	3	0
Iowa	36	30	3	0	2	1	0
Marquette	17	13	0	1	0	1	2
McGill	8	5	0	0	3	0	0
McMaster	1	0	0	0	0	0	1
Northwestern-Garrett	35	15	5	3	5	7	0
Pennsylvania	4	3	0	0	1	0	0
Princeton University	23	18	4	0	0	1	0
St. Michael's	5	3	0	0	0	0	2
St. Paul (Ottawa)	12	3	0	0	1	0	8
Syracuse	1	1	0	0	0	0	0
Temple	22	4	0	0	0	0	18
Vanderbilt	33	10	1	11	1	0	10
Yale	97	58	11	1	3	2	22*
Totals	658	373	68	33	51	30	103

* One year missing.

NOTE. Institutions awarding ten or more degrees, for which this information was not available: Boston, Brandeis, Chicago, Dropsie, Hartford, Yeshiva.

TABLE 12–8b

FIRST EMPLOYMENT OF DOCTORAL RECIPIENTS

Th.D./S.T.D./D.H.L.

	Degrees Granted 1965–69	Teaching in College or University	Teaching in Seminary	Teaching Unspecified	Priesthood, Ministry, Rabbinate	Other	NR
Dallas	20	3	8	0	6	2	1
Dominican	5	1	3	0	0	0	1
Emmanuel	12	7	1	1	2	1	0
General Theological	4	1	2	0	1	0	0
Grace	11	5	6	0	0	0	0
Graduate Theological	6	5	0	0	0	0	1
Harvard	40	18	17	1	3	0	1
Iliff	17	0	0	3	10	3	1
Knox	2	0	1	0	1	0	0
New Orleans	47	11	2	2	30	2	0
Princeton Theological	43	14	8	0	6	0	15
Southern Baptist	46	0	4	2	3	2	35
Southwestern Baptist	75	13	2	0	51	6	3
Union (N.Y.)	53	23	19	0	8	2	1
Union (Va.)	17	9	3	0	4	1	0
Totals	398	110	76	9	125	19	59

NOTE. Institutions awarding ten or more degrees for which this information was not available: Catholic University, Concordia, Jewish Theological.

TABLE 12-9

FALL 1969 ENROLLMENTS IN DOCTORAL PROGRAMS

	Ph.D.		Th.D./S.T.D./D.H.L.
100 or more doctoral students			
Chicago (Div.)	251*	Southwestern Baptist	120
Temple	173		
Fordham	130		
Yale	114		
Total	668		120
75-99 students			
Boston	94	Princeton Theological	96
Iowa	83		
Dropsie	83		
Claremont	78		
Total	338		96

TABLE 12-9—(Continued)

50-74 students	Ph.D.		Th.D./S.T.D./D.H.L.
Hartford	71	Graduate Theological	65
Graduate Theological	68	Southern Baptist	52
Harvard (Rel.)	67	Catholic	51
Emory	64		
Vanderbilt	59		
Drew	59		
Duke	58		
Columbia	52		
St. Paul (Ottawa)	52		
Notre Dame	51		
Total	601		168
25-49 students			
Northwestern-Garrett	48	Union (N.Y.)	45
McMaster	42	New Orleans Baptist	45
Catholic	41	Dallas	43
Harvard (NEL)	(est.) 30		
Marquette	38		
Hebrew Union	36		
Aquinas	35		
Ottawa	35		
Baylor	32		
Pennsylvania	30		
Syracuse	26		
Brigham Young	25		
Total	418		133
1-24 students			
Brown	24	Grace	24
St. Michael's	24	Harvard	21
Princeton	22	Lutheran (Chicago)	20
McGill	22	Union, Va.	18
Saint Louis	18	Jewish Theological	13
Southern Methodist	17	Iliff	13
Rice	16	Montreal	13
S. California	16	Emmanuel	12
Johns Hopkins	16	Dominican	10
Wisconsin	15	Chicago Theological	9
Montreal	15	General	8
Pittsburgh	15	Fuller	7
Chicago (NT & ECL)	10	Concordia	6
Stanford	7	Trinity	6
Case Western Reserve	7	Knox	4
Jewish Theological	3	Seabury-Western	2
Univ. of Calif., Santa Barbara	2		
Total	249		186

*The number of students reported for Chicago included 70 technically in Ph.D. status and 181 technically in M.A. status. Both need to be included here, however, since the M.A. is considered as integral to the Ph.D.; i.e., it is not a terminal degree and all M.A. students are considered to be working for the Ph.D.

NOTE. Enrollment figures not available from Brandeis, New York, Yeshiva, Laval, St. Mary's.

TABLE 12-10

PROPORTION OF DOCTORAL STUDENTS IN FULL-TIME RESIDENCE STUDY, 1969-1970*

70%-100%	%	50%-69%	%	1%-49%	%
Claremont	71	Aquinas	65	Baylor	33
Columbia	83	Brown	62	Case Western Reserve	33
Duke	71	Catholic	56	Chicago Theological	33
Fordham	76	Chicago	68	Concordia	22
Fuller	100	Emory	69	Drew	9
Harvard	86	Graduate Theological	67	Grace	32
Notre Dame	89	Hebrew Union	60	Lutheran (Chicago)	7
Princeton University	77	Iowa	57	McGill	33
Southern Baptist	88	Marquette	57	New Orleans Baptist	48
Southern Methodist	77	Northwestern-Garrett	58	Southwestern Baptist	26
Syracuse	89	Pennsylvania	67	Toronto GSTS	21
Union (N.Y.)	78	Princeton Theological	61		
Vanderbilt	86	Rice	69		
Wisconsin	78	Saint Louis	56		
Yale	80	Yeshiva	50		

*Schools with questionnaire response rates of 60 percent or more are included in this table. From institutions with response rates of 40-60 percent, we have the following indications of full-time residence study: Boston, 58 percent; Brandeis, 54 percent; Hartford, 70 percent; McMaster, 100 percent; St. Michael's, 73 percent; Southern California, 38 percent; Stanford, 75 percent; and Temple, 45 percent.

TABLE 12-11

PERCENTAGE OF PH.D. STUDENTS IN RELIGION
WITH PROFESSIONAL DEGREES* (1969-1970)

By Schools

	No. of Respondents	Percent with Professional Degree
Baylor	24	100
Case	6	100
Duke	51	96
Hebrew Union	25	96
Emory	64	94
Boston†	53	93
Northwestern-Garrett	45	91
Drew	45	89
Hartford‡	30	83
St. Louis	16	81
Vanderbilt	49	80
McGill	15	80
Aquinas	26	77
GTU	56	77
Claremont	58	76
Southern Methodist	13	69
Pennsylvania	24	67
Yale	82	67
Princeton	22	64
Southern California†	8	63
Rice	16	63
Iowa	60	62
Temple‡	82	59
Harvard (Rel.)	42	57
Brown	16	56
U. of Chicago	163	55
Stanford†	4	50
Harvard (NEL)†	16	50
Syracuse	19	47
Catholic	41	46
Columbia	42	43
Brandeis†	28	43
Fordham	79	39
Notre Dame	36	39
McMaster†	18	39
Marquette	28	36
St. Michael's	11	27
Wisconsin	9	11
Brigham Young‡	11	9
California, Santa Barbara	1	0

*Or the equivalent. Excluded from calculations: schools with response rates less than 40 percent. Unless otherwise noted, response rates are 60 percent or more.
†Denotes a response rate of 50-59 percent.
‡Denotes a response rate of 40-49 percent (Harvard NEL response rate is estimated).

13

Directions of Research

Has the burgeoning of doctoral research in religion meant a charting of new territories, or has it been mostly the populating of old lands? Where are the current frontiers? What interests dominate the work of young scholars (or are neglected by them)? Partial answers to these questions may be drawn from four main sources: an account of the Ph.D. dissertations supervised in religion and theology between 1940 and 1952; the dissertations accepted in religion and theology between 1965 and 1969; reports from current doctoral students identifying their fields of concentration; and statements from graduate faculty concerning both their own present and intended areas of research and the most important new developments in their fields.[1]

In the field of religion as a whole, it is apparent that some different emphases are emerging in Ph.D. research. Since 1940–1952, the proportion of students in the history of religions areas has increased fivefold, while the proportion in practical theology has been cut in half. Ph.D. specialization, in other words, contin-

---

[1] The *Review of Religion* Supplement, 1954, provides a list of 569 Ph.D. dissertations accepted for religion degrees 1940–1952; précis are given for 425 of the dissertations. Our own questionnaires to institutions yielded a nearly complete list of dissertation titles (Ph.D., Th.D., S.T.D., D.H.L.) for degrees awarded in religion and theology by the sixty-nine institutions in the study for the years 1965–1969—1,293 dissertations in all. Of the 1,965 doctoral students in 1969–1970 who responded to the questionnaire, 1,760 provided usable responses identifying fields of specialization. There were 614 reports from graduate faculty members, some with extensive comments on developments in their fields.

The first three data sources were coded according to the list of fields of specialization given in Chapter 11, Table 11–3, and are the bases for most of the summary in this chapter and for Table 13–1. The classification of dissertation topics is necessarily arbitrary in some instances, since dissertations frequently overlap fields and in some cases could be classified equally well in one or more fields (for example, theology or modern history of Christianity). The over-all tabulations nonetheless provide a reasonably accurate account. The statements by faculty members have been primarily used for making cautious predictions of trends, which are offered thus as estimates from the field rather than as independent judgments.

ues partly to move toward areas of academic demand. Small relative increases can be seen in theology, Bible, and Judaic–Islamic–Near East studies, though the latter may be due only to increased facilities. These modest gains contrast, for example, with decreases in philosophy of religion and history of Christianity. Contrasts between Ph.D. and Th.D./S.T.D. doctoral areas may be easily observed (see Table 13–1). The latter degree programs tend to group in the seminary quadrivium: Bible, history of Christianity, theology, and practical theology. The Ph.D. encompasses a broad spectrum, and it is likely that this diversity will become more and more pronounced.

It is remarkable, however, that even with the changes noted, doctoral students are grouped proportionally in roughly the same areas now as twenty-five years ago. The shifts that have occurred appear to be due not so much to massive changes of interest as to the opening up of new fields. But other internal changes have taken place. The increase in cross-disciplinary studies (both within and outside the field of religion) and the multiplicity of methodologies have conceptually expanded the meaning of such categories as "theology" and "Bible." These designations are not as distinct as they were even a generation ago. For example, what was theology of culture in 1945 is understood by some today simply as theology. Conclusions about general migrations of interest must therefore be qualified by data showing the actual range of interests in the various fields. It can be supposed that the sheer numerical increase has brought a greater variety of interests which has expanded the denotation and connotation of the older categories.

1. NEW STYLES: THREE FIELDS

Keeping in mind the general trend away from the seminary format and toward cross-disciplinary work, what areas seem to hold the most promise for the future of the entire field? That is, where are the new "styles" of religious studies being generated? The question can be partially answered by reviewing the subdisciplines where experimentation and academic "demand," or growth rate, coalesce. These are the so-called "history of religions," philosophy of religion, and religion and the behavioral studies.

As already noted, history of religions has experienced the highest growth rate of all fields (Table 13–1). Nearly one out of twelve present Ph.D. students locates himself in this area. Among younger Ph.D. students (those under twenty-eight) without a prior professional degree, this is the most favored field of all. By far the largest concentration is in Indian religions, followed by Buddhism and Chinese religions. In contrast, between 1940 and 1952 only seven dissertations, of which three dealt with Indian religion, were completed in this whole area in religion programs. Areas receiving scant attention are Graeco-Roman religions and primitive religions of North America, though the former are increasingly seen as an essential element in New Testament studies. No student reported specialization in Japanese religion (though some classified under Buddhism are studying it; see also Chapter 11). Several faculty suggest the need for greater consideration of African religions and for investigation of "westernized" forms of oriental faith.

TABLE 13-1
FIELDS OF DOCTORAL SPECIALIZATION

	Dissertations 1940-52	Dissertations 1965-69		Doctoral Students 1969-70	
	Ph.D. %	Ph.D. %	Th.D./S.T.D. %	Ph.D. %	Th.D./S.T.D. %
History of Religions	1.6	3.8	0.2	7.9	1.3
Judaic, Near Eastern, Islamic	3.7	5.3	2.1	5.4	0.0
(Judaic)		(3.2)	(1.2)	(3.5)	
(Islamic)		(0.7)	(0.2)	(0.7)	
Biblical Studies	17.0	18.6	35.8	18.9	37.0
(Old Testament)		(6.9)	(13.4)	(6.3)	(10.8)
(New Testament)		(7.2)	(17.9)	(9.3)	(21.8)
(Christian Origins)		(2.2)	(1.9)	(1.2)	(0.8)
History of Christianity	23.4	22.4	18.8	18.8	13.2
(Patristics)		(1.6)	(1.9)	(1.3)	(1.6)
(Medieval)		(1.2)	(0.2)	(0.4)	(0.0)
(Reformation)		(4.9)	(4.0)	(1.8)	(1.6)
(Roman Catholic)		(1.2)	(1.0)	(0.7)	(0.5)
(American)		(6.6)	(6.1)	(5.7)	(3.5)
Theological Studies	8.2	14.4	11.7	10.4	15.2
Philosophy of Religion	13.4	10.8	8.0	9.9	4.0
Ethics, Religion and Society	12.1	11.9	6.8	12.1	9.5
(Sociology of Religion)		(1.7)	(1.2)	(1.4)	(0.5)
Religion and Culture	6.3	4.8	1.9	6.8	1.8
(Religion and the Arts)		(1.5)	(0.7)	(3.1)	(0.3)
Practical and Pastoral Theology	11.2	6.6	14.1	5.2	14.3
Uncodable or N.R.	3.0	1.3	0.7	4.6	3.5
Total	99.9	99.9	100.1	100.0	99.8
	N = 425	N = 859	N = 426	N = 1469	N = 371

NOTE. The fields in parentheses show only some of the subdivisions in the larger areas; the corresponding percentages will not add up to the area totals.

The history of religions has also contributed (at least indirectly) to much of the recent experimentation with different methodologies and cross-disciplinary study. This is not suprising, since the field grew out of diverse attempts to devise adequate models for the understanding of religion; for instance, anthropological, structural, "phenomenological." Further, it has always availed itself of the resources of other disciplines, if only of language studies. An unusual example of this cross-disciplinary impact is a seminary-based program which attempts to combine practical (missionary) interest with linguistic analyses of African languages that are of use to both missionaries and linguists. The varied methods of history of religions, and to some extent even its diverse subjects, have become matters of concern in almost every other field. Comparative studies abound as Christian theism becomes more a problematic topic than a normative ideal. As one professor of Japanese Buddhism indicates, the "end of the Christian 'establishment' means an even more critical review of Christian categories." Some faculty manifest an interest also in the proliferation of occultism, astrology, and nonecclesiastical forms of popular faith. Many indicate that familiarity with another culture is fast becoming a *sine qua non,* particularly in the traditionally "Christian" areas of study.

Philosophy of religion, as "thinking philosophically on religiously significant topics," has evinced some of the same indefiniteness as theology (see below). Like history of religions, it can appeal to a variety of philosophical schools and to recently developed methodological advances to establish a focal point from which to assess issues and problems. Dissertations reflect a divergence between those that merely depict philosophical issues or patterns and those that "do philosophy." In the former, a strong "history of philosophy" trend appears. One of every four of the 117 philosophy of religion theses in the five-year span 1965–1969 dealt with Kierkegaard, Tillich, or Whitehead. There has been a fair number of dissertations in medieval philosophy, such as "Status of Theistic Propositions in William of Ockham" (though a singular dearth of medieval studies in the history of Christianity). American philosophers are by no means excluded, but there has been no special concentration on any figure or school, and in contrast to the years 1940–1952, American philosophy appears a less popular thesis topic.

The themes of critical philosophizing are fairly predictable, with one key exception. The main topics have included religious discourse, epistemology, and philosophical method. Surprisingly, such questions as self-identity and personality (for example, "Religious Languages and the Problem of Self") outnumber theistic problems like the nature of God or the arguments for God's existence. This is, however, in keeping with the marked "anthropocentric" trend in theology. Presumably, in dealing with this issue students of philosophy have greater access to the insights of the mind-body discussion, epistemology, and philosophical psychology.

Areas relatively neglected in the last five years are post-Kantian German idealism (except Schleiermacher), ancient philosophy, and the seventeenth- and eighteenth-century rationalists. Consideration of English philosophers has been limited almost exclusively to the twentieth century. Also, despite the desiderata expressed by some faculty, the topic of science and religion appears only rarely, though an exception, "Influence of Mathematics on Theology, as seen in Wittgenstein, Husserl, and Whitehead," is suggestive.

Perhaps as much as the history of religions, recent philosophy has contributed a certain style to the entire field of religion. Its issue-oriented questioning, its skepticism, and the emphasis on logical analysis have become increasingly the norm for inquiry in other areas, such as New Testament and theology. Here, too, there is amenability to cross-disciplinary experiments. One philosopher urges that "philosophy of religion should take more account of the social sciences, at least one." There are also suggestions that philosophy should extend its inquiries beyond theism to nontheistic religious phenomena. One might therefore expect the future philosopher of religion to experiment with logical and metalinguistic fervor in heretofore untapped areas of religious expression. Moreover, the possibility is present for the development of "philosophical" methodologies in connection with the relatively unique issues posed by non-Western traditions.

Though utilization of behavioral sciences occurs in all the fields, it is obviously more explicit in sociology of religion, psychology of religion, and in conjunction with psychology, in pastoral studies. Ethics also, insofar as it is oriented to social topics, must also be noted here.

Dissertations in ethics and in sociology of religion manifest roughly similar ranges of interest, namely, the examining of shifts of attitudes and values insofar as they reflect the over-all moral and religious concerns of a particular group or even society at large. Sociology of religion, however, tends toward techniques like computerized data analysis, while ethics deals with the issues more qualitatively. With the decline of ethics as a fashionable discipline in many philosophy departments, the field of religion has assumed greater responsibility for research in this area.

Many ethical studies are simply reviews of the work of one man, like R. Niebuhr, H. R. Niebuhr, Barth, Tillich, and Bonhoeffer. Numerous other theses reflect topical interests of the contemporary scene, such as "Towards an Ethical Understanding of Leisure in a Technological Society," though some are only indirectly relevant, like "Views of Selected Puritans 1560–1630 on Marriage and Sexuality." The themes run the gamut of the currently newsworthy: race, revolution, and most especially the ethical and religious implications of governmental policy. Several faculty see national and foreign policy as a fruitful area for further research. But one eminent faculty member laments "the regrettable replacement of conceptual analysis by relevancy and utopian revolutionary schemes." Other pregnant issues derive from the sexual revolution: adolescent sexuality, abortion, population control, and recent advances in the medical sciences. As in philosophy of religion, theoretical discussion has dealt mainly with questions of individual responsibility, value formation in the self, and ethical values generally associated with individual persons; for instance, "Failure and Capability in Love." Some ethicists indicate that comparative (cross-cultural) ethics may provide new territory for research.

Sociological techniques have been applied to three main groups: ministers, congregations, and denominations in a particular area (such as a state or a small foreign nation). A frequent underlying assumption seems to be that correlations in value shifts and changing attitudes, in a specific group, might evoke new styles of ministry and improved techniques of communication, like educational curricula and preaching. Such problems as "Leadership Differences in Selected Church Groups," "Leadership Expectations for the Methodist Minister in the Field of Social Ethics," and "Church in the Inner City in Phoenix" appear to reflect these concerns and sometimes a view of the church as dominantly a social agency. Faculty suggestions for future research fall into methodological and "material" categories. In the former, a respondent opines that sociology of religion is itself "an example of a field undergoing an 'identity crisis,' undecided as to whether students are sociologists (hard or soft empiricists) or religious (value oriented humanists)." The methods most often prescribed, however, tend toward the empiricist view and emphasize the standard techniques of data gathering, quantitative analysis, and case study, as well as relatively recent advances like game theory and "reflection-action" teaching methods. Suggested subject matters for research include the suburban church, role expectations in church leaders, alienating factors, and drugs. As in the field of history, some social scientists still face the question of admitting "socially committed values" to scientific inquiry.

To a large extent psychology of religion mirrors the same concerns as sociology, but on a more individual basis. It stresses factors which play a critical role in the development of personality—such as attitudes toward death (and bereavement), alienation, conceptual development—and the relation between psychological symptoms and religious belief, like "Attitudes toward Death as a Function of Development Stages," "Some Empirically Verifiable Correlates of the Christian Life as Derived from Protestant Thought," and "Psychotherapeutic Concepts and Theological Categories: P. Tillich and C. Rogers." A similar empiricist versus humanist dichotomy is present in this area, as one respondent notes: "Antibehavioral students of psychology are pushing the Religion and Personality Field (at Chicago) to a more humanistic, less clinical brand of psychology." Nevertheless, about half of the dissertation topics in this area seem to emphasize experimental method.

2. NOVELTY AND TRADITION

History of Christianity; Theology; Judaic, Near East, and Islamic Studies; Bible; Practical Theology.

Dissertations in the field of history of Christianity run the gamut from the early patristic era to the early twentieth century. They constitute, next to biblical studies, the largest category. Both the techniques and topics of "history" are seen as rather fluid, and many scholars indicate a willingness to experiment. Some feel that the discipline should explicitly admit value judgments into its treatment of data; others find social or "psychohistory" useful tools in dealing with religious phenomena.

There is a certain bifurcation in the field between what may be called "domestic chronicles"—histories of denominations or ecclesiastical figures, more or less confined within a specific religious tradition—and essays which attempt to set the religious tradition itself in a broader cultural context. Certainly the faculty believe the board cultural view of history to be a desideratum. Nevertheless, the former type of research is still very prevalent, particularly in the history of American religion, where the denominational pattern of inquiry seems almost the standard. Even studies of Catholicism, which are vastly outnumbered by Protestant themes, fit nicely into the "domestic chronicle" category.

Patristic and medieval studies have been mainly considerations of doctrine in a single figure, as "Salvation in Gregory Nazianzus" or "Redemption in the Writings of Peter Abelard." A promising development in patristics is the greater consideration given to the Graeco-Roman background, like "Paideia in Clement of Alexandria."

Notice should be taken of the comparatively poor representation of medieval studies. Only a dozen dissertations were completed in this area in 1965–1969. If one is to judge from our reports, the dark ages of Christianity are still rather dark and the whole millennium between Boethius and the pre-Reformation era is severely underrepresented in American religious scholarship.

By far the largest number of studies of the premodern era are devoted to the Reformation, with its antecedents and consequences. There is a slight preference in this subfield for studies of English developments, particularly in the seventeenth century. Several theses are given over to considerations of "social" themes, such as "Social Criticism by the English Clergy, 1600–1640." Wesley has been more popular as a thesis subject than Luther or Calvin. So-called "left-wing" reformation phenomena have been sparsely treated, but Pietism has been a popular topic. Perhaps due again to a "Protestant" bias, there have been very few theses on Tridentine and Counter Reformation topics. Besides the expressed interest in this area in "culture-context" history, some faculty see also a need for a more "problem-oriented" style of history, as opposed to simple description of events; that is, they explicitly encourage a reading of the past in terms of contemporary problems.

A prime question for American religious history is whether some of the intentions to consider "new" religious forms indigenous to American culture can be realized, or whether the "domestic chronicle" will be perpetuated. About half the dissertations on American religion have dealt with denominational topics. Intellectual biographies of ecclesiastical figures have also been popular.

The majority of dissertations directed to "church issues" have been discussions of practical theological questions, particularly ecumenism, ecclesiology, and, to a lesser extent, religious education. Given the atmosphere of American religious pluralism, there were surprisingly few efforts to locate the problems in the broader frame of American culture. (Exceptions included titles like "Property in American Protestant Thought" and "Attitudes of Princeton Theologians to Darwin and Evolution, 1859–1929.") In this field as a whole, a Protestant bias (or a Catholic apathy) is again evident. Only two studies of American Catholicism were to be found among eighty-three dissertations on religion in America.

One may expect an increased shift in the field of American studies from denominational to regional, ethnic, and political patterns. Black studies will certainly increase, along with studies of regions other than New England. New forms of cultural expression—youth movement, transplanted Eastern religions, and political ideologies—will gain more attention as religious phenomena. As one historian puts it: "Doctoral study of religious phenomena must begin to take into account religious practices wherever found and however bizarre." Economic and political structures will not only be assessed historically but be treated as "theological" developments. Throughout all this the ideal of "historical objectivity" may give way to the ideal of the *engagé Kulturkritker*; historical criticism will be involved more explicitly with the burden of making value judgments springing from a renewed social consciousness.

While God was dying, the study of "theology" provided a lavish threnody. For some it has seemed not only able to do without God but to do more and better without him. Nearly any phenomenon became "fair game" for the secularized theologian, who could preface his subject with "theology of" and proceed. Thus melodies have been keyed on "play," "sex," "technology," and whatever else might prove to be a surrogate for the former object of ultimate concern.

More conventionally, although some systematic work is being done in relation to patristic, medieval, and Reformation topics, theological studies have tended to concentrate on a few modern figures. Nearly a fifth of the 174 dissertations in theology, 1965–1969, dealt with Barth or Bultmann or Tillich. The question of research reduplication must again be sharply posed. Do four dissertations on Barth's anthropology, or three treatments of the knowledge of God in John Baillie, all stringently uphold the canons of originality? Other well-scrutinized figures were Yves Congar (two theses on his ecclesiology), Nels Ferré (two on *agape*), Jonathan Edwards (two on his Christology); and there have been multiple theses on Bonhoeffer, Brunner, and Hartshorne.

Among the problems taken up, ecclesiology and ecumenics were fairly common, taking a slight lead even over the many discussions of theological method (for instance, "Secularity and Theology: A Study in Theological Method"). The "problem of God" was secondary, as was Christology. Some efforts have been made to extend the concept of ecumenical theology to include the non-Western traditions.

What are the likely directions in theology? Faculty expect a continued openness to methodological experimentation; for example, incorporating psychology, anthropology, and even economics and political history. Methodological self-consciousness is pervasive. Theologians will look toward (or perhaps become) philosophers of religion, insofar as these latter deal with theologically pertinent topics. Strict limitation to Christian categories will be less fashionable. Current social concerns (like ecology) will continue to furnish topics for theological discussion. (Social and political awareness may become confused with theological acumen.) Inasmuch as some theological issues have been redistributed into other fields, such as history of Christianity and philosophy of religion, "theology" might come to mean thinking "theologically" on whatever subject seems pertinent. This type of theological free thinking will reinforce a radical self-questioning of the traditional theological endeavor.

The field variously called theology of culture, or religion and the arts, or theology and literature, which even more explicitly recognizes the susceptibility of the secular society as a subject for religious inquiry, has greatly increased in popularity. It is particularly favored, along with history of religions, among young Ph.D. students (age twenty-eight or under) who do not hold a professional degree. The principal focus in dissertation study has been literature, largely of the twentieth century. So-called existentialist authors (Sartre, Dostoevsky), the French theatre, and American novelists (Melville, Faulkner, S. Bellow) are frequent research subjects. A few dissertations prescind from both the modern and "literature" trends, such as "Spenerian Pietism and the Cantatas of J. S. Bach," or "Movements in the Church of England as Reflected in the Prose Fiction of the Eighteenth Century." But like theology, this field increasingly draws its subject matter from modern phenomena; indeed, there is the suggestion that theology and literature may be baptizing a new literature of theology.

Playing an intermediary role between history of religions and the more traditional "Christian" areas (like Bible) are Near East, Islamic, and Judaic studies. These three (with the possible exception of Islam) have a strong independent tradition of scholarship antedating their involvement in cross-disciplinary religious studies. Judaic research, which engages over 3 percent of Ph.D. students now in progress, is a combination of traditional Talmudic and Rabbinic studies with increasing efforts to view Judaism in its varying historical contexts. Some investigations relate to biblical concerns ("The Idea of God's Kingship in Jewish Thought"); others, to topical interests ("The Cominterm and Zionism in Palestine"). Similarly, the Near Eastern area continues to develop as an autonomous field, while making substantive contributions to biblical studies. Its efforts to reconstruct and depict the institutions of the ancient Near East have to a large extent forced a continuing evaluation and alteration of the historical categories operative in scriptural studies. Titles like "Hieros Gamos in the Ancient Near East" and "Old Babylonian Judiciary and Legal Procedure" evince the efforts of scholars in this field to recreate the history of the Near East as their primary aim, of which the relevance to scriptural study is a secondary spin-off.

In doctoral population, the field of biblical studies and early Christianity is the largest. Nearly one of every five Ph.D. students and more than one of three Th.D. students have been engaged in this field. For the last generation, the percentage has held steady for Ph.D. students.

Concentration in the canonical literature of Old and New Testament has led to much duplication, particularly in New Testament. For instance, in 1965–1969, no fewer than five dissertations were completed on Pauline eschatology, and three theses on Mark's passion narrative as well as two others on the parables of Mark. Besides exegesis, "second-order" analyses of previously formed exegetical and hermeneutical theories have been common. In both areas, traditional approaches (like *Heilsgeschichte*) are being subordinated to attempts to view the documents in their cultural context, though some New Testament studies are still oriented to theological categories such as ecclesiology.

Future advances in both fields, it is widely asserted, will be largely a result of utilizing "nonbiblical" discoveries. Old Testament will continue its interest in Ugaritic studies, archaeological finds, and apocalyptic traditions. Wisdom literature may be increasingly studied, particularly in connection with contemporary intertestamental phenomena. On the New Testament side, as one respondent notes, "Coptic will become a boom language" because of the publication of the Nag Hammadi documents. Computerization in text research may be more fully utilized . Qumran, Hellenistic and Roman history, and Judaic studies are also beginning to be presupposed as main areas of fertile research for New Testament scholars.

Despite the hopeful expansion of both material and method in the biblical fields, the question is still being raised whether there is in fact sufficient new material and supportive resources (such as language training, "on-site" research) to support the massive numbers of students in this field. One scholar laments that the Old Testament field "is prolific and sterile."

The traditional seminary fields in practical theology seem destined to continue to decline. Demand for doctorates in fields like liturgy, homiletics, and missions is limited more by ecclesiastic than by academic considerations (and the trend toward Doctor of Ministry as the first professional degree title will accelerate the decline of the Th.D. in some areas). In the practical theology areas, however, there are also signs of change. For example, missionary studies are increasingly cognizant of the sociology of "third world" culture and of linguistics, while a traditional area like homiletics is drawing on sophisticated research in "mass-media" communication. The survival of such fields as academic disciplines may well depend on their further interaction with developments in other theological and nontheological areas.

3. IN CONCLUSION

The preceding summary is altogether cursory and frequently impressionistic. It rests on a strictly limited body of data and is certainly not to be taken as an inclusive statement of the directions of religious studies in their numerous subdisciplines. Even from such a brief sketch, however, some issues that recur in doctoral research in the several fields are evident.

a. Redundancy and Neglect. In some fields, particularly biblical studies and theology, there appears to be extensive duplication of effort, with multiple theses being written on nearly identical topics. One of the reasons for this is the lack of good communication in the field as a whole (including both the universities and the theological schools) regarding dissertations proposed and in progress. Improved communication would at least expedite complementary rather than repetitive research. We presuppose a view of the thesis as original research, genuinely contributory to the scientific knowledge of the field. That assumption is disputable, particularly by those who would view the dissertation merely as a modest exercise in learning how to do research. But whether the traditional concept of the thesis is to be maintained or modified, it does not seem excusable to encourage dissertation research that is merely replicatory, or whose originality is purchased at the expense of significance and interest. The desirable diversity of viewpoints on any given issue is too often a pretext for unimaginative repetition. At the least, it is appropriate to ask for better direction of research. The request is especially pertinent since there are broad areas that are relatively uncharted.

One respondent puts the question appropriately: "In religious studies, why not isolate the problems that are worth solving (i.e., those that someone really wants answers to) and attack them?"

b. The Cross-Disciplinary Trend. Nothing is better attested than the attraction for many religion faculty of cross-disciplinary and interdisciplinary studies. Further, the lively developments in dissertation research that have escaped the peril of mere replication have often been those moving in this direction. Still, some ask whether the goal may be both oversold and abused. A theologian dealing with literature asserts: "So-called inter-disciplinary studies accomplish far less than they are made to boast, since in most cases they result from declining rather than ascending disciplines." Though we may dissent from such a universal judgment, it is a useful warning about the not infrequent loss of focus on any recognizable religious phenomena and the ready movement into problem areas in which religion by any interpretation is no more than secondary. Numerous dissertations (for example, "A Study of the Armenian Constitutional System in the Ottoman Empire, 1839–63" or "The Sense of Competence in Middle Adolescent Boys") reveals at best an oblique relation to religious studies. They are neither interdisciplinary nor cross-disciplinary nor even multidisciplinary.

c. Conceptual Indeterminism or New Styles of Thought? The changing patterns of graduate research, as well as the testimony of both faculty and students, point to a growing indefiniteness of some of the traditional categories, notably theology. The difficulty is again one of focus. Theology is plainly confronting its own identity crisis, with the consequence that a fair amount of research being done in the name of theology has moved on through the philosophy of religion into philosophical investigations that no longer have any concern with theological or religious questions. But the diversity of dissertation problems in other fields as well, like psychology of religion and history of Christianity, reveals that here, too, an eagerness to eschew religious commitments or ecclesiastical delimitations has often led to the circumventing of any explicit attention to what may even loosely be called dimensions of religious phenomena. From one point of view, then (and this is a judgment of numerous faculty), there are important threats to the very meaning of religious research from the absorption of this research into disciplines where religion is only a secondary interest. But on the other hand, the same conceptual indeterminism is in part a result of the emergence into prominence of new areas and new conceptions of religious studies, and it has been generated in part by the breaking down of traditional disciplinary lines. Thus the indeterminism is a function of the, as yet, incomplete attempts to formulate new models of coherence for interpreting the field as a whole. No good cause will be served by attempting to circumscribe such efforts, but new intelligible patterns of relation need to emerge. Here, as in other disciplines, it remains true both that the nature of the field determines the range of research and the research defines the meaning of a field.

APPENDICES

APPENDIX A

GRADUATE INSTITUTIONS SURVEYED

The following list comprises the institutions and doctoral programs that have been included in the study. The names are given in alphabetical order of the abbreviations commonly used. Where more than one degree or department is involved, appropriate notation has been made.

Aquinas	Aquinas Institute School of Theology, Dubuque, Iowa. Ph.D.
Baylor	Baylor University, Waco Texas
	Department of Religion. Ph.D.
Boston	Boston University, Boston, Mass.
	Division of Theological Studies. Ph.D.
Brandeis	Brandeis University, Waltham, Mass.
	Department of Near Eastern and Judaic Studies. Ph.D.
Brigham Young	Brigham Young University, Provo, Utah
(BYU)	Department of Ancient Scripture; Department of Church History and Doctrine. Ph.D.
Brown	Brown University, Providence, R.I.
	Department of Religious Studies. Ph.D.
U. Calif., S.B.	University of California at Santa Barbara, Calif.
	Department of Religious Studies. Ph.D.
Case Western	Case Western Reserve University, Cleveland, Ohio
	Department of Religion. Ph.D.
Catholic U.	Catholic University of America, Washington, D.C.
	Department of Religion. Ph.D.
	School of Theology. S.T.D.
Chicago	University of Chicago, Chicago, Ill.
	Department of New Testament and Early Christian Literature. Ph.D.
	Divinity School. Ph.D.
Chicago Theol.	Chicago Theological Seminary, Chicago, Ill. D.Th.
Claremont	Claremont Graduate School, Claremont, Calif.
	Faculty of Religion. Ph.D.
Columbia	Columbia University, New York, N.Y.
	Department of Religion. Ph.D.
Concordia	Concordia Seminary, St. Louis, Mo. Th.D.
Dallas	Dallas Theological Seminary, Dallas, Texas. Th.D.
Dominican	Dominican House of Studies, Washington, D.C. S.T.D.
Drew	Drew University, Madison, N.J.
	The Graduate School with the Theological School. Ph.D.
Dropsie	Dropsie University, Philadelphia, Pa. Ph.D.
Duke	Duke University, Durham, N.C.
	Department of Religion. Ph.D.
Emmanuel*	Emmanuel College, Toronto, Ontario, Canada. Th.D.

257

Emory   Emory University, Atlanta, Georgia
                        Division of Religion. Ph.D.
Fordham   Fordham University, Bronx, N.Y.
                        Department of Theology. Ph.D.
Fuller   Fuller Theological Seminary, Pasadena, Calif. Th.D.
General Theol.   General Theological Seminary, New York, N.Y. Th.D.
Grace   Grace Theological Seminary, Winona Lake, Ind. Th.D.
Graduate Theol.   Graduate Theological Union, Berkeley, Calif. Ph.D. and Th.D.
  (GTU)
Hartford   Hartford Theological Seminary. Ph.D.
Harvard   Harvard University, Cambridge, Mass.
  (Rel.)   Committee on Higher Degrees in the Study of Religion. Ph.D.
  (NEL)   Department of Near Eastern Languages and Literatures. Ph.D.
  (Div.)   Divinity School. Th.D.
Hebrew Union   Hebrew Union College, Cincinnati, Ohio. Ph.D.
Iliff   Iliff School of Theology, Denver, Colo. Th.D.
Iowa   University of Iowa, Iowa City, Iowa
                        School of Religion. Ph.D.
Jewish Theol.   Jewish Theological Seminary of America, New York, N.Y. Ph.D.
                        and D.H.L.
Johns Hopkins   Johns Hopkins University, Baltimore, Md.
                        Department of Near Eastern Studies, Ph.D.
Knox*   Knox College, Toronto, Ontario, Canada. Th.D.
Laval   University of Laval, Quebec, P.Q., Canada. Ph.D.
Lutheran   Lutheran School of Theology at Chicago, Chicago, Ill. S.T.D.
  (Chicago)
McGill   McGill University, Montreal, Canada
                        Faculty of Religious Studies. Ph.D.
McMaster   McMaster University, Hamilton, Ontario, Canada
                        Department of Religion. Ph.D.
Marquette   Marquette University, Milwaukee, Wis.
                        Department of Theology. Ph.D.
Montreal   University of Montreal, Montreal, P.Q., Canada
                        Faculty of Theology. Ph.D. and Th.D.
New Orleans   New Orleans Baptist Theological Seminary, New Orleans, La.
                        School of Theology. Th.D.
New York   New York University, New York, N.Y.
  (NYU)   Institute of Hebrew Studies. Ph.D.
Northwestern-   Northwestern University, Evanston, Ill.
  Garrett   Department of History and Literature of Religions. Ph.D.
                    Garrett Theological Seminary.
Notre Dame   University of Notre Dame, Notre Dame, Ind.
                        Department of Theology. Ph.D.
Ottawa   University of Ottawa, Ottawa, Ontario, Canada
                        Department of Religious Studies. Ph.D.
Pennsylvania   University of Pennsylvania, Philadelphia, Pa.
                        Department of Religious Thought. Ph.D.
Pittsburgh   University of Pittsburgh, with Pittsburgh Theological Seminary,
                        Pittsburgh, Pa. Ph.D.
Princeton   Princeton Theological Seminary, Princeton, N.J.   Th.D.
  Theol.
Princeton U.   Princeton University, Princeton, N.J.
                        Department of Religion. Ph.D.

Rice	Rice University, Houston, Texas Department of Religion. Ph.D.
St. Louis	St. Louis University, St. Louis, Mo. School of Divinity. Ph.D.
St. Mary's	St. Mary's Seminary and University, Baltimore, Md. Ph.D.
St. Michael's	University of St. Michael's College, Toronto, Ontario, Canada Institute of Christian Thought. Ph.D.
St. Paul	University of St. Paul, Ottawa, Ontario, Canada Faculty of Theology. Ph.D. and D.Th.
Seabury- Western	Seabury-Western Theological Seminary, Evanston, Ill. Th.D.
Southern Baptist	Southern Baptist Theological Seminary, Louisville, Ky. Th.D.
Southern Cal. (USC)	University of Southern California, Los Angeles, Calif. School of Religion. Ph.D.
Southern Methodist (SMU)	Southern Methodist University, Dallas, Texas Graduate Program in Religion. Ph.D.
Southwestern Baptist	Southwestern Baptist Theological Seminary, Fort Worth, Texas. Th.D.
Stanford	Stanford University, Stanford, Calif. Religious Studies Program (Humanities Special Program). Ph.D.
Syracuse	Syracuse University, Syracuse, N.Y. Department of Religion. Ph.D.
Temple	Temple University, Philadelphia, Pa. Department of Religion. Ph.D.
Trinity*	Trinity College, Toronto, Ontario, Canada Faculty of Divinity. Th.D.
Union (N.Y.)	Union Theological Seminary, New York, N.Y. Th.D.
Union (Va.)	Union Theological Seminary, Richmond, Va. Th.D.
Vanderbilt	Vanderbilt University, Nashville, Tenn. Department of Religion. Ph.D.
Wisconsin	University of Wisconsin, Madison, Wis. Buddhist Studies Program. Ph.D.
Yale	Yale University, New Haven, Conn. Department of Religious Studies. Ph.D.
Yeshiva	Yeshiva University, New York, N.Y. Bernard Revel Graduate School. Ph.D.

* These institutions are members of the Toronto Graduate School of Theological Studies (TGSTS) and have a combined program of doctoral studies.

APPENDIX B

UNDERGRADUATE INSTITUTIONS SURVEYED

In March, 1970, a seventeen-page questionnaire was mailed to the department chairman or program director at 873 four-year colleges and universities in the United States and Canada, which in response to a screening questionnaire had claimed to have the study of religion "organized within a special program or department." The names of these institutions are listed in five groups, relating to their responses to the questionnaires.

I

Eight institutions responded to a prepilot questionnaire, on the basis of which the final questionnaire was developed:

Princeton University, Princeton, N.J.; Bucknell University, Lewisburg, Pa.; Dickinson College, Carlisle, Pa.; Eastern Baptist College, St. David's Pa.; Pennsylvania State University, University Park, Pa.; University of Pennsylvania, Philadelphia, Pa.; Rosemont College, Rosemont, Pa.; University of Toronto, Toronto, Ontario.

II

Of the institutions responding to the main questionnaire before the cutoff date (May 4, 1970) chosen to permit computer descriptive tabulation, the following were identified as offering an undergraduate major in religion or a combined major (such as religion and philosophy), and their responses were used for a number of the detailed interpretations in Chapter 9.

Alabama: Birmingham Southern College, Huntingdon College, Judson College, University of Alabama. *Arkansas*: Hendrix College, John Brown University, Philander Smith College. *California*: Bethany Bible College, Biola College, California Baptist College, Chico State College, Claremont Men's College, College of the Holy Name, Hebrew Union College, Loma Linda University, Occidental College, Pacific Union College, Pepperdine College, St. John's College, St. Mary's College, San Fernando Valley State College, Scripps College, Simpson Bible College, Southern California College, Stanford University, University of California at Santa Barbara, University of Redlands, University of San Francisco, University of Santa Clara, University of the Pacific, Whittier College. *Colorado*: Loretto Heights College, University of Denver. *Connecticut*: Connecticut College, Fairfield University, Wesleyan University, Yale University. *District of Columbia*: American University, Catholic University of America, Georgetown University, George Washington University, St. Paul's College, Trinity College.

Florida: Bethune-Cookman College, Florida Memorial College, Florida Southern College, Florida State University, Rollins College, University of Florida, University of Miami, University of West Florida. *Georgia*: Agnes Scott College, Berry College, Clark College, Emory University, Georgia College at Milledgeville, LeGrange College, Paine College, Piedmont College, Shorter College, Tift College, Wesleyan College. *Hawaii*: The Church College of Hawaii. *Idaho*: College of Idaho, Northwest Nazarene College. *Illinois*: Augustana College, Aurora College, Blackburn College, Bradley University, College of St.

261

Francis, DePaul University, Elmhurst College, Eureka College, Greenville College, Illinois College, Illinois Wesleyan University, Jewish University of America, Lewis College, Loyola University, Millikin University, Mundelein College, Northwestern University, Olivet Nazarene College, Principia College, Southern Illinois University, Trinity College, Wheaton College. *Indiana*: Butler University, DePauw University, Earlham College, Fort Wayne Bible College, Franklin College of Indiana, Goshen College, Huntington College, Indiana Central College, Indiana University, Manchester College, Oakland City College, St. Mary-of-the-Woods College, St. Meinrad College, Taylor University, University of Notre Dame, Valparaiso University, Wabash College.

Iowa: Briar Cliff College, Buena Vista College, Coe College, Cornell College, Drake University, Iowa Wesleyan College, Luther College, Northwestern College, Simpson College, University of Dubuque, University of Iowa, Vennard College. *Kansas*: Baker University, Bethel College, Friends Bible College, Friends University, Kansas Wesleyan University, McPherson College, Marymount College, Mount St. Scholastica College, Ottawa University, St. Benedict's College, The College of Emporia, University of Kansas. *Kentucky*: Berea College, Centre College of Kentucky, Georgetown College, Thomas More College, Transylvania College, Union College, Western Kentucky University. *Louisiana*: Centenary College of Louisiana, Louisiana College.

Maine: Bowdoin College, St. Francis College. *Maryland*: Goucher College, Hood College, St. Joseph College, Western Maryland College. *Massachusetts*: Amherst College, Assumption College, Berkshire Christian College, Boston College, Boston University, Cardinal Cushing College, College of the Holy Cross, Emmanuel College, Gordon College, Mount Holyoke College, Newton College of the Sacred Heart, Tufts University, Wellesley College, Williams College. *Michigan*: Alma College, Andrews University, Aquinas College, Calvin College, Detroit Bible College, Hillsdale College, Hope College, Marygrove College, Michigan State University, St. Mary's College, University of Detroit, University of Michigan. *Minnesota*: Bethel College and Seminary, College of St. Benedict, College of St. Catherine, College of St. Scholastica, Concordia College (Moorhead), Hamline University, Macalester College, Minnesota Bible College, St. John's University, St. Mary's College, St. Olaf College, St. Paul Bible College. *Mississippi*: Blue Mountain College, Millsaps College, Mississippi State College for Women, Tougaloo College, William Carey College. *Missouri*: Avila College, Central Bible Institute, Culver-Stockton College, Evangel College, Lindenwood College, Marillac College, Missouri Valley College, Northeast Missouri State College, St. Louis University, Webster College, Westminster College, William Jewel College, William Woods College. *Montana*: Rocky Mountain College.

Nebraska: Concordia Teachers College, Creighton University, Dana College, Grace Bible Institute, Hastings College, Nebraska Wesleyan University. *New Hampshire*: Dartmouth College. *New Jersey*: Bloomfield College, Caldwell College for Women, Montclair State College, Upsala College. *New Mexico*: College of Santa Fe, Eastern New Mexico University. *New York*: Bard College, College of New Rochelle, Columbia University, Hamilton College, Hobart and William Smith Colleges, Houghton College, Iona College, Keuka College, Ladycliff College, Manhattan College, Manhattanville College, Nyack Missionary College, St. Lawrence University, Syracuse University, Wells College. *North Carolina*: Appalachian State University, Atlantic Christian College, Campbell College, Catawba College, Guilford College, High Point College, Mars Hill College, Meredith College, Methodist College, North Carolina Wesleyan College, Pfeiffer College, Piedmont Bible College, Queens College, Salem College, Shaw University, University of North Carolina, Wake Forest University, Wilmington College. *North Dakota*: University of North Dakota.

Ohio: Antioch College, Ashland College, Bluffton College, Case Western Reserve University, Central State University, Denison University, Hebrew Union College, Heidelberg College, Hiram College, Kenyon College, Lake Erie College, Malone College, Marietta College, Mount Union College, Muskingum College, Oberlin College, Ohio Dominican College, Ohio Wesleyan University, Otterbein College, The Cleveland State University, University of Dayton, Western College for Women, Wilmington College, Wittenberg University, Wright State University, Xavier University. *Oklahoma*: Bethany Nazarene College, Oklahoma Baptist University, Oklahoma Christian College, University of Tulsa. *Oregon*: George Fox College, Lewis and Clark College, Linfield College, Marylhurst College, Multnomah School of the Bible, Northwest Christian College, Reed College, Warner Pacific College.

Pennsylvania: Academy of the New Church, Albright College, Allegheny College, Bryn Mawr College, Cedar Crest College, Duquesne University, Eastern Pilgrim College, Elizabethtown College, Gettysburg College, Gwynedd-Mercy College, Haverford College, Juniata College, King's College, Lafayette College, La Salle College, Lebanon Valley College, Lincoln University, Lycoming College, Messiah College, Moravian College, Northeast Bible Institute, Sesquehanna University, Swarthmore College, Thiel College, University of Pennsylvania, University of Pittsburgh, Westminister College, Wilson College. *Puerto Rico*: Inter American University of Puerto Rico. *Rhode Island*: Barrington College, Brown University.

South Carolina: Central Wesleyan College, Columbia Bible College, Columbia College, Converse College, Erskine College, Newberry College, Presbyterian College, University of South Carolina, Winthrop College, Wofford College. *South Dakota*: Augustana College, Huron College, Mount Marty College, Sioux Falls College, Yankton College. *Tennessee*: Bethel College, Carson-Newman College, David Lipscomb College, Lambuth College, Lane College, Lee College, Maryville College, Scarritt College, Southwestern at Memphis, Tennessee Wesleyan College, Trevecca Nazarene College, Tusculum College, Vanderbilt University, William Jennings Bryan College. *Texas*: Abilene Christian College, Angelo State College, Austin College, Dallas Baptist College, East Texas Baptist College, Houston Baptist College, Howard Payne College, Huston-Tillotson College, Jarvis Christian College, LeTourneau College, McMurry College, Mary Hardin-Baylor College, Our Lady of the Lake College, Dominican College, Rice University, St. Mary's University of San Antonio, Southern Methodist University, Southwestern Union College, Southwestern University, Texas Christian University, Texas Lutheran College, Texas Wesleyan College, Trinity University.

Vermont: Middlebury College, Norwich University, Vermont College. *Virginia*: Bridgewater College, Eastern Mennonite College, Emory and Henry College, Lynchburg College, Mary Baldwin College, Randolph-Macon Women's College, Sweet Briar College, University of Virginia, Virginia Wesleyan College, Washington and Lee University. *Washington*: Seattle University, Whitworth College. *West Virginia*: Bethany College, Davis and Elkins College, Marshall University, Morris Harvey College, Salem College, West Virginia Wesleyan College. *Wisconsin*: Beloit College, Carroll College, Carthage College, Edgewood College, Northland College, St. Norbert College.

CANADA—*Alberta*: University of Alberta. *Manitoba*: St. Boniface College. *Nova Scotia*: St. Mary's University. *Ontario*: University of Ottawa, University of Waterloo, University of Windsor, Waterloo Lutheran University. *Prince Edward Island*: University of Prince Edward Island. *Quebec*: Bishop's University, McGill University, Sir George Williams University, University of Quebec.

III

Responses from the following institutions either arrived after the cutoff date or indicated that no undergraduate major was offered (although a special department or program existed). Forty-nine of the late returns proved to have an undergraduate major; this is indicated by an asterisk after the name of the institution. Information from all these questionnaires was used in certain of the studies in Chapter 9, particularly those relating to faculty characteristics.

Alabama: Florence State University, Livingston University, St. Bernard College, Stillman College. *Arizona*: Prescott College, University of Arizona. *Arkansas*: Arkansas College, Ouachita Baptist University*. *California*: California Lutheran College*, California State College at Bakersfield, California State College at Fullerton*, Loyola University, Pomona

College*, St. Joseph College, San Diego State College*, San Jose State College, University of California at Davis, University of California at Riverside, University of Southern California*, Westmont College*. *Colorado*: Temple Buell College. *Connecticut*: Albertus Magnus College, Quinnipiac College, Sacred Heart University, St. Joseph's College, Southern Connecticut State. *District of Columbia*: Gallaudet College. *Florida*: St. Leo College. *Georgia*: Brenau College. *Hawaii*: Chaminade College of Honolulu, University of Hawaii*. *Illinois*: Knox College, Lake Forest College, Maryknoll College, Monmouth College*, North Central College*, North Park College, Rockford College, Rosary College, St. Procopius College, University of Illinois.

Indiana: Anderson College*, Ball State University, Concordia Senior College, Indiana State University, St. Francis College. *Iowa*: Central College, Clarke College, Divine Word College, Grinnell College, Iowa State University, Marycrest College, Morningside College*, Mount Mercy College, Parsons College, St. Ambrose College, Westmar College*. *Kansas*: Bethany College, Kansas State Teachers College, Sacred Heart College, St. Mary of the Plains College, Southwestern College*, Tabor College*, Washburn University of Topeka. *Kentucky*: Bellarmine-Ursuline College, Brescia College. *Louisiana*: St. Joseph Seminary, Xavier University of Louisiana.

Maine: Nasson College. *Maryland*: College of Notre Dame of Maryland, Loyola College, Morgan State College, Mount St. Agnes College, Towson State College. *Massachusetts*: College of Our Lady of the Elms, Eastern Nazarene College*, Merrimack College, Northeastern University, Regis College, St. Hyacinth College and Seminary, Springfield College*, Stonehill College, Worcester Polytechnic Institute. *Michigan*: Kalamazoo College*, Western Michigan University*. *Minnesota*: Augsburg College*, Bemidji State College, Carleton College*, College of St. Thomas, Lea College on Lake Chapeau. *Mississippi*: Rust College, University of Southern Mississippi. *Missouri*: Fontbonne College, Maryville College of the Sacred Heart*, St. Mary's Seminary, St. Paul's College, Stephens College*, Washington University. *Montana*: Montana State University, University of Montana.

Nebraska: Chadron State College, Midland Lutheran College*, Union College*, University of Nebraska. *New Jersey*: College of St. Elizabeth, Don Bosco College, Douglass College at Rutgers*, Jersey City State College, Rutgers College in the State University*. *New York*: Adelphi University, Alfred University, Colgate University*, C. W. Post College, Dominican College of Blauvelt, D'Youville College, Fordham University*, Hofstra University, Kings College, LeMoyne College, Marist College, Marymount Manhattan College, Mercy College, Molloy Catholic College for Women, Mount St. Mary College, New York University*, Niagara University, St. Bonaventure University, St. Francis College, St. John Fisher College, Siena College, State University of New York. *North Carolina*: Belmont Abbey College, Bennett College, North Carolina State University, Pembroke State University, Sacred Heart College, University of North Carolina, Western Carolina University. *North Dakota*: Jamestown College, Mary College, North Dakota State University. *Ohio*: Borromeo Seminary of Ohio, Bowling Green State University, Kent State University, Mary Manse College, Miami University*, Notre Dame College, Ohio State University, St. John College of Cleveland, The College of Steubenville, The University of Toledo, University College, Urbana College, Wilberforce University. *Oklahoma*: Oklahoma Panhandle State College, Oklahoma State University of Agriculture. *Oregon*: Mount Angel College, Mount Angel Seminary, Oregon State University*, Pacific University*, University of Oregon, University of Portland, Willamette University. *Pennsylvania*: Allentown College of St. Francis de Sales, Beaver College*, Bloomsburg State College, Chatham College, Gannon College, Immaculata College, Lehigh University, Mercyhurst College, Millersville College, Muhlenberg College, St. Charles Borromeo Seminary, St. Fidelis College and Seminary, St. Francis College, St. Vincent College, Seton Hill College, University of Scranton, Ursinus College, Villa Maria College, Villanova University, Waynesburg College. *Puerto Rico*: Catholic University of Puerto Rico, College of the Sacred Heart.

Rhode Island: Providence College, Salve Regina College. *South Carolina*: Clemson

University, Lander College. *South Dakota*: South Dakota State University. *Tennessee*: East Tennessee State University, King College, Siena College, University of Tennessee*. *Texas*: Bishop College, North Texas State University, Paul Quinn College, Stephen F. Austin State College, Texas Tech University, University of St. Thomas*. *Vermont*: Champlain College, Lyndon State College. *Virginia*: College of William and Mary, George Mason College, Hampton Institute, Madison College, Old Dominion University, Radford College, Randolph Macon College*, Roanoke College, University of Richmond*, University of Virginia*, Virginia Union College.

Washington: St. Martin's College, The Sulpician Seminary of the Northwest, Whitman College. *West Virginia*: Alderson-Broaddus College. *Wisconsin*: Holy Family College, Marian College of Fond du Lac*, Milton College, University of Wisconsin—Milwaukee, Vitrebo College, Wisconsin State University—Eau Claire, Wisconsin State University—Oshkosh, Wisconsin State University—Stevens Point, Wisconsin State University—Whitewater.

CANADA—*British Columbia*: University of British Columbia*. *Manitoba*: University of Manitoba*. *New Brunswick*: Université de Moncton. *Newfoundland*: Memorial University*. *Nova Scotia*: Acadia University*, Mount St. Vincent University*, St. Francis Xavier University*. *Ontario*: Huron College, McMaster University*, Queen's University of Kingston*. *Quebec*: Loyola College, University of Sherbrooke*.

IV

The following institutions did not respond to the main questionnaire but did respond to a brief follow-up questionnaire sent in the fall of 1970. Those identifying themselves as offering an undergraduate major are indicated by an asterisk.

Alabama: Samford University*, Spring Hill College. *Arkansas*: Harding College*. *California*: LaVerne College*, Pasadena College*, St. Patrick's College. *Connecticut*: Trinity College*. *Florida*: Biscayne College*, Florida Agricultural & Mechanical University*. *Georgia*: Mercer University*, Morris Brown College, Oglethorpe College, University of Georgia*, West Georgia College. *Illinois*: Barat College of the Sacred Heart*, McKendree College, MacMurray College*, National College of Education, Quincy College*, St. Xavier College*, Trinity Christian College. *Indiana*: Bethel College*, Hanover College*, Marian College*, Marion College*, St. Joseph's College*, St. Joseph's College—Calumet Campus, St. Mary's College*. *Iowa*: University of Northern Iowa. *Kansas*: St. Mary College*, Sterling College*, Wichita State University*. *Kentucky*: Campbellsville College*, Catherine Spalding College*, Pikeville College. *Louisiana*: Loyola University*. *Maine*: Bates College*, Colby College. *Maryland*: Washington College. *Massachusetts*: Smith College*. *Michigan*: Albion College, Eastern Michigan University, Mercy College of Detroit*, Olivet College*, Sacred Heart Seminary, Spring Arbor College. *Minnesota*: College of St. Teresa*, Concordia College (St. Paul)*. *Mississippi*: Mississippi College*. *Missouri*: Central Methodist College*, Immaculate Conception Seminary, Missouri Baptist College, Rockhurst College, The School of the Ozarks*. *Montana*: Carroll College, College of Great Falls.

Nebraska: College of St. Mary. *New Hampshire*: Mount St. Mary College, Notre Dame College, St. Anselm's College. *New Jersey*: Drew University*, Glassboro State College. *New Mexico*: University of Albuquerque. *New York*: Canisius College*, College of Mount St. Vincent, College of St. Rose*, Good Counsel College, Hartwick College*, Marymount College, Roberts Wesleyan College, Rosary Hill College*, St. John's University*, Vassar College*. *North Carolina*: Barber-Scotia College, Greensboro College*, Lenoir Rhyne College*, St. Andrew's Presbyterian College*. *Ohio*: College of Wooster*, John Carroll University*, Ohio University, The Pontifical College Josephinum*. *Oklahoma*: Northeast State College, Oklahoma City University*, Phillips University*. *Pennsylvania*: Holy Family College, Washington and Jefferson College, Wilkes College. *Rhode Island*: Our Lady of Providence Seminary. *South Carolina*: Benedict College. *South Dakota*: University of South Dakota. *Tennessee*: Belmont College*, Southern Missionary College*,

Union University*. *Texas*: Baylor University*, East Texas State University, Hardin-Simmons University*, Southwest Texas State University, University of Texas at El Paso. *Utah*: Westminster College*. *Vermont*: Marlboro College*, University of Vermont*. *Virginia*: Hampden-Sydney College*, Hollins College*. *Washington*: Pacific Lutheran University*, Walla Walla College*. *West Virginia*: West Liberty State College, Wheeling College*. *Wisconsin*: Alverno College*, Holy Redeemer College, Lakeland College*, Lawrence University*, Mount Mary College*, Ripon College, St. Francis de Sales College*.

V

The following institutions, which had initially indicated an undergraduate program, did not respond to either the main questionnaire or the follow-up.

Alabama: Athens College, Troy State University. *Arkansas*: Shorter College, University of Arkansas at Little Rock. *California*: Chapman College, Immaculate Heart College, Marymount College, Mills College, Pacific College, San Francisco College for Women, University of San Diego. *Colorado*: Colorado College, Regis College. *Connecticut*: St. Basil's College, University of Hartford. *District of Columbia*: Dunbarton College of Holy Cross, Southeastern University. *Florida*: Florida Technical University, Stetson University, University of Tampa. *Georgia*: Morehouse College. *Illinois*: College of Jewish Studies, Concordia Teachers College, University of Chicago. *Indiana*: University of Evansville. *Iowa*: Loras College, Wartburg College. *Kentucky*: Asbury College, Cumberland College, Kentucky Wesleyan College. *Louisiana*: St. Mary's Dominican College.

Maryland: Columbia Union College, Mount St. Mary's College. *Massachusetts*: Anna Maria College for Women, Emerson College. *Michigan*: Madonna College, Nazareth College, Siena Heights College. *Minnesota*: Golden Valley Lutheran College, Gustavus Adolphus College. *Mississippi*: Mississippi State University. *Missouri*: Cardinal Glennon College, Drury College, Notre Dame College, Park College. *Nebraska*: Doane College. *New Jersey*: Alma White College, Georgian Court College, Paterson State College, St. Peter's College, Seton Hall University, Shelton College. *New York*: Barnard College, Mater Dei, Nazareth College of Rochester, St. Joseph's College for Women, St. Thomas Aquinas College, Skidmore College, University of Rochester, Wagner College. *North Carolina*: Davidson College, Elon College, Johnson C. Smith College, Warren Wilson College, Winston-Salem State University. *North Dakota*: Mayville State College. *Ohio*: Capital University, Defiance College, Ohio Northern University, Ursuline College for Women. *Oklahoma*: Bartlesville Wesleyan College, East Central Nazarene College, Oklahoma City Southwestern College.

Pennsylvania: Cabrini College, Chestnut Hill College, College Misericordia, Franklin and Marshall College, Marywood College, Temple University. *Rhode Island*: Catholic Teachers College. *South Carolina*: Bob Jones University, Claflin College, Coker College, Furman University, Limestone College, Morris College. *Tennessee*: Christian Brothers College, Fisk University, Knoxville College, University of the South. *Texas*: Incarnate Word College, Southwestern Assemblies of God College, University of Corpus Christi, Wayland Baptist College, West Texas State University, Wiley College. *Utah*: Brigham Young University. *Vermont*: St. Michael's College. *Virginia*: Virginia Polytechnic Institute. *Washington*: Fort Wright College of the Holy Name, Gonzaga University, Seattle Pacific College, University of Puget Sound. *West Virginia*: West Virginia State College. *Wisconsin*: The Cardinal Stritch College.

BIBLIOGRAPHY

This is not intended as a comprehensive or definitive bibliography. However, most works cited in the text are included. Titles preceded by an asterisk are especially recommended. Some brief annotations are provided.

Academic and Financial Status of Graduate Students, Spring 1965. Department of Health, Education, and Welfare, Office of Education. Washington: U.S. Government Printing Office, 1967.

Adler, Cyrus, editor. *The Jewish Theological Seminary of America.* Semicentennial volume. New York: Jewish Theological Seminary of America, 1939.

Alexander, W. J., editor. *The University of Toronto and its Colleges, 1827-1906.* Toronto: University Library, 1906.

Allen, Elliott B. "The Roman Catholic Seminary: Changing Perspectives in Theological Education," *Canadian Journal of Theology,* XIV (1968), 159–168.

Alumni Bulletin of the Union Theological Seminary, Vols. 1 ff., 1925 ff.

American Association of Theological Schools in the United States and Canada (formerly Conference of Theological Seminaries of the United States and Canada). *Bulletin,* Vols 1 ff., December, 1920 ff.

American Council on Education. *A Fact Book on Higher Education.* Washington: 1970.

Annuaire de l'Université-Laval. Quebec, 1857 ff.

Annual Reports of the President and Treasurer of Harvard College. Cambridge, Mass., 1894 ff.

Armstrong, Maurice W., Lefferts A. Loetscher, and Charles A. Anderson, editors. *The Presbyterian Enterprise: Sources of American Presbyterian History.* Philadelphia: Westminster, 1956.

Bach, Marcus. *Of Faith and Learning: The Story of the School of Religion at the State University of Iowa.* Iowa City: School of Religion, 1952.

Bacon, B. W. *The Yale University School of Religion.* 1914. *See* Anson Phelps Stokes.

Baetke, Walter. *Aufgabe und Struktur der Religionswissenschaft.* Part 3, pp. 206-228.

Bainton, Roland. "Yale and German Theology in the Middle of the Nineteenth Century," *Zeitschrift für Kirchengeschichte,* LXVI (1954–1955), 294–302.

————. *Yale and the Ministry: A History of Education for the Christian Ministry at Yale from the Founding in 1701.* New York: Harper, 1957.

*Band, Arnold J. "Jewish Studies in American Liberal-Arts Colleges and Universities," *American Jewish Yearbook,* LXVII (1966), 1–30. A recent and basic survey.

Beach, Waldo. "Graduate Study in Religion at Duke University," *Journal of Bible and Religion,* XXXI (1963), 36–39.

Beazley, Richard. *Numbers and Characteristics of Employees in Institutions of Higher Education.* Washington: U.S. Government Printing Office, 1969.

Berelson, Bernard. *Graduate Education in the United States.* New York: McGraw-Hill, 1960.

Bridston, Keith R., and Dwight W. Culver. *Pre-Seminary Education: Report of the Lilly Endowment Study.* Minneapolis: Augsburg, 1965.

Brief to the Royal Commission on Education of the Province of Quebec. Submitted under the authority of the Board of Governors, and with the approval of the Senate, November 29, 1961. Montreal: McGill University.

Brown, William Adams. *The Education of American Ministers.* Vol. I, *Ministerial Education in America: Summary and Interpretation.* New York: Institute of Social and Religious Research, 1934.

——. "The Responsibility of the University for the Teaching of Religion," *Yale Divinity Quarterly,* XVI (1919–1920), 141–157.

Burge, E. J. "Recent Higher Degrees in Theology," *Theology,* LXVIII (1965), 431 ff.

Cartter, Allan M. *An Assessment of Quality in Graduate Education.* Washington: American Council on Education, 1966.

——. "Scientific Manpower for 1970–1985," *Science,* CLXXII (April, 1971), 132–140.

——. "The Supply of and Demand for College Teachers," *Journal of Human Resources,* Vol. I, No. 1 (1966), pp 22–38.

Cass, James, and Max Birnbaum. *Comparative Guide to American Colleges.* New York: Harper and Row, 1969.

Catholic University of America Year Book. Washington: 1899 ff.

Chittenden, Russell H. *History of the Sheffield Scientific School of Yale University 1846–1922.* 2 vols. New Haven: Yale University Press, 1928.

Christ, Frank L., and Gerard E. Sherry, editors. *American Catholicism and the Intellectual Ideal.* New York: Appleton-Century-Crofts, 1961.

Coffin, Henry Sloane. *A Half Century of Union Theological Seminary 1896–1945: An Informal History.* New York: Scribner's, 1954.

Committee on Undergraduate Teaching. *The Importance of Teaching: A Memorandum to the New College Teacher.* New Haven: Hazen Foundation, n.d.

Conway, John S. "The Universities and Religious Studies," *Canadian Journal of Theology,* V (1959), 269–272.

Council on the Study of Religion. *Bulletin,* Vols. 1 ff., 1970 ff.

Cragg, Gerald R. "The Present Position and the Future Prospects of Canadian Theology," *Canadian Journal of Theology,* I (1955), 5–10.

Crismon, Leo T. *Graduate Theses of Southern Baptist Theological Seminary 1894–1962.* N.p., n.d.

Davis, Moshe. "Jewish Religious Life and Institutions in America (A Historical Study)," in Louis Finkelstein, editor, *The Jews: Their History, Culture, and Religion,* 3rd ed. New York: Harper, 1960. I, 488–587. A concise history, with bibliography.

Deferrari, Roy J. "The Origin and Development of Graduate Studies under Catholic Auspices," in Roy J. Deferrari, editor, *Essays on Catholic Education in the United States.* Washington: Catholic University of America Press, 1942. Pp. 195–215.

Dexter, F. B. *Sketch of the History of Yale University.* New York: Holt, 1887.

Dirks, J. Edward. "Trends in Teaching Religion in Independent and Church Related Colleges and Universities," *Religious Education,* LIV (1959), 164–170.

Doctorate Recipients from United States Universities 1958–1966. Publication 1489. Washington: National Academy of Sciences, 1967.

Doerne, Martin, editor. *Grundriss des Theologiestudiums.* 3 vols. Gütersloh: Bertelsmann, 1948–1952.

Dropsie University. *Bulletin,* Philadelphia, 1970–1972.

Earned Degrees Conferred: 1967–68. Part A—Summary Data. Department of Health, Education, and Welfare, Office of Education. Washington: U.S. Government Printing Office, 1969.

Elbogen, Ismar. "American Jewish Scholarship: A Survey," *American Jewish Yearbook,* XLV (1943–1944), 47–65.

*Ellis, John T. *American Catholicism.* ("The Chicago History of American Civilization.") 2nd ed., rev. Chicago: University of Chicago Press, 1969. A concise account.

————. "American Catholics and the Intellectual Life," *Thought*, XXX (1955), 351–388.
*————. *Essays in Seminary Education*. Notre Dame, Ind.: Fides, 1967. Offers a history of Roman Catholic theological training and reflections on present-day seminaries and on "The Priest as Intellectual."
————. *The Formative Years of the Catholic University of America*. Washington: American Catholic Historical Association, 1946.
————, editor. *Documents of American Catholic History*. Milwaukee: Bruce, 1956.
Fairchild, H. N., editor. *Religious Perspectives in College Teaching*. New York: Ronald, 1952. Essays by George Thomas, E. Harris Harbison, *et al.* on "religious perspectives" in the teaching of a variety of subjects in the arts and sciences.
Fairweather, E. R. "Canadian Journal of Theology: 1955–70," *Canadian Journal of Theology*, XVI (1970), 127–128.
Feilding, Charles. "Twenty-Three Theological Schools: Aspects of Canadian Theological Education," *Canadian Journal of Theology*, XII (1966), 229–237.
Foster, O. D. "Canadian Theological Colleges and American Schools of Religion," *Christian Education*, V (1922), 281–303.
————. "Denominational Cooperation in Religious Education at State Universities," *Christian Education*, V/3 (December, 1921), 12–20.
————. "Schools of Religion at State Universities," *Christian Education*, V/7 (April, 1922), 183–193. Early statements on the teaching of religion in state schools.
Garrett Biblical Institute Bulletin, Vols. I ff., 1913 ff.
Gaustad, Edwin S. *Historical Atlas of Religion in America*. New York: Harper, 1962.
Good, Edwin M. "The Purpose of Religious Studies in General Education," *Journal of General Education*, XIII (1961), 180–200.
Goodspeed, Thomas W. *A History of the University of Chicago: The First Quarter-Century*. Chicago: University of Chicago Press, 1916.
*Grant, G. P. "The Academic Study of Religion in Canada," in R. H. Hubbard, editor, *Scholarship in Canada, 1967: Achievement and Outlook*. Toronto, University of Toronto Press, 1968.
**Guide to Graduate Study: Programs Leading to the Ph.D. Degree*. 4th ed. Robert Quick, editor. Washington: American Council on Education, 1969.
Handlin, Oscar. *Adventure in Freedom: Three Hundred Years of Jewish Life in America*. New York: McGraw-Hill, 1954.
Handy, Robert T. *The American Religious Depression 1925–1935*. ("Facet Books—Historical Series," Vol. 9.) Philadelphia: Fortress, 1968. First published in *Church History*, XXIX (1960), 3–16.
Harrison, Paul M. "The Role of Scholarship in Religion," in C. Conrad Cherry and John Y. Fenton, editors, *Religion in the Public Domain*. Proceedings of the Pennslyvania State University consultation, 1966, pp. 70–92.
Hartzell, Karl D., and Harrison Sasscer, editors. *The Study of Religion on the Campus of Today: Selected Papers from the Stony Brook Conference on Religion as an Academic Discipline*. Washington: Association of American Colleges, 1967.
Harvard University, Faculty of Arts and Sciences. *Report of the Committee on the Future of the Graduate School*. March, 1969.
Harvey, Van A. "Reflections on the Teaching of Religion in America," *Journal of the American Academy of Religion*, XXXVIII (1970), 17–29.
Herbermann, Charles G. "The Faculty of the Catholic University," *American Catholic Quarterly Review*, XIV (1889), 701–715.
Herrmann, Wolfgang, and Gerd Lautner, editors. *Theologiestudium—Entwurf einer Reform*. Munich: Kaiser, 1965.
Hess, H. E., and H. E. Tödt, editors. *Reform der theologischen Ausbildung*. Im Auftrag der Gemischten Kommission für die Reform des Theologiestudiums. 7 vols to date. Stuttgart and Berlin: Kreuz, 1967–1970.
*Holbrook, Clyde A. *Religion, a Humanistic Field*. ("The Princeton Studies: Humanistic Scholarship in America.") Englewood Cliffs, N.J.: Prentice-Hall, 1963.

269

Howard, Oswald. *The Montreal Diocesan Theological College: A History from 1873 to 1963.* Montreal: McGill University Press, 1963.

Hudson, Winthrop S. *Religion in America.* New York: Scribner's, 1965.

Hughes, Everett C. *Men and Their Work.* Glencoe: Free Press, 1958.

Jacob, E. *Revue de l'Enseignement Supérieur,* 1962, pp. 103–106.

Jencks, Christopher, and David Riesman. *The Academic Revolution.* Garden City: Doubleday Anchor Books, 1969.

The Jesuit Relations and Allied Documents: Travels and Explorations of the Jesuit Missionaries in New France. Edited by R. G. Thwaites. 73 vols. Cleveland: Burrows, 1896–1901.

Jewish Theological Seminary of America. *Register,* 1966–1969.

Kelly, Robert L. *Theological Education in America: A Study of One Hundred Sixty-One Theological Schools in the United States and Canada.* New York: Doran, 1924. The first comprehensive study of Protestant seminaries.

Kitagawa, Joseph M. "The Making of a Historian of Religions," *Journal of the American Academy of Religion,* XXXVI (1968), 191–202.

Klaperman, Gilbert. *The Story of Yeshiva University: The First Jewish University in America.* London: Macmillan, 1969.

Lampe, M. Willard. *The Story of an Idea: The History of the School of Religion at the University of Iowa.* Iowa City: State University of Iowa, 1963. Bulletin 806.

Lanczkowski, G. *Religionswissenschaft als Problem und Aufgabe.* ("Sammlung gemeinverständlicher Vorträge," No. 244.) Tübingen: Mohr, 1965.

Langevin, Gilles. "L'Évolution récente et l'état actuel de l'enseignment de la théologie au Canada français: Documents," *Canadian Journal of Theology,* XIV (1968), 169–179.

Lee, C. B. T., editor. *Improving College Teaching.* Washington: American Council on Education, 1967.

Loetscher, Lefferts A. *The Broadening Church: A Study of Theological Issues in the Presbyterian Church since 1869.* Philadelphia: University of Pennsylvania Press, 1957. Treats doctrinal controversies at Princeton Seminary, Union, *et al.*

Lupton, H. E. *Literature of Religious Education.* Sutton, Warwick: R. E. Trust, 1970.

McCluskey, Neil G., editor. *The Catholic University: A Modern Appraisal.* Notre Dame, Ind.: University of Notre Dame Press, 1970.

MacGregor, Geddes. "Graduate Study in Religion and the University of Southern California," *Journal of Bible and Religion,* XXX (1962), 109–114.

McGuire, Martin R. P. "Catholic Education and the Graduate School," in Roy J. Deferrari, editor, *Vital Problems of Catholic Education in the United States.* Washington: Catholic University of America Press, 1939.

Macintosh, Douglas C. "The Department of Religion in the Graduate School," *Yale Alumni Weekly,* XXXIII (1922), 128.

*McLean, Milton D., editor. *Religious Studies in Public Universities.* Carbondale: Central Publications, Southern Illinois University, 1967. Interpretative essays plus excerpts from college catalogues on religion programs and course offerings.

MacLennan, Hugh, editor. *McGill: The Story of a University.* London: Allen and Unwin, 1960.

Macmillan, Cyrus. *McGill and Its Story 1821–1921.* London and New York: John Lane, and Toronto: Oxford University Press, 1921.

Martin, D., editor. *A Sociological Year Book of Religion in Britain.* Vols. I, II, III. London: SCM, 1968, 1969, 1970.

Martin, J. A. "The Graduate Study of Religion in the Seminary Environment," *Journal of Bible and Religion,* XXXI (1963), 320–328.

Martin, J. A., and Ann B. Martin. "The Role of Religion in Some Colleges and Universities of the East." Unpublished article. Association of Teachers of Religion in Higher Education, 1961.

Maurault, Olivier. *Le Grand Séminaire de Montréal.* Montreal: Grand Séminaire, 1940.
May, Mark A. *The Education of American Ministers.* Vol. II. *The Profession of the Ministry: Its Status and Problems.* Vol. III. *The Institutions that Train Ministers.* New York: Institute of Social and Religious Research, 1934.
————, and Frank K. Shuttleworth. *The Education of American Ministers.* Vol. IV, Appendices. New York: Institute of Social and Religious Research, 1934.
Mayhew, Lewis. *Graduate and Professional Education, 1980: A Survey of Institutional Plans.* New York: McGraw-Hill, 1970.
Mémorial du Cinquantenaire (1914–1964) de l'École des Langues Orientales Anciennes de l'Institut Catholique de Paris. ("Travaux de l'Institut Catholique de Paris," Vol. X) Paris, 1964.
Mémorial du Cinquantenaire (1919–1969) de la Faculté de Théologie Catholique. Strasbourg: Le Roux, 1970.
Michaelsen, Robert. *Piety in the Public Schools: Trends and Issues in the Relationship between Religion and the Public Schools in the United States.* New York: Macmillan, 1970.
————. "Reflections on the Graduate Program in Religion," *Journal of Bible and Religion,* XXX (1962), 224–231.
————. *The Scholarly Study of Religion in College and University.* New Haven: The Society for Religion in Higher Education, 1964.
*————. *The Study of Religion in American Universities: Ten Case Studies with Special Reference to State Universities.* New Haven: The Society for Religion in Higher Education, 1965.
————. "The Supreme Court and Religion in Public Higher Education," *Journal of Public Law,* XIII (1964), 343–352.
Morison, S. E., editor. *The Development of Harvard University since the Inauguration of President Eliot, 1869–1929.* Cambridge: Harvard University Press, 1930.
Mueller, William A. *A History of Southern Baptist Theological Seminary.* Nashville: Broadman, 1959.
Nash, George. "A Description of the 1,444 Accredited Four-Year Institutions of Higher Education." Unpublished report. Bureau of Applied Social Research, Columbia University, 1969.
Niebuhr, H. Richard, Daniel D. Williams, and James H. Gustafson. *The Advancement of Theological Education.* New York: Harper, 1957.
Nowlis, Vincent, Kenneth E. Clark, and Miriam Rock. *The Graduate Student as Teacher.* Washington: American Council on Education, 1968.
Pelikan, Jaroslav, *et al. Religion and the University.* Toronto: University of Toronto Press, 1964.
Power, E. J. *A History of Catholic Higher Education in the United States.* Milwaukee: Bruce, 1958.
Prentiss, G. L. *The Union Theological Seminary in the City of New York: Its Design and Another Decade of Its History.* Asbury Park, N.J.: Pennypacker, 1899.
Problèmes et méthodes d'Histoire des Religions. Mélanges publiés par la Section des Sciences religieuses à l'occasion du centenaire de l'École pratique des Hautes Études. Paris: Presses universitaires de France, 1968.
Proosdij, B. A. van. "A Century of the History of Religions in the Netherlands: An Ecological Outline," in *Books in Religion* (Leiden: Brill, 1970), pp. i–xi.
Quarterly Calendar. See University of Chicago.
Ramsey, Paul. "Princeton University's Graduate Program in Religion," *Journal of Bible and Religion,* XXX (1962), 291–298.
————. "The Status and the Advancement of Theological Scholarship in America," *Christian Scholar,* XLVII (1964), 7–23.
————. "Theological Studies in College and Seminary," *Theology Today,* XVII (1961), 466-484.

————, editor. *Religion*. ("The Princeton Studies: Humanistic Scholarship in America.") Englewood Cliffs, N.J.: Prentice-Hall, 1965.

*Ramsey, Paul, and John F. Wilson, editors. *The Study of Religion in Colleges and Universities*. Princeton: Princeton University Press, 1970.

Reed, T. A., editor. *A History of the University of Trinity College Toronto 1852–1952*. Toronto: University of Toronto Press, 1952.

Religion in the Public Schools. American Association of School Administrators. New York: Harper, 1964. Includes a survey of the important court decisions.

Rochemonteix, Camille de. *Les Jésuites et la Nouvelle-France au XVIIe siècle d'après beaucoup de documents inédits*. 3 vols. Paris: Letouzey et Ané, 1895–1896.

Roose, Kenneth, and Charles Anderson. *A Rating of Graduate Programs*. Washington: American Council on Education, 1970.

Roy, Pierre-Georges, editor. *LaVille de Québec sous le Régime Français*. 2 vols. Quebec: Redempti Paradis, 1930.

Rudolph, K. "Die Problematik der Religionswissenschaft als akademisches Lehrfach," *Kairos*, XI (1967), 22–42.

St. Charles Seminary, Overbrook: A History of the Theological Seminary of Saint Charles Borromeo, Overbrook, Philadelphia, 1832–1943 . . . Philadelphia: St. Charles Seminary, 1943.

Schreuder, O. "Trends in the Sociology of Religion in the Netherlands, 1960–69," *Sociologia Neerlandica*, VI (1970), 129–136.

Scott, H. A. *Bishop Laval*. London and Toronto: Oxford University Press, 1926.

Sexton, John E., and Arthur J. Riley. *History of Saint John's Seminary, Brighton*. Boston: Roman Catholic Archbishop of Boston, 1945.

Shipps, Howard Fenimore. *A Short History of Asbury Theological Seminary*. Berne, Ind.: Herald Press, 1963.

Silverman, L. J. and S. Metz. *Selected Statistics on Educational Personnel*. Department of Health, Education, and Welfare. Washington: U.S. Government Printing Office, 1970.

Sissons, C. B. *A History of Victoria University*. Toronto: University of Toronto Press, 1952.

Sizer, Theodore R., editor. *Religion and Public Education*. Boston: Houghton Mifflin, 1967.

Sloyan, Gerard S. "The New Role of the Study of Religion in Higher Education: What Does It Mean?" *Journal of Ecumenical Studies*, VI (1969), 1–17.

Smart, Ninian. "Religion as a Subject," *Church Quarterly*, II (1970), 227 ff.

Smith, Huston. "The Interdepartmental Approach to Religious Studies," *Journal of Higher Education*, XXXI (1960), 61–68.

Spivey, Robert A. "Modest Messiahs: The Study of Religion in State Universities," *Religious Education*, LXIII (1968), 5–12.

Stokes, Anson Phelps. *University Schools of Religion*. n.p., 1914. Reprinted from *Religious Education*, IX (1914), 323–335. Bound with B. W. Bacon. *The Yale University School of Religion*.

Storr, Richard J. *Harper's University: The Beginnings. A History of the University of Chicago*. Chicago: University of Chicago Press, 1966.

The Study of Religion in College and University and Its Implications for Church and Seminary. New York: National Council of Churches, 1967.

Sweet, William Warren. "The Rise of Theological Schools in America," *Church History*, VI (1937), 260-274.

"Theological Scholarship" (editorial). *Canadian Journal of Theology*, I (1955), 139-140.

Union Seminary in the Church of Christ: A Statement Issued by the Authority of the Board of Directors of the Union Theological Seminary in the City of New York. August, 1915.

Union Theological Seminary Bulletin, Vols. I ff, New York, 1917 ff.
United States Bureau of the Census. *Current Population Reports*. Series P-20, No. 79. Washington, 1958.
University of Chicago. *Quarterly Calendar*, Vols. 1 ff., 1892 ff.
————, *University Record*, Vol. 1 ff, 1896 ff.
University of Toronto. *Graduate Studies in the University of Toronto: Report of the President's Committee on the School of Graduate Studies 1964–1965*. Toronto: University of Toronto Press, 1965.
Vachon, Louis-Albert. *Mémorial*. Quebec: Presses de l'Université Laval, 1963. Includes a sketch of the history of the Quebec seminary as well as documents and other materials on the seminary and Laval University.
Waardenburg, J. D. J. "Phenomenology of Religion in Holland, 1885-1965," *Numen* (1971-1972).
Wahlquist, John T. *Innovations in the Preparation of College Teachers*. Bloomington, Ind.: Phi Delta Kappa, 1970. Describes Master of Philosophy and Doctors of Arts programs and the role of teaching assistants.
Wallace, W. Stewart. *A History of the University of Toronto 1827-1927*. Toronto: University of Toronto Press, 1927.
*Walsh, H. H. *The Christian Church in Canada*. Toronto: Ryerson, 1956. Historical introduction to Canadian Christianity and the development of religion study in Canada.
Walter, Erich A. *Religion and the State University*. Ann Arbor: University of Michigan Press, 1958.
Walters, Everett, editor. *Graduate Education Today*. Washington: American Council on Education, 1965. Essays and data on various aspects of graduate education.
Weigel, Gustave. "American Catholic Intellectualism—A Theologian's Reflections," *Review of Politics*, XIX (1957), 275-307. On the relation between ecclesiastical authority and scholarship, and hindrances to American Catholic scholarship.
Weigle, Luther A. "A Survey of Contemporary Theological Education," in American Association of Theological Schools, *Bulletin* 5 (September, 1926), pp. 11-18.
Welch, Claude. "Identity Crisis in the Study of Religion? A First Report from the ACLS Study," *Journal of the American Academy of Religion*, XXXIX (1971), 3-18.
————. "Reflections on the Academic Study of Religion: Patterns, Problems, and Prospects," *ACLS Newsletter*, XIX/6, (October, 1968), pp. 1-8.
————. "Why a Council on the Study of Religion?" Council on the Study of Religion, *Bulletin*, Vol. I/1 (June, 1970), pp. 3-5.
Wernle, Paul. *Einführung in das theologische Studium*. 3d, rev. ed. Tübingen: Mohr, 1921.
Wevers, John W. "Canadian Universities and the Teaching of Religion," *Canadian Journal of Theology*, II (1956), 151-162.
White, Morton. *Religion, Politics and the Higher Learning*. Cambridge: Harvard University Press, 1959.
Williams, George Hunston, editor. *The Harvard Divinity School: Its Place in Harvard University and in American Culture*. Boston: Beacon, 1954.
Yale Divinity Quarterly, XVI (1919-1920), 133 ("The School Resumes its Old Name").
Yale Pot-Pourri. Vol. XXXIII. New Haven: Yale University, 1898.
Yearbook of American Churches: Information on All Faiths in the U.S.A. Edition for 1970. Edited by Constant H. Jacquet, Jr. New York: National Council of Churches, 1970.

Index

273

F

Fairweather, E. R., 133
Feilding, C., 132
Fern, W., 119, 120
Ferré, N., 251
Financial support, 7, 79-81, 89, 212ff.
Ford, J., 120
Fordham University, 62, 69, 70, 75, 79, 80, 87, 89, 93, 186, 222, 225, 231, 235, 237, 239, 240
Foreign students, 65, 207f.
Foster, O. D., 132
Freud, S., 53, 59, 196
Fromm, E., 152
Fuller Theological Seminary, 67, 69, 94, 224, 227, 231, 235
Full-time study, 69-70, 89, 213, 234-243
Fund for Theological Education, viii

G

Gaustad, E. S., 122
Garrett Theological Seminary, x, 33, 44. See also Northwestern University
Gottheil, R., 123
General Theological Seminary, 78, 94, 224, 226, 230, 238, 240
Glock, C., xii
Gibbons, B., xiii
Grace Theological Seminary, 67, 69, 70, 80, 95, 227, 231, 236, 238, 240, 241, 242
Graduate Record Examination, 65, 198, 210
Graduate Theological Union, ix, x, 35, 36, 38, 61, 67, 69, 75, 78, 83, 84, 87, 89, 92, 93, 223, 224, 226, 231, 236, 238, 239, 240, 241, 242, 243
Grant, F. C., 126, 132
Graeco-Roman religions, 53, 245
Gustafson, J., 13

H

Hall, J. W., 60
Handy, R. T., 124
Harrelson, W., v
Harrison, P. M., 84-85, 86
Harnock, A., 23
Harper, W. R., 119
Hartford Theological Seminary, 27, 46, 60, 63, 78, 91, 115, 223, 226, 235, 237, 239, 241, 242, 243
Hartshorne, C., 251
Hartzell, K. D., and H. Sasscer, 55, 127, 166

Harvard University, x, 35, 36, 39, 44, 60, 62, 67, 68, 69, 70, 78, 80, 84, 87, 89, 90, 113, 114, 119, 120, 122, 125, 186, 223, 226, 227, 230, 231, 232, 237, 238, 239, 240, 241, 242, 243
Harvard Committee on the Future of the Graduate School, 74
Harvey, V. A., 20
Hebrew Union College, x, 34, 68, 78, 80, 91, 122, 186, 223, 226, 231, 235, 237, 239, 241, 243
Hegel, G. W. F., 16
Heintz, J. G., 135, 136
Herbermann, C. G., 121
Heffner, R., v
Hermann, W. and G. Lautner, 152
Hess, H. E. and H. E. Todt, 152
Higher Education Act of 1965, 85
Hinduism, 53, 60, 62, 189, 192, 194, 195, 196
Hisch, E. G., 123
Historical studies (Christian), 109, 189, 190, 191, 192, 194, 195, 220ff., 245, 246, 249-253
History of Religions. See also religions of India, Buddhism, comparative religions, Chinese religions, Japanese religions, primitive religions. 20, 24, 34, 61, 158, 162, 189, 190, 191, 192, 194, 195, 220ff., 247f., 252
Hodge, C., 116
Hoens, D. J., 134, 157
Holbrook, C., vii, 17, 127, 166, 198
Howard, O., 131
Hudson, W. S., 116
Hughes, E. C., 32
Husserl, E., 248

I

Iliff School of Theology, 39, 67, 70, 90, 224, 227, 236, 238, 240, 241
Indian, religions of, 160, 220, 245. See also Hinduism
Indiana University, 27, 51
Institute of Islamic Studies, 61
Interdisciplinary studies, 6, 46, 52, 55-56. See also cross-disciplinary studies
Iowa, University of, x, 34, 50, 61, 67, 68, 70, 78-79, 87, 89, 91, 95, 124, 178, 179, 186, 222, 225, 230, 237, 239, 240, 243
Islamic studies, 34, 59, 61, 62, 63, 81, 159, 160, 189, 191, 192, 194, 195, 196, 220ff., 245, 246, 249-253

J

Jacob, E., 139
James, W., 53, 120
Japanese religions, 53, 60, 61, 192, 220ff., 245
Jastrow, M., 123
Jencks, C., and D. Riesman, 19, 28, 44, 48, 82
Jewish studies, see Judaic studies
Jewish Theological Seminary, x, 34, 35, 45, 67, 70, 78, 91, 122, 223, 224, 226, 227, 231, 233, 235, 236, 240, 241
Johns Hopkins University, 62, 67, 68, 90, 222, 225, 230, 232, 241
Johnson, R., v
Judaic studies, 20, 21, 22, 34, 54, 83, 95, 128, 189, 191, 192, 194, 196, 220ff., 245, 246, 249-253
Jung, C. J., 53, 59

K

Keane, J. J., 122
Kelly, R. L., 117, 118
Kennedy School of Missions, 61
Kent Fellowship Program, 15, 212
Kierkegaard, S., 240
Kings College, 130, 132
Klaperman, G., 215
Klausner, S., ix, xii
Knox College, x, 67, 231, 232, 236, 240, 241

L

Lambert, R. D., 56
Lampe, W. M., 124
Lanczkowski, G., 153
Langerak, E., v
Laval, Bishop, 129
Laval, University of, 90, 129, 130, 224, 227, 232, 235
Langevin, G., 132
Lawrence, D. H., 196
Leo XIII, Pope, 122
Length of time in study, 70-73, 234-243
Levi-Strauss, C., 53
Library resourcs, x, 8, 77-79, 89
Lilly Endowment Study, 208
Loisy, A., 137
Luce Foundation, ix, xiii
Luther, M., 250
Lutheran School of Theology at Chicago, 69, 70, 94, 224, 227, 231, 236, 241
Lupton, H. E., 154
Lyon, D., 123

M

McCluskey, N. G., 122
McGiffert, A. C., 127
McGill University, 31, 61, 62, 67, 68, 70, 75, 87, 92, 131, 226, 231, 235, 237, 239, 241, 242, 243
MacGregor, G., 125
Macintosh, D. C., 120
MacLean, M., vii, 31, 166, 179
MacLennan, H., 131
McMaster University, 58, 61, 67, 69, 75, 80, 83, 87, 92, 93, 222, 225, 231, 239, 241, 242, 243
Macmillan, C., 131
Malinowski, B., 53
Marquette University, 35, 68, 69, 80, 92, 93, 186, 222, 225, 231, 235, 241, 242
Martin, D., 154
Martin, J. A., v, 60, 125
Marx, K., 16, 152, 146
Mather, C., 114
Mather, I., 114
Maurault, O., 129
May, M. A., 126
May, W., v, 48, 118
Mayhew, L., 31
Michaelsen, R., vii, viii, 31, 125, 127, 166, 179, 195
Michigan State University, 178
Montreal, University of, ix, 35, 67, 70, 223, 224, 226, 231, 241
Moore, G. F., 119, 197
Morison, S. C., 119, 120
Morris, R. P., 126
Mueller, W. A., 121, 126
Miller, M., 23

N

Nash, G., 170ff.
National Academy of Sciences, 31, 47, 71
National Association of Biblical Instructors. See American Academy of Religion
National Defense Education Act, 85
National Endowment for the Humanities, 85
National Foundation for Jewish Culture, 129
Near Eastern religions, 34, 53f., 90, 189, ch. 11, 249ff.
New Orleans Baptist Theological Seminary, 39, 67, 70, 95, 224, 227, 230, 240, 242
New Testament Studies, 18, 82, 189, 191, 193, 194, 195, 196, 220ff., 245, 246, 248, 252

Weber, M., 53
Welch, C., 128
Welch, T., xiii
Wevers, J. W., 132
Wernle, P., 152
Wesley, J., 250
Wesleyan University, 51
Western Michigan University, 178
Whitehead, A. N., 247, 248
Widengren, G., 159
Williams, G. H., 114, 118
Wilson, B., 154
Wisconsin, University of, 61, 67, 69, 83, 89, 92, 93, 222, 225, 232, 235 241, 242
Wittgenstein, L., 248

Wolfson, H. A., 124
Woodrow Wilson Fellowship Program, 212
World religions, See history of religions
Wright, C., 114

Y

Yale University, 21, 31, 39, 40, 41, 44, 50, 58, 60, 63, 67, 68, 69, 70, 75, 78, 80, 84, 87, 89, 90, 113, 114, 115, 125, 127, 134, 135, 186, 223, 226, 230, 235, 237, 239, 243
Yeshiva University, 67, 90, 223, 226, 235, 239, 241, 242

WESTMAR COLLEGE LIBRARY

93915

BL
41
.W4